BREAKFAST AROUND THE WORLD

Alaska to Zambia

475 Recipes from 43 Countries

Richard S. Calhoun

ISBN 0-941367-46-0
Peach Blossom Publications

DEDICATION

My wife,
Daisy,
who helped me taste-test every recipe.

My Daughter,
Floramaria,
who helped to prepare the book for publication

My friend,
Louise Ulmer,
who did the final editing

Richard S. Calhoun has collected more than 1,300 different breakfast recipes from around the world. His collection continues grow. Some of his favorite recipes are presented in this cookbook. He also writes food and health articles for children and parenting publications. Is the co-author of *The ABC's of Food* reference book for middle grade and high school students, and author of *Cheechako: An Alaskan Adventure.*

COVER PHOTO: A hearty *Irish* breakfast begins with a bowl of oatmeal, followed by *fudge* (potato cakes) with *ulster fry* (Irish bacon, banger sausages, black and white breakfast puddings, tomatoes and eggs) with toasted wheat bread. (*Shannon Traditional photo*)

BREAKFAST AROUND THE WORLD

INTRODUCTION, Page 1

Chapter I **BARS, CRULLERS & OTHER DELIGHTS**, Page 2

Chapter II **BEVERAGES** (fruit & hot), Page 14

Chapter III **BISCUITS & SCONES** (plus toppings), Page 22

Chapter IV **BREADS** (tea bread, yeast breads & spreads), Page 37

Chapter V **CEREALS** (ready-to-eat, hot, baked & fried), Page 60

Chapter VI **COFFEE CAKES, STRUDELS & SWEET CAKES**, Page 81

Chapter VII **DOUGHNUTS, FRITTERS & FRIED BREADS**, Page 96

Chapter VII **DUMPLINGS & DOUGHS THAT ARE STEAMED OR BAKED**, Page 108

Chapter IX **EGGS** (casseroles, omelets & quiche), Page 117

Chapter X **FRENCH TOAST**, Page 145

Chapter XI **FRUIT** (plus toppings), Page 152

Chapter XII **MEAT & SEAFOOD** (beef, pork, poultry, fish, seasonings), Page 160

Chapter XIII **MUFFINS**, Page `195

Chapter XIV **PANCAKES & CREPES**, Page 205

Chapter XV **PUDDINGS**, Page 222

Chapter XVI **VEGETABLES**, Page 230

Chapter XVII **WAFFLES**, (plus toppings), Page 241

AND: Kid's Breakfast Club with 19 easy fun-to-make recipes, page 246
Cookbooks & Magazines, Page 252
Mail Order Sources, Page 253
Acknowledgements, Page 254

INTERNATIONAL RECIPE INDEX, Page 256

HEALTHY BREAKFAST IDEAS

Some breakfast recipes can be high in calories, fats, salt and sugar. If this is a concern, I offer a few tips to make your breakfast enjoyable and tasty.

BEVERAGES: Coffee, tea and hot chocolate can be sweetened with a sugar substitute without adding any calories. Some of these substitutes are 200 or more times sweeter than sugar, so use with care..

BAKING: In most recipes, an equal amount of applesauce can replace an equal amount vegetable oil or shortening. Egg substitutes can replace eggs, use one-fourth cup of substitute for each egg requested in the recipe. When replacing sugar, I use Splenda® as some other substitutes will lose their sweetness when heated and others can be bitter when heated.

BREAD: When making bread most recipes call for sugar, honey or other sweetener. Sugar is yeast food that helps the dough to rise. As you will note, not much sugar is used, however, you can cut the sugar in half without affecting the yeast. Salt on the other hand helps to control the action of the yeast by slowing the rising time. You can cut the amount of salt in half. I have never used a sugar or salt substitute in baking bread.

DAIRY: Nonfat or low-fat milk can replace whole milk in most recipes with out affecting the taste of the finished product. Also nonfat and low-fat cottage cheese and sour cream can be used in place of higher fat dairy products. The final taste just won't be as rich, but you will still receive all the calcium. Nonfat and low-fat yogurt can be used to replace sour cream, and nonfat and low-fat ricotta can be used to replace cottage cheese.

EGGS: Egg substitute can be used in most baking recipes. One egg equals one-fourth cup of egg substitute. Also you can replace one whole egg with two egg whites in baking recipes. When you still want the richness and taste of a whole egg, mix two egg whites with one whole egg. This equals two eggs. Also boil or poach eggs instead frying.

MEAT: Use low fat cuts whenever possible (ground round in place of hamburger, ground turkey to replace ground beef, etc.). Replace pork bacon with turkey bacon. Broil, rather than frying meat helps to reduce fat intake. There are also some soy products that are quite good and make great replacements.

PRESERVES: Jelly, jam and preserves are fat-free. However, they do contain sugar calories. There are both sugar-free and low sugar preserves available at the supermarket. Those made with fruit juice tend to be tastier, but can still be high in sugar calories. Read the label and compare.

BUTTERMILK PANCAKES

The following recipe serves four or three pancakes each. By using substitutes in parentheses you will cut the calories from 261 to 162, fat from 19% to 3%, and salt from 25% to 13%. Carbohydrates remain about the same.

1 cup all-purpose flour
1 cup buttermilk (4 tablespoons cultured buttermilk + 1 cup water)
1 egg (1/4 cup egg substitute)
4 teaspoons sugar (4 teaspoons sugar substitute)
3 tablespoons vegetable oil (3 tablespoons applesauce)
1 teaspoon baking powder
½ teaspoon baking soda
½ teaspoon salt (eliminate or use a salt substitute)

INTRODUCTION

Even though most nutritionists claim breakfast is the most important meal of the day, in many countries people are just now discovering breakfast. In most parts of Europe, it is customary to rise early and go to work with little or nothing to eat. Those who do eat a breakfast, have fruit juice and coffee or tea, with or without bread. An example: in the French countryside after working for awhile, it is traditional to have *casse-croue,* meaning to "break crust." In Paris the custom is to have *panade,* which is leftover bread from the previous dinner. In America we have a "coffee break" and usually includes something sweet such as a doughnut. The French breakfast is called *petit de jeuner* and is enjoyed at the noon hour. The meal is more like a Sunday brunch in the United States with grilled meats, omelets, pastries, croissants, fresh fruit, "cafe au lait" (coffee with milk), and a glass of Burgundy wine. This noon time breakfast is practiced in many other countries as well. The most popular breakfast in the United States is: orange juice, bacon and eggs, toast, coffee or tea If you take a close look at this menu, it's not American, because none of the foods originated from America. Oranges and other citrus fruits came from Asia. Eggs we eat today come from chickens, and chickens , as well at hogs, also originated in Asia.. Toast is made from wheat flour, and it is believed wheat originated in the Euphrates Valley, now part of Iraq. Coffee came from Abyssinia, now Ethiopia, and tea is native to China. Today, all these foods are now grown in many parts of the world.

However, if you stop and ask: what did the Native Americans have for breakfast before the Europeans arrived? Native fruits, such as berries and pumpkin, venison, duck or turkey eggs, cornmeal made into flat cakes or hot cereal, and tea made from bark or leaves.

As the Europeans migrated, they brought their recipes. And many brought their ingredients, animal or plant, to their new home and shared their cuisine with neighbors. The colonists came to substitute European ingredients with American ingredients (i.e., cornmeal for wheat flour), and rewrote their recipes with some of America's new ingredients.

Breakfast isn't just bacon and eggs. There are a variety of breads, grains, meats, fruits and vegetables. Breakfast doesn't have to be boring. As you look through this book, you will note many of the recipes are from various regions of the United States. Most have connections to other countries, while some relate to Native American foods. Some of the recipe ingredients might sound a bit strange. I think the late Clyde LeBlanc, author of *The Good Earth Cookbook,* in his chapter, "Thoughts of a Cajun Breakfast," says it best, "If that is what you got, you eat it." No longer does breakfast need to be called "The Most Important Meal of the Day," but instead, "The Most Enjoyable Meal of the Day." And that is what this book is all about, sharing and bringing the best of what the world has to offer for breakfast to your table. I do hope you enjoy.

Richard S. Calhoun

CHAPTER I

BARS, CRULLERS & PASTRIES

Everyone has been in this situation. You're on the go and there's no time for breakfast. That's no excuse, because with a little planning, you can make some breakfast bars and other delights ahead of time, and as you go out the door grab one or two. True, some of the recipes are a bit high in both calories and fat, but they will give you the needed energy to make it until lunch. Eating something is better than nothing and some of the recipes are even quite healthy.

Apple Bars (*Washington*), 3

Breakfast in Italy

Chocolate Almond Biscotti (*Italy*), 3

Chocolate Chunk, White Chocolate Chip Cookies (*USA*), 4

Crullers (*Netherlands)*), 4

Danish Pastry (*Denmark), 5*

Basic Danish Dough with Sugar Icing, 5

Spandavers, 6

Trekanters, 7

Cockscombs

Fastelavnsboller & variations, 7

Fromajardis & Crispers (*Minorca*), 8

Granola Bars (*Missouri*), 9

Kolaches (*Germany*), 9

Monster Cookies (*Illinois), 10*

Peach Crunch Bars (*Kansas*), 10

Pecan Crescents (*Mississippi*), 11

Poffertjes (*Netherlands*), 11

Old Fashioned Dutch Letters (*Netherlands)*, 12

Rugalach *(Israel)*, 12

S'More Bars (*USA*), 13

Waffeltoerichen (*Germany*), 13

APPLE BARS

Makes 25 squares

Hope Abadie of Chelan, Washington solved her breakfast problem by making a good supply of these apple bars using ingredients the family likes the most.

1/2 cup margarine
1 cup sugar
1 egg, beaten
1 cup tart apples, chopped

1 cup peanuts
1 cup flour
1/2 teaspoon baking soda
1/2 teaspoon baking powder

1 teaspoon cinnamon

1. In a large bowl, cream margarine and sugar.
2. Beat in egg.
3. Stir in apples and peanuts.
4. In a small bowl, combine flour, soda, baking powder, and cinnamon.

5. Mix the apple and flour mixtures together.
6. Pour into a greased 10x10-inch pan.
7. Bake for 40 minutes at 350°F.
8. Cool, cut into 2x2-inch squares.

NUTRITION FACTS per square: 121 calories, 10% calories from fat, 6.8g total fat (49%), 1.1g saturated fat (6%), 13.6g carbohydrates (5%), 2.3g protein (5%), 6mg iron (3%), 8.5mg cholesterol (3%), .7g fiber (3%), 79mg sodium (3%), 17mg calcium (2%), zero vitamin C and 164 IU vitamin A (3%).

BREAKFAST IN ITALY

Emily Baldwin of New York City's *Balducci's*, says Italians are not real breakfast eaters. Fresh fruit, biscotti, and a cup of coffee; that's about it! Biscotti means "twice baked." They are hard crunchy cookies that originated in Tuscany. They are traditionally dunked in espresso, cappuccino, *vin santo*, or as the Americans sometimes do, eaten plain with milk.

Nina Balducci enjoys a big hunk of "*Pane di Casa*" with sweet butter and a cup of coffee. *Pane di Casa* is an authentic old-fashioned, sourdough bread. It is baked in a brick oven on a stone slab and has a firm, toasty crust marked by cracks and ridges. "*Prosciutto*" bread is also very popular. Usually baked in a ring, it is filled with small chunks of prosciutto ham. Some Italians wrap a paper-thin slice of this ham around a melon wedge or quartered ripe pears and occasionally add a squeeze of lemon.

CHOCOLATE ALMOND BISCOTTI

Makes about 4 dozen

You can make biscotti at home with this recipe from the *Nestle Beverage Company*.

1 cup whole almonds
2 1/4 cups flour
1 teaspoon baking powder
1/4 teaspoon baking soda
1/4 teaspoon salt

1/2 cup butter, melted
3 eggs
2 tablespoons Nescafe® Classic Coffee Crystals
1 tablespoon orange zest, grated
2 cups Nestle Quik® chocolate powder

1. Preheat oven to 350° F.
2. Arrange almonds on a large baking sheet. Bake about 10 minutes; cool.
3. In a medium bowl, combine flour, baking powder, soda and salt; set aside.
4. In a large bowl, beat chocolate powder, butter, eggs, coffee crystals and orange zest until mixed.

5. Add half of flour mixture; mix well. Use wooden spoon to blend in remaining flour.
6. Stir In almonds.
7. Divide dough into thirds.
8. Place 1/3 of the dough on sheet of waxed paper.

9. Roll dough into log, about 1/2x12-inches. Repeat to form 3 logs.
10. Place logs on greased baking sheet 2-inches apart; flatten logs to 1-inch thickness.
11. Bake 22 to 25 minutes or until baked through.
12. Cool 20 minutes; cut diagonally into 5/8-inch wide slices.
13. Return to baking sheet(s).
14. Bake at 300°F for 25 minutes.
15. Turn off oven; let stand in oven 1 hour to dry.

NUTRITION FACTS per biscotti: 52 calories, 19 calories from fat2.4g total fat (4%), .6g saturated fat (3%), 13.3mg cholesterol (4%), 30.4mg sodium (1%), 7.2g carbohydrates (2%), 1.5g fiber (6%), 2.3g protein (5%), zero vitamins A and C, 22mg calcium (2%) and 1mg iron (5%).

Nestle Quik and Nescafe are registered trademarks of the Nestle Beverage Company

CHOCOLATE CHUNK/WHITE CHOCOLATE CHIP COOKIES
Makes about 2 dozen

Sallie and *Welling Clark* are the innkeepers at *Holden House*, in Colorado Springs, Colorado. They keep a cookie jar filled 24 hours a day for their guests.

3/4 cup brown sugar
3/4 cup butter or margarine
2 eggs
1 teaspoon vanilla

2 1/2 cups flour
1 teaspoon baking soda
6 ounces chocolate chunks
5 ounces vanilla chips

¼ cup walnuts, chopped

1. Preheat oven to 375° F.
2. Cream brown sugar and butter (can be soften in a microwave for 1 minute on high).
3. Add eggs and vanilla. Mix well.
4. Add flour and soda to the sugar egg mixture and mix well.
5. Add chocolate chunks, vanilla chips and walnuts.
6. Place with well-rounded teaspoonfuls on an ungreased cookie sheet.
7. Bake for 10 to 12 minutes or until slightly brown on top.

NUTRITION FACTS per cookie: 191 calories, 93 calories from fat, 10.8g total fat (17%), 6g saturated fat (30%), 33mg cholesterol (11%), 119mg sodium (5%), 22.8g carbohydrate (8%), .8g fiber (3%), 2.8g protein (6%), 247 IU vitamin A (5%), zero vitamin C, 14mg calcium (1%) and 1.2mg iron (7%).

> **What is "white chocolate?** The so-called "white" chocolate is actually cocoa butter. The white chocolate you buy in block form contains sugar, cocoa butter, nonfat milk powder, milk fat, soy lecithin (an emulsifier) and vanilla.

CRULLERS

The cruller is sort of a sister to the doughnut and is found in recipes throughout Europe. Crullers have made their way to Mexico where they are called *churros* and are squeezed out of a decorator tube into a pot of hot fat. In France they are made into a round shape and come out almost like a cream puff (cream puffs are baked, crullers are fried). *Alice Merrymen* from Summersville, West Virginia makes her crullers similar to the Dutch version. Her crullers puff up like little pillows when fried and have a taste much like cream puffs. For another cruller recipe see POFFERTJES, page 11..

2 eggs
1/2 cup cream, sweet or sour
1/2 cup milk
1 teaspoon baking soda

1 teaspoon salt
1/4 cup sugar
3 1/2 to 4 cups flour
Powdered sugar (optional)

Cinnamon/sugar mixture (optional)

1. In a large bowl, beat the eggs, add cream and milk.
2. In another bowl, sift dry ingredients and combine with liquid, using just enough flour to make the dough that can be rolled, but still remains soft.
3. Mix well and let stand for 2 hours.
4. Turn out on floured board and roll to 1/4-inch thick.

5. Cut into strips about 1x6-inches. Can be fried as a single strip or two strips can be layered, sealed at each end and twisted before frying.
6. Fry in deep fat or vegetable oil until brown on both sides.
7. Drain on absorbent paper towels and dust with powdered sugar or a cinnamon/sugar combination, if desire.

Every cook has a mixture of cinnamon and sugar for such occasions. Other cooks like to first sprinkle the cinnamon and than top with sugar. A mixture is usually is one cup of sugar to one tablespoon of cinnamon.

DANISH PASTRY

A quote from a Danish cookbook: *"Out of deference to the English-speaking world we have quite happily agreed to the use of the term 'Danish Pastry' to describe the goodies which decorate the windows in the bakeries. Among ourselves, however, we call it Wiererbröd (Viennese Bread), which seems to puzzle visitors. Quite frankly, we are happy to let the visitor go on being puzzled and not delve too deeply into the matter, for there is a risk of someone digging up evidence that a master baker in Vienna thought up the recipe before we did."* Bodil Hartmann from the office of *Royal Danish Consulate General* says, *"These pastries are fattening."* Bodil is right. They are! The problem is that because these pastries are so delicious, no one can eat just one. The dough takes time to prepare, however, once you make it, you will think the time well worth the effort.

BASIC DANISH DOUGH

With this recipe you can make several recipes as follows, as well as the simple one called *"wienerbrodsdejg"* with sugar icing. This pastry turns out better with margarine, but butter can, of course be used.

1 cup cold milk
2 ounces fresh yeast or 3 packages dry yeast
1/4 cup sugar
2 eggs

1 pound margarine or butter, soften
5 cups flour
1 egg for brushing
1/2 cup flour to roll dough in

1. In a large bowl, work the yeast, sugar and eggs together with the fingers in the milk, then sift in the 5 cups of flour with your fingers.
2. Knead until you have dough that slides smoothly in the hands.
3. Sprinkle flour on the bread board and place the dough on it.
4. Form the margarine into a square and place on top of the dough.

5. Pack the dough up over the margarine to form a square once again. Roll out to a rectangle about 1/2- inch thick.
6. Fold inwards a third from one end and another third from the other end overlapping on top of the first so that the dough is in three layers.
7. The dough has now been rolled once. Repeat twice more in exactly the same way.
8. Set to cool for 15 minutes.
9. Cut into four equal pieces.

You now have sufficient dough to make about 45 pastries in 4 different varieties.

NUTRITION FACTS per pastry, without toppings and fillings: 142 calories, 79 calories from fat, 8.8g total fat (14%), 1.7g saturated fat (8%), 14.9mg cholesterol (5%), 102.7mg sodium (4%), 13.4g carbohydrates (4%), zero fiber, 2.4g protein (5%), 362 IU vitamin A (7%), zero vitamin C, 14mg calcium (1%) and .8mg iron (4%).

SUGAR ICING

3 cups powdered sugar
3 tablespoons boiling water

1. Sift sugar.

2. Stir into the water until a smooth mass is obtained.

Color and taste can be varied by mixing in lemon, cocoa, etc.

A teaspoon of icing will add about 31 calories per pasty.

SPANDAUERS
Makes 10 Spandauers

Take note: Eat them as oven-fresh as possible for they were not designed to be kept in a container, no matter how airtight!

1 piece of Danish dough
Egg, beaten

Raspberry jam
Chopped nuts

Sugar icing

1. Roll the dough out to a rectangle about 20-inches long by 6-inches wide.
2. Cut down lengthways into 2 strips.
3. Cut each strip into 5 equal parts, thus forming a total of 10 squares of dough.
4. Fold in the four-corners of each towards the center and press down well.
5. Place on baking sheet with plenty of space between each.

6. Brush with egg.
7. Place a dot of jam in the middle of each and sprinkle with a few chopped nuts.
8. Set aside to rise for about 15 minutes.
9. Bake in 350°F oven until golden brown and crisp.
10. When cold, spread a spoonful of sugar icing on each.

The topping will add about 24 calories to each spandauer.

TREKANTERS

1 piece of Danish dough
Pastry filling

Chopped nuts
Egg well beaten for brushing

Sugar icing

1. Roll out dough and cut into 10 squares as for the spandauers.
2. Put a dot of pastry filling in the center of each square and fold over, forming a triangle.
3. Press the two edges well together and make 5 slashes in each with a knife.
4. Brush with egg and sprinkle a few chopped

nuts in the middle.
5. Place on baking sheet and allow to rise for about 15 minutes.
6. Bake in 350°F oven until golden brown and crisp.
7. When cold, spread a teaspoon of sugar icing on the top of each.

PASTRY FILLING

1/2 cup butter

1/2 cup sugar

1 teaspoon vanilla

1. Cream sugar and butter.

2. Stir in vanilla and the filling is ready for use.

This filling will add about 120 calories to each trekanter.

TREKANTERS and **COCKSCOMBS** are basically turnovers. If you desire, you can make larger pastry squares and put in a larger amount of filling. Also, canned pie fillings can be used.

COCKSCOMBS

1 piece of Danish dough
Apple jam

Chopped nuts
Sugar icing

1. Roll out and cut dough into 10 squares as for spandauers.
2. Place a teaspoonful of apple jam in the center of each.
3. Fold over once across the middle and press the two edges well together.
4. Make 5 slashes in this edge with a knife.

5. Place on baking sheet and brush with egg.
6. Sprinkle with a few chopped nuts.
7. Allow the dough to rise for about 15 minutes.
8. Bake in a 350°F oven until golden brown.
9. When cold, spread a teaspoon of sugar icing on each.

FASTELAVNSBOLLER

A quote from a Danish cookbook: *"Our Shrovetide celebrations consist mainly in antics round a barrel in which we pretend there is a cat (in olden times there was a cat) and in using the occasion as a good excuse for a bit of serious cake-eating. We like to eat these buns (in English called carnival buns) to replenish all the energy expended on the cat and the barrel, but even if you can not supply this local color, we think you will like them anyway!"*

1 piece of Danish dough
Raisins

Candied peel, chopped
Egg, beaten

Sugared water

1. Roll out dough and cut as spandauers.
2. In the middle of each square of dough drop a few raisins and chopped candied peel.
3. Fold in the four-corners towards the center.
4. Place on baking sheet with the four-corners facing downwards.

5. Press well.
6. Brush with egg.
7. Set aside for about 15 minutes.
8. Bake in a 350°F oven until golden brown.
9. Remove from oven and brush with a little sugared water.

VARIATIONS: The filling can be varied to suit your taste. Try your favorite jam or preserves, sweetened cream cheese or chocolate chips. You can also glaze them with different flavored and colored icings. As you see, the combinations are endless. Also other shapes and sizes can be made. For example, **Bear Claws.** Cut strips about 3 by 5-inches wide. Fill the center the length of the strip with canned almond filling. Fold over and press the edges together. Slash each piece 3 or 4 times about an inch from the edge and bake as above recipes.

A teaspoon will add about the following calories:

- 16 calories for jelly or jam,
- 17 calories for chocolate chips,
- 16 calories for cream cheese,
- 26 calories for sweeten cream cheese,

- 16 calories for walnuts,
- 16 calories for candied citrus peel,
- 9 calories for raisins

FROMAJARDIS
Makes 36 fromajaris

When the *Minorcans* arrived in San Augustine, Florida, during the 16th century, they kept alive many of their traditions of their homeland. On Easter Eve, strolling men with guitars serenaded families beneath balconies and open windows. The singers extended baskets on long poles filled with small cakes and bottles of orange wine. These cakes were cheese stuffed pastries called *"fromajardis."* The recipe is from the *Century Souvenir Company* of San Augustine.

FILLING

1 pound cheddar cheese, grated
2 tablespoons flour
6 eggs, beaten

2 tablespoons sugar
1/4 teaspoon nutmeg
1/4 teaspoon cayenne pepper

1. In a bowl, combine all ingredients.

RICH PASTRY

This is an excellent pastry for pie crusts and other recipes requiring a crust.

6 cups flour
1 tablespoon salt
2 tablespoons baking powder
6 tablespoons sugar
1 pound shortening

Pinch of nutmeg (optional)
1/2 cup water
Butter
Sugar
Paprika

1. In a large bowl, mix flour, salt, baking powder and sugar.
2. Cut in shortening.
3. Blend in nutmeg, if desired.
4. Add water to the mixture, 1 tablespoon at a time, mix with a fork.
5. Form into a ball and let it rest for a few minutes.
6. Roll out crust to a little less than 1/4 inch thick.

7. Cut dough in 5-inch circles.
8. Place 1 tablespoon of filling on one half of each circle, fold over and flute.
9. Cut a small, cross shaped vent.
10. Place on ungreased cookie sheet.
11. Brush with butter, sprinkle with sugar and paprika.
12. Bake at 375°F until brown and melted cheese comes through cross shaped vents.

NUTRITION FACTS per fromajardis: 289 calories, 186 calories from fat, 20.7g total fat (32%), 7.3g saturated fat (37%), 52.1mg cholesterol (17%), 340.2mg sodium (14%), 19.5g carbohydrates (6%), zero fiber, 6.4g protein (13%), 239 IU vitamin A, zero vitamin C, 155mg calcium (16%) and 1.3mg iron (7%).

CRISPEES

Crispees are nearly always served along with the fromajardis.

Rich Pastry
Nutmeg
Sugar

Egg, beaten
Cinnamon

1. With left over pastry from the fromajardis, add a dash or two of nutmeg, and roll out to about ¼ inch thick.
2. Cut out circle with a biscuit cutter.
3. Pinch up edges to make a rim.

4. Brush with egg and sprinkle with cinnamon and sugar.
5. Bake in a 375°F oven until brown.

GRANOLA BARS

Kay Gibson of Watson, Missouri found that these bars make the prefect on-the-go breakfast. For that extra treat, she always adds chocolate chips.

4 cups rolled oats, uncooked
1 ½ cup walnuts, chopped
1 cup brown sugar
¾ cup butter or margarine, melted
1 teaspoon vanilla

½ cup honey
1 teaspoon salt
1 tablespoon wheat or rice bran
1 cup chocolate chips (optional)

1. In a large bowl, combine well all ingredients, mix well.
2. Press mixture into a well-greased jelly roll pan, 15 ½ x 10 ½-inches.

3. Bake at 450°F for 7 to 10 minutes or until light golden brown.
4. Cool in pan, cut into 75 bars.

NUTRITION FACTS per bar: 73 calories, 36 calories from fat, 4.2g total fat (6%), 1.7g saturated fat (8%), 4.9mg cholesterol (2%), 48.2mg sodium (2%), 8.4g carbohydrates (3%), .7g fiber (3%), 1.4g protein (3%), 81 IU vitamin A (2%), zero vitamin C, 7mg calcium (1%) and .4mg iron (2%).

VARIATIONS: You can replace part of the oats with rolled grains, such as rye, barley and wheat. Replace the cinnamon with other spices, such as allspice, cloves and nutmeg. You can add you choice of nuts by replacing walnuts with almonds, coconut, hazelnuts, pecans, or peanuts. Also seeds can replace the walnuts, such as sunflower or sesame seeds. Honey can be replaced with corn syrup or molasses. Raisins can be replaced with other dried fruits, such as apples, apricots, dates, peaches, or pears.

KOLACHES
Makes about 2 ½ dozen

In the German community of Fredericksburg, Texas, *Mrs. W. A. Nettle* still makes this old country recipe.

1/2 cup milk, scalded
½ cup sugar
1 teaspoon salt
½ teaspoon mace (optional)
½ lemon rind, grated

2 packages yeast
½ cup of warm water
2 egg, beaten,
½ cup margarine, melted
4 ½ to 5 ½ cups flour

1. In a large bowl, combine milk, sugar, salt, mace and lemon rind. Cool to lukewarm.
2. Stir yeast into warm water; let stand 5 minutes. Add to milk mixture.
3. Stir in eggs and margarine and enough flour to make a soft dough.
4. Knead on lightly floured board until smooth and elastic.
5. Cover and let rise in warm place until double in bulk.

6. Punch down, cover and let rise for 30 minutes more.
7. Shape into 2-inch balls, flatten slightly and place on greased cookie sheets 2 inches apart.
8. Cover and let rise 30 minutes.
9. Make a large depression in each with fingertips and fill with cottage cheese filling.
10. Bake at 375°F about 20 minutes or until golden.

Other suitable fillings are apricot preserves, cherry preserves, etc. and stewed fried fruit, mashed and sweetened to taste.

COTTAGE CHEESE FILLING

1 ½ cups cottage cheese
2 egg yolks
½ teaspoon mace (optional)

½ cup raisins

1 tablespoon lemon rind, grated
1 tablespoon lemon juice
1 ½ tablespoons sugar

1. Process cheese in electric blender until smooth (or press through a fine sieve).

2. Add remaining ingredients except raisins and blend well.

3. Stir in raisins.

NUTRITION FACTS per kolach: 193 calories, 39 calories from fat, 4.3g total fat (7%), 1g saturated fat (5%), 29.9mg cholesterol (10%), 160.7mg sodium (7%), 34.1g carbohydrates (11%), .5g fiber (2%), 4.9g protein (10%), 181 IU vitamin A (4%), 1mg vitamin C (1%), 24mg calcium (2%) and 1.3mg iron (7%).

MONSTER COOKIES
Makes about 60 cookies

Danna Bransky of Bensenville, Illinois says: "*My cookies don't look like monsters. They just feed a lot of monsters!*"

6 eggs, beaten
1 pound brown sugar
2 cups sugar
2 teaspoons corn syrup
1 1/2 teaspoons vanilla

9 cups rolled oats
1 pound mini chocolate chips
1 pound mini M&M's
1/2 pound butter, melted
4 teaspoons baking soda

1 1/2 cups peanut butter

1. Preheat oven to 350°F.
2. In a very large mixing bowl, combine oats, sugars and baking soda. Blend well.
3. Add eggs, vanilla, syrup, butter and peanut butter.
4. Add chocolate chips and M&M's.
5. Blend well tossing all ingredients to form a soft mixture.

6. Drop by small spoonfuls onto lightly greased cookie sheets, leaving a 2-inch space between cookies.
7. Bake for 8 to 10 minutes or until a very light brown.
8. Remove from oven, remove cookies with a spatula and cool on paper towels. They will stiffen as they cool.

Keep in air tight containers. They also freeze well.

NUTRITION FACTS per cookie: 246 calories, 99 calories from fat, 11.5g total fat (18%), 4.2g saturated fat (21%), 30.7mg cholesterol (10%), 164.6mg sodium (7%), 33.7g carbohydrates (11%), 2.3g fiber (9%), 4.9g protein (10%), 169 IU vitamin A (3%), zero vitamin C, 34mg calcium (3%) and 1.2mg iron (7%).

PEACH CRUNCH BARS

The fruity taste of peaches highlights these breakfast bars from *Kansas State Board of Agriculture.*

1 cup flour
1 cup whole wheat flour
1/2 cup brown sugar
1 1/2 cups granola

1/2 cup honey
1/2 cup margarine, melted
3 cups peaches, peeled, fresh, frozen, thawed or canned, drained

1/2 cup of peach preserves

1. Grease 9-inch square baking pan.

3. Stir in honey and margarine until mixture is crumbly.

2. Combine flours, sugar and granola in a large bowl.

4. Press half the mixture into the baking pan and arrange sliced peaches on top.

5. Cover with preserves.
6. Sprinkle remaining mixture on the top.

7. Bake at 350 F for 30 minutes.
8. Cool in pan before cutting into 12 bars.

NUTRITION FACTS per bar: 330 calories, 104 calories from fat, 12.1g total fat (19%), 2.1g saturated fat (10%), zero cholesterol, 99.2mg sodium (4%), 54.5g carbohydrates (1850, 3.9g fiber (15%), 4.8g protein (10%), 545 IU vitamin A (11%), 4mg vitamin C (7%), 28mg calcium (3%) and 1.8mg iron (10%).

PECAN CRESCENTS
Makes 40 crescents

Mr. and Mrs. Harry Sharp from the *Duff Green Mansion* in Vicksburg, Mississippi serves these pecan goodies to their guests.

1/2 cup butter, divided
2 teaspoons cinnamon
3/4 cup brown sugar
1/4 cup water

1/2 cup pecans, chopped
2 packages crescent refrigerated rolls (total 8 rolls)
1/4 cup sugar

1. In the oven, melt 5 tablespoons of butter in a 9x13-inch pan.
2. Sprinkle brown sugar over the butter and add the pecans.
3. Sprinkle with water.
4. Separate dough into rectangles.

5. Mix remaining butter, sugar and cinnamon. Spread this mixture on the dough.
6. Roll up each rectangle. Using a thread, slice each into 5 pieces.
7. Place cut dough in pan.
8. Bake at 375°F for 20 minutes.
9. Flip out of pan onto wax paper.

NUTRITION FACTS per crescent: 78 calories, 35 calories from fat, 4g total fat (6%), 1.7g saturated fat (8%), 6.2mg cholesterol (2%), 83.3mgsodium (3%), 10g carbohydrates (3%), .5g fiber (2%), 1.1g protein (2%), 88 IU vitamin A (2%), zero vitamin C, 18mg calcium (2%) and .5mg iron (3%).

Did you know that the pecan is a native tree from North America? They are found native from South Carolina to Arizona, mostly along the rivers and along the Gulf Coast. This area is offered called the "pecan belt." There are both hand and soft shell varieties. When it comes to Southern cooking, pecans are always the first choice.

POFFERTJES

Mina Baker-Roelofs from Pella, Iowa makes these Dutch home-style crullers with special iron molds. You can made this recipe by frying in hot fat, and they will still come out light and fluffy.

1/4 cup sugar
1 teaspoon salt
1/4 cup fat
1 cup hot water

1 teaspoon orange rind, grated
1 cup flour
3 eggs
Powdered sugar

1. Put sugar, salt, fat, rind and water in a saucepan.
2. Heat to boiling point.
3. Add flour and mix well.
4. Cook until thick (like cream puffs) stirring constantly.
5. Cool slightly. Add 1 egg at a time, beating hard after each addition.

6. Press through pastry bag on to a well greased square of heavy paper, one at a time.
7. Turn paper upside down and let cruller drop into 375°F fat.
8. Fry 6 to 7 minutes until well puffed and delicate brown.
9. Drizzle with powdered sugar.

OLD FASHIONED DUTCH LETTERS

In *Holland*, they are called "*banket*." There are many variations with different fillings from almonds to sweet potatoes. *Josie Vander Pol* of Pella, Iowa makes this version the most. She says it is important to age the filling prior to use.

FILLING

1 pound almonds
2 cups sugar

1/2 lemon rind, grated
3 eggs

1. Grind blanched almonds through a fine food chopper.

2. Add sugar, lemon rind and eggs.
3. Place in a jar and refrigerate for 4 to 5 weeks.

DUTCH CRUST

2 cups flour
1 cup butter

1/2 to 3/4 cup water
Sugar

1. In a large bowl, cut butter into flour and add enough water to make a soft dough.
2. Cool in refrigerator for 1/2 hour.
3. Remove and roll out. Put back in refrigerator for another 1/2 hour.
4. Repeat procedure once again (total of 3 times). This makes the *banket* flaky.
5. After final roll out, cut dough in strips 14x4-inches.

6. Spread filling down center of each strip and roll up from the long side and seal by brushing one edge with water to help it stick.
7. Place on greased cookie sheets; form each roll in a "S" shape.
8. Brush with beaten egg and sprinkle with sugar.
9. Prick with a fork every 2 inches.
10. Bake at 375°F for 25 minutes or until golden.
11. Cool on wire racks.

RUGELACH
Makes about 40

On Fridays, the smell of the aroma of the "*rugelach*" is on every street corner in *Israel*. People are eager to buy them for the weekend and will line up at their neighborhood bakery to get them hot out of the oven.

5 cups flour
1/2 pound margarine
2 ounces fresh yeast

3/4 cup sugar, divided
3 eggs, beaten
2 cups milk or water

1. Mix yeast with 1 teaspoon of sugar and 1/2 cup of lukewarm milk (or water) until yeast starts bubbling.

2. Mix in rest of the ingredients and knead until dough is not sticky.
3. Cool in refrigerator for at least 2 hours.

FILLING

Jam

1/3 cup cocoa

1 cup sugar

1. Mix sugar and cocoa together.
2. Roll dough into a flat sheet.
3. Spread jam on dough and spread the sugar mixture on top.

4. Cut into small triangles and roll starting from the base of the triangle.
5. Place a cookie sheet.
6. Bake at 375°F until golden, about 25 to 35 minutes.

S'MORE BARS

Do you want to make the kids happy? Serve them these bars from the *Diamond Walnut Growers* and the kids will think they are sitting around a camp-fire, telling scary stories as a full moon rises above the horizon.

¾ cup flour
3/4 cup graham cracker crumbs
1/2 cup sugar
1/2 cup butter or margarine

1 egg, beaten
1 cup miniature marshmallows
1 cup walnuts, coarsely chopped
1 cup semi-sweet chocolate pieces

1. Heat oven to 350°F.
2. Grease a 9-inch square pan.
3. In a large bowl, combine flour, graham cracker crumbs, and sugar.
4. Using a pastry blender or fork, cut in butter until mixture resembles fine meal.
5. Blend in egg.
6. Spread in the greased pan.

7. Bake for 15 to 20 minutes or just until top is lightly browned.
8. Remove from oven; immediately top with marshmallows, walnuts and chocolate pieces.
9. Return to oven for 2 minutes to soften chocolate.
10. Swirl chocolate over marshmallows and walnuts.
11. Cool until chocolate is set; cut into 20 bars.

NUTRITION FACTS per bar: 179 calories, 96 calories from fat, 11.2g total fat (17%), 4.7g saturated fat (24%), 22.9mg cholesterol (8%), 70.7mg sodium (3%), 19.1g carbohydrates (6%), .9g fiber (4%), 3g protein (6%), 207 IU vitamin A (4%), zero vitamin C, 10mg calcium (1%) and .9mg iron (5%).

WAFFELTOERICHEN

This recipe might be the most difficult one in the book. Once you master the frying, then you will appreciate the Europeans who brought this recipe to America. You will need a *rosette wafer iron* to make them. Here's what to look for if you develop a problem:

• If waffeltoerichens do not come off easily from iron, they are not fried long enough.
• If they have blisters that absorb fat, eggs are beaten too much.
• If they drop off into shortening from iron, iron is not deep enough in shortening.
• If batter will not stick to iron, iron is too hot.
• If waffeltoerichen is not crisp, it has been fried too quickly.

Cora Habenicht lives in the Texas German town of Fredericksburg and makes these wafers on special occasions. These thin, crisp wafers are enjoyed in other European countries, especially the *Scandinavian* countries.

2 eggs
2 teaspoons sugar
1/2 teaspoon salt
1 cup milk
1 cup flour

Shortening for frying
Powdered sugar for dusting
Nuts, chopped
Whipped topping

1. In a heavy, deep skillet heatshortening to 390°F to 400°F to cover the wafer iron.
2. Meanwhile beat eggs <u>slightly</u> with sugar and salt.
3. Add milk and flour to make a thin batter; beat until smooth.
4. Heat wafer iron hot shortening, dip into batter, not letting the batter come over the top of the iron.

5. Return iron to the hot shortening, thoroughly covering the iron for at least 20 seconds, but not over 35 seconds.
6. Remove rosette from iron with a piece of clean cheese cloth or paper towel.
7. Dust with sugar or fill with whipped topping and chopped nuts.

CHAPTER II

BEVERAGES

Today, orange juice is the number one choice for fruit beverage. That was not always the case, apple juice was number one until the 1950s when frozen orange juice concentrate was introduced. During America's early years, a lot of water was contaminated, and apple juice or apple cider was consumed at all meals. There are other treats, such as smoothies, coolers and shakes. Some of these treats provide two or three healthy servings from the food guide pyramid.

FRUIT BEVERAGES

Almond Fruit Smoothie (*USA*) 15

Banana Breakfast (*Mexico*) 15

Citrus Cooler (*Iowa*) 15

Good Morning Bracer (*California*) 16

Pineapple Frost (*Louisiana*) 16

Peach Freeze (*Texas*), 16

Slippery Monkey (*Texas*) 17

Tropical Orange Drink (*Tropics*) 17

HOT BEVERAGES

Almond Cappuccino & variation Orange Cappuccino (*Italy*) 17

Cafe-au-Lait & Cafe Noir (*French Louisiana*) 18

Cafe Vienna (*Austria*) 18

Dotted Swiss Cocoa (*Switzerland*) 18

Hot Chocolate (*France*) 19

Hot Spices Tea (*USA*) 19

Irish Coffee (*Ireland*) 19

Breakfast in *Mexico*

Mexican Coffee (*Mexico*) 20

Mint Tea (*Israel*) 20

Spiced Apple Cider (*Pennsylvania*) 21

Turkish Coffee (*Israel*) 21

COLD BEVERAGES

ALMOND FRUIT SMOOTHIE
Makes 4 servings

In this recipe from the *Azar Nut Company*, there are several servings from the fruit group, a serving from the dairy group, almonds from the meat group, and wheat germ from the cereal group. It's low in calories and fat, high in vitamin C, and with some protein and minerals. And it tastes great!

1 3/4 cups orange juice
1/4 cup nonfat yogurt
2 cups fresh, frozen or canned fruit (strawberries, bananas peaches, etc.)

1/4 cup of almonds, chopped, toasted
1 tablespoon honey
1 tablespoon wheat germ
2 ice cubes, crushed

1. Combine all ingredients in a blender.

2. Blend until smooth.

NUTRITION FACTS per serving: 154 calories, 5.3 total fat (8%), 29% calories from fat, .5g saturated fat (3%), 25g carbohydrates (8%), 3.2g fiber (13%), 4.2g protein (8%), 14mg sodium (1%), 77mg calcium (7%), 1.1mg iron (6%), 238 IU vitamin A (4%), and 97mg vitamin C (161%).

BANANA BREAKFAST
Makes 1 serving

Shelia D. Chavez of Livermore, California created "Desayuno con Platano" for her "Mexican Heritage Cookbook Complemented with Wine." A quick, high protein and energy breakfast drink for those on the go.

1 to 1 1/2 cups cold milk
1 egg

2 teaspoons sugar (optional)
1 banana

1 or 2 dashes cinnamon

1. Mix in blender on high for 30 seconds.

2. Pour into glass.

NUTRITION FACTS per serving: 399 calories, 138 calories from fat, 15.8g total fat (24%), 8.1g saturated fat (41%), 254mg cholesterol (85%), 213.7mg sodium (9%), 49.9g carbohydrates (17%), 2.7g fiber (11%), 17.5g protein (35%), 794 IU vitamin A (16%), 13mg vitamin C (22%), 396mg calcium (40%) and 1.2mg iron (7%).

CITRUS COOLER
Makes 8 servings

Barbara and Marsha Stensvad served guests in their 1898 *Victorian Chestnut Charm Bed and Breakfast Manor* in Atlantic, Iowa this refreshing cooler.

8 whole apricots, fresh or canned, drained
8 ounces orange juice
8 ounces pineapple juice

Crushed ice
Club soda or sparkling mineral water
8 cherries

1. Pierce apricots on all sides with fork.
2. Place an apricot in the bottom of each the 8 large chilled wine glasses.
3. Pour juices in pitcher and stir gently.

4. Equally divide juice mixture over apricots in glasses.
5. Fill each glass slightly more than halfway with crushed ice.
6. Add a splash or two of the soda.
7. Garnish with a cherry.

GOOD MORNING BRACER
Makes 1 serving

The *California Dried Plum Board* offers a beverage that most kids love, but don't tell them there are prunes (now called "dried plums) in it. This low fat, high vitamin and mineral morning beverage has a similar taste as the original Dr Pepper® soft drink.

1/4 cup prune juice
1/4 cup unflavored low-fat yogurt
4 pitted dried plums
1 tablespoon frozen orange juice concentrate

1 tablespoon frozen cranberry juice concentrate
1 tablespoon unprocessed bran
4 ice cubes
2 tablespoons sparkling water, chilled

1. Add juice, yogurt, dried plums, concentrates and bran to a blender; blend smooth.

2. Add ice; blend smooth.
3. Pour into a tall glass; stir in sparkling water.

NUTRITION FACTS per serving: 204 calories, 11 calories from fat, 1.3g total fat (2%), .6g saturated fat (3%), 3.5mg cholesterol (1%), 45mg sodium (2%), 47.2g carbohydrates (16%), 4.7g fiber (19%), 4.9g protein (10%), 721 IU vitamin A (14%), 27mg vitamin C (45%), 134mg calcium (13%) and 2.1mg iron (12%).

PINEAPPLE FROST
Makes 12 servings

Planning a brunch? *Jan Lugenbuhl* of Metairie, Louisiana serves this delicious starter at family gatherings.

3 cups pineapple sherbet, softened
16 ounces canned pineapple, crushed, drained

2 cups half and half
2/3 cup light corn syrup

1 quart ginger ale, chilled

1. In a blender or food processor, mix sherbet, pineapple, half and half, and corn syrup until pineapple is very finely chopped.
2. Pour into a medium bowl, cover, an until firm.

3. One hour before serving, remove from freezer. Place mixture in a 3 quart container, pour ginger ale over, and stir to make a slush.

NUTRITION FACTS per serving: 218 calories, 50 calories from fat, 5.8g total fat (9%), 3.5g saturated fat (18%), 18.4mg cholesterol (6%), 66.7mg sodium (3%), 42.1g carbohydrates (14%), .5g fiber (2%), 1.9g protein (4%), 230 IU vitamin A (5%), 7mg vitamin C (12%), 74mg calcium (7%) and .4mg iron (2%).

PEACH FREEZE
Makes 2 servings

If you attend the "Night in Old Fredericksburg" celebration in Fredericksburg, Texas, stop by the *P & J Peach Booth* to sample this delicious drink. If you wish, you can make it at home.

2 cups peaches, sliced
2/3 cups milk

1 teaspoon vanilla
½ cup sugar

Ice

1. Combine all ingredients in a blender and fill with ice.

2. Blend until smooth and still thick.
3. Do not over blend.

Makes 2 servings.

NUTRITION FACTS per serving: 319 calories, 25 calories from fat, 2.9g total fat (4%), 1.7g saturated fat (9%), 11.1mg cholesterol (4%), 40.4mg sodium (2%), 72.8g carbohydrates (24%), 3.4g fiber (14%), 3.9g protein (8%), 1012 IU vitamin A (20%), 12mg vitamin C (20%), 106mg calcium (11%) and .3mg iron (2%).

SLIPPERY MONKEY
Makes 2 serings

Alisa G. Zavala of Plano, Texas suggests this starter for you and a friend.

1/4 fresh cantaloupe, sliced
1 banana
3 fresh strawberries

1/2 cup orange or pineapple juice
1/3 cup skim milk
Dash of cinnamon or nutmeg

1. Mix all ingredients in a blender.
2. Blend until frothy.

3. Serve immediately

NUTRITION FACTS per serving: 185 calories, 12 calories from fat, 1.5g total fat (2%), .2g saturated fat (1%), zero cholesterol, 30.5mg sodium (1%), 43.1g carbohydrates (14%), 7.2g fiber (29%), 4.4g protein (9%), 2466 IU vitamin A (49%), 191mg vitamin C (319%), 99mg calcium (10%) and 1.3mg iron (7%).

TROPICAL ORANGE DRINK
Makes 2 servings

In many tropical countries, orange juice is often mixed with milk with the addition of an egg. This is breakfast to many with an excellent source for vitamin C and a good source for protein.

1 cup orange juice
1 raw egg (wash shell before cracking)

1 cup milk

1. Place all ingredients in a blender, blend until smooth.

NUTRITION FACTS per serving: 168 calories, 61 calories from fat, 6.8g total fat (11%), 3.4g saturated fat (17%), 122.8mg cholesterol (41%), 92.5mg sodium (4%), 18.9g carbohydrates (6%), .3g fiber (1%), 8g protein (16%), 560 IU vitamin A (11%), 63mg vitamin C (105%), 172mg calcium (17%), and .7mg iron (4%).

HOT BEVERAGES

Basically there are four kinds of hot beverages: chocolate, coffee, tea and cider. Each country has their-own specialties. I am only presenting a few, as there are a lot of country to country crossovers combinations.

ALMOND CAPPUCCINO
Makes 1 serving

The *Hershey* kitchens present this Italian favorite. Note the orange *cappuccino* variation. While they might not be Italian, you can experiment with other extracts to create your own flavors.

1 tablespoon HERSHEY'S® European Cocoa
1/2 cup vanilla ice cream
1 1/2 teaspoons sugar

1 1/2 teaspoons powdered instant coffee
3/4 cup milk
1/4 teaspoon almond extract

1. In small saucepan, combine cocoa, sugar and instant coffee; stir in milk.
2. Add ice cream; heat to serving temperature.

3. Do not boil.
4. Add almond extract.
5. Serve immediately.

If desired, mixture may be placed in a blender and mixed until frothy.

ORANGE CAPPUCCINO

1. Delete almond extract.
2. Add 1/4 teaspoon orange extract
3. 1/4 teaspoon vanilla.

The late Clyde LeBlanc from Houma, Louisiana presented two coffees, "cafe-au-lait" and "cafe noir." in his "The Good Earth Cookbook" that have their roots from France. In his own words, here's how he made them:

CAFE-AU-LAIT & CAFÉ NOIR

Cafe-au-lait (coffee with milk) is served in a large china cup with milk of equal parts of strong hot coffee and good fresh cream (or milk) scaled well and very hot. These are often poured from two matching pots at the same moment, one being held in each hand. If the cream is not fresh and sweet it will curdle. The cafe-au-lait is sweetened, if desired, when served.

NUTRITION FACTS per cup: 77 calories, 36 calories from fat, 4.1g total fat (6%), 2.5g saturated fat (13%), 16.6mg cholesterol (6%), 62.1mg sodium (3%), 6.2g carbohydrates (2%), zero fiber, 4.1g protein (8%), 154 IU vitamin A (3%), 1mg vitamin C (2%), 148mg calcium (15%) and .1mg iron (1%).

It is most important that the coffee pot be perfectly clean inside as well as outside because stale oils will give coffee a rancid flavor (most peculiar and unpleasant to the taste). Over heating also spoils the flavor. Water must be freshly drawn and boiling briskly when poured over grounds. Serve café noir in tiny china cups (called *demi-tasse*) hot and strong and sweetened with loaf sugar. You have a real cup of *Creole cafe noir*. This is generally an early morning or afternoon drink.

CAFE VIENNA
Makes 1 serving

Picture sitting by *Austria's* blue Danube River at an outdoor Vienna café, sipping a cup a coffee. That's what the people at *Nestle® Beverage Company* pictured when they developed this recipe.

3 cups brewed hot coffee or 2 tablespoons instant
coffee in 3 cups hot water
2 cinnamon sticks

4 whole cloves
Whipped cream, sweeten
Cinnamon

1. Pour hot coffee over cinnamon sticks and cloves.
2. Hold in coffee warmer or over low heat for at least 15 minutes.

3. Fill coffee cups with spiced coffee.
4. Spoon large dollops of whipped cream and sprinkle cinnamon on top.

DOTTED SWISS COCOA
Makes 1 serving

The American Dairy Association offers this simple, yet delicious cocoa that kids really enjoy.

1 envelope hot cocoa mix
3/4 cup milk

3 tablespoons whipped cream
Cinnamon candy hearts

1. Put milk in a 2 cup glass measuring cup.
2. Microwave on high 1 1/2 minutes.
3. Use a wire whisk to beat cocoa mix into hot milk until foamy.

4. Pour into a mug.
5. Drab whipped cream on top.
6. Sprinkle with cinnamon candies.
7. Drink immediately.

HOT CHOCOLATE
Makes 6 servings

Even though chocolate originated in the America's, it took the Europeans to add life to this delicious drink. The *French* did it up right with a hint orange and cinnamon.

1 quart milk
Grated zest from 1 large orange
3 sticks cinnamon or 1/4 teaspoon ground cinnamon

4 ounces semi-sweet chocolate
6 tablespoons Grand Marnier
Whipped cream for garnish (optional)

1. In a small saucepan over low heat, slowly scald the milk with the orange zest and cinnamon.
2. Remove the sticks.
3. In a blender, combine the hot milk with the .

chocolate and Grand Marnier.
4. Blend on slow speed until very smooth, about 30 seconds.
5. Serve immediately in warm mugs and top with whipped cream, if desired.

NUTRITION FACTS per serving (without whipped cream): 245 calories, 108 calories from fat, 11g total fat (17%), 6.7g saturated fat (33%), 22.1mg cholesterol (7%), 81.9 sodium (3%), 25.6g carbohydrates (9%), 1.2g fiber (5%), 6.2g protein (12%), 218 IU vitamin A (4%), 4mg vitamin C (7%), 205mg calcium (20%), and .7mg iron (4%).

HOT SPICED TEA
Makes 4 servings

Brew your favorite tea, add the goodness of honey and a bit of spice to this recipe from the *National Honey Board*.

4 cups freshly brewed tea
1/4 cup honey
4 whole cloves

4 cinnamon sticks
4 slices citrus fruit (optional)

1. Combine tea, honey, cinnamon and cloves in a saucepan; simmer 5 minutes.

2. Serve hot with citrus garnish.

NUTRITION FACTS per serving: 67 calories, zero fats, cholesterol and sodium, 18.2g carbohydrates (6%), zero fiber, protein, vitamin A and C and calcium, .2mg iron (1%).

IRISH COFFEE
Makes 4 servings

For that special brunch, make this all time favorite from Ireland from the *Coffee Development Group* kitchens.

1 1/2 cups hot coffee
8 teaspoons sugar

4 ounces Irish whiskey
Whipped cream

1. Warm 4 wine glasses or mugs in hot water; dry the glasses and place 2 teaspoons of sugar in each glass.
2. Pour in hot coffee to within 2 inches of rim.
3. Mix sugar and coffee.

4. Add 1 ounce whiskey to each glass and stir.
5. Top each serving with 2 tablespoons of softly whipped cream.
6. Serve immediately.

Did you know that coffee originated in Abyssinia (now Ethiopia)? These tropical plants are now grown throughout the tropics regions of the world. Coffee bushes were first cultivated in Arabia. Brazil is the largest coffee grower.

BREAKFAST IN MEXICO

In Mexico, ingredients from the Spanish and the Aztec have been combined to make an unique breakfast. The Aztec contributed beans, corn, tomatoes, avocados and pumpkins; while the Spanish introduced rice, olives and almonds.

Corn is the key ingredient and is made into a meal called "*masa*," which are corn kernels soaked in lime water, dried, then ground into a powder. *Masa* is used for making tortillas and tamales.

In some regions of Mexico, sweet tamales are often served for breakfast.

The word tortilla comes from Spain and is an omelet, however, in Mexico, it is a pancake type of bread. Some tortillas are also made from flour, which is preferred over corn in some parts of Mexico. Tortillas are available in many parts of the United States, however, best to make them fresh. Many supermarkets stock both corn and flour *masas* in the Mexican food section.

Fried beans are served as a side dish with most breakfast main courses.

MEXICAN COFFEE
Makes 4 servings

Let's go south of the border for this treat from the *National Honey Board*.

4 cups hot strong, espresso-style coffee
3/4 cup half & half
1/3 cup honey

2 tablespoons unsweetened cocoa
1 teaspoon cinnamon
Sweetened whipped cream (optional)

Chocolate shavings (optional)

1. Combine hot coffee, half and half, honey, cocoa and cinnamon in blender and blend 1 minute on high.

2. Pour into mugs; garnish with whipped cream and chocolate shavings, if desired.

NUTRITION FACTS per serving without the toppings: 157 calories, 46 calories from fat, 5.6g total fat (9%), 3.5g saturated fat (17%), 16.7mg cholesterol (6%), 25mg sodium (1%), 28.1g carbohydrates (9%), 1.3g fiber (5%), 2.2g protein (4%), 199 IU vitamin A (4%), 1mg vitamin C (1%), 64mg calcium (6%) and .8mg iron (5%).

MINT TEA
Makes 4 servings

Mint tea is enjoyed at breakfast, since it has a cooling effect during *Israel's* hot summer months, plus it is a natural thirst quencher any time during the day.

2 1/2 tablespoons sugar
2 teaspoons mint leaves

4 shakes lemon salt
5 cups boiling water

4 tea bags

1. In a teapot or carafe put sugar, tea bags, mint and lemon salt.

2. Add boiling water, cover and let steep.

NUTRITION FACTS per serving: 39 calories, zero calories from fats, cholesterol and sodium, 9.7g carbohydrates (3%), zero fiber, .4g protein (1%), zero vitamin A, 1mg vitamin C (1%), 6mg calcium (1%) and .3mg iron (2%),

Did you know that tea is native to China? Tea is now grown throughout the Orient and parts of Africa. There are three basic teas: black, green, and oolong. Tea is a member of the *camellia* genus. Black tea is the most popular, followed a dozen varieties such as Ceylon, Ear Gray (a blend) and Sumatra. The best teas are grown above 6500 feet in the hot, humid mountains.

SPICED APPLE CIDER
Makes 16 servings

In the German *Kitchen Kettle Village* in Intercourse, Pennsylvania, stop by the *Jam & Relish Kitchen* and pick up some of their apple cinnamon jelly to make this delicious drink. It's great either hot or chilled!

1 gallon of apple cider   5 ounces apple cinnamon jelly

6 whole cloves

1. Heat cider, jelly and cloves until jelly melts.

. Keeps well for 1 week in the refrigerator.

NUTRITION FACTS per serving: 141 calories, 7 calories from fat, .8g total fat (1%), .2g saturated fat (1%), zero cholesterol, 14mg sodium (1%), 35g carbohydrates (12%), 1.2g fiber (5%), .3g protein (1%), zero vitamin A, 4mg vitamin C (7%), 34mg calcium (3%) and 1.1mg iron (6%).

Cider is made from ground up apple, pear and/or peach pulp. The juice is then pressed from the pulp. The juice is fermented (hard). By English standards, American cider isn't cider all, but merely juice. The alcoholic content of hard cider varies from 2% to a potent distilled spirit called "applejack" (90g alcohol and one cup has 628 calories, but zero fats, vitamins and minerals) or cider brandy. In Colonial times, cider was the national beverage, made so by the abundance of apples, pears, and peaches. In a good year, a single village of forty families might put up 3,000 barrels of cider in the 1720s. As it aged, it became more intoxicating, but at least it was preserved to help people through the long winters. Cider is also made into a sweet version, which is pasteurized so it won't spoil. Also American cider contains preservatives to keep it from fermenting beyond the legal limit. The sweet cider has 177 calories per cup,

---

TURKISH COFFEE
Makes 1 serving

The drinking of *Turkish* coffee has become part of the national folklore in *Israel*. Songs have been composed about the coffee and its *feenjan* pot. This pot has a long handle, is wide at the bottom and narrow toward the top. Drinking it at the end of breakfast is a well established custom in *Israel*.

1 tablespoon Turkish coffee, finely ground   Cardamon pods to taste
1 teaspoon sugar (more or less to suit your taste)   1 1/4 cups boiling water

1. Thoroughly mix coffee and sugar in a feenjan or a deep saucepan.
2. Add the boiling water, stir well.
3. Add cardamon pods (experiment to achieve desired taste).
4. Bring coffee to a boil.
5. When the foam on top begins to rise, remove coffee from heat until it settles and repeat process by boiling once more.
6. Pour into a coffee cup, spooning in some of the foam.
7. The coffee grounds will sink to the bottom of the cup; do not stir them up.
8. Serve immediately.

May be multiplied by the number of cups required. Turkish coffee and feenjan pots can be found at most stores specializing in Middle Eastern foodstuffs and some spice shops.

NUTRITION FACTS per serving: 29 calories, zero fats, cholesterol and sodium 6.4g carbohydrates (2%), zero fiber, .7g protein (1%), zero vitamins A and C, 8mg calcium (1%) and .2mg iron (1%).

BISCUITS & SCONES

Scones made by Scottish immigrants are believed to be the forerunner of the American biscuit. Scones are made with butter, and usually have eggs and cream as the liquid, whereas biscuits are more basic with shortening in place of butter, and seldom are eggs or cream used as part of the liquid.

It is important that biscuit and scone doughs needs a minimum of handling or they can become heavy and tough, instead of light and fluffy. While some kneading is required, keep it to a minimum. The type of flour used is the key to flakiness. All purpose flour is a combination of soft and hard wheat and produces the flakiest product, which is preferred in the northern United States. In the South a crumbly product is preferred, hence only soft flour is used.

BISCUITS

Angel Biscuits (*Kansas*) 23

Beaten Biscuits (*Virginia*) 23

Buttermilk Biscuits (*USA*) 24

Variations

Bacon Biscuits 24

Cheddar Cheese Biscuits 24

Drop Biscuits 24

Fruited Biscuits 24

Herb & Spiced Biscuits 24

Nutty Biscuits 24

Flaky Cinnamon Biscuits (*USA*) 25

Breakfast in Ireland

Irish Soda Bread (*Ireland*), 25

Jimmy's Biscuits (*Louisiana*) 25

Norwegian Flatbread (*Norway*) 26

Pinwheels (*USA*) 26

Potato Biscuits (*Illinois*) 27

Sourdough Biscuits (*Texas*) 27

Spicy Turkey Sausage Biscuits (*USA*) 28

Sweet Potato Biscuits (*Virginia*) 28

SCONES

Chalet Luise Scones (*Canada*) 29

Cinnamon Scones (*cruise ship*) 29

English Breakfast Scones (*California*) 30

Glazed Raisin Scones with Lemon Butter (*North Carolina*) 30

Golden Pumpkin Scones (*USA*) 31

Good Morning Scones (*Canada*) 32

Layered Jam Biscuit Bake (*USA*) 32

Variation - Cinnamon Pecan 33

Orange Scones (*Oregon*) 33

Scottish Potato Scones (*USA*) 33

BISCUIT & SCONE TOPPINGS

Blueberry Jam (*USA*) 34
Gooseberry Jam (*Canada*) 35
Marmalade (*France*) 35

Pear Preserves (*USA*) 35
Quince Jam (*Mississippi*) 35
Rhubarb & Strawberry Jam (*Canada*) 36

BISCUITS

BISCUIT TIPS

• Do not over blend the shortening with the flour. The result should look like course crumbs. Over blending will reduce the flakiness.
• Knead with your finger tips and gently. Never knead more than a dozen times.
• Roll or pat out the dough lightly. Do not roll out thinner than 1/2-inch unless instructed to do so.
• Dip the biscuit cutter in the flour between each cut.
• Biscuit is done when both the top and bottom are golden brown.

Biscuits are best when served immediately. They should be hot enough so the butter will melt into them.

ANGEL BISCUITS
Makes about 30 biscuits

Early day leavening agents were not always dependable, so many bakers added yeast to biscuit recipes to insure they would be light and fluffy. Yeast also gives this recipe by *Teresa Flora* of Sawyer, Kansas, extra flavor not found in regular baking powder biscuits.

5 cups unsifted flour	1 package yeast
¼ cup sugar	1 tablespoon baking powder
1 teaspoon salt	1 teaspoon baking soda
1 cup shortening	2 teaspoons warm water

2 cups buttermilk

1. In a small bowl, dissolve yeast in 2 teaspoons of warm water.
2. In a large bowl combine all dry ingredients.
3. Cut shortening into flour mixture until crumbly.
4. Add yeast and buttermilk.
5. Turn onto floured surface, knead 4 or 5 times.

6. Roll out to ½-inch thick. Cut with 2 ½ inch biscuit cutter.
7. Place on an ungreased cookie sheet, cover and let rise in warm place, free from drafts, for 10 to 15 minutes.
8. Bake at 475°F for 10 to 15 minutes, until tops are golden brown.

NUTRITION FACTS per biscuit: 151 calories, 65 calories from fat, 7.2g total fat (11%), 1.8g saturated fat (9%), zero cholesterol, 167.1mg sodium (7%), 18.6g carbohydrates (6%), zero fiber, 2.8g protein (6%), zero vitamin A and C, 56mg calcium (6%) and 1.1mg iron (6%).

BEATEN BISCUITS
Makes 24 biscuits

Contrary to all biscuit theories, the dough of these old fashion biscuits are beaten with a mallet for about an hour and are served cold. If you have a kneader, as does *Steamers Seafood Restaurant* on Chincoteague Island, Virginia, run the dough back and forth until rather soft and perfectly smooth. Try making them by hand at least once!

3 cup flour	3 teaspoons butter
1/2 teaspoon sugar	3 teaspoons shortening
1/2 teaspoon salt	1/2 cup cold milk

1/2 cup cold water

1. Sift flour, sugar and salt in a mixing bowl.
2. Add butter and shortening and blend with a pastry blender.
3. Add milk and water and toss mixture with a fork.
4. Knead dough for about 15 minutes.

5. Place dough on a floured board and beat with a mallet for about an hour. When ready, the dough is smooth and glossy.
6. Roll into balls about the size of a walnut.
7. Place on a baking sheet and prick each biscuit one time with a fork.
8. Bake for 30 minutes in a 325°F oven.

NUTRITION FACTS per biscuit: 87 calories, 3.5g total fat (5%), 1.5g saturated fat (7%), 5mg cholesterol (1.5%), 12g carbohydrates (4%), 2g protein (3.5%), 62mg sodium (2.5%), 9mg calcium (5%), 1mg iron (4%) and 60 IU vitamin A (1%).

BUTTERMILK BISCUITS
Makes 12 biscuits

The easiest, and the most popular biscuit is the buttermilk biscuit. Follow this recipe by *SACO Foods, Inc.* and they will always come out light and flaky.

3 tablespoons dry cultured buttermilk powder
2 teaspoons baking powder
1/2 teaspoon soda
2 cups flour

1 teaspoon salt
2 teaspoons sugar
1/3 cup shortening
2/3 cup water

1. Preheat oven to 450°F.
2. Sift dry ingredients together into a mixing bowl.
3. Cut in shortening thoroughly until mixture resembles cornmeal.
4. Add water and mix until dough is pliable.

5. Turn dough on a lightly floured surface and knead lightly for about 30 seconds (20 to 25 times).
6. Roll or pat 1/2-inch thick, no less.
7. Cut with floured 2 1/2-inch biscuit cutter.
8. Place close together on an ungreased baking sheet.
9. Bake 10 to 12 minutes or until golden brown.

NUTRITION FACTS per biscuit: 136 calories, 54 calories from fat, 6g total fat (9%), 1.5g saturated fat (8%), zero cholesterol, 300.7mg sodium (13%), 17.7g carbohydrates (6%), zero fiber, 2.8g protein (6%), zero vitamin A and C, 82mg calcium (8%) and 1.1mg iron (6%).

VARIATIONS

Add a little excitement to the buttermilk biscuit recipe by adding an extra ingredient or two.

BACON BISCUITS: Add 6 slices of cooked crisp bacon, crumbled to dry ingredients.
CHEDDAR CHEESE BISCUITS: Add 1/2 to 1 cup of grated cheese to dry ingredients.
DROP BISCUITS: Increase water to 1 cup. Do not knead. Drop by tablespoons on an ungreased cookie sheet.
FRUITED BISCUITS: Add up to 1/2 cup of chopped dried fruit, such as apples, apricots, dates, raisins, etc. If desired, add 1/4 teaspoon of cinnamon.
HERB AND SPICED BISCUITS: Add 1/2 to 1 teaspoon of your favorite seeds, spice or herbs to dry ingredients, such as allspice, basil, caraway, cinnamon, cloves, curry, nutmeg, poppy seeds, rosemary, sesame seeds, etc.
NUTTY BISCUITS: Add about 1/2 cup of chopped almonds, peanuts, pecans, or walnuts to dry ingredients.

> **The biscuit term** has many meanings. In America it is baked dough. In Europe it refers to a cookie or a cracker. In Italy it is frozen desert. The word in French means "twice cooked," and refers to a thin, flat bread used by shipboard travelers, known as "pilot bread."

FLAKY CINNAMON BISCUITS

Make the buttermilk biscuit recipe.

Butter, melted   Cinnamon
                          Brown sugar

1. Roll out to about 1/4 inch thick.
2. On one half, brush with melted butter, sprinkle lightly with cinnamon and brown sugar; fold over.

3. Roll out one more time and repeat with butter, cinnamon and brown sugar; fold over.
4. Cut with biscuit cutter and proceed as with buttermilk biscuits.

BREAKFAST IN IRELAND

The hearty Irish breakfast is as varied and full of flavor and character as Ireland itself. From the northern reaches of Donegal to the rolling green hills of County Kerry, distinctive regional breakfast specialties have evolved over the centuries.

The bountiful breakfast, as it is known today, originated in the 19th century and was called *"The Fry."* This includes a combination of pork, potatoes, grains and dairy products, along with a pint of ale. Today it is the same, but in most cases minus the ale. Bacon, sausage, puddings, oats, potatoes, breads and cheeses are the mainstays.

IRISH SODA BREAD
Makes 1 loaf

This giant biscuit, the largest of the biscuits, is served to guests at *Ashing Cottage*, Spring Lake, New Jersey, by *goodie and Jack Stewart.*

4 cups flour   1 cup raisins
1 tablespoon baking powder   2 tablespoons caraway seeds
1 teaspoon salt   2 eggs
3/4 teaspoon baking soda   8 ounces plain yogurt
                          1/2 cup water

1. Preheat oven to 350°F and grease a deep, round casserole dish.
2. In a large bowl, combine together all dry ingredients including the raisins and caraway.
3. In a separate bowl beat eggs, yogurt and water.
4. Add egg mixture to the dry ingredients.

5. Knead lightly adding a little flour if to sticky.
6. Form into a round, put into casserole bowl and cut an "X" into the top with a sharp knife.
7. Bake for 1 hour and 15 minutes or until golden brown.
8. Best if served the following day. Slice very thin and serve with butter or honey butter.

NUTRITION FACTS per slice (based on 16 slices per loaf): 162 calories, 14 calories from fat, 1.6g total fat (2%), .6g saturated fat (3%), 28.4mg cholesterol (9%), 277mg sodium (12%), 32.4g carbohydrates (11%), .7g fiber (3%), 5g protein (10%), 61 IU vitamin A (1%), 1mg vitamin C (1%), 99mg calcium (10%) and 2mg iron (11%).

JIMMY'S BISCUITS
Makes 6 servings

In Louisiana's Cajun country, *Jimmy Provost*, along with his wife *Betty*, host guests at their *Wildlife Gardens* in Gibson with a number of specialties that includes this easy to make drop biscuits.

2 cups prepared biscuit mix   7-UP®   ¼ cup margarine

1. Preheat an iron skillet on top of the stove.
2. Melt the margarine.
3. Mix the biscuit recipe per package instructions with amount of liquid called for, but use 7-UP instead of the liquid stated. The consistency of the batter should be soft.
4. Spoon tablespoons of the batter into the hot skillet.
5. Bake in a 375°F oven until golden brown on top.
6. Turn onto a platter quickly.

NUTRITION FACTS per serving: 228 calories, 115 calories from fat, 12.9g total fat (20%), 1.3g saturated fat (7%), zero cholesterol, 555.3mg sodium (23%), 25.5g carbohydrates (8%), zero fiber, 2.8g protein (6%), 311 IU vitamin A (6%), zero vitamin C, 56mg calcium (6%) and .7mg iron (4%).

FLATBREAD
Makes 6 circles

In some European countries, cookies are called "biscuits." Well, this recipe is neither a cookie, nor a biscuit, but is closer to a biscuit than a bread. For some tasty variations to this *Norwegian* recipe, make flatbread with only white flour or only rye flour or substitute 2/3 cup cornmeal for 2/3 cup flour.

1 1/3 cups whole wheat flour
1 1/3 cups white flour
1/4 cup vegetable oil

1 teaspoon baking soda
1/2 teaspoon salt
3/4 to 1 cup buttermilk

1. Combine first 5 ingredients in a bowl; mix well.
2. Add only enough buttermilk to make a stiff dough.
3. Knead dough for 30 seconds on a well floured surface.
4. Roll about 1/4 cup of the dough into a ball and then pat it down into a flat circle.
5. Keep the remaining dough covered so it doesn't become too dry.
6. With a floured stockinet-covered rolling pin on a well floured surface, roll dough into a very thin 10-inch circle.
7. If dough sticks on the surface or the rolling pin, dust it with more flour.
8. Place flatbread on an ungreased cookie sheet.
9. Score dough circle with a knife, making triangles, squares or whatever shapes you prefer.
10. Bake at 350°F for 8 to 10 minutes.
11. Flatbread should be crisp and slightly brown around the edges.
12. Cool on wire rack and repeat with remaining dough.

Break into pieces, serve plain or with desired topping, such as butter or cheese.

NUTRITION FACTS per circle: 189 calories, 60 calories from fat, 6.8g total fat (10%), .9g saturated fat (5%), zero cholesterol, 281mg sodium (12%), 28g carbohydrates (9%), 2.2g fiber (9%), 5g protein (10%), zero vitamins A and C, 33mg calcium (3%) and 1.6mg iron (9%).

PINWHEELS

With buttermilk biscuit dough, you can make small cinnamon rolls that will melt in your mouth.

Buttermilk biscuit recipe, page 24
Brown sugar

Cinnamon or other spices
Raisins

Walnut or pecans, chopped

1. Roll out dough, to about 16x8-inches, by1/4-inch thick.
2. Sprinkle brown sugar, spices, raisins, and/or nuts and roll up jelly roll style.
3. Cut into 12 equal pieces and place in muffin cups or an 8x10-inch baking pan.
4. Bake at 450°F for about 12 to 15 minutes or until golden brown.

NOTE: Brown sugar, cinnamon, raisins and nuts can be replaced with a thin layer of your favorite jam, finely chopped apples and other ingredients.

POTATO BISCUITS
Makes about 4 dozen biscuits

Are you too busy to fix breakfast? *Danna Bransky* of Bensenville, Illinois suggests to prepare this recipe the night before and bake in the morning.

1 1/2 cups plain mashed potatoes (no milk or seasonings)
4 eggs, slightly beaten
2 packages yeast
1/2 cup warm water
2/3 cup sugar

1/2 cup butter, melted
1 tablespoon salt
2 cups potato water
1 cup warm milk
1/2 cup shortening, melted

8 to 10 cups flour

1. Cook potatoes in water; drain and save liquid.
2. In a large bowl, mash potatoes.
3. Add the rest of the ingredients, except flour.
4. Stir in flour, a cup at a time until mixture gradually becomes an elastic ball.
5. Grease ball of dough lightly. Cover with waxed paper. Let rise until it doubles in size. This will raise in the refrigerator over night.

6. Punch down, roll out to 1/2-inch thick (no less).
7. Cut with biscuit cutter.
8. Let rise in a warm place until doubled.
9. Bake 350°F for 20 minutes.

NUTRITION FACTS per biscuit: 140 calories, 46 calories from fat, 5.1g total fat (8%), 2.1g saturated fat (10%), 23.6mg cholesterol (8%), 180.3mg sodium (8%), 20.3g carbohydrates (7%), .3g fiber (1%), 3.2g protein (6%), 115 IU vitamin A (2%), zero vitamin C, 14mg calcium (1%) and 1.1mg iron (6%).

SOURDOUGH BISCUITS
Makes 30 biscuits

Picture a group of cowboys lined up at a chuck wagon waiting for a plate full of scrambled eggs, country sausage and a handful of sourdough biscuits. You can experience that with a visit to the *Figure 3 Ranch* in Claude, Texas. Here's how *Anne Christian* makes her biscuits.

5 cups flour
2 1/2 cups sourdough starter
1 teaspoon sugar

1 teaspoon baking soda
1/2 teaspoon salt
1/4 cup vegetable oil

1. Place flour in a large and make a well in the flour.
2. Pour starter into the well and add all other ingredients.
3. Stir until mixture no longer picks up flour.
4. Cover and let rise 3 to 4 hours, or overnight.
5. Place dough on floured board and roll to 1/2

inch thickness.
6. Cut out biscuits and place in a large greased cast-iron Dutch oven.
7. Set by the campfire to rise for 1 to 2 hours.
8. Place hot lid on oven, set oven on hot coals, and place some coals on the lid.
9. Cook until brown, about 5 to 8 minutes.

NUTRITION FACTS per biscuit: 119 calories, 2g total fat (3%), .3g saturated fat (1%), zero cholesterol, 22g carbohydrates (7%), 3g protein (6%), 79mg sodium (3%), 5mg calcium, 1.4mg and iron (7%)

SOURDOUGH STARTER

1 package dry yeast
1 1/2 cups warm water

2 teaspoon sugar
1 1/2 cups flour

1. In a nonmetal crock mix yeast, water, sugar and flour.

2. Cover and let it rise for about 12 hours.

NOTE: If a Dutch oven and a campfire are not handy place biscuits on a cookie sheet, cover and let rise in a warm place, uncover and bake at 400°F until golden brown.

TURKEY SAUSAGE BISCUITS SPICY
Makes 12 biscuits

Are you looking for more protein for breakfast, but without the fat? *Deborah Lund* of the *National Turkey Federation* suggests you try this recipe.

1 pound turkey breakfast sausage, casings removed
2 1/4 cups biscuit mix

1/2 cup oat bran
1 cup reduced-fat cheddar cheese, grated
1/2 teaspoon red pepper flakes

1/3 cup skim milk

1. In medium non-stick skillet, over medium heat, break up and sauté turkey 5 to 6 minutes or until no longer pink; remove from heat and drain.
2. In medium bowl combine turkey sausage, biscuit mix, oat bran, cheese and pepper flakes.
3. Add milk, stirring just until moistened.

4. Coat 12x15-inch baking sheet with cooking spray.
5. Drop approximately 1/3 cup of dough for each biscuit onto baking sheet.
6. Bake in middle of 450°F oven for 12 to 15 minutes or until browned.

NUTRITION FACTS per biscuit: 194 calories, 63 calories from fat, 6.7g total fat (10%), 1.9g saturated fat (10%), 23.5mg cholesterol (8%), 757.1mg sodium (32%), 19.4g carbohydrates (6%), 1.3g fiber (5%), 12.4g protein (25%), 41 IU vitamin A (1%), zero vitamin C, 126mg calcium (13%) and 2mg iron (11%).

SWEET POTATO BISCUITS
Makes 24 biscuits

Here's a special breakfast treat that *Jackie Russell* from Chincoteaggue Island, Virginia makes for her family.

2 cups flour
4 teaspoons baking powder
1 teaspoon salt

2 tablespoons sugar
2 heaping tablespoons shortening
1 1/2 cups sweet potatoes, cooked, mashed

1 cup milk

1. In a large bowl, mix flour and other dryingredients.
2. Cut in shortening.
3. Add sweet potatoes and blend well.
4. Add liquid, a little at a time to make a soft dough (if sweet potatoes are dry, recipe might require a bit more liquid).

5. Roll on floured board and cut with a biscuit cutter.
6. Place on a greased baking sheet and bake at 400°F for 15 to 20 minutes until brown.

NUTRITION FACTS per biscuit: 66 calories, 1.5g total fat (2.5%), .6 saturated fat (2.5%), 1.5mg cholesterol (.5%), 12g carbohydrates (4%), 1.5g protein (3%), 155mg sodium (7%), 43mg potassium, 72mg calcium (7%), .6mg iron (3%), 2mg vitamin C (3%) and 1,643 IU vitamin A (33%).

Did you know the sweet potato is not related to the yam? Yes, they are two different species, however, can be interchanged in recipes. The sweet potato originated in tropical America and was cultivated by Native Americans long before the Europeans arrived.

SCONES

Scones, like biscuits, originated in America, with recipes making it back to Europe. Scones are quite popular in Britain, especially at tea time. The British like scones with butter and jam. In the county of Devonshire, a large dollop of thick Devonshire cream is preferred.

SCONE TIPS

• Handling and care of scone dough is basically the same as for biscuits (see BISCUIT TIPS, page 23).
• When butter is used, it should be chilled.
• Scone dough is generally patted out in a circle, not rolled, and cut into wedges.
• If the dough is cut with a round biscuit cutter, gather remaining dough, make a ball, gently pat it into a circle about 1/2-inch thick and cut into wedges.

CHALET LUISE SCONES
Makes 4 servings

On the menu at *Chalet Luise* in Whistler, B.C., Canada, hosts *Luise and Eric Zinsli* serve these scones to their guests.

1 3/4 cups flour
2 1/4 teaspoons baking powder
Sugar
1 teaspoon vanilla
1/4 cup salted butter, cut into pieces, at room temperature

1/4 cup raisins
1/4 cup candied orange or lemon peel
1/4 cup almonds, sliced
1/2 cup whipping cream or half & half
1 egg
2 tablespoons milk

1. Preheat oven to 450°F.
2. Sift flour, baking powder and 2 tablespoons of sugar into a large bowl.
3. Using finger tips rub butter into flour until mixture resembles course meal.
4. Stir in raisins, peel and nuts.
5. Make a well in the center.
6. In a small bowl, blend cream with egg and vanilla and pour into the well.
7. With a large fork mix until incorporated.
8. Gather dough into ball and flatten.

9. Roll out on lightly floured board to 1/2 inch thick.
10. Cut with cookie cutter in 2 inch rounds. Reroll scraps and cut into six equal wedges.
11. Place on lightly buttered baking sheet.
12. Lightly brush with milk and sprinkle with sugar.
13. Place in oven, reduce to 400°F and bake about 15 minutes or until golden brown.
14. Serve warm with butter and jam.

NUTRITION FACTS per serving: 602 calories, 258 calories from fat, 29.1g total fat (45%), 15g saturated fat (75%), 125.6mg cholesterol (42%), 369.6mg sodium (15%), 77.2g carbohydrates (26%), 2.3g fiber (9%), 10.3g protein (21%), 962 IU vitamin A (19%), 1mg vitamin C (1%), 265mg calcium (26%) and 3.6mg iron (20%).

CINNAMON SCONES
Makes 8 wedges

These scones are featured in the *Princess Cruises Cuisine Cookbook* and are served shipboard to passengers.

2 cups flour
2 teaspoons baking powder
1/2 teaspoon baking soda
1/2 teaspoon salt
1/2 cup butter or margarine

1 egg, separated
3 tablespoons honey
1/3 cup buttermilk
1 tablespoon sugar
1/4 teaspoon cinnamon

1. Preheat oven to 400°F.
2. In a large bowl stir together first four ingredients.
3. Cut in butter until the mixture is the consistency of coarse crumbs.
4. In a small bowl, beat egg yolk with honey and buttermilk until blended.
5. Add buttermilk mixture to the flour mixture, stirring lightly only until dough clings together.
6. Using floured hands, lightly shape dough into a flattened ball.
7. Roll or pat out on a floured board to a circle about 1/2-inch thick and 8 1/2-inches in diameter.

8. Using a floured knife, cut into 8 equal wedges. Place them slightly apart on a greased baking sheet.
9. In a small bowl, beat egg white slightly to a froth.
10. In another small bowl, blend sugar and cinnamon.
11. Brush scones lightly with egg white, then sprinkle them with the cinnamon mixture.
12. Bake for 10 to 12 minutes, or until golden brown.

NUTRITION FACTS per wedge: 259 calories, 110 calories from fat, 12.4g total fat (19%), 7.4g saturated fat (37%), 57.6mg cholesterol (19%), 438mg sodium (18%), 32.9g carbohydrates (11%), zero fiber, 4.5g protein (9%), 471 IU vitamin A (9%), zero vitamin C, 109mg calcium (11%) and 1.8mg iron (10%).

ENGLISH BREAKFAST SCONES
Makes about 12 scones

Innkeeper *Lisa Smith* of the *Country Garden Inn* in Napa, California, held a "bake off" at the Inn. This was the best. One of the secrets for scones is that all ingredients should be very cold.

3 cups self raising flour
1/2 cup butter
1/2 teaspoon salt

1/2 cup sugar
2 eggs
1/2 cup milk

1. In a food processor, process flour and butter until crumbly.
2. Add salt and sugar, pulse 2 times to mix.
3. Add cold milk and cold eggs.
4. Pulse until dough "just" forms.
5. Roll out onto floured surface 1-inch thick.

6. Cut with round biscuit cutter.
7. Place on an ungreased cookie sheet.
8. Bake at 350°F for 18 to 25 minutes or until golden brown.

NUTRITION FACTS per scone: 228 calories, 82 calories from fat, 9.1g total fat (14%), 5.2g saturated fat (26%), 57.2mg cholesterol (19%), 578.4mg sodium (24%), 32.1g carbohydrates (11%), 1g fiber (4%), 4.5g protein (9%), 351 IU vitamin A (7%), zero vitamin C, 124mg calcium (12%) and 1.6mg iron (9%).

GLAZED RAISIN SCONES WITH LEMON BUTTER
Makes 16 scones

Liz Oehser, innkeeper at the *Buttonwood Inn* in Franklin, North Carolina serves these scones to her guests.

2 cups flour
Sugar
2 1/2 teaspoons baking powder
1/2 teaspoon salt

1/2 cup butter or margarine, slightly softened
3/4 cup raisins
2 eggs, divided
1/4 to 1/3 cup milk

1. Preheat oven to 400°F.

2. In large bowl mix flour, 1/4 cup sugar, baking powder and salt.

3. Cut in butter until mixture resembles coarse crumbs.
4. Mix in raisins.
5. In small bowl, mix 1 egg and 1 egg yolk; reserve remaining white in another bowl.
6. Mix eggs into flour mixture.
7. Mix in enough of the milk to make the dough that holds together.
8. Turn onto lightly floured surface and knead 5 or 6 times.
9. Halve dough.
10. Pat each half into a circle 1/2 inch thick.
11. Cut each circle into 8 wedges.
12. Place, spaced apart, on lightly greased baking sheet.
13. With fork beat reserved egg white until bubbly.
14. Brush scones with white; sprinkle generously with additional sugar.
15. Bake 14 to 18 minutes until golden brown.
16. Serve warm with lemon butter and fruit preserves.
17. To reheat scones, place on baking sheet in preheated 350°F oven.
18. Heat about 5 minutes until warm.

NUTRITION FACTS per scone (made with lemon butter): 152 calories, 59 calories from fat, 6.6g total fat (10%), 3.8g saturated fat (19%), 42.4mg cholesterol (14%), 192mg sodium (8%), 20.9g carbohydrates (7%), .3g fiber (1%), 2.8g protein (6%), 259 IU vitamin A (5%), zero vitamin C, 68mg calcium (7%) and 1.1mg iron (6%).

LEMON BUTTER

This lemon butter recipe is not only great on scones, but you will enjoy it on muffins and toast as well.

4 eggs
Pinch of salt
3 lemons, juiced & rind grated
2 cups sugar
1/2 cup butter or margarine

1. Melt butter in top of double boiler.
2. In a bowl, beat eggs with a pinch of salt.
3. Beat in sugar, lemon juice and rind.
4. Continue to beat for several minutes.
5. Stir into melted butter.
6. Cook and stir until thick.
7. Pour into glass jars and refrigerate.
Keeps for several weeks.

NUTRITION FACTS per tablespoon: 44 calories, 15 calories from fat, 1.7g total fat (3%), 1g saturated fat (5%), 17mg cholesterol (6%), 18.6g sodium (1%), 7.3g carbohydrates (2%), zero fiber, .5g protein (1%), 76 IU vitamin A (2%), 6mg vitamin C (9%), zero calcium and iron.

GOLDEN PUMPKIN SCONES
Makes 8 servings

The *Nestle® Beverage Company* have taken the American pumpkin and incorporated into this delicious scone recipe.

2 cups flour
1/2 cup brown sugar
2 teaspoons baking powder
1/2 teaspoon baking soda
1/4 teaspoon salt
3/4 teaspoon cinnamon
1/4 teaspoon nutmeg
1/4 teaspoon allspice
1/4 cup margarine or butter
1/2 cup golden raisins or currants
1 egg
3/4 cup canned pumpkin
2 tablespoons buttermilk
1 egg white, beaten
Sugar (optional)

1. Combine flour, brown sugar, baking powder, soda, salt and spices in a large bowl.
2. Using a pastry blender, cut in margarine until mixture is crumbly.
3. Stir in raisins.
4. Beat egg, pumpkin and buttermilk in a small bowl.
5. Add liquid ingredients to flour mixture; mix well.

6. Press dough into 3/4-inch thick circle on lightly floured surface.
7. Cut with 2-inch biscuit cutter.
8. Place dough on ungreased baking sheet.
9. Brush tops with egg white; sprinkle with sugar, if desired.

10. Bake in preheated 400°F oven for 10 to 12 minutes or until wooden pick comes out clean.
11. Remove from baking sheet; cool on wire rack.

NUTRITION FACTS per scone: 132 calories, 32 calories from fat, 3.6g total fat (5%), .7g saturated fat (4%),14.2mg cholesterol (5%), 172.7mg sodium (7%), 22.6g carbohydrates (8%), .6g fiber (2%), 2.7g protein (5%), 2850 IU vitamin A (57%, 1mg vitamin C (1%), 62mg calcium (6%) and 1.3mg iron (7%).

GOOD MORNING SCONES
Makes 8 servings

John and Donna Ortiz are the innkeepers at *Riordan House Bed and Breakfast* in Penticton, B.C., Canada. The following recipe is served regularly to their guests. Note, the dough is scooped, like drop biscuits.

4 cups flour
2 tablespoons baking powder
2 tablespoons sugar
1 pinch of salt
1/2 cup margarine

1 big handful of raisins, candied peel, blueberries, strawberries or any seasonal fruit
1 1/4 cup milk
1 teaspoon vanilla
2 eggs

1. In a large bowl, mix flour, baking powder, sugar and salt together.
2. Cut in margarine with finger tips or pastry blender.
3. Mix fruit into the dry mixture.
4. Whip milk, vanilla, and eggs together.

5. Add the milk mixture to the dry ingredients until moisten
6. Scoop large tablespoon portions onto lightly greased baking sheet.
7. Bake for 20 minutes at 350°F.

NUTRITION FACTS per serving: 426 calories, 130 calories from fat, 14.5g total fat (22%), 3.3g saturated fat (16%), 58.3mg cholesterol (19%), 442.7mg sodium (18%), 64.5g carbohydrates (22%), .5g fiber (2%), 9.8g protein (20%), 595 IU vitamin A (12%), 1mg vitamin C (1%), 326mg calcium (33%) and 3.8mg iron (21%).

LAYERED JAM BISCUIT BAKE
Makes 8 servings

The name says "biscuits," the ingredients says "scones," but it bakes like a "coffee cake." Recipe courtesy of *Sun-Maid Growers of California*.

2 cups flour
2 tablespoons sugar
1 tablespoon baking powder
1/4 teaspoon salt
1/2 cup butter or margarine

1/2 cup milk
2 eggs, beaten
3/4 cup currants or raisins
1/2 cup thick strawberry or blueberry jam
Butter, melted (optional)

Sugar (optional)

1. Heat oven to 425°F.
2. Grease an 8 or 9-inch round cake pan.
3. In a large bowl, combine flour, sugar, baking powder and salt.
4. Using pastry blender or a fork, cut in butter until mixture resembles coarse crumbs.

5. Add milk, eggs and currants; stir just until dry ingredients are moistened.
6. With floured hands, pat half of dough into bottom of greased pan; press dough 1/4-inch up sides.
7. Spread dough with jam.

8. Roll out remaining double and top the jam; spread evenly.
9. Using a sharp knife, score dough into 8 wedges.
10. Brush top with melted butter and sprinkle with sugar, if desired.
11. Bake for 20 to 25 minutes or until toothpick inserted in center comes out clean. Serve warm.

NUTRITION FACTS per serving: 342 calories, 119 calories from fat, 13.5g total fat (21%), 7.8g saturated fat (39%), 85.9mg cholesterol (29%), 351.4mg sodium (15%), 51.1g carbohydrates (17%), 1.1g fiber (5%), 6.1g protein (12%), 539 IU vitamin A (11%), 3mg vitamin C (4%), 175mg calcium (18%) and 2.4mg iron (13%).

CINNAMON PECAN VARIATION

1 cup brown sugar
1 teaspoon cinnamon

2 tablespoons butter
1/3 cup pecans, chopped

1. Omit jam.
2. Combine brown sugar and cinnamon.
3. Using pastry blender or a fork, cut in butter.
4. Stir in pecans.
5. Sprinkle bottom layer of dough with cinnamon mixture.

ORANGE SCONES
Makes 8 servings

Innkeeper *Peggy Kuan* from the *Chanticleet Inn* in Ashland, Oregon has put a new twist on eggs benedict (see ORANGE EGGS BENEDICT, page 126) by replacing the English muffin with an orange scone. Of course this scone is just as delicious without the eggs benedict.

2 cups flour
2 teaspoons baking powder
1/2 teaspoon salt
2 tablespoons orange zest, grated

1/4 cup butter, chilled
2 eggs
1/3 cup heavy cream

1. Preheat oven to 425°F.
2. In a bowl, mix flour, baking powder and salt.
3. Cut in butter until mixture resembles coarse meal.
4. Mix in eggs, one at a time.
5. Add cream and orange zest.
6. Turn dough out onto a lightly floured surface.
7. Knead dough until smooth, about 2 minutes.
8. Roll out 3/4-inch thick.
9. Cut scones with 3-inch round cookie cutter.
10. Bake 15 to 20 minutes until golden brown and crusty.

NUTRITION FACTS per scone: 207 calories, 87 calories from fat, 9.7g total fat (14%), 5.5g saturated fat (28%), 77.2mg cholesterol (26%), 302mg sodium (13%), 25g carbohydrates (8%), zero fiber, 5.1g protein (10%), 394 IU vitamin A (8%), 2mg vitamin C (4%), 109mg calcium (11%) and 1.8mg iron (10%).

SCOTTISH POTATO SCONES
Makes 12 wedges

America's *Scottish* pioneers are credited for creating the scone. The scone recipe made its way back to *Scotland* where potatoes were added.

1 1/2 cups flour
1/3 cup butter or margarine
1 cup potatoes, cooked, mashed, cooled, unseasoned

2 teaspoons baking powder
1/2 teaspoon salt
1 egg, well beaten
Milk

1. In a large bowl, sift flour, salt and baking powder together.
2. Add mashed potatoes.
3. Cut in butter lightly.
4. Add the egg and if necessary a little milk to make a soft dough.
5. Divide dough into 3 parts and roll into rounds half an inch thick.

6. Cut each into 4 pie-sized wedges.
7. Place on ungreased baking sheet

8. Bake in a 400°F oven for about 10 minutes or until lightly browned.
9. Split open, butter, and serve hot.

NUTRITION FACTS per wedge: 127 calories, 57 calories from fat, 6.4g total fat (10%), 3.5g saturated fat (18%), 31.9mg cholesterol (11%), 258.6mg sodium (11%), 15.1g carbohydrates (5%), .4g fiber (1%), 2.6g protein (5%), 248 IU vitamin A (5%), 1mg vitamin C (2%), 68mg calcium (7%) and .9mg iron (5%).

BISCUIT & SCONE TOPPINGS

BLUEBERRY JAM

Recipe courtesy of the *North American Blueberry Council.*

2 1/2 cups fresh or dry-pack frozen blueberries
3 cups sugar

1/3 cup orange juice
1 tablespoon lemon juice

3 ounces of fruit pectin

1. Wash blueberries.
2. Crush blueberries in an enamel pan.
3. Add sugar and fruit juices.
4. Mix well.
5. Bring to full rolling boil.

6. Boil hard for 1 minute, stirring constantly.
7. Remove from heat.
8. Stir in pectin.
9. Seal in hot sterilized jars.
10. Refrigerate. Can be stored for 2 months.

NUTRITION FACTS per tablespoon: 59 calories, zero fats, cholesterol and sodium, 15.4g carbohydrates (5%), .2g fiber (1%), zero protein and vitamin A, 2mg vitamin C (3%), zero calcium and iron.

GOOSEBERRY JAM

This recipe comes from *Betty Hamilton's* grandmother and is served to guests at *Hamilton Bed and Breakfast* at Port Hardy, B.C. Canada.

4 cups gooseberries
1/2 cup orange juice

Grated rind from one orange
3 cups sugar

1. Wash berries in cold water.
2. Remove stems and blossom ends.
3. In a large pot, add gooseberries, rind, juice, and cook until berries are soft.

4. Add the sugar, bring to a boil.
5. Boil until thick and clear, about 20 to 25 minutes.
6. Pour into sterilized jars and seal.

NUTRITION FACTS per tablespoon: 28 calories, zero fats, cholesterol and sodium, 7.1g carbohydrates, .3g fiber, zero protein and vitamin A, 3mg vitamin C (4%), zero calcium and iron.

MARMALADE
Makes 2 pints

Recipe courtesy of *Grand Marnier Liqueurs.*

4 Valencia juice oranges, well scrubbed
2 lemons, well scrubbed

6 cups water
About 5 cups sugar

1/2 cup Grand Marnier

1. Cut the oranges and lemons in half and remove the seeds.
2. Cut the fruit into 1/4 inch strips, so that each slice has some fruit on the rind.
3. In a large sauce pan, combine the fruit and water and bring to a simmer over moderate heat and cook for 5 minutes.
4. Remove from the heat and let stand at room temperature for at least 8 hours, overnight is better.

5. Measure the fruit mixture.
6. For each cup of fruit, add one cup of sugar.
7. Return the fruit mixture to the saucepan, stir in the sugar and simmer over low heat, stirring constantly, until a jelly thermometer registers 200 F, about 20 to 30 minutes.
8. Stir in the Grand Marnier.
9. Spoon the hot marmalade into very clean, hot canning jars and seal with paraffin.

Marmalade can be refrigerated, but should be used within 1 week. The flavor of the marmalade will intensify upon standing in the sealed jars.

NUTRITION FACTS per tablespoon: 72 calories, zero fats, cholesterol and sedum, 17.6g carbohydrates (6%), zero fiber, protein and vitamin A, 6mg vitamin C (10%), 5mg calcium (1%) and zero iron.

PEAR PRESERVES
Makes 1 pint

Recipe courtesy of The *Sugar Association, Inc.*

3 cups pears, chunked   1 cup sugar

1. Night before: peel and cut up pears in a container of cold water.
2. Drain off water and put pears in a non-metal container.
3. Cover with sugar and refrigerate overnight.
4. Next day: There should be a lot of syrup in the pear mixture.
5. In a large pot, cook pear syrup mixture over medium- low heat (stirring and being careful not

to scorch) about 3 hours or until pear mixture thickens and pears become translucent tender.
6. To preserve, pour into hot, sterilized jars and seal.
7. Process 15 minutes at simmering.
8. Or store covered in refrigerator and use as a spread within 1 week.

NUTRITION FACTS per tablespoon: 33 calories, zero fats, cholesterol and sodium, 8.6g carbohydrates (3%), .4g fiber (1%), zero protein and vitamin A, 1mg vitamin A, zero calcium and iron.

QUINCE JAM
Makes 4 half pints

"Quinces are full of natural pectin and make wonderful jams and jellies," says *Arie Farr* of Hattiesburg, Mississippi.

3 yellow quince   3 cups sugar
2 apples   1/4 cup cinnamon Redhot candies
Water to cover

1. Peel, core quince and apples; cut into small pieces.
2. Cover with water and boil until fruit is soft.
3. Press through a sieve or food processor and remove all lumps.

4. Add sugar and bring to a boil, stirring constantly.
5. Reduce heat to prevent spattering.
6. Add Redhots and cook until candies have melted. 1

7. When the jam is thick, test for doneness by pouring a small quantity on a cold plate.
8. Jam is done when no rim of liquid separates around the jam on the plate.

9. Pour hot jam into hot sterilized 1/2 pint jars and seal.

NUTRITION FACTS per tablespoon: 22 calories, zero calories from fat, zero fats, cholesterol and sodium, 5.8g carbohydrates (2%), 1g fiber (1%), zero protein, vitamins and minerals.

RHUBARB & STRAWBERRY JAM

Lorne and Betty Hamilton prepares this jam for their guests at *Hamilton Bed and Breakfast*, Port Hardy, B.C., Canada.

4 cups rhubarb, cut up
1 cup crushed pineapple

3 cups sugar
1 package strawberry gelatin

1. In a large pot, boil together rhubarb, pineapple and sugar for 30 minutes.
2. Remove from the stove and add the gelatin.

3. Stir well.
4. Pour into sterilized jars and seal.

NUTRITION FACTS per tablespoon: 29 calories, zero fats, cholesterol and sodium, 7.5g carbohydrates (2%), zero fiber, protein and vitamin A, 1mg vitamin C (1%) and zero calcium and iron.

JAMS, JELLIES AND PRESERVES

You can make your own jams, jellies and preserves at home. The success will depend on the kind and condition of the fruit, and how you plan to store it.

Some recipes call for pectin (you purchase this at the supermarket). Pectin is a substance found in citrus, apples and sugar beets. Using pectin helps you to make larger yields with less cooking time. Without pectin, the fruit has to be boiled a very long time to reduce the liquid in the fruit so it will thicken. Pectin is available both in a liquid and powdered forms. Liquid pectin is added after the fruit has been cooked. Powdered pectin on the other hand is added to the unheated fruit.

When purchasing the pectin, instructions on how to use with the fruit you have chosen will be given. It is important to follow the recipes exactly for the best success. When cooking the fruit it is important to stir continually to prevent the fruit-sugar combination from sticking but, more importantly, from scorching. Once scorched, about all you can do it toss the mixture in the garbage.

Some jams and jellies can be made without cooking. However, storage can be a problem. Best to freeze what you are not going to eat in a month or two. No cooked jams can be stored in the refrigerator for several months, but are best when first made.

You must prepare jars and lids properly. They must be covered with hot boiling water and kept hot until ready to be filled. You can seal most jams with paraffin. Again, follow instructions on the paraffin package. It is best to melt paraffin in a double boiler.

Canning jars also come with instruction on how to seal in a water bath.

IMPORTANT: Before your first jam making be sure to read all instructions and have all necessary ingredients and equipment before you start.

CHAPTER IV

BREADS

There are two basic breads, one leavened with baking powder and/or baking soda and called "tea breads." The second are breads leavened with yeast, and called "yeast breads."

TEA BREADS

Boston Brown Bread (*USA*) 38

Cinnamon Crunch Walnut (*USA*) 39

Coconut (*British Virgin Islands*) 39

Crunchy Banana Bread (*USA*) 40

Fruited Pumpkin Bread (Nebraska) 40

Guatemala Banana (*Guatemala*) 41

Hazelnut Maple Bread (*USA*) 41

Lemon Thyme Zucchini (*Canada*) 42

Rogge Brood (*Netherlands*) 42

Sally's Hawaiian Bread (*California*) 42

Texas Corn Bread (*Texas*) 43

West Indies Hot Bread (Caribbean) 43

YEAST BREADS

Bagels (*Israel*) 44

Baked Passover Bagels (*Israel*) 45

Cajun Hot Tomato Bread (*Louisiana*) 45

Caramelized Onion (*California*) 46

Cheese & Wine Bread (*California*)

Danish Light Rye Bread (*Denmark*) 47

Danish Sourdough Dark Rye Bread (*Denmark*) 47

Danish White Bread (*Denmark*) 48

Danish Whole Wheat (*Denmark*) 49

English Muffin Loaves (*England*) 49

French & Italian(*France & Italy*) 50

Breakfast in Israel

Hope's Egg Bread with Challah variation (*Israel*) 51

Julebrod (*Norway*) 51

Kulich with Pashka (*Russia*) 52 & 53

Oatmeal Apple Bread (*Iowa*) 54

Pain Campagnard Aux Pommes (*France*) 54

Sourdough Bread (*Alaska*) 55

Swedish Rye Bread (*Sweden*) 56

Weihnachtsstollen (*Germany*) 56

Homemade Yeast (Texas)57

BREAD SPREADS

Cinnamon Cream Cheese (*USA*) 57

Fruit Spread (*Washington*) 58

Fruity Cream Cheese Spread (*USA*) 58

Ham & Cheese Spread (*Kansas*) 58

Honey Blueberry Spread (*USA*) 59

Honey Hazelnut Spread (*USA*) 59

Strawberry Spread (New York) 59

TEA BREADS

Tea breads are leavened with baking powder and/or baking soda, not yeast. They are called tea breads because they are generally served at afternoon teas. Like muffins, tea breads have not gained in wide world popularity. Tea breads make great breakfast breads and many have a similar texture to muffins. In fact, many muffin and tea bread recipes can be interchanged. Tea breads are best made a day ahead of time prior to slicing. Most tea breads can be enjoyed at room temperature, warmed in the oven or microwave, or toasted.

BOSTON BROWN BREAD
Makes 1 loaf (16 slices)

This Colonial staple is made with three flours and is usually served with baked beans. Brown breads are usually steamed. This one from the test kitchens of *Sun-Maid Growers of California* is baked in a loaf pan.

1 cup milk
2 teaspoon cider vinegar
1/2 cup flour
2/3 cup whole wheat flour
1/3 cup yellow cornmeal
1/4 cup brown sugar

1 teaspoon baking soda
1/2 teaspoon salt
1/3 cup molasses
1/4 cup vegetable oil
1 cup raisins
1/2 cup walnuts, chopped

1. Preheat oven to 350°F.
2. Grease an 8 1/4 x 4-inch loaf pan.
3. In a bowl, combine milk and vinegar; set aside.
4. In a large bowl, combine flours, brown sugar, soda and salt; mix well.
5. Add milk mixture, molasses and oil; stir just until dry ingredients are moistened.

6. Fold in raisins and walnuts. Spoon batter into pan.
7. Bake for 40 to 45 minutes or until toothpick inserted in center comes out clean.
8. Cool in pan 10 minutes.
9. Remove from pan and cool completely on wire rack.

NUTRITION FACTS per slice: 159 calories, 55 calories from fat, 6.4g total fat (10%), .9g saturated fat (5%), 2.1mg cholesterol (1%), 157.7mg sodium (7%), 24.1g carbohydrates (8%), 1.4g fiber (6%), 3.1g protein (6%), 43 IU vitamin A (1%), 1mg vitamin C (1%), 43mg calcium (4%) and 1.2mg iron (7%).

MICROWAVE METHOD

1. Prepare recipe as above.
2. Grease a 2-cup glass measure.
3. Spoon in 1 1/2 cups of batter.
4. Cover with plastic wrap, venting spout.
5. Microwave at medium (50%) for 6 to 7 minutes or until toothpick inserted in center comes out clean; rotate dish halfway through.

6. Let stand 2 minutes; turn out bread; cool on wire rack.
7. Repeat with remaining batter.
8. Slice in rounds to serve.

Would you like to steam this bread the old Boston way? You can. You will need two 28 ounce or three 20 ounce fruit cans. Wash and grease the canned. Divide the batter among the chosen cans, cover tightly with foil and place on a rack in a deep kettle. Pour in boiling water to a depth of 1-inch. Place on stove top and with low heat, steam for about 3 hours, adding more boiling water as needed. Remove can from the kettle, remove the foil and place the cans in a 450°F preheated oven for 5 minutes. Remove bread from the pans, cool on a wire rack, wrap and store overnight before cutting.

CINNAMON CRUNCH WALNUT LOAF
Makes 1 loaf (16 slices)

This fragrant loaf by the *Diamond Walnut Growers, Inc.,* is worthy of important gift wraps and bake sales.

1 1/2 cup walnuts, chopped
1 tablespoon butter, melted
1 cup sugar, divided
2 teaspoons cinnamon
3 cups flour

4 1/2 teaspoons baking powder
1/2 teaspoon salt
1/4 cup shortening
1 egg, lightly beaten
1 1/4 cups milk

1. Preheat oven to 350°F.
2. Grease a 9x5-inch loaf pan.
3. In a bowl, combine walnuts and butter.
4. Add 1/4-cup sugar and cinnamon; mix well to coat walnuts; set aside.
5. In another bowl, combine remaining sugar, flour, baking powder and salt; cut in shortening.
6. In a third bowl, combine egg and milk; blend well.
7. Add to flour mixture; stir just until dry ingredients are moistened.
8. Fold in walnut mixture.
9. Spoon into greased pan.
10. Bake for 65 to 70 minutes or until toothpick inserted in center comes out clean.
11. Cool in pan for 10 minutes.
12. Remove from pan and cool on wire rack.

NUTRITION FACTS per slice: 257 calories, 103 calories from fat, 11.7g total fat (18%), 2.2g saturated fat (11%), 17.8mg cholesterol (6%), 190mg sodium (8%), 33.3g carbohydrates (11%), .7g fiber (3%), 6.3g protein (13%), 106 IU vitamin A (2%), 1mg vitamin C (1%), 134mg calcium (13%) and 1.8mg iron (10%).

COCONUT BREAD
Makes 2 loaves

When you think about the tropics, what first comes in your mind? That's right, palm trees swaying in the breeze. The good people of the *British Virgin Islands* have taken the coconuts from these palms and have made a delicious tea bread.

2 cups coconut, grated
1 teaspoon salt
3/4 cup sugar
1/2 teaspoon nutmeg
1/2 teaspoon cinnamon

Milk or water*
4 cups flour
2 eggs, beaten
3 teaspoons baking powder
1 teaspoon vanilla

2/3 cup shortening, melted

1. In a bowl, sift flour, salt and baking powder together.
2. Add spices, coconut and sugar.
3. In another bowl, mix shortening, eggs and vanilla.
4. Add to flour mixture.
5. Add enough milk to make a stiff, but pliable dough.
6. Knead on a floured board. Shape in 2 loaves and bake in greased tins in a 350°F oven until brown.

NUTRITION FACTS per slice: 142 calories, 57 calories from fat, 6.4g total fat (10%), 2.6g saturated fat (13%), 13.8mg cholesterol (5%), 118.7mg sodium (5%), 19.2g carbohydrates (6%), .2g fiber (1%), 2.3g protein (5%), zero vitamins A and C, 41mg calcium (4%) and .9mg iron (5%).

*VARIATION: Replace liquid with canned crushed pineapple.

CRUNCHY BANANA BREAD
Makes 1 loaf (16 slices)

Amy Scherber thinks that most people with enjoy this sweet, moist loaf with a good banana flavor and the golden color of wheat.

1 cup flour
3/4 cup whole wheat flour
1/2 cup oat bran
1/2 cup cornmeal
1 tablespoon baking powder
1/2 teaspoon salt

1 1/4 cups ripe banana, mashed
1/2 cup honey
1/2 cup non-fat milk
3 tablespoons vegetable oil
3 egg whites

1/2 cup walnuts

1. Preheat oven to 350°F.
2. Grease a loaf pan.
3. In a large bowl, combine flours, oat bran, cornmeal, baking powder and salt.
4. In a separate bowl, whisk together the banana, honey, milk, oil and egg whites.
5. Add to the dry ingredients along with the walnuts.
6. Stir just until moistened.
7. Pour the batter into the loaf pan and bake for 65 to 70 minutes or until tested done.
8. Cool 10 minutes in the pan. Remove to a wire rack.

NUTRITION FACTS per slice: 172 calories, 45 calories from fat, 5.3gtotal fat (8%), .6g saturated fat (3%), zero cholesterol, 150.2mg sodium (6%), 29.5g carbohydrates (10%), 2.2g fiber (9%), 4.6g protein (9%), 59 IU vitamin A (1%), 2mg vitamin C (3%), 83mg calcium (8%) and 1.3mg iron (7%).

Did you know the banana originated in the Malaysian jungles? It is believed the first Europeans to eat bananas were members of Alexander the Great's expedition to India in 327 B.C. It was the Portuguese traders that carried the roots from Africa to the Canary Islands, and it was Franciscan Frier Tomas de Berlanga who bought the roots to the Caribbean in 1516. Today there are some 30 species of bananas. Some cannot be eaten raw, and must be cooked.

FRUITED PUMPKIN BREAD
Makes 2 loaves (32 slices)

Christie Miller of Dunbar, Nebraska says her family likes the combination of pumpkin, banana and pecans in this tea bread. There's just a hint of spice.

3/4 cup butter, softened
1 1/4 cups sugar
3 eggs
3/4 cup canned pumpkin
3/4 cup ripe banana, mashed

3 cups flour
1 1/2 teaspoons baking soda
1 teaspoon salt
1 teaspoon pumpkin pie spice or nutmeg
1 cup pecans, chopped

1/8 teaspoon walnut flavoring

1. In a bowl, beat butter and sugar until creamy.
2. Add eggs and beat well.
3. Stir in pumpkin, banana and walnut flavoring.
4. In another bowl, sift flour with soda, salt and spice and mix into the creamed mixture.
5. Stir in nuts.
6. Grease and flour 2 loaf pans.
7. Spoon in batter and bake at 350°F for 1 hour.

NUTRITION FACTS per slice: 146 calories, 63 calories from fat, 7.2g total fat (11%), 3g saturated fat (15%), 31.4mg cholesterol (10%), 175.4mg sodium (7%), 18.9g carbohydrates (6%), .5g fiber (2%), 2.2g protein (4%), 243mg vitamin A (5%), 1mg vitamin C (1%), 8mg calcium (1%) and .7mg iron (4%).

GUATEMALA BANANA BREAD
Makes 1 loaf (16 slices)

Dusty Stoughton of Wilmington, California picked up this recipe on a trip to Guatemala.

4 cups bananas, mashed
1/2 cup coconut milk
1/2 cup butter, melted
3 cups flour

2 teaspoons baking powder
1/2 teaspoon salt
1/2 teaspoon vanilla
1/2 cup raisins (optional)

1/2 cup cashews, chopped (optional)

1. In a large bowl, combine flour, baking powder and salt.
2. Stir in bananas, coconut milk, vanilla and butter.

3. Fold in raisins and cashews, if desired.
4. Pour into a greased 5x9-inch loaf pan.
5. Bake at 350 F for 1 hour and 15 minutes or until tested done.

NUTRITION FACTS per slice with raisins and cashews: 227 calories, 86 calories from fat, 9.9g total fat (15%), 5.7g saturated fat (28%), 15.3mg cholesterol (5%), 173.2mg sodium (7%), 33.3g carbohydrates (11%), 1.8g fiber (7%), 3.6g protein (7%), vitamin A (5%), vitamin C (9%), calcium (6%) and iron (9%).

HAZELNUT MAPLE BREAD
Makes 2 loaves (32 slices)

The test kitchens of the *Hazelnut Marketing Board* have combined the popular European hazelnut with bananas from the tropics and the flavor of maple from America's northeast in this delicious tea bread.

2 cups flour
2 teaspoons baking powder
1/2 teaspoon salt
1/2 cup sugar
1/4 cup butter or margarine, softened
1/4 cup hazelnut butter

2 eggs
1/4 cup maple syrup
1 teaspoon vanilla
1/2 teaspoon maple extract
1/2 cup bananas, mashed
1/4 cup milk

1/2 cup hazelnuts, roasted, coarsely chopped

1. In a bowl, sift together flour, baking powder and salt; set aside.
2. In a large bowl cream sugar and butter until smooth.
3. Beat in hazelnut butter, eggs, maple syrup, vanilla and maple extract.
4. Mix in bananas in three additions, alternately mix in the dry ingredients and milk.

5. Fold in hazelnuts.
6. Divide the batter between 2 greased loaf pans.
7. Bake in 350°F oven for 30 to 35 minutes or until golden and toothpick inserted into the center comes out clean.
8. Cool on rack.

NUTRITION FACTS per slice: 86 calories, 32 calories from fat, 3.6g total fat (6%), 1.2g saturated fat (6%), 17.4mg cholesterol (6%), 75.9mg sodium (3%), 12.2g carbohydrates (4%), .2g fiber (1%), 1.7g protein (3%), 80 IU vitamin A (2%), zero vitamin C, 34mg calcium (3%) and .7mg iron (3%).

Did you know the hazelnut is native to Europe. The name "hazel" comes from the Anglo-Saxon word *haesil,* meaning headdress. The nut resembled a Roman headdress or helmet. Americans refer to the wild variety as hazelnuts, while they say "filbert' for the cultivated kind. Hazelnuts are drier than almonds, hence are easy to grind into meal.

LEMON THYME ZUCCHINI BREAD
Makes 2 loaves

In the late summer *Chef Bernard Casavant* of the *Chateau Whistler Resort* in Whistler, British Columbia, *Canada* gathers lemon thyme from his herb garden to make this delicious bread for guests at the resort's *Wildflower Cafe.*

3 1/2 cups flour
1 tablespoon cinnamon
1 teaspoon nutmeg
1 teaspoon baking soda
1 teaspoon baking powder
1/2 teaspoon salt
3/4 cup raisins
2 eggs

1/3 cup vegetable oil
3/4 cup low fat plain yogurt
1/4 cup milk
1 cup brown sugar
2 teaspoons vanilla
2 pounds zucchini, unpeeled, finely shredded
1/2 cup fresh lemon thyme, stems removed, finely chopped

1. Combine flour, cinnamon, nutmeg, baking soda, baking powder, salt and raisins in a large bowl.
2. In another large bowl, beat eggs until foamy.
3. Beat in oil, yogurt, milk, sugar and vanilla.
4. Stir in the zucchini and lemon thyme.
5. Add to flour mixture and stir until combined.

6. Pour batter into 2 well greased 8x4-inch loaf pans.
7. Bake in 350°F oven for 55 minutes or until toothpick inserted into center comes out clean.
8. Remove from pan and let cool thoroughly before slicing.

NUTRITION FACTS per slice: 113 calories, 26 calories from fat, 2.9g total fat (5%), .5g saturated fat (2%), 13.6mg cholesterol (5%), 96.7mg sodium (4%), 19.6g carbohydrates (7%), .7g fiber (3%), 2.7g protein (5%), 144 IU vitamin A (3%), 3mg vitamin C (5%), 52mg calcium (5%) and 1.8mg iron (10%).

ROGGE BROOD

This rye bread recipe was bought to America from the province of Friesland in the *Netherlands.* This Dutch bread is best sliced thin, buttered, and when topped with cheese, is called houtsnip. *Hilma Schagen Schakel* from Pella, Iowa says, "This is a very heavy, dark, coarse bread."

1 cup white flour
3 cups cracked rye
1 teaspoon baking soda

1/2 teaspoon salt
1 cup dark cane syrup
3 cups buttermilk

1. In a bowl, combine all ingredients.
2. Pour into a large well greased loaf pan with the bottom lined with wax paper.

3. Let it rest for 1 hour.
4. Bake in a 300°F oven for 5 hours.

SALLY'S HAWAIIAN BREAD
Makes 2 loaves

Sally Dumont serves this sweet bread to her guests at the *Silver Rose Inn*, Calistoga, California.

1 cup vegetable oil
2 cups sugar
3 eggs
2 1/2 cups flour
1 teaspoon baking soda

1 teaspoon cinnamon
2 teaspoons vanilla
1 cup canned crushed pineapple, drained
1 cup coconut, grated
2 cups carrots, grated

1. In a bowl, cream oil, sugar and eggs until light.

2. In another bowl, sift together flour, soda and cinnamon.

3. Add to creamed mixture.
4. Gently fold in vanilla, pineapple, coconut and carrots.

5. Divide batter in two well greased loaf pans.
6. Let batter rest for 30 minutes.
7. Bake in 350°F oven for 1 hour.

NUTRITION FACTS per slice: 169 calories, 73 calories from fat, 8.3g total fat (13%), 1.7g saturated fat (8%), 19.9mg cholesterol (7%), 22.8mg sodium (1%), 22.4g carbohydrates (7%), .7g fiber (3%), 1.8g protein (4%), 3733 IU vitamin A (75%), 2mg vitamin C (3%), 20mg calcium (2%) and .7mg iron (4%).

TEXAS CORN BREAD

Unlike most tea breads, corn breads are best enjoyed hot from the oven. This recipe from *Texas* produces a moist bread. This recipe can also be baked in muffin tins, baking time 15 to 20 minutes.

¾ cup flour
¼ cup cornmeal
2 teaspoons baking powder
¼ teaspoon salt

1 tablespoon sugar
1 egg
½ cup milk
1 cup canned cream-style corn

2 tablespoons vegetable oil or butter, melted

1. Mix dry ingredients in a large bowl; set aside.
2. Whisk together remaining ingredients in a medium bowl.
3. Stir into dry ingredients until moistened.

4. Pour into a greased 8x8-inch baking pan.
5. Bake in a 450 °F preheated oven for 25 to 30 minutes or until golden brown.
6. Cut into 9 pieces. Serve warm.

While still hot, top with 4 tablespoons of honey butter, if desired.

NUTRITION FACTS per piece: 122 calories, 38 calories from fat, 4.3g total fat (7%), .9g saturated fat (4%), 25.5mg cholesterol (8%), 234.9mg sodium (10%), 18.4g carbohydrates (6%), .6g fiber (2%), 3.1g protein (6%), 96 IU vitamin A (2%), 1mg vitamin C (2%), 97mg calcium (10%), 1mg iron (5%).

WEST INDIES HOT BREAD
Makes 10 servings

Cheryl Juchniewicw of *Waldo's Bistro Restaurant* of Punda Gorda, Florida presents the ultimate in corn breads. A word of caution when working with chilies, wear rubber gloves and discard all seeds. Most of the heat is in the seeds. If you like a very hot pepper, you can substitute one of the peppers for a habanero pepper.

2 cups cornmeal
1/2 cup sugar
2 cups flour
3 tablespoons butter, softened
1 scotch bonnet or jalapeno pepper, chopped
1 cup cheddar cheese, shredded

2 cups milk
1/2 cup roasted garlic covered with olive oil
2 red onions, chopped
1 sweet red pepper, chopped
2 eggs
1/4 cup vegetable oil

1. Preheat oven to 400°F.
2. Combine all dry ingredients in a mixing bowl.
3. Stir in remaining ingredients except oil.

4. Place 8-inch skillet in oven with oil until very hot.
5. Pour batter and bake for 40 to 50 minutes until done.

NUTRITION FACTS per serving: 428 calories, 144 calories from fat, 16.1g total fat (25%), 6.6g saturated fat (33%), 70.2mg cholesterol (23%), 145.8mg sodium (6%), 59.6g carbohydrates (20%), 3.2g fiber (13%), 11.7g protein (23%), 1355 IU vitamin A (27%), 44mg vitamin C (73%), 173mg calcium (17%) and 2.9mg iron (16%).

YEAST BREADS

If this is your first try to make bread, I suggest you pick out an easy recipe, such as French bread or Danish white bread. Also read several recipes to get a feel how other breads are made. You will soon understand the kneading that is required to make a good loaf. Generally, bread is finished baking when it is golden brown and when tapped on the top, sides and bottom it sounds hollow.

BAGELS
Makes 20 bagels

These doughnut-shaped breads are part of *Jewish* cuisine. Today, bagels come in many flavors. This recipe is the basis for other recipes, some using different flours, seasonings, seeds, herbs, and dried fruits such as raisins and blueberries. Plain bagels are great toasted and topped with cream cheese and smoked salmon, however, you can top them with anything you like. *Christie Miller* from Dunbar, Nebraska says. *"Bagels take time to prepare, but are lots of fun to make. Let the kids make other shapes, such as letters or bread sticks."*

4 to 5 cups flour	1 egg yolk
3 tablespoons sugar	1 1/2 cups very warm water (125 F to 130 F)
1 tablespoon salt	1 tablespoon honey
1 package quick-rising yeast	1 egg white, beaten

1 tablespoon cold water

1. In a large bowl mix together 1 1/2 cups flour, sugar, salt, and yeast.
2. Gradually add egg yolk and water, and beat for 2 minutes at medium speed with an electric beater.
3. Add 1/2 cup more flour and beat at high speed for 2 minutes.
4. Add enough additional flour by hand to make a soft and malleable, but not dry, dough.
5. Turn dough onto a floured board.
6. Knead for 8 to 10 minutes (add more flour if dough is too sticky).
7. Place dough in an ungreased bowl.
8. Cover and let rise for 20 minutes (dough will not be doubled).
9. Punch down and turn onto a floured board.
10. Divide dough in half.
11. Divide each half into about 10 equal parts.
12. One at a time, shape each into a smooth ball, tucking excess dough underneath.
13. Flatten ball in a 2 1/2-inch diameter disc.
14. With floured hands, poke a hole through center of disc with finger, and enlarge hole to about 1-inch in diameter by twirling dough on floured surface while keeping light contact with the surface with the tip of your finger (for an easier, but less professional looking bagel, roll each piece between your hands to make a rope; pinch the ends together to form circles).
15. Place on ungreased baking sheets.
16. Cover and let rise for 20 minutes (not until double).
17. Preheat oven to 375°F.
18. In a large shallow pan boil 2 quarts water and stir in honey.
19. Lower to medium heat.
20. Transfer bagels to pot with slotted spoon and boil in batches of three or four at a time and simmer for 7 minutes.
21. Place on a cooling rack for about 5 minutes, then place on ungreased baking sheets.
22. Bake bagels for 10 minutes.
23. Remove from oven, brush with a mixture of egg white and water, and return to oven.
24. Bake for about 20 minutes longer, or until they are golden brown and sound hollow when tapped.
25. Cool on wire racks.
26. To serve split and toast.

NUTRITION FACTS per bagel: 118 calories, 5 calories from fat, .6g total fat (1%), .1g saturated fat (1%), 10.6mg cholesterol (4%), 323.8mg sodium (13%), 24.5g carbohydrates (8%), .2g fiber (1%), 3.5g protein (7%), zero vitamin A and C, 6mg calcium (1%) and 1.4mg iron (8%).

BAKED PASSOVER BAGELS
Makes 12 bagels

During the *Jewish Passover*, there are a number of dietary laws from the Bible that must be followed. Note with these bagels, flour has been replaced with matzo meal. This recipe is from *Manischewitz*, producer of Jewish foods.

1 cup boiling water
1/2 cup pareve margarine
2 cups matzo meal

2 tablespoons sugar
1 1/4 teaspoons salt
3 eggs

1. Place water and margarine into a 3 quart saucepan.
2. Heat over medium heat until margarine is melted.
3. Combine the dry ingredients and add all at once to the saucepan.
4. Stir briskly until dough forms a ball and leaves sides of the pan.
5. Remove from heat.
6. Add the eggs one at a time, stirring in each one thoroughly before adding the next.
7. Put dough into a bowl and place plastic wrap directly onto dough.

8. Let stand at room temperature for 15 minutes.
9. Divide dough into 12 equal pieces.
10. Shape each piece of dough into a 6-inch log.
11. Form a circle and secure the ends by pinching the dough together.
12. Place on a greased cookie sheet.
13. Bake in a preheated 375 F oven for 50 minutes or until golden brown.
14. With a sharp knife, piece each bagel twice on opposite sides to release steam.
15. Cool on a wire rack.
16. Store in an airtight container.

NUTRITION FACTS per bagel: 250 calories, 85 calories from fat, 9.4g total fat (14%), 1.8g saturated fat (9%), 53.1mg cholesterol (18%), 327.3mg sodium (14%), 35.3g carbohydrates (12%), 1.2g fiber (5%), 5.6g protein (11%), 390 IU vitamin A (8%), zero vitamin C, 14mg calcium (1%) and 1.4mg iron (8%).

CAJUN HOT TOMATO BREAD
Makes 2 loaves

Amelia S. Meaux from Crowley, Louisiana says, *"Cajun food can be quite spicy. It's the Bloody Mary mix in this recipe that adds the heat. If you want a mild bread, replace with either tomato juice or vegetable cocktail. If you want more heat, add a one or two chopped jalapeno peppers."*

1 cup Bloody Mary mix
1 cup water
1 package active dry yeast
1/3 cup honey
1/4 cup vegetable oil

1/4 cup green onion tops, chopped
1/4 cup fresh parsley, chopped
1 garlic clove, minced
1 teaspoon salt
5 to 6 cups flour

1. In a small saucepan, combine Bloody Mary mix and water.
2. Cook over low heat to 105°F to 115°F (no hotter or you will kill the yeast).
3. Pour into large mixing bowl and add yeast; stir until dissolved.
4. Add honey, oil, onions, parsley, garlic and salt; mix well.
5. Add 1 cup flour and stir until smooth.
6. Stir in more flour until a firm dough is formed.
7. Knead on lightly floured board about 5 minutes.
8. Shape into a ball and place in a large greased bowl; turn to grease all sides.

9. Cover bowl and set in a warm place to rise for about 1 hour or until doubled in size.
10. Punch down and divide into 2 equal parts.
11. Shape each piece into a loaf and place in a greased loaf pan.
12. Cover and let rise in a warm place about 1 hour or until doubled in size.
13. Bake at 400°F about 30 minutes or until loaves have a hollow sound when tapped and crust is brown.
14. Remove from pans and cool on wire rack.

CARAMELIZED ONION BREAD
Makes 3 loaves

Rosemary Campiformio makes this bread at her *Saint Orres Restaurant* in Gualala, California. She says, *"It's the onions that are caramelized with sugar to achieve the delicate, yet distinctive flavor in this bread."*

3 tablespoons butter
2 red onions, thinly sliced
1/2 cup sugar
1 package dry yeast
1 tablespoon sugar
1 cup warm water

4 teaspoons rosemary, finely chopped
1/2 cup roasted garlic with olive oil*
1 teaspoon salt
2 egg whites
3 to 3 1/2 cups bread flour
2 tablespoons butter, melted

1. In a pan, place 3 tablespoons of butter, red onions and 1/2 cup of sugar.
2. Sauté on high until the onions are sweet and golden brown.
3. Set aside to cool.
4. In a large bowl, mix yeast with warm water and 1 tablespoon of sugar.
5. Add rosemary, garlic and oil, salt and egg whites.
6. With mixer running on slow, add flour, 1/2 cup at a time to make a soft dough.
7. Add remaining flour by hand, mixing until flour mixture leaves te sides of the bowl.
8. Turn out on a floured board and knead until smooth and no longer sticky.

9. Place in a greased bowl, cover with a towel and let dough rise at room temperature until doubled, about 40 minutes.
10. Divide dough into three parts and roll out to an 8-inch circle.
11. Place 1/3 of the onion mixture on each round.
12. Roll the dough up forming a loaf.
13. Be sure to fold under and secure the ends to prevent the onions from seeping out while rising and cooking.
14. Let rise uncovered until double.
15. Bake in 350 F oven for about 30 minutes.
16. Brush with melted butter while still hot.

NUTRITION FACTS per slice: 67 calories, 17 calories from fat, 2g total fat (3%), .8g saturated fat (4%), 3.2mg cholesterol (1%), 59.6mg sodium (2%), 10.8g carbohydrates (4%), .5g fiber (2%), 1.7g protein (3%), 47 IU vitamin A (1%), 1mg vitamin C (2%), 7mg calcium (1%) and .6mg iron (3%).

*ROASTED GARLIC

1. To roast garlic, take 2 whole garlic heads, wrap in foil and roast in a 375°F oven for 1 hour.
2. When cool to handle, pinch each clove so that the roasted garlic slips out.

3. Mix roasted garlic with 2 tablespoons of olive oil.

CHEESE & WINE BREAD
Makes 1 loaf

From California's Napa Valley, comes a very delicious egg-rich bread made with wine. This is one of more than 200 recipes from the *Sharpsteen Museum Cookbook*. This bread makes excellent toast.

3 to 4 cups flour
1 package yeast
1 cup dry white wine
1/2 cup margarine or butter
2 teaspoons sugar

1 teaspoon salt
3 eggs at room temperature
1 cup Monterey Jack cheese cut into 1/4 inch cubes

1. In a large mixer bowl, combine 1 1/2 cups of flour and the yeast.
2. In a sauce pan, heat wine, margarine, sugar and salt to 115°F to 120°F, stirring constantly until margarine almost melts.
3. Add to flour/yeast mixture.
4. Add eggs, beat at low speed for 1/2-minute, scraping sides of bowl constantly.
5. Beat 3 minutes at high speed.
6. By hand, stir in cheese and remaining flour.
7. Mix well with a wood spoon.
8. Turn out onto floured surface and knead, adding flour until dough no longer is sticky or until smooth and elastic.
9. Place in lightly greased bowl, turning once to grease surface.
10. Cover and let rise in a warm place (about 80°F) until doubled in bulk, about 1 1/2 hours.
11. Punch dough down, cover and let rest for 10 minutes.
12. Shape into an 8-inch round loaf.
13. Place in a greased 9-inch pie plate, cover and let rise in a warm place until double in bulk, about 40 minutes.
14. Bake in 375°F oven for about 40 minutes, cover with foil after 20 minutes if browning too fast.

NUTRITION FACTS per slice: 190 calories, 86 calories from fat, 9g total fat (14%), 5.2g saturated fat (26%), 61.4mg cholesterol (20%), 242mg sodium (10%), 19g carbohydrates (6%), .2g fiber (1%), 5.7g protein (11%), 340 IU vitamin A (7%), zero vitamin C, 64mg calcium (6%) and 1.5mg iron (8%).

DANISH LIGHT RYE BREAD
Makes 1 loaf

This *Danish* bread, is the type of bread known in the United States as *Jewish rye*. Rye flour lacks the gluten of wheat flour, hence, this bread will be dense. Best sliced thin and toasted. Great topped with cream cheese, *Danish* cream cheese of course.

1 ounce fresh yeast or 1 1/2 packages dried yeast
1/3 cup lukewarm water
1 cup buttermilk
1 teaspoon salt

1 teaspoon sugar
1 tablespoon ground caraway
3 1/3 cups rye flour
Egg, beaten or cold coffee

1. In a bowl, dissolve the yeast in the water.
2. Add the buttermilk, salt, sugar and caraway.
3. Add half of the flour and knead the dough well, adding more flour a little at a time.
4. Cover the dough and let it rise until double.
5. Knead the dough lightly and shape it into a loaf.
6. Put it in a greased loaf pan and let it rise for 20 minutes.
7. Brush with beaten egg.
8. Bake on the lowest rack in a 400°F oven for 25 minutes.
9. Cool on a baking rack.

NUTRITION FACTS per thin slice: 162 calories, 8 calories from fat, .9g total fat (1%), .2g saturated fat (1%), zero cholesterol, 101.3mg sodium (4%), 35g carbohydrates (12%), 6.6g fiber (27%), 4.6g protein (9%), zero vitamins A and C, 25mg calcium (2%) and 1mg iron (6%).

DANISH SOURDOUGH DARK RYE BREAD
Makes 3 loaves

When making *Danish* sourdough bread, it takes about 24 hours of mixing and rising before baking. But it is worth it. Many *Danes* consider it something of a sport to be able to make bread for years from the same sourdough. It is kept in a glass in the refrigerator and can stay fresh for about 3 weeks. It can be frozen for up to 3 months, taken out 2 days before use, and thawed in the refrigerator. When used, save a bit for the next loaf.

SOURDOUGH STARTER

3/4 cup rye flour

2/3 cup plain yogurt

1 tablespoon coarse salt

1. Mix together all ingredients in a non-metallic bowl.

2. Cover with plastic wrap and set in a warm place for 2 to 3 days until the dough bubbles.

BASIC DOUGH

Aged sourdough starter
1 quart lukewarm water
3 3/4 cups whole wheat flour

1 tablespoon salt
3 3/4 cups flour

1. In a bowl, dilute the sourdough starter with the water.
2. Add salt and flours.
3. Cover and let the dough rise 12 hours.

4. If for some reason the dough did not rise, add 3 packages of yeast to the 1 1/3 cups of lukewarm water (following recipe ingredients) and knead in the rye flour

RYE BREAD DOUGH

1 1/3 cups lukewarm water
Brush with a little vegetable oil

5 cups rye flour

1. Add the water and rye flour to the basic dough.
2. The dough will be to soft, so you will not be able to that knead it with the hands.
3. Take 1 cup of the dough as a starter for the next bread.
4. Pour the dough into a greased 3-quart loaf pan, cover, and let rise for 10 to 12 hours.

5. Brush the bread with oil and prick with a fork.
6. Put the loaf pan in a cold oven.
7. Set the temperature at 350°F and bake for 1 1/2 to 2 hours.
8. Wrap the bread in a clean dish towel and cool on a baking rack.

NUTRITION FACTS per slice: 113 calories, 5 calories from fat, .6g total fat (1%), .1g saturated fat (1%), zero cholesterol, 253.2mg sodium (11%), 23.9g carbohydrates (8%), 2.9g fiber (12%), 3.6g protein (7%), zero vitamins A and C, 12mg calcium (1%) and 1.1mg iron (6%).

DANISH WHITE BREAD
Makes 3 loaves

In Europe you will find this recipe as a basic white bread. There are some differences from country to country because of the flours used and how they are milled. In *Denmark*, white bread is in its purest form made with wheat flour. While this recipe does not contain them, many bakers add a few wheat kernels, giving the bread a coarser consistency.

1 ounce fresh yeast or 1 1/2 packages dried yeast
1 1/4 cups milk
2 tablespoons butter
Egg, beaten or cold coffee

1 teaspoon salt
1 teaspoon sugar
3 1/3 cups flour

1. In a bowl, dissolve the yeast in a little of the cold milk.
2. In a saucepan, melt the butter and add to the rest of the milk.
3. Stir it into the yeast mixture.
4. Add the salt, sugar and half of the flour.
5. Knead the dough until soft and elastic, adding more flour.

6. Cover the dough and let it rise until double.
7. Knead the dough lightly and put it in a greased loaf pan.
8. Let it rise for 30 minutes.
9. Brush with egg and slash the loaf lengthwise.
10. Bake the bread on the lowest rack in at 450°F oven for 30 minutes.

48

11. Turn the bread out of the pan and cool it.

NUTRITION FACTS per slice: 122 calories, 21 calories from fat, 2.4g total fat (4%), 1.3g saturated fat (7%), 6.4mg cholesterol (2%), 158.1mg sodium (7%), 21.3g carbohydrates (7%), .2g fiber (1%), 3.5g protein (7%), 78 IU vitamin A (2%), zero vitamin C, 28mg calcium (3%) and 1.3mg iron (7%).

DANISH WHOLE WHEAT BREAD
Makes 1 leaf

This recipe is similar to the white bread. However, buttermilk is used in place of milk and whole wheat flour in place of white flour.

1 ounce fresh yeast or 1 1/2 packages dried yeast
1/3 cup lukewarm water
1 cup buttermilk
2 tablespoons vegetable oil

1 teaspoon salt
1 teaspoon sugar
1 cup whole wheat flour
2 -2/3 cups white bread flour

Brush with beaten egg or cold coffee

1. In a bowl, dissolve the yeast in the water.
2. Add the buttermilk, oil, salt, and sugar.
3. Stir in the wheat flour and half of the bread flour.
4. Knead the dough until it is soft and elastic, adding more flour.
5. Cover the dough and let it rise until double.
6. Knead the dough, shape it into a loaf, and put it in a greased loaf pan.

7. Let the loaf rise for 30 minutes.
8. Brush with egg and slash the loaf lengthwise with a sharp knife.
9. Bake the bread on the lowest rack in the oven at 450°F for 30 minutes.
10. Turn the bread out of the pan and cool it on a baking rack.

NUTRITION FACTS per slice: 132 calories, 21 calories from fat, 2.4g total fat (4%), .4g saturated fat (2%), zero cholesterol, 150.7mg sodium (6%), 23.3g carbohydrates (8%), 1.6g fiber (7%), 4.4g protein (9%), zero vitamins A and C, 24mg calcium (2%) and 1.4mg iron (8%).

ENGLISH MUFFIN LOAVES
Makes 3 loaves

So you like *English* muffins (see MUFFIN chapter, page 200), but don't have the time to make them. *SACO Foods* has your answer. These loaves are easy to make, no kneading, no double rising, just mix, place dough in cans, let rise, and bake.

6 cups flour
2 packages yeast
1 tablespoon sugar
2 teaspoons salt

1/2 cup cultured buttermilk powder
1/4 teaspoon baking soda
2 1/2 cups water, warmed to 120 F to 130 F
Cornmeal

1. In a large bowl combine 3 cups of flour, yeast, sugar, salt, buttermilk powder and soda.
2. Add the warm water to dry ingredients and beat at low speed until blended.
3. Continue to beat at medium speed for 2 minutes.
4. By hand, add remaining flour, one cup at a time, to make a stiff dough.

5. Divide dough in three 1-pound coffee cans (see NOTE) that have been greased and sprinkled with cornmeal.
6. Sprinkle tops of dough with corn meal.
7. Cover, let rise in warm place for 30 minutes.
8. Bake on bottom rack of oven at 400°F for 25 minutes.
9. Immediately remove from cans and cool.
10. To serve, slice thick and toast.

NOTE: Other can sizes can be used, just fill about half full and follow same instructions. Kids like to use small fruit cans. Tall juice cans also make excellent loaves. And yes, you can use bread loaf pan as well.

NUTRITION FACTS per slice: 69 calories, 3 calories from fat, .4g total fat (1%), zero saturated fat and cholesterol, 102.4mg sodium (4%), 13.5g carbohydrates (4%), .6g fiber (2%), zero vitamin A and C, 18mg calcium (2%) and .8mg iron (5%).

FRENCH AND ITALIANS BREADS
Makes 2 loaves (32 slices)

There's nothing more basic than *French* and *Italian* breads. Main ingredients are flour, water and yeast. About the only difference is *Italian* bread has more sugar as compared to *French* bread.

About 5 cups flour
1 teaspoon sugar for French bread,
or 1 tablespoon sugar for Italian bread
1 tablespoon salt
2 packages yeast

1 1/2 tablespoons vegetable oil
1 3/4 cups warm water (120 F to 130 F)
Cornmeal
Vegetable oil (optional)
1 egg white

1 tablespoon water

1. In a large bowl, combine 1 cup flour, sugar, salt and yeast.
2. In a measuring cup, mix vegetable oil and warm water.
3. Slowly add the liquid to the dry ingredients, beating with an electric mixer for about 2 minutes.
4. Add 1 cup of dry ingredients and beat at high speed for another 2 minutes.
5. By hand, stir in remaining dry ingredients, a little at a time, until a stiff dough.
6. On a floured board, knead in as much flour to make a smooth, elastic, none sticky dough.
7. Cover dough with plastic wrap and a towel and let the dough rest for 20 minutes.
8. Divide dough into two equal parts.

9. On the floured board, roll each half into an oblong, about 15-inches long.
10. Beginning on the wide side, roll up dough, tuck ends underneath, and taper ends.
11. Sprinkle cornmeal on a greased cookie sheet.
12. Place formed dough on the cookie sheet.
13. For a soft crust, brush dough with vegetable oil, if desired.
14. Loosely cover dough with plastic wrap.
15. In a warm place, let dough rise until double, about 1 hour.
16. Combine egg white and 1 tablespoon of water, and brush loaves.
17. Bake in a preheated 450°F oven for about 20 minutes or until done.
18. Cool on wire racks.

NUTRITION FACTS per slice: 84 calories, 8 calories from fat, .9g total fat (1%), .1g saturated fat (1%), zero cholesterol, 202.8mg sodium (8%), 16g carbohydrates (5%), .5g fiber (2%), 2.8g protein (6%), zero vitamins A and C, zero calcium, and 1.2mg iron (7%).

VARIATIONS

- Bread can have 3 to 4 diagonal cuts just prior to baking.
- Egg white mixture can be brushed on loaves about half way through baking.
- Dough can be made in rolls.
- Bread or rolls can be topped with sesame seeds.
- While baking, dough and oven can be sprayed lightly with water 3 or 4 times. This will makes a crispy crust.
- Brush with milk for a softer crust.
- For more color, brush with honey.
- Dough can be frozen for up to a month and a half for future baking.

HOPE'S EGG BREAD
Makes 3 loaves (48 slices)

Hope Irvin Marston, from Black River, New York, says, *"You can use this recipe to make Jewish Challah bread for the Sabbath or special holidays. You can also cut my egg bread in thick slices to be used for French toast."*

2 packages quick rise yeast
1/2 cup sugar
1 3/4 cups warm water
2 cups whole wheat flour

1 teaspoon salt
4 eggs, beaten
1/2 cup butter, melted, cooled
5 1/2 cups bread flour

1. Combine yeast and sugar in large bowl.
2. Add warm water and stir until yeast is dissolved.
3. Add whole wheat flour, salt, eggs, and butter and beat by hand until smooth.
4. Continue to add flour until the dough forms a ball you can knead.
5. Knead on a lightly floured board for 10 minutes.
6. Grease a bowl with shortening.
7. Place dough in the bowl and turn once to coat it with shortening.

8. Cover dough with a heavy towel and let rise in a warm spot until the dough doubles.
9. When doubled, turn it on onto a lightly floured surface and divide it into thirds.
10. Shape into loaves and place in 3 loaf pans.
11. Let rise until level with the top of the pans.
12. Bake at 350°F for 30 minutes or until brown.
13. Remove from oven, turn out of pans, and grease all sides with butter.
14. Cool on baking racks.

NUTRITION FACTS per slice: 106 calories, 24 calories from fat, 2.7g total fat (4%),, 1.4g saturated fat (7%), 22.8mg cholesterol (8%), 158.6mg sodium (7%), 17.3g carbohydrates (6%), 1.1g fiber (5%), 3.3g protein (7%), 98 IU vitamin A (2%), zero vitamin C, 7mg calcium (1%) and 1mg iron (6%).

CHALLAH BREAD VARIATION
Makes 2 loaves

1 egg yolk, beaten with 1 teaspoon water

Poppy seeds

1. In step #9, divide dough in half.
2. Divide each half into thirds.
3. With your hands roll each third to a rope about 12- inches in length.
4. Braid the 3 ropes, pinch the ends to seam and place on a greased cookie sheet.
5. Cover and let rise until double.

6. Brush with the egg yoke and sprinkle with poppy seeds.
7. Bake in a 375°F oven for about 40 minutes or until golden brown.
8. Cool on wire racks.

JULEBROD

A special treat served for the *Norwegian* Christmas breakfast is julebrod. This Christmas bread makes wonderful toast.

1 cup raisins
1 cup candied red & green cherries cut into thirds
or assorted candied fruit
2 packages active dry yeast
1 tablespoon sugar
1/4 cup warm water
1/2 cup blanched almonds, finely chopped

2 cups milk
1/2 cup shortening
1/2 cup sugar
2 teaspoons salt
2 teaspoons cardamon seed, ground
6 1/2 to 8 cups flour

1. In a bowl, soften raisins in a small amount of hot water for about 5 minutes; drain.
2. Prepare cherries by shaking them in a bag with a little flour.
3. In a small bowl dissolve yeast with 1 tablespoon sugar and warm water.
4. In a saucepan, scald milk.
5. Stir in shortening and let it cool for about 15 minutes.
6. When milk has cooled, pour into a big mixing bowl.
7. Add 1/2 cup sugar, salt, cardamon; stir.
8. Add yeast; stir.
9. Add 2 cups of flour, candied cherries, raisins and almonds; mix well.
10. Continue to add more flour, 1 cup at a time, stirring until dough leaves the sides of the bowl.
11. Turn dough out on a floured board and knead well.
12. Use as much remaining flour as it takes to produced a springy, elastic texture.
13. Place dough in a greased bowl and cover with a damp towel.
14. Place the bowl in a warm place and let the dough rise until double.
15. Punch down and let it rise until double again.
16. Punch down once more and cut into 2 equal sections.
17. Knead each section well.
18. Form round loaves and place them on a cookiesheet.
19. Cover with a damp cloth and let rise until double once again.
20. In a preheated 350°F oven bake for about 35 minutes or until tops are golden brown.

NUTRITION FACTS per slice: 189 calories, 47 calories from fat, 5.3g total fat (8%), 1.3g saturated fat (6%), 2.1mg cholesterol (1%), 13mg sodium (1%), 31.8g carbohydrates (11%), .6g fiber (2%), 4.3g protein (9%), zero vitamins A and C, 32mg calcium (3%) and 1.6mg iron (9%).

KULICH WITH PASHKA
Makes 1 loaf

This bread is enjoyed in *Russia* during the Easter holidays. At one time, Kulich was considered so delicate that bakers placed pillows around the dough to prevent it from falling. The initials "XV" are placed on top of the bread either in design with frosting or thin strips of dough. The XV meaning is, "Christ is risen." The top slice of this special Easter bread is served to a guest of honor or a senior member of the family. Makes great toast!

1 package dry yeast	2 1/4 cups flour
1/4 cup water, warmed to 110 F to 115 F	1 egg, slightly beaten
1/4 cup butter or margarine, softened	1/2 teaspoon vanilla
1/4 cup sugar	1/4 teaspoon cardamon
1 teaspoon salt	1/4 cup red candied cherries, chopped
1/4 cup milk, scalded, cooled to lukewarm	1/4 cup green candied cherries, chopped

1 tablespoon almonds, toasted, chopped

1. In a bowl, soften yeast in warm water; let stand for 10 minutes.
2. Combine butter, sugar and salt in a bowl.
3. Add cooled scalded milk and stir until butter is melted.
4. With electric mixer (or by hand), beat 1/2 cup flour into milk mixture.
5. Stir in the yeast, then beat in egg, vanilla and cardamom.
6. Add remaining flour gradually by hand with a wooden spoon, mixing thoroughly after each addition.
7. Place in a greased bowl, cover, place in a warm place and let it rise until double, about 2 hours.
8. Punch down and let it rise again until almost doubled, about 45 minutes.
9. Turn dough onto a lightly floured surface, mix in cherries and almonds; knead 15 times.
10. Shape dough into a ball and place in a well greased 1-pound coffee can or tall 46-ounce fruit juice can.
11. Cover and let rise again until doubled in bulk, about 30 minutes.
12. Bake at 350°F for 45 minutes or until bread is well browned.

13. Cool in the can for 15 minutes, then turn out onto a wire rack to cool completely.
14. Blend some powdered sugar with milk until smooth.
15. Spoon the icing over the Kulich and allow it to drip down the sides.
16. Garnish top with whole red candied cherries.
17. Slice and spread with paskha.

NOTE: For the children, top with vanilla glaze and a dozen jelly beans, if desired.

PASHKA

In *Russia, kulich* is usually served with Easter cheese, called *Pushka. Pushka* is also served as a dessert.

16 ounces cream cheese, softened
1/2 cup butter, softened
1 cup large curd cottage cheese
1/2 cup sugar
1 tablespoon lemon peel, finely shredded

1 tablespoon orange peel, finely shredded
1 teaspoon vanilla
1/3 cup red candied cherries, chopped
1/4 cup golden raisins
2 tablespoons candied pineapple, diced

1/4 cup almonds, toasted, chopped

1. In a bowl, combine first 7 ingredients; beat until smooth.
2. Mix in remaining ingredients.
3. Line cheese cloth in a colander.
4. Spoon mixture into the cheese cloth and place colander in a shallow pan for drainage.
5. Cover and place in the refrigerator to allow to drain and for the flavors to blend for at least 12 hours.

OATMEAL APPLE BREAD
Makes 3 loaves

Here's a recipe you probably won't find in any cookbook, that is until now. This bread is served to guests at *Chestnut Charm Bed and Breakfast* by *Barbara and Martha Stensvad* in Atlantic, Iowa. Their flour is ground from grain at the nearby 1848 Danish windmill.

1/3 cup raisins
2 tablespoons rum
1 teaspoon sugar
2 tablespoons molasses
1/2 cup apple juice
1/3 cup brown sugar
1 tablespoon salt
1 1/3 cups apple cider

2 tablespoons butter, melted
2 packages yeast
5 1/2 to 6 cups bread flour
1/2 teaspoon cinnamon
1 1/2 cups rolled oats
3/4 cup apple, finely chopped
1/2 cup walnuts, chopped
1 egg white

1 tablespoon water

1. In a small bowl, mix raisins and rum.
2. Cover; set aside 3 to 4 hours or overnight to soak.
3. In a heavy sauce pan mix sugars, molasses, salt, juices and butter.
4. Heat to 110°F.

5. Mix in a medium bowl, 3 cups of bread flour, yeast, and cinnamon.
6. Add warm liquid mixture and mix well.
7. Add oats, apple and walnuts and mix well.
8. Add remaining flour, a little at a time to make a soft dough.
9. Turn out dough onto a lightly floured surface.
10. Kneed dough 8 to 10 minutes or until smooth and elastic.
11. Place dough in a large greased bowl, turning all sides.
12. Let rise until double in a warm place.

13. After an hour, punch down and kneed 30 seconds.
14. Divide dough and shape into 3 greased loaf pans.
15. Let rise again until double in a warm place.
16. Mix egg white with water and brush glaze on top of the raised dough.
17. Baked in a 375°F for 35 to 40 minutes or until bread sounds hollow when tapped on sides and bottom.
18. If bread is browning too quickly, put a foil tent over it.
19. Remove from pans and cool on racks.

NUTRITION FACTS per slice: 111 calories, 17 calories from fat, 1.9g total fat (3%), .4g saturated fat (2%), zero cholesterol, 141mg sodium (6%), 19.9g carbohydrates (7%), .7g fiber (3%), 3.5g protein (7%), zero vitamin A and C, 11mg calcium (1%) and 1.2mg iron (7%).

PAIN CAMPAGNARD AUX POMMES
Makes 3 loaves

Thierry Tellier, the pastry chef for *la Madeleine French Bakery and Café*, Dallas, Texas says, *"Apples provide just the right flavor to give the real taste of country cooking. This is an excellent bread, as well as a great breakfast toast. The bread sounds sweet because of the fruit and cider, but it isn't. The apples merely add a subtle flavor. Preparation is only 30 minutes, however, this bread requires 7 hours of rising time and can not be hurried."*

3 packages dry yeast
6 tablespoons lukewarm water (105 F to 115 F)
2 cups apple cider

1 2/3 cups rye flour
1 2/3 cups whole wheat flour

1. In a bowl, sprinkle yeast over the warm water.
2. Set aside, in a warm place, for 5 minutes to proof.
3. Mixture will become foamy as the yeast begins to work.

4. In a bowl, mix yeast together with rye and wheat flours and cider.
5. Set this aside for 6 hours to create a "sponge."

6 ¾ cups bread flour
5 teaspoons salt

1 to 2 cups water
2 apples, peeled, cored, diced

6. After 6 hours add bread flour, salt and 1 cup of water (more water might be needed).
7. Add dough.
8. Combine well, then mix in the apples.
9. Knead dough in the mixer with a dough hook at medium speed for 5 minutes or by hand for 10 minutes.
10. Place dough in an oiled bowl, cover and let rise 30 minutes or until double in size.
11. Punch down and divide into 3 equal pieces.
12. Form into loaves either using bread pans or shape into a round loaf.

13. Grease the pans and place dough in them and let rise for 30 minutes or until doubled in size.
14. Bake the bread in a preheated 375°F oven for 40 minutes or until cooked through.
15. To test, thump or knock on the loaf, it will sound hollow when done.
16. The loaf will have a crusty exterior and a golden color.
17. Cooking times can vary with the size of the loaf made.

NUTRITION FACTS per slice: 107 calories, 5 calories from fat, .5g total fat, zero saturated fat, cholesterol and sodium, 22.1g carbohydrates (7%), 1.9g fiber (7%), 3.5g protein (7%), zero vitamin A and C, 7mg calcium (1%) and 1.3mg iron (7%).

SOURDOUGH BREAD
Makes 2 loaves

Sourdough, is a word that means different things to different people. To an *Alaskan* it means a "*pioneer."* To a *baker* it means "*a fermented dough that is kept from one baking to another."* And to a *connoisseur* it might mean a "*delicious tasting bread*." The words "sour" and "dough" are Germanic words, "sour" referring to "salt" and "dough" referring to "knead." This is how I made sourdough bread when I lived in *Alaska.*

1 package dry yeast
1 1/2 cups warm water
1 tablespoon sugar
5 to 6 cups flour
1 cup sourdough starter at room temperature

(see PANCAKES, page 220)
Sourdough Hotcakes recipe for Sourdough
Starter recipe)
2 teaspoons salt
1/2 teaspoon baking soda

1. In a large mixing bowl soften yeast with warm water and sugar, about 5 minutes.
2. Add starter, salt, soda and 2 cups flour.
3. Beat at medium speed with electric mixture for about 2 minutes.
4. By hand, stir in additional flour to make a stiff dough.
5. Place on a floured surface and knead for about 7 minutes.
6. Shape into a ball and place in a greased bowl; turning once to grease all sides.
7. Cover and let rise in a warm place for about 2 hours or until double in bulk.
8. Punch down, divide in half and shape into two round or oblong loaves.

9. Place on greased baking sheet that has been lightly sprinkled with cornmeal.
10. With a sharp knife make several slashes on top of the loaves.
11. Cover with a cloth and let rise in a warm place for about 1 1/2 hours or until almost double.
12. Bake in preheated 400°F oven for 35 to 40 minutes.
13. Cool on wire racks.
14. If you want a crusty bread, spray the inside of the oven with water several times during baking.
15. For a soft crust, brush with butter as it cools onthe wire racks.

NUTRITION FACTS per slice: 95 calories, 2 calories from fat, zero fats and cholesterol, 153.6mg sodium (6%), 19.9g carbohydrates (7%), zero fiber, 2.8g protein (6%), zero vitamin A, C and calcium, and 1.2mg iron (7%)

NOTE: Sourdough can turn almost any yeast bread into a sourdough bread. Just add 1 cup of sourdough starter and ½ teaspoon of soda to the recipe. Once you have mastered the making of starter, you might want to experiment by adding a little sugar and see if it improves the taste or not. The bacteria reacts different to the various ingredients across the country. Also rise time will vary, a bit slower in cool weather like Alaska, but faster in a warmer climate like America's south.

SWEDISH RYE BREAD
Makes 1 loaf (16 slices)

Rye flour has its own unique taste with a somewhat heartier flavor than wheat, yet the nutritional values are about the same. This recipe comes from the *Arrowhead Mills* test kitchens.

2 cups rye flour
1 cup scalded milk
2 1/2 teaspoons sea salt
2 tablespoons molasses or honey
1 tablespoon caraway seeds

2 tablespoons vegetable oil
1 cup water
1 package dry yeast
3 1/2 cups bread flour

1. In a bowl, blend milk with salt, molasses and oil.

2. Add water.
3. When cool, add yeast and bread flour.

4. Blend until smooth.
5. Stir in caraway seeds.
6. Gradually add rye flour.
7. Mix by hand to a medium stiff dough.
8. Turn onto a floured surface and knead until smooth.
9. Place in oiled bowl.
10. Cover and let rise until doubled in size.
11. Punch down and let it rise again.
12. Punch down one more time.
13. Shape and place in oiled 9x5-inch loaf pan, let rise until doubled in size.
14. Bake at 375°F for 30 to 40 minutes.

NUTRITION FACTS per slice: 188 calories, 27 calories from fat, 3g total fat (5%), .6g saturated fat (3%), 2.1mg cholesterol (1%), 303.6mg sodium (13%), 34.6g carbohydrates (12%), 3g fiber (12%), 5.7g protein (11%), zero vitamins A and C, 34mg calcium (3%) and 1.9mg iron (11%).

Did you know that rye is a cereal grass? The whole rye grain is used to make alcoholic liquors, such as some kinds of vodka and whiskey. To make rye bread, the grain is ground into a flour. Since rye flour doesn't have the gluten to make bread rise, it must be mixed with wheat flour. Breads made will all rye flour are quite heavy and can be moist. The original pumpernickel bread was made with all rye flour and was quite heavy. Today pumpernickel has some rye, but mostly wheat flour and is colored with molasses and/or cocoa. Rye flour is also used to make crackers and cookies .Rye flour is quite popular in Northern Europe, because it can grow in colder climates than wheat. When the new settlers came to America, their first choice for flour was made from corn. When wheat didn't do well, they planted rye and mixed the rye flour with corn flour and this bread was known as "rye'n'Injun." Rye grass was a boon to mankind because it will grow in Nordic regions, in mountains and on poor soil.

WEIHNACHTSSTOLLEN
Makes 3 loaves

This German Christmas bread recipe comes from *Mrs. Alex Wambach* of Fredericksburg, Texas.

2 packages yeast
2 cups milk, scalded, cooled to 120°F
10 cups flour
2 1/2 cups butter, divided
1 cup sugar
1 teaspoon salt
4 eggs
1 tablespoon orange or lemon rind, grated
1 cup raisins
1 1/2 cups candied fruit
1 1/2 cups blanched almonds, chopped

1. In a bowl, dissolve yeast in warm milk.
2. Stir in 1 cup flour.
3. Let rise about 1/2 hour.
4. In another bowl, cream 2 cups of butter with sugar and salt.
5. Add eggs, one at a time and beat well after each.
6. Add rind.
7. Combine the two mixtures and add enough flour to make a soft dough.
8. Mix in raisins, fruit and almonds.
9. Add more flour until smooth and elastic.
10. Turn out on floured board, knead gently 4 to 6 minutes.
11. Place in warm, greased bowl; let rise in warm place until doubled, 1 1/2 to 2 hours.
12. Punch down, knead 2 to 4 minutes.
13. Divide dough into 3 or 4 parts.
14. Roll each into an oblong, 1/2 inch thick; brush with melted butter.
15. Fold long sides together; press down edges.
16. Place in large, greased pans and let rise 1 to 1 1/2 hours or until doubled.
17. Brush with remaining melted butter.
18. Bake in 350°F oven for 40 minutes or until golden brown.
19. While still hot, brush on thin icing made with 2 cups powdered sugar mixed with about 1/3 cup of milk. May also be decorated with candied fruit or nuts.

NUTRITION FACTS per slice: 205 calories, 86 calories from fat, 9.7g total fat (15%), 4.9g saturated fat (25%), 33.7mg cholesterol (11%), 118gmg sodium (5%), 26.5g carbohydrates (9%), .5g fiber (2%), 3.7g protein (7%), 299 IU vitamin A (6%), zero vitamin C, 28mg calcium (3%) and 1.2mg iron (7%)

MAKING HOMEMADE YEAST

Mrs. Chas. F. Kiehne, says "*You can use these yeast cakes with any yeast recipe, but use double the amount called for and allow for a longer rising time.*" *Mrs. Jacob Gold, Sr.* says, "*Bread doughs are best prepared the day before and allowed to rise overnight.*" Both ladies are from Fredricksburg, Texas.

1 yeast cake, homemade or compressed
1 pint water, warmed
1 tablespoon cornmeal
1 tablespoon sugar

1 teaspoon salt
1 pint buttermilk
1 cup flour
1 cup water

Cornmeal

1. In a bowl, dissolve the yeast cake in the warmed water.
2. Add cornmeal, sugar and salt.
3. Let stand overnight.
4. In the morning bring the buttermilk to a boil.
5. In a bowl, mix the flour and water to make a smooth batter.
6. Pour this into the boiling milk, stirring constantly and cook until thick.
7. Remove from the heat and let it cool.

8. Combine with the yeast mixture and set in a warm place until it ferments.
9. Work in enough cornmeal to make a stiff dough.
10. Form into a long roll, 1 1/2 inches across and cut into cakes about 1/2 inch thick.
11. Dry in the shade.
12. Place in cloth sack and hang it out to dry in a cool place.
13. This will keep about 1 month.
14. Or freeze for up to 4 months.

Did you know that yeast is a living organism that floats in the air all around you? Yeast is so tiny, a couple thousand packed tightly would take up less than a quarter inch of space. Yet, when mixed with liquid and sugar or starch, yeast converts to carbon dioxide and alcohol and begins to ferment. Yeast in bread dough tries to push its way out, thus making the bread dough rise. Yeast also turns grapes, fruit and grains into wine, beer and liquor. Yeast is considered fungi, just like mushrooms. They all belong to the same living things. Active dry yeast is available on supermarket shelves in small packets and by bulk in jars. Moist compressed yeast is kept in the refrigerator section. When using yeast to make bread, care must be taken not to get it too hot, because heat will kill it. Liquids should be less than 120°F for dried yeast and under 90°F for compressed yeast. Also if the raising place exceeds 145°F, it will kill the yeast. Hence, when the risen bread dough is placed in a preheated oven, the yeast is killed immediately and the bread holds its shape. If the bread is placed in a cold oven, it will continue to rise until the heat kills the yeast. This sometimes will make the bread rise too much, causing large air pockets.

BREAD SPREADS

CINNAMON CREAM CHEESE SPREAD

Cream cheese cuts the calories in half and the fat by about 25% as compared to butter. An excellent spread for biscuits, muffins, tea breads, and toast. Recipe courtesy of *McCormick/Shilling*.

8 ounces cream cheese, softened
1/2 teaspoon cinnamon

1 1/2 teaspoons sugar
1 teaspoon orange extract

1. Combine all ingredients.

2. Refrigerate

FRUIT SPREAD

Andrea Levy of Redmond, Washington uses this spread instead of jam on bread and in recipes.

1 cup fresh berries (strawberry, raspberry or blackberry), crushed or pureed

1/4 cup frozen fruit juice concentrate (apple, orange or pineapple)

1. Bring juice concentrate (do not add water) to boil in a small sauce pan.
2. Add berries and simmer uncovered for about 1 hour.
3. Stir frequently so that fruit does not stick to the bottom of the pan.
4. Cool slightly, pour into a sterile container.
5. The spread can be stored in the refrigerator for 1 to 2 weeks.

FRUITY CREAM CHEESE SPREAD
Makes 2 1/2 cups

Recipe courtesy of *The Sugar Association, Inc.*

1 apple, finely chopped
1 tablespoon lemon juice
8 ounces cream cheese

2 tablespoons sugar
1 teaspoon cinnamon
1/2 cup raisins

1 carrot, shredded

1. In a bowl, mix apples and lemon juice to prevent browning; set aside.
2. With a mixer, blend cream cheese, sugar and cinnamon.
3. With a spoon, add raisins, carrot and apple; mix well.

Store tightly covered in refrigerator for up to 4 days.

HAM & CHEESE SPREAD

Teresa Flora of Sawyer, Kansas likes this spread on both toast and biscuits.

1 cup margarine, room temperature
1/2 teaspoon poppy seed
1 teaspoon prepared mustard

2 ounces ham, minced
1/2 pound cheddar cheese, grated
1/2 teaspoon dried onion flakes

1 teaspoon Worcestershire sauce

1. In a bowl, beat all ingredients together until creamy.
2. Store in refrigerator. Can be frozen.
3. Before serving, heat in oven or microwave until cheese is melted

HONEY BLUEBERRY SPREAD
Makes 2/3 cup

Recipe courtesy of the *National Honey Board.*

1/2 cup fresh or frozen blueberries, thawed   1/4 cup honey, divided
1/2 cup butter or margarine, softened

1. In a saucepan, bring blueberries and 2 tablespoons of honey to boil over medium-high heat stirring constantly.
2. Cook 3 to 4 minutes or until mixture thickens and is reduced by half.

3. Cool.
4. Blend in remaining honey.
5. Beat in butter.
6. Refrigerate.

NUTRITION FACTS per tablespoon: 110 calories, 79 calories from fat, 9.1g total fat (14%), 5.7g saturated fat (28%), 24.5mg cholesterol (8%), 93.4mg sodium (4%), 8g carbohydrates (3%), .2g fiber (1%), zero protein, 350 IU vitamin A (7%), 1mg vitamin C (2%), zero calcium and iron

HONEY HAZELNUT SPREAD
Makes 1 1/4 cups

Recipe courtesy of the *National Honey Board.*

1/2 cup honey   1/2 cup butter or margarine, soften
1/2 cup hazelnuts, roasted, skinned, ground

1. Roast hazelnuts in a flat pan at 325°F for 15 minutes or until skins blister and nuts are lightly colored.
2. Cool slightly; rub between palms of hands or with clean towel to remove skins.

3. Grind hazelnuts.
4. In a bowl, cream honey and butter.
5. Stir in hazelnuts.
6. Refrigerate.

NUTRITION FACTS per tablespoon: 84 calories, 54 calories from fat, 6.3g total fat (10%), 3g saturated fat (15%), 12.3mg cholesterol (4%), 46.7mg sodium (2%), 7.4g carbohydrates (2%), .2g fiber (1%), .5g protein (1%), 173 IU vitamin A (3%), zero vitamin C, 7mg calcium (1%) and .1mg iron (1%).

STRAWBERRY SPREAD
Makes 1 1/2 cups

Hope Irvin Marston from Black River, New York has replaced butter on her toast with this spread.

1/2 cup margarine or butter, soften   10 ounce package frozen strawberries, thawed
1/3 cup powdered sugar

1. Drain juice from thawed berries.
2. In a bowl, beat margarine until creamy.
3. Gradually add berries, beating well after each addition.

4. Beat in sugar.
5. Chill.

NUTRITION FACTS per tablespoon: 51 calories, 33 calories from fat, 3.8g total fat (6%), .7g saturated fat (3%), zero cholesterol, 44.8mg sodium (2%), 4.5g carbohydrates (1%), .2g fiber (1%), 158 IU vitamin A (3%), 4mg vitamin C (6%), zero calcium and iron.

CHAPTER V

CEREALS

Cereals are made from edible grass seeds, which are called cereal grains. This includes barley, corn, oats, rice, rye and wheat. While not true cereals, buckwheat and millet are also eaten as cereals. If you stop and think, cereals are the most important of all foods, since they feed both man and animal. Without cereal there would be no biscuits, bread, coffee cakes, doughnuts, pancakes, waffles, and that's just for breakfast. For dinner there would be no pasta, rice, cakes and crusts for your favorite pie. Cereals also provide the highest percentage of carbohydrates of any of the plant foods, plus protein, vitamins and minerals, all with almost no fat.

Cereals are divided into two groups, ready-to-eat, also known as cold cereals, and hot cereals. Commercially packaged cereals are available in both groups. For a change of pace create some excitement with these cereal grains.

READY-TO-EAT CEREALS

Cereal tips (*information*) 61

Make Your Own Ready-to-Eat Cereals (*USA*) 61

Basic Honey Granola 62

plus 6 variations 62

Muesli (*Switzerland*) 63

Birchermuesli (*Mississippi)*) 63

Crystal Muesli (*cruise ship*) 63

Seabourn Muesli (*cruise ship*) 63

Trail Mixes:64

Dried Corn Snack (*California*) 64

Trail Mix Cereal (*Washington*) 65

Vim & Vigor Mix (*Kansas*) 65

HOT CEREALS

Arroz con Leche (*Mexico*) 65

Cornmeal Pap(British Virgin Islands) 66

Egg Pilau (*Minorcan*) 66

Groundnut Porridge (*Zambia*) 67

Halwa (*Pakistan*) 67

Irish Oatmeal (*Ireland*) 68

Millet (*Mali*) 68

Nasi Lemar (*Singapore*) 68

Oatmeal (*USA*) 69

Okra Fungi (*British Virgin Islands*) 69

Breakfast in Cyprus

Pourgori (*Cyprus*) 70

Rice Oatmeal (*New York*) 71

Risengrynsgrot (Norway) 71

Rolled Grains (USA) 71

Barley 71

Wheat 71

Steel-Cut Oats (*Ireland*) 72

Absolute Apples 72

Other Topping Ideas 73

Steel-Cut Oats Cooking Short Cuts 73

Swedish Rice Porridge (*Sweden*) 73

Swiss Oatmeal (*Switzerland*) 73

Wheat Berries (*Utah*) 74

BAKED & FRIED CEREALS

Baked Oatmeal (*Pennsylvania*) 74

Cajun Couche Couche (*Louisiana*) 75

Cheese Grits Casserole (*Louisiana*) 75

Coo-Coo (*Trinidad & Tabago*) 76

Fried Cornmeal Mush (*Indiana*) 76

Fried Grits (Southern *USA)* 76

Irish Oatmeal Soufflé (*Ireland*) 77

Jalapeño Garlic Cheese Grits

(*Louisiana*) 77

Meatless "Sausage" Patties (*USA*) 78

Nasi Gureng (*Singapore*) 78

Rice & Shine (*New York*) 79

Scrapple (*Pennsylvania)* 79

Sweetenin' Pone (West Virginia) 80

READY-TO-EAT CEREALS

A few tips for commercially made cereals:

- If the cereal has lost it's crispness, pour the cereal on a cookie sheet and place in a 400°F oven for a couple of minutes.
- If you normally top your cereal with granulated sugar, for a change of pace try brown sugar, cinnamon, honey, or maple or fruit-flavored syrup.
- Fresh fruit makes a great addition to cereal, sliced bananas, berries, or your favorite fruit.
- If you think you need more protein, mix an egg with one cup of milk in a sauce pan, heat it gently, but do not cook the egg, then cool the milk in the refrigerator, and pour it on your cereal.
- If your kids are picky eaters, instead of plain milk or cream, use chocolate milk. Also you can top their cereal with miniature marshmallows, gumdrops, jelly beans, or a few maraschino cherries.

Some of the above tips also work well with hot cereals.

MAKE YOUR OWN READY-TO-EAT CEREALS

Some cereals you will eat with milk or cream. While others you might enjoy more if eaten dry out of hand.

GRANOLAS are early day dry cereals before flaked cereals were invented. They are wholesome, but can contain too much fat and sugar. They can be made almost fat free by replacing vegetable oils with applesauce.

MUESLI is similar to granola, except the ingredients are not cooked. Some cooks like to make muesli the night before and refrigerate, while others like to add the fresh fruit and other ingredients just prior to serving.

TRAIL MIXES are eaten out of hand. Let the kids have fun making combinations out of supermarket cereals. Mix with dried fruits, nuts and marshmallows. These mixtures will stay fresh if placed in a sealed container.

COLD CEREALS

BASIC HONEY GRANOLA
Makes 10 servings

Granola is easy to prepare, quite healthful, and with variations different taste treats can be experienced.

4 cups rolled oats
1/4 cup wheat germ (optional)
1/4 cup dried skim milk (optional)
1 tablespoon cinnamon
1/2 cup walnuts, chopped

1/2 cup honey
2 teaspoons vanilla
1/2 cup applesauce, vegetable oil, or butter (melted)
1 cup raisins

1. Combine oats, wheat germ, dried milk, cinnamon and walnuts in a large bowl.
2. In a small bowl combine honey, vanilla, and applesauce with a fork.
3. Pour over the oats mixture.
4. Blend well until all flakes are coated.
5. Spread mixture on foil on a baking sheet.
6. Bake in a 300°F preheated oven for about 20 to 25 minutes or until flakes are golden brown.

7. Turn every 7 to 10 minutes so flakes will brown evenly.
8. DO NOT OVERBAKE.
9. Mixture might be a little sticky when done, but will crisp up when cool.
10. Pour baked mixture back into a large bowl and stir in the raisins.
11. Cool completely on a baking sheet.
12. When cool, store in an airtight container and refrigerate.

VARIATIONS

The fun thing about making granola is you can vary the ingredients to suit your taste.

1. Replace the oats all or part with a mixture of rolled grains: rye, barley and wheat with oats.
2. Replace cinnamon with other spices. Adjust amount to suit your taste: 2 teaspoons nutmeg, 1 teaspoon allspice, 1/2 teaspoon cloves, or 1 teaspoon vanilla (combine vanilla with honey/oil mixture).
3. Your choice of nuts: almonds, coconut, hazelnuts, peanuts, pecans, walnuts or use a combination of nuts.
4. Honey can be replaced with light or dark corn syrup, maple sysrup, brown sugar, or molasses.

5. Vanilla can be increased as desired for a more vanilla taste. Also, other extracts such as lemon, strawberry, or maple can be used
6. There are all kinds of dried and candied fruits: apples, apricots, dates, peaches, pears, etc., that can be used either in place of or in combination with the raisins.
7.. Up to one more cup of dry ingredients can be added, such as: 1/4 cup oat bran, 1/2 cup sesame seeds, 1/2 cup sunflower seeds, 1/2 cup pine nuts, or increase the nuts and dried fruits to suit your taste.

NUTRITION FACTS per serving with applesauce: 289 calories, 51 calories from fat, 6g total fat (9%), .7g saturated fat (3%), zero cholesterol, 0.7mg sodium (1%), 53.9g carbohydrates (18%), 5.2g fiber (21%), 8.9g protein (18%),121 IU vitamin A (2%), 1mg vitamin C (2%), 76mg calcium (8%), and 2.4mg iron (13%).

NUTRITION FACTS per serving with olive oil (extra light olive oil is suggested if you do not like the olive oil flavor): 375 calories, 144 calories from fat, 16.7g total fat (26%), 2.1g saturated fat (11%), zero cholesterol, 20.3mg sodium (1%), 51.3g carbohydrates (17%), 5.1g fiber (20%), 8.8g protein (18%), 120 IU vitamin A (2%), 1mg vitamin C (2%), 76mg calcium (8%), and 2.4mg iron (13%),

NUTRITION FACTS per serving with butter: 359 calories, 129 calories from fat, 15g total fat (23%), 6.3g saturated fat (32%), 25.1mg cholesterol (8%), 112.9mg sodium (5%), 51.3g carbohydrates (17%), 5.1g fiber (20%), 9g protein (18%), 463 IU vitamin A (9%), 1mg vitamin C (2%), 78mg calcium (8%), and 2.4mg iron (13%).

MUESLI

In the early 1900s, Dr. Bircher, a renowned authority on nutrition, created muesli. In became popular in the 1950s, mostly as a dessert. Dr. Bircher used sweetened condensed milk and yogurt, instead of milk as used today.

Like granola, muesli recipes vary and there are many variations. In addition to the following recipes, some cooks like to add dried fruit (apricots, plums raisins, etc.), oats can be replaced partially with other rolled grains (wheat, barley, rye, etc.), commercially made dried cereals (corn flakes, shredded wheat, oat rings, etc.), wheat germ, brown sugar, and spices.

BIRCHERMUESLI
Makes 8 servings

Billie Hilburn Sartin of Clarksdale, Mississippi created this version for the *Mississippi College Cookbook with Special Distinction.*

1/4 cup sweetened condensed milk
1/4 cup lemon juice
1/4 cup rolled oats
1/2 teaspoon lemon rind, grated
1 cup fresh or frozen strawberries, drained

1/2 cup pecans, chopped (optional)
8 ounce canned, crushed pineapple, drained
2 red apples, grated with peeling
2 bananas, grated or mashed
Whipped cream (optional)

1. Mix milk, lemon juice, oats, lemon rind, strawberries, pecans and pineapple; refrigerate.

2. At serving time, add apples and bananas.
3. Top with whipped cream, if desired.

NUTRITION FACTS per serving with pecans, but without whipped cream: 159 calories, 52 calories from fat, 6.2g total fat (9%), 1g saturated fat (5%), 3.2mg cholesterol (1%), 13.1mg sodium (1%), 26.2g carbohydrates (9%), 2.9g fiber (11%), 2.7g protein (5%), 93 IU vitamin A (2%), 22mg vitamin C (37%), 41mg calcium (4%) and .7mg iron (4%).

CRYSTAL MUESLI
Makes 8 servings

Aboard *Crystal Cruise* ships, they make their muesli fresh prior to serving.

1 cup low fat milk
2/3 cup rolled oats, lightly toasted
12 ounces nonfat yogurt
1/3 cup honey
1/3 cup orange juice
3 apples, grated

1 pound assorted berries
2 bananas, sliced
2 tablespoons hazelnuts, chopped
2 tablespoons apples, chopped
2 tablespoons raisins
2 tablespoons sunflower seeds

1. Soak the oats in the milk for 30 minutes.
2. Mix with the yogurt, honey and orange juice.

3. Add remaining ingredients and serve chilled.

NUTRITION FACTS per serving: 222 calories, 31 calories from fat, 3.6g total fat (6%), .6g saturated fat (3%), 2mg cholesterol (1%), 50.3mg sodium (2%), 45g carbohydrates (15%), 4.8g fiber (19%), 6.2g protein (12%), 160 IU vitamin A (3%), 43mg vitamin C (72%), 148mg calcium (15%) and 1.1mg iron (6%).

Did you know oats grow best in a damp climate? That is why they grow so well in Ireland and Scotland. Oats has a hard outer shell with a soft interior. The oats are kiln dried to help loosen the hull that also develops the oats nutty flavor. The gains are cleaned and the hulls removed. Oat bran is made from the hulls. Packaged oats found in the supermarket are the grains with the hull removed and flattened between heated rollers. Flattened oats, also known as rolled oats, are made into hot cereal and added to baking recipes. Some oat grains are steel cut into granules rather than flattened. Steel cut oats take longer to cook and can not be used in baking unless precooked.

SEABOURN MUESLI
Makes 10 servings

Chef de Cuisine, *Paul Mooney,* aboard *Seabourn Cruise* ships prepares part of his muesli the night before and adds a few more ingredients at serving time.

1 1/2 cups hazelnuts, flaked
1 3/4 cups rolled oats
2 pounds red apples, grated
1/3 cup brown sugar
1/4 cup honey

1 1/2 cups milk
1 cup yogurt
Juice & zest of one lemon
Juice & zest of one orange
Pinch cinnamon

1. Place all of the ingredients in a bowl and mix; refrigerate overnight.

Per Serving
2 tablespoons whipped cream
1/2 cup of mixed berries
1/2 sliced banana
Coconut flakes, toasted

2. At serving time add whipped cream, berries and banana to each serving.

3. Sprinkle top with the coconut

NUTRITION FACTS per serving: 289 calories, 112 calories from fat, 13.3g total fat (20%), 1.8g saturated fat (9%), 5mg cholesterol (2%), 21.5mg sodium (1%), 41g carbohydrates (14%), 5.1g fiber (21%), 6g protein (12%), 141 IU vitamin A (3%), 14mg vitamin C (24%), 98mg calcium (10%) and 1.5mg iron (8%).

TRAIL MIX

Trail mixes are easy to make, some require cooking, others just mix and enjoy.

DRIED CORN SNACK
Makes 8 servings

This chewy and nutty-sweet natural snack was conceived by *Renee Shepherd* and *Fran Raboff* for their book, *Recipes From A Kitchen Garden.* It is perfect for both breakfast and afternoon snacks.

8 large ears of fresh corn, cut from the cob,
about 7 to 8 cups
3 tablespoons sugar

2 teaspoons salt
¼ cup milk

1. Combine all ingredients in a heavy-bottomed saucepan.
2. Bring to a boil, lower heat to simmer and cook for 15 minutes, stirring frequently.

3. Pour into a shallow greased baking pan and dry in a low 250°F oven for about 1 ½ hours, stirring occasionally. Corn should be light golden brown when done.
4. store in covered container.

NUTRITION FACTS per serving: 149 calories, 11 calories from fat, 1.4g total fat (2%), .3g saturated fat (2%), zero cholesterol, 541mg sodium (23%), 34.9g carbohydrates (12%), 3.5g fiber (14%), 4.6g protein (9%), 196 IU vitamin A (4%), 9mg vitamin C (15%), 16mg calcium (2%) and .6mg iron (3%).

Did you known that corn first grew wild in Mexico as a grass? The Aztecs cultivated into corn.

TRAIL MIX CEREAL

Andrea Levy of Redmond, Washington said her kids always got up too late for breakfast. So she serves them this on-the-go breakfast with a single serving container of milk, orange juice or apple juice. *Andrea* varies the ingredients to keep the mix interesting.

1 cup raisins or other dried fruits
1 cup peanuts, unsalted

¼ cup sunflower seeds, unsalted, toasted
1 cup oat rings, shredded squares, etc.

1 cup corn puffs

1. Mix all of the ingredients together and store in a large closed container. This mixture can be eaten dry as a finger food or in a bowl with milk or cream.

NUTRITION FACTS per ¼ cup: 177 calories, 91 calories from fat, 10.7g total fat (16%), 1.4g saturated fat (7%), zero cholesterol, 111.3mg sodium (5%), 18.5g carbohydrates (6%), 2.2g fiber (9%), 4.3g protein (9%), 78 IU vitamin A (2%), 1mg vitamin C (2%), 37mg calcium (4%) and 1.2mg iron (7%).

VIM & VIGOR MIX
Makes 5 servings

Almost every kid will enjoy this trail mix version by the *Kansas State Board of Agriculture.*

2 1/2 quarts popped popcorn
1/3 cup honey or apple jelly
1/2 cup peanut butter

1/2 cup dried milk
2 tablespoons sunflower seeds, toasted
1/2 cup raisins

1. Keep popped popcorn warm in a 200°F oven.
2. Heat honey in a small sauce pan; stir in peanut better and dried milk.

3. In a large bowl, combine popcorn, sunflower seeds, and raisins.
4. Pour the honey mixture over popcorn mixture and toss to mix.

HOT CEREALS

On those cold, windy days, nothing warms the bones more like a hot bowl of cereal. It is important to follow directions accurately or the cereal might be lumpy. For the most part cereal should be added to boiling water, except for is oats, which can be added to either cold water or boiling water. It's best not to rush the cooking process, as most of the grains are uncooked and require the full cooking times. Many of the hot cereal recipes in this chapter are called "porridge," which is oatmeal boiled in water or milk until thick.

ARROZ CON LECHE
Makes 6 servings

This Mexican rice is served at all meals and can be served chilled, hot or at room temperature. On special occasions *Elsa Foglio* of the *Mexican Government Tourist Office* likes to add a tablespoon of brandy.

1 cup long-grain white rice
3 cups water
1 cinnamon stick
1 tablespoon lime or orange peel, sliced in very fine julienne strips

Pinch of salt
4 cups milk
1 1/2 cups sugar or to taste
1/3 cup raisins
1 teaspoon vanilla

Ground cinnamon, for garnish (optional

1. Place rice in a large saucepan with the water, cinnamon, lime peel and salt.
2. Bring to a boil, cover, lower the heat and cook until most of the water has been absorbed.
3. Stir in the milk and sugar, cook, stirring constantly (about 30 minutes), over low heat until the mixture thickens.
4. Add the raisins and vanilla and cook for an additional 2 minutes.

5. Remove from the heat and let it cool for 20 minutes. Mixture will be thin. For thicker rice, add 1/4 cup more of rice or reduce milk to 3 1/2 cups.
6. Transfer to a platter or individual bowls. Refrigerate leftovers.
7. Sprinkle lightly with cinnamon before serving, if desired.
8. May be topped with cream or milk.

NUTRITION FACTS per serving: 431 calories, 50 calories from fat, 5.7g total fat (9%), 3.5g saturated fat (17%), 22.1mg cholesterol (7%), 82.9mg sodium (3%), 89g carbohydrates (30%), 1g fiber (4%), 7.8g protein (16%), 207 IU vitamin A (4%), 3mg vitamin C (5%), 213mg calcium (21%) and 1.8mg iron (10%).

VARIATION

For a richer, more custard-like flavor, beat an egg into the milk before adding it to the cooked rice. This will increase calories to 444 and cholesterol to 57.5mg (19%).

CORNMEAL PAP
Makes 4 servings

Monica Allen of the *British Virgin Islands* enjoys a bit of sugar and spice with her cornmeal.

1 cup milk
1 cinnamon stick
1/4 cup sugar
1 teaspoon margarine

*1 cup water
1 cup cornmeal
1 teaspoon salt
1/2 cup raisins (optional)

1. Bring to a boil the milk, *water, salt and cinnamon.
2. Add cornmeal slowly, stirring constantly to prevent lumping.
3. Add sugar, margarine and raisins, and continue stirring until mixture begins to thicken.

4. Lower heat, cover, cook for 10 to 15 minutes, stirring occasionally. If Pap is too thick for your taste add more liquid, equal amounts of water and milk up to 2 cups. *Also to prevent lumping add the 1 cup of cold water to cornmeal before adding to boiling liquid

NUTRITION FACTS per serving, with raisins: 275 calories, 32 calories from fat, 3.6g total fat (6%), 1.5g saturated fat (8%), 8.3mg cholesterol (3%), 577.2mg sodium (24%), 56.5g carbohydrates (19%), 3.3g fiber (13%), 5.5g protein (11%), 260 IU vitamin A (5%), 1mg vitamin C (2%), 85mg calcium (8%) and 1.9mg iron (10%).

EGG PILAU
Makes 4 servings

When the *Minorcans* colonized Saint Augustine, Florida, one of their hot cereals was this recipe. According to the late *Helen E. Becker,* pilau (pronounced pur-lo) was made with a number of ingredients (also see MEAT recipes, page 175), all of which contained rice.

2 cups chicken broth
1 teaspoon salt
1 cup rice
1/4 cup butter

Dash of pepper
3 eggs, lightly beaten
4 slices bacon, cooked, crumbled
Chives, minced

1. In a large pot add the broth, salt and rice.

2. Cover closely and simmer until the rice has absorbed all the broth, about 20 minutes.

3. Add the butter, pepper and eggs.

4. Mix thoroughly and served with bacon and chives.

NUTRITION FACTS per serving: 411 calories, 181 calories from fat, 19.9g total fat (31% DV), 9.8g saturated fat (49%), 196.7mg cholesterol (66%), 1580mg sodium (66%), 41.1g carbohydrates (14%), 1.4g fiber (6%), 15.6g protein (31%), 699 IU vitamin A (14%), 3mg vitamin C (4%), 44mg calcium (4%) and 3.2mg iron (18%)

GROUNDNUT PORRIDGE
Makes 4 servings

In parts of *Africa*, peanuts are called "groundnuts." Since milk is in short supply, this porridge is a common milk substitute for *Zambian* babies. Even though it is not rich in calcium, it does provide some calcium, as well as protein and iron. Groundnut porridge is also eaten as a breakfast food for children and adults. *Hope Irvin Marston* of Black River, New York found this recipe on a trip to *Zambia*.

2 1/4 cups boiling water
1 cup cold water
1 cup white cornmeal

1/2 cup peanuts, coarsely ground or chunky peanut butter

1. Bring to a boil in a medium saucepan the 2 1/4 cups of water.
2. In a small bowl, combine cornmeal and 1 cup of water to make a smooth paste.
3. Slowly add cornmeal to boiling water, stirring constantly.

4. Reduce heat and simmer 3 minutes.
5. Add the peanuts and simmer 3 to 5 minutes more.
6. Serve with salt, sugar, brown sugar, honey, butter or milk.

NUTRITION FACTS per serving: 230 calories, 84 calories from fat, 9.6g total fat (15%), 1.3g saturated fat (7%), zero cholesterol and sodium, 29.8g carbohydrates (10%), 4.1g fiber (16%), 7.6g protein (15%), zero vitamins A and C, 19mg calcium (2%) and 2.3mg iron (13%).

HALWA
Makes 6 servings

"Pakistanis enjoy halwa with cholay and puri," says *Shazia Hazan* Karachi, *Pakistan, "especially on weekends. Just the flavor in the air will cause people to line up at your kitchen window with plates in hand."*

1 cup semolina or flour
2 cups sugar
3 cups water

1/3 cup raisins
2/3 cup vegetable oil

1. Heat the oil in a pan or a wok.
2. Add the semolina (white all-purpose flour can be substituted, but it's better with semolina) and stir continually.
3. When the semolina becomes golden brown, remove from the heat.
4. Pour the water into another pan, add the sugar

and raisins
5. Simmer until the sugar is completely dissolved.
6. Pour this thin syrup over the semolina while stirring.
7. Return to the heat and stir until the semolina thickens and takes the form of a very thick paste

Enjoy the last puri with a bowl of halwa (see DOUGHNUTS, FRITTERS & FRIED BREADS for PURI, page 104 and VEGETABLES for CHOLAY recipes, page 235).

IRISH OATMEAL
Makes 4 servings

The most important meal of the day is started with a piping hot bowl of oatmeal or "porridge" as it is known in Ireland.

1 1/3 cups quick cooking oatmeal   4 cups cold water or low fat milk

1. Combine oats and water in a saucepan.   2. Bring to a boil, stirring constantly, for 3 to 5 minutes or until thicken

Serve with milk or light cream, brown sugar or honey, fruits and nuts, as desired.

NUTRITION FACTS per serving: 104 calories, 15 calories from fat, 1.7g total fat (1.7g), .3g saturated fat (2%), zero cholesterol and sodium, 18.1g carbohydrates (6%), 2.9g fiber (11%), 4.3g protein (9%), 27 IU vitamin A (1%), zero vitamin C, 14mg calcium (1%) and 1.1mg iron (6%).

MILLET
Makes 4 servings

While millet is not one of the cereal grasses, it is enjoyed as a hot cereal in *Mali* as does *Hope Irwin Marston* of Black River, New York. Millet is available in most health food stores.

1 cup millet   1/3 cup dry milk powder   3 cups water

1. Rinse millet in warm water.   4. Stir in millet and heat to boiling. Reduce heat
2. Let millet drain for 5 minutes.   and simmer 10 minutes, stirring occasionally.
3. Combine dry milk and water in a saucepan.   5. Let stand 10 minutes.

Serve millet with milk, honey butter or applesauce.

NUTRITION FACTS per serving: 215 calories, 12 calories from fat. 1.4g total fat (2%), .3g saturated fat (2%), 3.9mg cholesterol (1%), 109.5mg sodium (5%), 38.8g carbohydrates (13%), 1.6g fiber (6%), 11.4g protein (23%), 440 IU vitamin A (9%), 1mg vitamin C (2%), 255mg calcium (25%) and .8mg iron (5%).

NASI LEMAR
(Fragrant Rice Simmered in Coconut Milk)
Makes 6 servings

Nasi Lemak is basically a long grain rice porridge that is simmered in coconut milk and seasoned with *pandan* leaves. Delicious garnishes that accompany the rice include *ikan bilis* (crisp fried anchovies) mixed with fried peanuts, cucumber and slices of hard boiled egg. This dish, topped with *sambal udang* (prawns sautéed in chile shallot sambal), is eaten for breakfast in *Singapore*.

Because of the garnishes, *nasi lemar* can be eaten as a main breakfast course, as well as an enjoyable dinner.

Singaporeans also make porridges with chicken, fish and pork (see MEAT chapter, pages 171 and 190).

2 cups long grain rice   1/4 cup anchovies, fried crisp
3/4 cup coconut milk (if canned, shake can well)   1 cup peanuts, deep fried
1 1/4 cups water or to cover rice by 1 inch   Pinch of sugar
Salt   1 cucumber, sliced
2 fresh or frozen pandan leaves   1 pound prawns, sautéed in chile & shallots
3 eggs, hard cooked, sliced

1. Put rice in a large bowl and rinse it with cold water until the water looks clear; drain thoroughly.
2. Combine the rice, coconut milk, water and 1/2 teaspoon of salt in a saucepan.
3. Boil over high heat until there is no water left on the surface of the rice.
4. Tie each pandan leaf into a knot and place them on top of the rice.
5. Cover the pot, reduce the heat, and simmer until steam no longer seeps through the cover, about 10 minutes.

6. Turn off the heat and allow the rice to finish cooking for another 10 minutes. Do not remove the cover.
7. Combine the anchovies and peanuts; season to taste with salt and sugar.
8. Fluff the rice with a wet wooden spoon; discard pandan leaves.
9. For each serving, put 1 cup of rice on a banana leaf (or a plate). Scatter a small portion of the anchovy mixture, cucumber, prawns and egg on top. Serve hot or at room temperature

NUTRITION FACTS per serving: 508 calories, 208 calories from fat 23.5g total fat (36%), 9.2g saturated fat (46%), 227.2mg cholesterol (76%), 168.3mg sodium (7%), 48.2g carbohydrates (16%), 3.4g fiber (13%), 27.9g protein (56%), 408 IU vitamin A (8%), 5mg vitamin C (8%), 112mg calcium (11%) and 5.2mg iron (29%).

OATMEAL
Makes 2 servings
Recipe can be doubled

In our hurried world, some things are cooked too fast. Oatmeal is one of those foods that should be cooked slowly. This is the way my grandmother use to make for me in my youth.

1 3/4 cups water
1 cup oats

1/8 teaspoon salt
2 tablespoons raisins

1. Mix all ingredients together and put on the top part of a double boiler.

2. Cook over simmering water for about one hour.

NUTRITION FACTS per serving: 183 calories, 23 calories from fat, 2.6g total fat (4%), .5g saturated fat (2%), zero cholesterol, 135.9mg sodium (6%), 34.3g carbohydrates (11%), 4.7g fiber (19%), 6.8g protein (14%), 42 IU vitamin A (1%), zero vitamin C, 26mg calcium (3%), and 1.9mg iron (10%).

OKRA FUNGI
Makes 6 servings

Okra for breakfast? Don't knock it until you've tried it. The people of the *British Virgin Islands* enjoy it cooked with cornmeal. Give it a try. You might like it too!

4 okras, washed, cut up
1 teaspoon salt

1 tablespoon margarine
2 1/2 cups waters

1 1/4 cups cornmeal

1. In a sauce pan, boil okras in water.
2. Add salt and slowly sprinkle the cornmeal over the boiling water, stirring briskly to prevent lumping.

3. Add margarine, cover and steam on low for about 12 minutes, stirring occasionally.
4. Serve hot.

NUTRITION FACTS per serving: 125 calories, 22 calories from fat, 2.4g total fat (4%), .4g saturated fat (2%), zero cholesterol, 378.9mg sodium (16%), 22.9g carbohydrates (8%), 2.3g fiber (9%), 2.6g protein (5%), 248 IU vitamin A (5%), 2mg vitamin C (3%), 9mg calcium (1%) and 1.3mg iron (7%).

BREAKFAST IN CYPRUS

Cyprus, an island in the eastern Mediterranean, has been the cross roads for many invaders, foreign settlers and traders for more than 3,000 years. People from Greece, Turkey, Armenia, Lebanon, Syria, Italy and of late France and Great Britain brought their influences and their recipes. Because of the mild climate, the island produces a huge variety of foods. Figs, beans, chick peas, herbs, olives, dates, almonds and nuts date back to the Bible and are everyday foods.

Cypriots cook with less oil than their Mediterranean neighbors and their diet is a healthy one, except for maybe their love of syrup soaked pastries. Everything is cooked fresh daily, and the quality of the produce is superb. As many Cypriot housewives say, *"If it isn't fresh, we don't want it."* Depending on the time of the year, oranges, grapefruit, lemons, strawberries, black cherries, plums, apricots, peaches, nectarines, watermelon and grapes of many varieties are found fresh in the market.

Cypriot families still produce almost everything they need, from *pourgouri* (cracked wheat) to cheese, home baked breads and smoked cured pork. For those in a hurry, fast food is something stuffed into a pita bread pocket.

Loukanika, a Cyprus sausage, varies in flavor depending on where it is made. The meat content is lean and usually crushed coriander and other spices are added. Before being smoked, the sausages are soaked in red wine. Some sausages, such as *pastourma*, are spiced with hot peppers and fenugreek.

Cyprus breads can contain various ingredients such as olives, mint, onions, sesame paste and sausage, and many are coated with seeds. Many of the pastries are soaked in syrup, such as rose water syrup to orange flower water syrup or even honey.

Besides wine, coffee is consumed by almost everyone. Coffee is made similar to Turkish coffee (see BEVERAGES, page 21), but without the spices. However, the coffee beans come from Brazil and are of course ground fresh daily. Cypress coffee is very strong and is always served with a glass of cold water.

POURGOURI
Makes 8 servings

On the island of *Cyprus*, cracked wheat is prepared from hulled wheat. The grain is steamed until partly cooked, then dried before being ground. Pourgouri is enjoyed at all meals and can be eaten with eggs in place of potatoes or grits. Recipe courtesy of *Permanent Mission of Cyprus to the United Nations.*

2 tablespoons olive oil	8 ounces bulgar cracked wheat
1 onion, finely sliced	1 1/2 cups chicken stock
1 ounce vermicelli or angel hair pasta	Salt & pepper to taste

1. Heat the oil in a heavy-based pot and sauté the onion for a couple of minutes until it softens, but not brown.
2. Stir in the vermicelli, breaking it with your hands.
3. Continue to fry with the onion for two minutes until it begins to absorb the oil.

4. Rinse the bulgar under cold water, then add to the pot.
5. Add the stock and seasonings.
6. Cover and simmer gently for 8 to 10 minutes or until all the stock is absorbed.
7. Turn off heat and let the pourgouri sit for 10 minutes before serving

NUTRITION FACTS per serving: 150 calories, 23% calories from fat, 4g total fat (6%) .6g saturated fat (3%), zero cholesterol, 25g carbohydrates (8%), 5.4g fiber (22%), 5g protein (10%), 219mg sodium (9%), 21mg calcium (2%), .9mg iron (5%), and 1mg vitamin C (1%).

Did you know that bulgur cracked wheat is also known as "ala?" Bulgur is cracked wheat that has been partially cooked. It is good as a breakfast hot cereal with milk and sugar, makes a wonderful chilled salad, or a side dish cook with vegetables. It's easy to cook. Use one part bulgur with two parts water and simmer for 5 minutes, fluff, cover and let it sit for 10 minutes.

RICE OATMEAL
Makes 2 servings

Jennifer Jones of Homer, New York, says, *"This is my children's favorite breakfast."* Jennifer shared the recipe with her sister-in-law who manages a high school cafeteria that serves breakfast. It made such a hit that it is now on the regular menu.

1 cup cooked rice
1 cup milk
1/4 cup rolled oats

1/4 cup brown sugar
2 teaspoons butter
Pinch of cinnamon

1. Combine all ingredients in a saucepan.
2. Cook and stir over moderately high heat until mixture boils and thickens to desired consistency.

3. Serve with additional milk and sugar if desired.

NUTRITION FACTS per serving: 297 calories, 80 calories from fat, 8.8g total fat (14%), 5.1g saturated fat (25%), 26.8mg cholesterol (9%), 102.6mg sodium (4%), 45.5g carbohydrates (15%), 1.5g fiber (6%), 8.4g protein (17%), 307 IU vitamin A (6%), 1mg vitamin C (2%), 167mg calcium (17%) and .8mg iron (4%).

RISENGRYNSGROT
Makes 4 servings

This rice porridge recipe from *Norway* is simple to make. *Berit Lunde* from the *Norwegian Information Service* likes to liven it up with raisins, cinnamon, brown sugar, honey or thick cream.

4 cups milk
1/2 teaspoon salt

1 cup white rice, cooked
2 teaspoons butter

1. Combine milk and salt in a sauce pan and bring to a boil over medium heat.
2. Add the cooked rice and butter.
3. Boil for 15 minutes at medium heat, stirring constantly.

4. Cover and turn heat to low, simmer for 4 minutes, stirring occasionally.
5. Serve hot, sprinkled with sugar and cinnamon or with milk and a teaspoon of butter.

NUTRITION FACTS per swerving: 233 calories, 92 calories from fat, 10.2g total fat (16%), 6.3g saturated fat (31%), 38.3mg cholesterol (13%), 406.3mg sodium (17%), 25.7g carbohydrates (9%), .2g fiber (1%), 9.4g protein (19%), 379 IU vitamin A (8%), 2mg vitamin C (4%), 298mg calcium (30%) and .2mg iron (1%).

ROLLED GRAINS

Like oats, many grains are rolled flat and make wonderful hot cereals. *Foster Boyd* from *Arrowhead Mills* suggests you try rolled barley or rolled wheat for a change of pace.

BARLEY
Makes 4 servings

1 cup rolled barley
3 cups water

1/2 teaspoon salt (optional)
1/2 cup dried fruit, apples, dates, raisins, etc.

1. Bring water to a boil.
2. Slowly add the barley and salt.
3. Lower heat and cover, simmer for 20 to 25 minutes or until all water is absorbed.

4. If you like, add dried fruit for the last 5 minutes of cooking time.

WHEAT
Makes 4 servings

1 cup rolled wheat
1 teaspoon vegetable oil
1/4 teaspoon salt (optional)
3 cups boiling water

Sesame seeds, roasted (optional)
Sunflower seeds (optional)
Pecans or walnuts (optional)
Raisins (optional)

1. Sauté wheat in oil until golden brown.
2. Add water and salt.
3. Cook covered over a low heat for 30 minutes.

4. Stir occasionally.
5. Serve with a sprinkling of sesame seeds, sunflower seeds, nuts or raisins, if desired.

NUTRITION FACTS per serving: 168 calories, 17 calories from fat, 2.1g total fat (3%), .3g saturated fat (1%), zero cholesterol, 134.2mg sodium (6%), 32.7g carbohydrates (11%), 6.1g fiber (24%), 7.4g protein (15%), zero vitamin A and C, 12mg calcium (1%) and 1.7mg iron (10%).

STEEL-CUT OATS
Makes 4 servings

In *Ireland*, the oat grains are not all rolled, most are cut into little nuggets. According to *Paul Germann*, the American distributor for *McCann's Irish Oatmeal*, this gives the oat nuggets a distinctive taste, sort of a nutty flavor, and because there is less handling, retains all the nutritional value.

4 cups boiling water
1 cup steel-cut oats
1 teaspoon salt

1. After bringing water to a boil, stir in salt and oats.

2. Once the oats starts to thicken, reduce heat and simmer for 30 minutes, stirring occasionally.
3. Do not overcook.

Traditionally oatmeal is served with fresh buttermilk, but is just as good with milk, cream, brown sugar, honey or butter. Steel-cut oats can also be made in a double boiler.

ABSOLUTE APPLES
Makes 4 servings

There are many ways to enjoy steel-cut oats. Try this recipe for full enjoyment.

1 cup uncooked steel-cut oats
1 cup dried apple slices
1 cup apple juice
3 cups water
1/4 cup honey

1 1/4 teaspoons cinnamon, divided
1/4 teaspoon cardamon
1 cup fresh apples, chopped
3 tablespoons unsalted butter

1. Stir oats, dried apples, apple juice, 3/4 teaspoon cinnamon and cardamon into boiling water.
2. Cook until thickened.
3. Reduce heat and simmer 30 minutes.
4. Pour into individual bowls.

5. Sauté fresh apples in butter and 1/2 teaspoon of cinnamon.
6. Once apples are tender, stir in honey.
7. Top cooked oats with the fresh apple mixture.
8. Serve with warm cream or milk.

OTHER TOPPING IDEAS

These suggestions are for individual servings. From the Middle east try yogurt, honey and toasted pine nuts; for a Vermont taste add banana and maple syrup; and for a Southern touch top with molasses and poached dried fruits in orange juice or fresh peaches.

STEEL-CUT OATS COOKING SHORTCUTS

Judith Choate, noted author and cooking authority, has found ways to cut preparation time with steel-cut oats. She recommends the following:

1. Cook up five days worth and refrigerate. To reheat individual servings, place in a microwave safe bowl and set the microwave on high for 2 to 3 minutes.
2. Before retiring for the night, bring 1 cup of oats to a boil in 4 cups of water. Remove from heat, cover and place in an oven set on warm. The next morning, the piping hot oatmeal is ready to serve. Or place mixture in a crock pot and set on low.
3. Place oats in a preheated 300°F oven and toast for about 20 minutes. Store toasted oats in a tightly covered container and in a cool spot. Toasted oats can cut cooking time in half.
4. Use a pressure cooker. Add 1 cup of pre-toasted oats to 3 1/2 cups water, 1 tablespoon of unsalted butter and a pinch of salt in the pressure cooker. Pressure cook for about 5 minutes, following manufacturer's instructions.
5. Place steel-cut oats in a food processor. A few turns of the metal blade will break up the grains and will reduce the cooking time by at least 5 minutes.

SWEDISH RICE PORRIDGE
Makes 4 servings

Like their Norwegian neighbors, the *Swedes* also enjoy rice porridge for breakfast, but like to spice it up a bit with a hint of cinnamon. This recipe is from the courtesy of the *Swedish Travel and Tourism Council*.

1 1/3 cups water	1 cinnamon stick
1 teaspoon salt	2/3 cup rice
1 tablespoon butter	2 2/3 cups milk

1 tablespoon sugar

1. Boil water with salt, butter and cinnamon.
2. Add rice and simmer covered for about 10 minutes.
3. Add milk and continue to simmer on very low heat for another 30 to 40 minutes until milk is absorbed. Stir occasionally so it does not burn.
4. Add the sugar and stir.
5. Serve with milk, sugar and cinnamon.

NUTRITION FACTS per serving: 250 calories, 77 calories from fat, 8.5g total fat (13%), 5.2g saturated fat (26%), 29.8mg cholesterol (10%), 643.1mg sodium (27%), 35.4g carbohydrates (12%), .4g fiber (2%), 7.6g protein (15%), 312 IU vitamin A (6%), 2mg vitamin C (3%), 204mg calcium (20%) and 1.4mg iron (8%).

SWISS OATMEAL
Makes 4 servings

Dr. Bircher of *Switzerland* invented muesli, which is eaten uncooked. *Arrowhead Mills* presents a cooked version.

3 cups water	1 1/3 cups rolled oats
1 cup mixed dried fruit, chopped	2 tablespoons honey
1 teaspoon salt	2 tablespoons wheat germ

1/4 cup almonds, slivered & toasted

1. Bring water to a boil; stir in fruit, salt and honey.
2. Bring to boil again, add oats; stir; lower heat to simmer.
3. Cover and simmer 15 minutes, stir before .

4. Serve and sprinkle each serving with 1 1/2 teaspoons of wheat germ and 1 tablespoon almonds.
5. Serve with milk or cream.

serving.

NUTRITION FACTS per serving: 261 calories, 56 calories from fat, 6.6g total fat (10%), .8g saturated fat (14%), zero cholesterol, 540.4mg sodium (23%), 47.1g carbohydrates (16%), 4.5g fiber (18%), 7.1g protein (14%), 660 IU vitamin A (13%), 1mg vitamin C (2%), 51mg calcium (5%) and 2.4mg iron (13%).

WHEAT BERRIES
Makes 8 servings

At the *La Sal Mountain Guest Ranch* in La Sal, Utah, innkeeper *Barbara Redd* serves steamed wheat berries to her guests.

2 cups wheat berries, washed

5 cups hot water

1 teaspoon salt

1. In the evening, put all ingredients in a crock pot and cook on low all night.

2. Serve with honey, milk or cream

NUTRITION FACTS per serving: 145 calories, 4 calories from fat, .5g total fat (1%), zero saturated fat and cholesterol, 266.9mg sodium (11%), 31.1g carbohydrates (10%) zero fiber, 3.4g protein (7%), zero vitamin A, C and calcium and .4mg iron (2%).

BAKED AND FRIED CEREALS

Once the cereal grains have been cooked, many are eaten as is, while other ingredients can be added to create new and exciting breakfast treats.

BAKED OATMEAL
Makes 8 servings
For 4 servings, cut recipe in half

In the *Pennsylvania Dutch Country* baked oatmeal is served in both the homes and restaurants. This recipe comes from the *Kling House Restaurant* located in the *Kitchen Kettle Village* in Intercourse, Pennsylvania. For those who do not really care for oatmeal, will find this special treat delightful.

2/3 cup vegetable oil
1 cup sugar or brown sugar
2 eggs, beaten
4 cups rolled oats
1 tablespoon baking powder

1 teaspoon salt
1 1/2 cups milk
2 apples, chopped
1 cup walnuts, chopped
1 teaspoon cinnamon

1. In a large bowl, mix oil, sugar and eggs thoroughly, then add the remaining ingredients.

2. Pour the mixture into a greased baking pan
3. Bake at 350°F for 25 to 30 minutes

NUTRITION FACTS per serving: 724 calories, 309 calories from fat, 35.3g total fat (54%), 5g saturated fat (25%), 59.4mg cholesterol (20%), 443mg sodium (18%), 87g carbohydrates (29%), 1.9g fiber (7%), 20g protein (40%), 292 IU vitamin A (4%), 3mg vitamin C (5%), 245mg calcium (25%) and 4.7mg iron (26%).

CAJUN COUCHE COUCHE
This real Cajun breakfast serves 4

This old fashioned *Cajun* breakfast treat is a thick, crusty breakfast cereal made with a fried cornmeal batter and is a great way to start the day. Originally made of *Moroccan* grain, couscous, it was the main dish served to the *African* slaves. *Goldie Comeaux* of *Mulate's Cajun Restaurant* in Breaux Bridge, Louisiana says *"Couche Couche (pronounced kosh-kosh} also makes a great late night snack."*

2 cups cornmeal
1 1/2 teaspoons salt
1 tablespoon baking powder
1 1/2 cups water

1/4 cup vegetable oil
Bacon, fried crisp
Milk
100% cane syrup or sugar

1. Thoroughly mix the cornmeal, salt and baking powder.
2. Add water and blend well.
3. In a heavy skillet, heat the oil on high until it is hot.
4. Add the cornmeal mixture.

5. Reduce heat to medium and cook until a crust forms, then give it a good stir and reduce the heat to low.
6. Cover and simmer for 15 minutes.
7. Serve hot with milk and 100% cane syrup (or sugar) mixed in and bacon on the side.

NUTRITION FACTS per serving: 254 calories, 1g total fat (2%), 54g carbohydrates (18%), 5g fiber (20%), 6g protein (12%), 1076mg sodium (45%), 260mg calcium (26%), 3.3mg iron (18%) and 285 IU vitamin A (5%).

CHEESE GRITS CASSEROLE
Makes 8 servings

In the *Southern United States*, grits are standard fare for breakfast. Grits can be served hot in a bowl, topped with milk and sugar; or served with eggs and bacon in place of potatoes and usually topped with gravy. *Jan Lugenbuhl* of Metairie, Louisiana likes to serve this casserole on special occasions.

1 cup water
2 cups milk
3/4 cup quick-cooking grits
3 eggs, beaten well

1/2 cup sharp Cheddar cheese, shredded
3 tablespoons margarine or butter
1/4 teaspoons salt
1/4 teaspoon red pepper

4 ounces ham, cooked, finely diced

1. In a saucepan, bring milk and water to a boil over medium heat.
2. Stir in grits. Bring to a boil again, reduce heat to medium-low. Cook, stirring occasionally, until thick.
3. Remove from heat, cool then add eggs

cheese, margarine, salt, pepper and ham; stir until well blended.
4. Pour into a greased 1 1/2 quart baking dish.
5. Bake in a 350°F preheated oven for 30 minutes or until set and lightly puffed.

NUTRITION FACTS per serving: 212 calories, 111 calories from fat, 12.2g total fat (19%), 4.6g saturated fat (23%), 103.5mg cholesterol (35%), 400.9mg (17%), 15.3g carbohydrates (5%), zero fiber, 10g protein (20%), 533 IU vitamin A (11%),5mg vitamin C (8%), 136mg calcium (14%) and 1.1mg iron (6%).

Did you know that grits is dried, ground hominy and is available in fine or coarse grinds? Some grits must be soaked for up to an hour prior to cooking. Fast-cooking grits are just poured into boiling water, and will be ready to eat in minutes. There are also "instant" grits in packets for microwave cooking. Grits need only butter, salt and pepper for seasoning when served as a side dish. For a hot breakfast cereal, top with milk and sugar. In the south, grits are often served with gravy in place of hash brown potatoes.

COO-COO
Makes 6 servings

Nancy Pierre from *Trinidad and Tobago* likes to fry coo-coo made with *conquintay* (a flour made from green bananas called *plantains*) or *cassava* (a flour made *yuca*). Coo-coo can also be made with cornmeal. Cooked coo-coo can be served as a hot cereal or molded, refrigerated, then sliced and fried. Coo-coo is often served with fish, such as herring or shad.

1 cup conquintary, cassava flour or cornmeal
1 cup water (increase to 1 1/2 cups with
cornmeal)

1/2 teaspoon salt
1 tablespoon butter
6 okra, sliced (optional)

1. Bring to a boil 1 cup of water and salt in a sauce pan.
2. Remove from the heat and slowly stir in the flour until smooth (if cornmeal is used, first moisten it with 1/2 cup water before stirring into the hot water).
3. In another saucepan, cook okra in salted water until tender; drain.

4. Add okra to the flour mixture and put back on medium heat and bring to a boil, stirring constantly.
5. If eaten as a hot cereal, top with butter.
6. To fry, first mould in a greased bread pan, refrigerate overnight, slice, and fry in a little butter.

NUTRITION FACTS per serving made with cornmeal: 101 calories, 20.5% calories from fat, 1.2g total fat (3%), 1.2g saturated fat (6%), 5.1mg cholesterol (2%), 18g carbohydrates (6%), 1.7g fiber (7%), 2g protein (4%), 199.4mg sodium (8%), 3mg calcium, 1mg iron (5%) and 166 IU vitamin A (3%).

FRIED CORNMEAL MUSH
Makes 4 servings

The *Palmer House,* a *Swiss Restaurant* in Berne, Indiana, offers fried cornmeal mush to their guests.

4 cups water, divided

1 teaspoon salt

1 cup corn meal

1. Bring 3 cups of water to a boil.
2. In a bowl add the cornmeal, salt and 1 cup of cold water.
3. Stir cornmeal mixture into boiling water.
4. Reduce heat and cook for about 15 to 20 minutes, stirring occasionally, until thick.

5. Pour mixture into a greased loaf pan.
6. Cool, refrigerate overnight.
7. Remove from pan and slice about 1/2-inch thick.
8. Fry in hot skillet until brown.
9. Top with syrup, butter or molasses.

NUTRITION FACTS per serving without suggested toppings: 126 calories, 5 calories from fat, .6g total fat (1%), zero saturated fat and cholesterol, 534mg sodium (22%), 26.8g carbohydrates (9%), 2.6g fiber (10%), 2.9g protein (6%), 142 IU vitamin A (3%), zero vitamin C and calcium, and 1.4mg iron (8%).

FRIED GRITS
Makes 4 servings

Like cornmeal mush, cooked grits can also be fried.

1 cup quick-cooking grits
4 cups water

8 slices bacon, cooked, crumbed
Butter, margarine, or bacon drippings

1. Bring water to a boil, slowly stir in grits.

2. Simmer about 5 minutes until thick.

3. Stir in bacon bits.
4. Pour cooked grits into a greased loaf pan, cool and refrigerate overnight.
5. Unmold and cut into 1/2-inch slices.

6. Fry in a skillet over medium-high heat, in small amount of butter, for about 10 minutes on each side until golden brown.
7. Serve with honey or syrup

NUTRITION FACTS per serving: 243 calories, 87 calories from fat, 9.6g total fat (15%), 4g saturated fat (20%), 18.4mg cholesterol (6%), 231.5mg sodium (10%), 31.1g carbohydrates (10%), zero fiber, 7.3g protein (15%), 279 IU vitamin A (6%), 4mg vitamin C (7%), zero calcium and 1.8mg iron (10%).

IRISH OATMEAL SOUFFLÉ
Makes 6 servings

Chef Michael Foley from *Le Perigord and Printer's Row* in Chicago, Illinois has created a soufflé that combines the best of the *Irish* Fry breakfast with oatmeal, cheese and bacon.

4 tablespoons unsalted butter, divided
1 tablespoon flour
1 cup milk
3/4 cup quick cooking oatmeal
1/2 cup cheddar cheese, grated
1/3 cup low-fat cream cheese
1/2 cup bacon, chopped, fried crisp

4 eggs, separated (yolks beaten, whites stiffly beaten)
1 tablespoon fresh flat leaf parsley, chopped
1 teaspoon prepared mustard
1/4 teaspoon salt or to taste
1/2 teaspoon cayenne red pepper
Freshly ground black pepper to taste

1. Using 2 tablespoons of butter, grease an 8-inch soufflé dish. Dust with flour; set aside.
2. Place milk and remaining butter in a saucepan over medium high heat and heat until almost boiling.
3. Slowly stir in oatmeal. Cook, stirring constantly, for about 4 minutes or until thick.
4. Remove from heat and beat in the cheeses.
5. When well combine, stir in bacon, beaten egg yolks, parsley, mustard and seasonings.

6. Fold beaten egg whites in thirds, taking care not to deflate the whites.
7. When incorporated, but not overly mixed, spoon into prepared soufflé dish.
8. Place in a cold oven. Turn heat to 350°F and bake, undisturbed, for about 40 minutes or until center is still slightly soft, soufflé has risen and is set.
9. Serve immediately.

NUTRITION FACTS per serving: 368 calories, 253 calories from fat, 28.1g total fat (43%), 13.5g saturated fat (68%), 201.4mg cholesterol (67%), 574.3mg sodium (24%), 11.4g carbohydrates (4%), 1.2g fiber (5%), 17.2g protein (3450, 861 IU vitamin A (17%), 7mg vitamin C (12%), 161mg calcium (16%) and 1.8mg iron (10%).

JALAPEÑO GARLIC CHEESE GRITS
Makes 6 servings

Hosts *Kay and Cliff LaFrance* from the 1820 *Boscobel Cottage Bed and Breakfast Inn* in Monroe, Louisiana offers this casserole to their guests.

1 cup grits
4 cups water
1 teaspoon salt

6 ounce roll jalapeño cheese
6 ounce roll garlic cheese
1/4 cup butter

1. Add grits to boiling, salted water; reduce heat and cook for 4 to 5 minutes, stirring frequently.
2. Add cheeses and butter until melted and mixture is well blended.

3. Bake uncovered in 1 1/2 quart casserole at 350°F for 30 minutes.

MEATLESS "SAUSAGE" PATTIES
Makes 8 patties

Arrowhead Mills offers this meatless sausage recipe for those concerned about calories and fat.

2 cups cooked Bulgur wheat
1/4 cup whole wheat flour
1 tablespoon crushed basil leaves
1 egg

3/4 teaspoon sage
3/4 teaspoon poultry seasoning
Salt to taste
3/4 cup cheddar cheese, grated (optional)

1. Mix the cooked Bulgur wheat, flour, eggs, seasonings and cheese together.
2. Chill mixture for 10 minutes.
3. Form into 8 patties and roll in whole wheat .

flour.
4. Fry in a small amount of vegetable oil (or use non- stick spray) until lightly browned. Cook like hamburger meat.

Leftovers may be wrapped in individual packages and reheated.

NUTRITION FACTS per patty: 105 calories, 38 calories from fat, 4.4g total fat (7%), 2.5g saturated fat (12%), 37.7mg cholesterol (13%), 143.2mg sodium (6%), 11.9g carbohydrates (4%), 2.6g fiber (11%), 5.4g protein (11%), 212 IU vitamin A (4%), zero vitamin C, 100mg calcium (10%) and 1.1mg iron (6%).

NASI GORENG
Makes 6 servings

Every cook in *Asia* has leftover rice to make fried rice. Fried rice originated in *China* and every Asian country has its own version. Nasi Goreng, a blend of *Indonesian* and *Malay* cooking styles, is filled with shrimp, peas, carrots, cabbage and eggs. This version uses two kinds of rice, plain steamed long grain and coconut simmered rice (all of one type of rice can be used). In *Singapore* this dish is served at breakfast with a crisp fried egg, sunny side up. Recipe courtesy *Singapore Tourist Promotion Board.*

1 1/2 cups cooked long grain rice, cold
1 1/2 cups coconut simmered rice, cold (see Nasi Lemak in HOT CEREALS, page 68)
2 tablespoons oil from red chile paste or vegetable oil
1 tablespoon garlic, chopped
1 cup cabbage, cut into 3/4 inch cubes
1/4 pound medium shrimp, cut into thirds

1 egg
1/4 cup cooked carrots, diced 1/4 inch
1/4 cup peas, blanched
1 tablespoon red chile paste
1 tablespoon Thai fish sauce
1 teaspoon salt
Pinch of sugar
Crisp shallot flakes

1. Put the rice in a plastic bag and gently press the lumps to separate the grains; set aside.
2. Preheat a wok over medium heat. When hot, add the oil and garlic; sauté until lightly brown.
3. Toss in the cabbage and stir-fry for 1 minute or until it begins to wilt.
4. Add the shrimp and stir-fry until they turn bright orange, about 30 seconds.

5. Increase the heat to high, push the ingredients up the sides of the wok, and crack the egg into the middle. Lightly scramble it in the middle of wok until it begins to set.
6. Add the rice, carrots, peas, red chile paste, fish sauce, salt and sugar.
7. Stir fry until the rice is evenly coated with the sauce.
8. Garnish with crisp shallot flakes. Serve hot.

NUTRITION FACTS per serving: 271 calories, 101 calories from fat, 11.2g total fat (17%), 5.3g saturated fat (26%), 64.5mg cholesterol (22%), 404.7mg sodium (17%), 33.6g carbohydrates (11%), 1.5g fiber (6%), 8.8g protein (18%), 2622 IU vitamin A (52%),15mg vitamin C (25%), 41mg calcium (4%) and 1.4mg iron (8%).

RICE & SHINE
Makes 4 servings

Jennifer Jones of Homer, New York makes this delicious breakfast casserole for a Sunday brunch.

2 cups warm cooked rice
2 eggs, beaten
1 tablespoon milk or cream
1 tablespoon chives, finely chopped

1/4 teaspoon salt
1/4 teaspoon paprika
Dash of pepper
4 slices bacon, fried crisp, crumbled

1. Butter a 1 quart casserole dish.
2. Combine the ingredients, except the bacon and pour into the casserole dish.

3. Place the dish in a shallow pan of water in the oven and bake at 325°F for 20 to 30 minutes, until firm.
4. Remove from the oven and sprinkle bacon over the top. Serve immediately.

NUTRITION FACTS per serving: 209 calories, 56 calories from fat, 6.1g total fat (9%), 2g saturated fat (10%), 112.2mg cholesterol (37%), 269.8mg sodium (11%), 29.2g carbohydrates (10%), .5g fiber (2%), 8g protein (16%), 283 IU vitamin A (6%), 3mg vitamin C (5%), 30mg calcium (3%) and .7mg iron (4%).

Did you know that rice is native to India and Southeast Asia? These ancient grains are now the chief source of food for half the world's population. Rice grows best in semi-marsh areas, but will grow in lesser qualities on land with a good rainfall. One advantage of rice over other grains is that it takes less milling prior to being eaten. Only the husks need to be removed for brown rice. Further milling to make white rice removes some of the important nutrients, especially the B and E vitamins and minerals. The word "rice" comes originally from the Arabic word *ruz* by way of the Greek and Latin *oryza* and finally, the French *ris*. Rice was brought to America in the middle 17th century. It was first grown in the low country of South Carolina. Today it is an important crop in Arkansas, California, Louisiana, and Texas. Rice can be cooked on the stovetop, steamed, or baked. American wild rice is not a member of the Asian rice family; it is a marsh grass.

SCRAPPLE
Makes 34 slices

Scrapple is quite popular in the *Pennsylvania Dutch Country*. The *Amish* seldom waste any part of the pig, hence much the of scraps sometimes find its way into this dish.

1 pound pork bones (neck, knuckles, etc.)
1 pound pork shoulder
1 onion, chopped
2 garlic cloves, chopped

3 quarts water
2 teaspoons salt
1 teaspoon pepper
1 teaspoon sage, dried

3 cups cornmeal

1. In a large pot, boil bones, pork, onion and garlic for about 2 to 2 1/2 hours.
2. Drain, reserve the broth, chill.
3. Remove the meat from the bones.
4. Place all of the meat in a blender, blend thoroughly.
5. Remove fat from the chilled broth; discard.
6. Pour 2 quarts of the chilled broth in a large pot.

7. Add the meat and seasonings, bring to a boil.
8. In the 1 quart of the remaining broth (add water if not enough broth), mix the cornmeal to a smooth paste.
9. Slowly stir the cornmeal into the boiling broth.
10. Reduce heat to medium, simmer until thickened, stirring constantly.
11. Cover, reduce heat to low, cook about 20 minutes, stirring often.

12. Pour into 2 greased bread pans, cool and refrigerate overnight.

13. Remove cornmeal from the pans, with a sharp knife, cut into 1/2 inch slices.

14. In a hot skillet, fry slices in butter or bacon fat until golden brown on both sides.

15. Top with syrup, if desires.

NUTRITION FACTS per slice without syrup: 66 calories, 13 calories from fat, 1.5g total fat (2%), .5g saturated fat (2%), 6.6mg cholesterol (2%), 147.9mg sodium (6%), 9.7g carbohydrates (3%), 1g fiber (4%), 3.1g protein (6%), 51 IU vitamin A (1%), zero vitamin C, 6mg calcium (1%), and .6mg iron (3%).

Pork is the flesh of the swine, more commonly called pig or hog. The meat is light pink when raw, however, turns white when cooked, and is often referred to as "the other white meat." Technically pork is considered red meat. Depending upon the cut, pork can be fried, roasted, broiled, braised and barbecued. Pork is also smoked and while you might call this smoked ham, ham is really the rear leg cuts. Hence, ham is available both fresh and cured. Just as the Amish in Pennsylvania have shown us in tasty recipes, almost every part of the pig can be eaten.

SWEETNIN' PONE
Makes 8 servings

Throughout the southeastern United States various cornmeal dishes were created. Sweetnin' Pone was one the popular ones. *Geri Beal* from Summerville, West Virginia would prepare this recipe for her friends at the *Memorial United Methodist Church.*

4 cups cornmeal
1/2 cup sugar
1 tablespoon salt
4 cups boiling water
1 cup flour

1 cup buttermilk
2 eggs, beaten
2 teaspoons baking powder
1 teaspoon baking soda, dissolved in a little warm water

1 tablespoon butter, melted

1. Place cornmeal, sugar and salt in a bowl.
2. Add boiling water and stir until smooth. Let stand overnight in warm place to "work."
3. In the morning, add flour, buttermilk, eggs, baking powder, soda and butter.

4. Mix well and pour into a well greased 10- inch skillet.
5. Bake in preheated 450°F oven for 15 minutes.
6. Remove from oven and turn upside down on a plate, serve when cool.

NUTRITION FACTS per serving: 402 calories, 38 calories from fat, 4.2g total fat (7%), 1.6g saturated fat (8%), 58mg cholesterol (19%), 1112.3mg sodium (46%), 80g carbohydrates (27%), 5.1g fiber (20%), 10.1g protein (20%), 428 IU vitamin A (9%), zero vitamin C, 134mg calcium (13%) and 3.9mg iron (22%).

Did you know the early settlers to America learned to dry corn from the Native Americans? Dried corn must be soaked in water overnight before boiling. Many farmers still dry corn kernels to be stored for the winter months. The corn must be kept in a dry, cool place or it will mold. The dried kernels are ground into a course meal, and called "cornmeal." Most corn is either white or yellow. There are other colors; one of the most popular is blue. All three are available in most supermarkets. All can be used to make cornmeal mush, polenta, cornbread and muffins. White and yellow cornmeals keep their color during cooking, while blue cornmeal turns lavender when cooked. For fun, make some purple pancakes for the kids with blue cornmeal. Blue cornmeal is higher in protein than white or yellow. Cornmeal is a good source for fiber, protein, vitamin A and iron.

CHAPTER VI

COFFEE CAKES, STRUDELS & SWEET CAKES

A whole book could be written just on coffee cakes that are enjoyed around the world. Many of these recipes also make fine desserts.

Apfelstrudel (*Austria*) variation: Cream Strudel 82

Ambrosia Coffee Cake (*USA*) 83

Ann's Rich Rolls (*Kansas*) 83

Blueberry Gingerbread Coffee Cake (*Vermont*) 84

Cobblers Delight (*Hungry*) 84

Coriander Spice Coffee Cake (*California)* 85

Cream Cheese Apple Torte (*Utah*) 85

Crumb Coffee Cake (Pennsylvania) 86

Curd Cake (*Sweden*) 86

Danish Pastry Bread (*Denmark*) 87

Empanadas de Pina (*El Salvador & Mexico*) 88

Gingerbread with Filbunke (*Sweden*) 88

Grandma Hazel's Shoo Fly Coffee Cake (*Maryland*) 89

Honey Pecan Sticky Buns (*USA) 90*

Lazy Daisy Coffee Cake (*Washington*) 90

Quesadilla Salvadorena (*El Salvador*) 91

Raisin Coffee Cakes (*California*) 91

Raspberry Cream Cheese Coffee Cake (*Iowa*) 92

Rhubarb-Strawberry Coffee Cake (*Norway*) 92

Breakfast in Norway

Shahi Tukra (*Pakistan*) 93

Spiced Banana Bundt Cake (*California*) 94

Swedish Applecake with Vanilla Sauce (*Sweden*) 95

APFELSTRUDEL
Makes 12 servings

This apple strudel is the *Austrian* version of something the *Turks* were concocting when they were not busy laying siege to Vienna. Recipe courtesy *Austrian National Tourist Office.*

STRUDEL DOUGH

Many recipe books suggest you purchase ready-made strudel sheets at the supermarket. The choice is yours, but if you want to give it a try, here's the recipe.

2 cups bread flour
Pinch salt

3 tablespoons vegetable oil
2/3 cup water, lukewarm

1. Combine flour, salt, oil and water and knead into medium-firm dough.
2. Divide into 3 small round loaves, brush each loaf with melted butter and let rest for 1 hour.
3. Roll the dough leaves with a rolling pin, then stretch rolled dough on the floured strudel cloth sheet with the backs of hands until paper thin.
4. Coat 2/3 of dough sheet with buttered breadcrumbs, spread apple filling over remaining 1/3 of dough.

5. Tear off edges, shape strudel into roll by lifting strudel sheet.
6. Place strudel on a buttered baking sheet and brush with melted butter.
7. Bake strudel for 60 minutes in a 400°F oven or until golden brown.

NUTRITION FACTS per serving with apple filling: 597 calories, 233 calories from fat, 26.4g total fat (41%), 13.5g saturated fat (68%), 54.3mg cholesterol (18%), 494.9mg sodium (21%), 85.7g carbohydrates (29%), 7.1g fiber (28%), 6.9g protein (14%), 852 IU vitamin A (17%), 15mg vitamin C (26%), 48mg calcium (5%) and 2.7mg iron (15%).

APPLE FILLING

4 1/2 pounds apples, peeled, cored, sliced
2/3 cup sugar
3 tablespoons dark rum

1 cup raisins
1/8 teaspoon cinnamon
2 lemons, juice and peel, grated

1. Mix all ingredients and blend together well.

BUTTERED BREADCRUMBS

2/3 cup butter, soften

1 cup bread crumbs

1. Blend butter and bread crumbs together to make a soft paste.

2. Or, spread butter on strudel dough and sprinkle with the bread crumbs.

CREAM STRUDEL

Monika Pacher from the Salon of *Culinary Arts at the New York Coliseum* suggests using the same recipe as the apple strudel but replacing the apple filling with the cream filling.

2 cups ricotta
1 cup sour cream

1/2 cup sugar
1/2 cup raisins

2 eggs, beaten

1. Mix all ingredients well and fill as with apple strudel.

AMBROSIA COFFEE CAKE
Makes 9 servings

Mary R. Humann from the *National Honey Board* says, *"Honey is nature's natural sweetener and will keep the coffee cake moist for several days."*

3 tablespoons butter or margarine, softened
2/3 cup honey, divided
1/4 cup coconut, flaked
1/3 cup pineapple, crushed, drained
1/4 cup shortening

1 egg
1/2 cup milk
1/2 teaspoon vanilla
1 1/2 cups flour
1 1/2 teaspoons baking powder

1/2 teaspoon salt

1. In small mixing bowl, blend together butter and 1/3 cup of honey.
2. Add coconut and pineapple; mix thoroughly; set aside.
3. In small bowl, place 1/3 cup honey and shortening.
4. Blend on low speed.
5. Add egg, milk and vanilla.
6. Beat on low speed until well blended, scraping sides and bottom of bowl several times.
7. Add flour, baking powder and salt.
8. Continue to mix on low speed until dry ingredients are moistened.
9. Beat on medium speed for 2 minutes.
10. Grease 8x8-inch pan. Dust bottom with flour.
11. Spread batter in the pan.
12. Spoon honey-coconut-pineapple mixture carefully over top of batter, spreading evenly.
13. Bake at 350°F for 30 to 35 minutes or until coffee cake tests done.
14. Serve warm.

NUTRITION FACTS per serving: 264 calories, 100 calories from fat, 11.5g total fat (18%), 4.9g saturated fat (25%), 35.7mg cholesterol (12%), 233.1mg sodium (10%), 38.6g carbohydrates (13%), .3g fiber (1%), 3.5g protein (7%), 196 IU vitamin A (4%), 1mg vitamin C (2%), 82mg calcium (8%) and 1.3mg iron (7%).

ANN'S RICH ROLLS
Makes 24 servings

Teresa Flora from Sawyer, Kansas makes these very rich cinnamon rolls for her family and friends. She suggests the more times you punch down the dough and let it rise, the better the rolls will be. Teresa usually makes the dough in the morning, punches it down several times, and bakes it in the afternoon.

1 cup milk
1/2 cup sugar
2 packages yeast
5 to 5 1/2 cups flour

Butter or shortening
1 1/2 teaspoons salt
1/2 cup warm water
2 eggs, beaten

1. Boil milk, add 1/2 cup butter, sugar and salt: set aside to cool.
2. Dissolve yeast in warm water.
3. When milk has cooled, add yeast to milk mixture with eggs and 1/2 cup flour.
4. Beat until smooth.
5. By hand with a wooden spoon, add more flour until mixture leaves the sides of the bowl.
6. Turn out on floured board and knead until satiny, adding more flour as necessary.
7. Put in a greased bowl, turning to grease all sides. Let rise until double. Punch down and le it rise one more. Repeat, punch down and let it rise one or more times.
8. Spread 1/4 of the filling in each of two 9x13-inch baking pans.
9. Divide dough in half.
10. Roll on floured board until 1/4-inch thick.
11. Spread with 1/4 of the filling.
12. Roll up jelly roll style.
13. Cut into 1-inch slices and place in the first baking pan. Continue with second half of the dough, place in second pan.
14. Let rise until double.
15. Bake at 375°F for 15 to 20 minutes.
16. While still hot, invert pan on to serving platter.

FILLING

2/3 cup butter
2 teaspoons cinnamon

1 1/2 cups brown sugar
4 teaspoons light corn syrup

1. Mix all ingredients in saucepan.

2. Cook over low heat until sugar is dissolved..

NUTRITION FACTS per roll: 242 calories, 88 calories from fat, 9.9g total fat (15%), 5.9g saturated fat (29%), 42.9mg cholesterol (14%), 239.5mg sodium (10%), 34.8g carbohydrates (12%), .4g fiber (2%), 4g protein (8%), 373 IU vitamin A (7%), zero vitamin C, 32mg calcium (3%) and 1.7mg iron (10%).

BLUEBERRY GINGERBREAD COFFEE CAKE
Makes 12 servings

Paul and Lois Dansereau, the innkeepers at *Silas Griffith Inn* in Darby, Vermont, takes advantage of the areas blueberries and add it to a gingerbread recipe.

2 cups fresh or frozen blueberries
1/4 cup sugar
1/4 cup vinegar
1 cup sour cream
3 cups flour
1 cup brown sugar
2 teaspoons baking soda

2 teaspoons ginger
1/2 teaspoon salt
1/2 teaspoon cinnamon
1/4 teaspoon mace
4 eggs, slightly beaten
1/4 cup molasses
1 cup butter, melted, cooled

1. Preheat oven to 350°F.
2. In a small bowl, toss berries with sugar and vinegar.
3. Let stand at room temperature for 1 hour.
4. Drain well, reserving berries and juice.
5. Set berries aside.
6. In a large bowl, stir juice into sour cream.
7. In another bowl, combine flour, brown sugar, soda, ginger, salt, cinnamon and mace; set aside.

8. Stir eggs, molasses and butter into sour cream mixture.
9. Add to flour mixture and beat until fluffy and smooth.
10. Carefully fold in blueberries.
11. Grease a bundt or angel food pan, fill pan with batter and bake 1 hour or until tested done.
12. Cool on rack.
13. Dust with confectioners sugar just before serving.

NUTRITION FACTS per serving: 409 calories, 189 calories from fat, 21.3g total fat (33%), 12.5g saturated fat (63%), 120.2mg cholesterol (40%), 494mg sodium (21%), 49.5g carbohydrate (17%), .8g fiber (3%), 6.3g protein (13%), 853 IU vitamin A (17%), 3mg vitamin C (6%), 67mg calcium (7%) and 2.4mg iron (14%).

COBBLER'S DELIGHT
Makes 6 servings

In *Hungary* pasta is added to make a most unusual and delicious strudel.

11 ounces vermicelli
Pinch of salt
1 1/3 cups sugar, divided
12 eggs, separated
1/2 lemon, juice & rind, grated
1 teaspoon vanilla

2/3 cup raisins
1/3 cup sour cream
6 bread rolls, crusts removed, cubed
Ready-made strudel leaves
Vegetable oil
1 tablespoon butter

1. In a pot, cook the vermicelli in salted water.

2. Rinse and drain; set aside.

3. In a large bowl, blend thoroughly half of the sugar with the egg yolks, lemon rind and juice, vanilla, raisins and sour cream.

4. In another large bowl, beat the egg whites with remaining sugar until stiff.

5. Mix together the vermicelli, bread cubes, sour cream mixture and fold in the beaten egg whites.

6. Grease a baking pan.

7. Oil the strudel leaves on both sides.

8. Place strudel leaves in the pan in such a way that after the filling in poured in, the strudel leaves will fold over and cover the filling.

9. Pour in the filling and cover with the strudel leaves.

10. Dot the top with butter and bake it in a 350°F oven for 30 to 40 minutes.

11. Cut it while still hot and serve.

NUTRITION FACTS per serving: 731 calories. 137 calories from fat, 15.4g total fat (24%), 5.2g saturated fat (26%), 430.7mg cholesterol (144%), 325.9mg sodium (14%), 128.7g carbohydrates (43%), .8g fiber (3%), 20.8g protein (42%), 738 IU vitamin A (15%), 3mg vitamin C (5%), 90mg calcium (9%) and 4.1mg iron (23%).

CORIANDER SPICE COFFEE CAKE
Makes 12 servings

Renee Shepherd and *Fran Raboff,* authors of *Recipes From a Kitchen Garden,* says, *"This is a moist, delicate cake that keeps very well and actually improves in flavor the second and third day."*

2 1/2 cups flour, sifted
2 teaspoons soda
1 teaspoon salt
2 teaspoons ginger
1 teaspoon cloves
1 teaspoon cinnamon
1 teaspoon coriander
1/2 cup sugar

1/2 cup butter, melted
1 cup molasses
2 eggs, slightly beaten
1/2 cup raisins
1/2 cup walnuts, chopped
1/3 cup candied orange peel, chopped
1 cup boiling water
Powdered sugar (optional)

1. Preheat oven 350°F.

2. Grease a 9x13-inch baking pan.

3. In a medium bowl, sift flour, soda, salt and spices together; set aside.

4. In a large bowl blend sugar with melted butter.

5. Beat in molasses and eggs.

6. Stir in raisins, walnuts and orange peel.

7. Add sifted dry ingredients and hot water alternately to egg mixture, beating after each addition until just combined.

8. Don't over mix.

9. Pour into pan and bake for 30 minutes or until a cake tester inserted in center comes out clean.

10. Sprinkle with powdered sugar, if desired.

NUTRITION FACTS per serving: 352 calories, 110 calories from fat, 11.8g total fat (18%), 5.2g saturated fat (26%), 61.2mg cholesterol (20%), 487.1mg sodium (20%), 53g carbohydrates (1850, .7g fiber (3%), 5.3g protein (11%), 357 IU vitamin A (7%), 1mg vitamin C (1%), 76mg calcium (8%) and 3.1mg iron (17%).

CREAM CHEESE APPLE TORTE
Makes 8 wedges

Marie Ruesch of Salt Lake City, Utah calls this easy-to- make recipe a torte, but your kids will call it a pizza.

9 frozen rolls, thawed & soft
8 ounces cream cheese, soften
1/2 cup sugar, divided
1 egg, beaten

1 teaspoon vanilla
20 ounce canned apples, sliced, drained
1/2 teaspoon cinnamon
1/4 cup almonds, sliced

1. Preheat oven to 350°F.

2. Knead rolls into one ball.

3. Roll dough into a 14-inch circle and place on a greased pizza pan.

4. Mix cream cheese, 1/4 cup sugar, egg and vanilla together.

5. Spread on dough.

6. Combine apples, 1/4 cup sugar and cinnamon.

7. Place on top of cheese mixture.
8. Sprinkle with almonds.

9. Bake for 25 to 30 minutes until golden brown.
10. Cut into 8 wedges and serve.

NUTRITION FACTS per wedge: 303 calories, 134 calories from fat, 15.2g total fat (23%), 7.2g saturated fat (36%), 58mg cholesterol (19%), 289.5mg sodium (12%), 36.6g carbohydrates (12%), 2.2g fiber (9%), 6.6g protein (13%), 454 IU vitamin A (9%), 1mg vitamin C (1%), 80mg calcium (8%) and 1.9mg iron (10%).

CRUMB COFFEE CAKE
Makes 8 servings

In you stop by for a hardy breakfast at the *Bird-in- Hand Restaurant* in *Pennsylvania Dutch Country* you will start with a bowl of baked oatmeal, followed by deep fried scrapple, and you will probably finish the breakfast with this crumb coffee cake.

1 3/4 cup brown sugar
1 1/4 cup flour
1/3 cup shortening
1 teaspoon cinnamon
4 eggs

Pinch of salt
1/8 teaspoon baking powder
1 teaspoon vanilla
1 cup buttermilk
1/8 teaspoon baking soda

1. In a large bowl, mix brown sugar, flour and shortening into fine crumbs; set aside.
2. Measure out 1 cup of this mixture and add the cinnamon; reserve for the topping.
3. In a large bowl, mix eggs, salt, baking powder and vanilla with a mixer at slow speed.
4. Add the brown sugar mixture; mix well.

5. Dissolve soda in the buttermilk and add to the mixture.
6. Mix well and pour in a greased 9x13-inch baking pan.
7. Sprinkle the reserved crumbs on top.
8. Bake at 350°F for about 40 minutes.

NUTRITION FACTS per serving: 312 calories, 98 calories from fat, 11g total fat (17%), 3g saturated fat (15%), 107mg cholesterol (36%), 88mg sodium (4%), 48g carbohydrates (16%), .2g fiber (1%), 6.2g protein (12%), 170 IU vitamin A (3%), zero vitamin C, 92mg calcium (9%) and 2mg iron (11%).

CURD CAKE
Makes 6 servings

This is *Sweden's* answer to a cheesecake that is made with cottage cheese, instead of cream cheese.

1/4 cup almonds, chopped
4 eggs, beaten
3 tablespoons sugar

3 tablespoons wheat flour
1 pound cottage cheese
1 cup whipping cream, whipped

1. Prepare almonds; set aside.
2. In a bowl, beat eggs with sugar.
3. Add flour and cottage cheese and blend thoroughly.
4. Blend in whipped cream and almonds.

5. Pour into a buttered 1-quart ovenproof dish.
6. Bake at 400°F for about 1 hour.
7. Serve the curd cake lukewarm directly from the dish.

Top with berries or jam, if desired.

NUTRITION FACTS per serving: 347 calories, 217 calories 24.5g total fat (38%), 11.6g saturated (58%), 202.4mg cholesterol (67%), 365.4mg sodium (15%), 15.2g carbohydrates (5%), 1.5g fiber (6%), 17.8g protein (36%), 848 IU vitamin A (17%), zero vitamin C, 120mg calcium (12%) and 1.1mg iron (6%).

Did you know that cottage cheese can be made from either whole or nonfat milk? Cottage cream is available in large or small curd, salted, unsalted, with fat or nonfat. When cream is add to the nonfat cottage cheese, it will contain fat.

DANISH PASTRY BREAD
Makes 16 servings

Instead of making small individual pasties, *Robin Belliston* of Hyde Park, Utah, prefers to make large loaves, and than slice into individual servings.

2 loaves wheat or white frozen bread dough
Vanilla pudding

Crumble topping

Almond filling
Egg white

1. Thaw loaves, shape into 2 balls.
2. Let rise 1 hour.

3. While bread is rising prepare pudding, filling and topping.

VANILLA PUDDING

2 tablespoons flour
1/4 teaspoon salt
1/3 cup sugar

1 cup milk
1 egg yolk
1 teaspoon vanilla

1. Blend sugar, flour and salt in a small sauce pan.
2. Stir in milk.
3. Cook over medium heat, stirring constantly.

4. When it boils, stir in a small amount into egg yolk, than stir in egg yolk into pan.
5. Stir and cook 1 minute. more
6. Remove from heat, add vanilla; set aside to cool

ALMOND FILLING

1 tablespoon butter, soften   3 tablespoons sugar   1/4 teaspoon almond extract

1. Mix all ingredients together in a small bowl; setaside.

CRUMBLE TOPPING

1 tablespoon butter, soften
2 tablespoons flour

2 tablespoons sugar
2 tablespoons almonds, slivered

1. Mix all ingredients together in a small bowl; set aside.

ASSEMBLING

1. Roll each loaf into a 14x7-inch rectangle.
2. Spread half of the vanilla pudding on each loaf, leaving 1 1/2 inches at sides unspread.
3. Divide almond filling in half, dropping by 1/2 teaspoons on top of pudding.
4. Make 6 to 7 cuts down each side about 1 inch into dough. Have the same number of cut on each side.
5. Fold end in.

6. Lace bread, tucking in each side so filling doesn't escape.
7. Place on lightly greased cookie sheet.
8. Beat egg white and brush on top.
9. Top each loft with 1/2 of the crumble topping.
10. Let rise for 10 minutes.
11. Bake at 375°F for 15 to 20 minutes or until golden brown

NUTRITION FACTS per serving: 138 calories, 34 calories from fat, 3.8g total fat (6%), 1.6g saturated fat (8%), 19.5mg cholesterol (6%), 190.4mg sodium (8%), 22.9g carbohydrates (8%), .7g fiber (3%), 3.2g protein (6%), 93 IU vitamin A (2%), zero vitamin C, 50mg calcium (5%) and 1mg iron (5%).

EMPANADAS DE PINA
Makes 36 empandas

Daisy Aguilar says, "Empanadas (turnovers) are found throughout Latin America. In *El Salvador* we usually bake them, while in *Mexico* they are generally fried."

PINEAPPLE FILLING

1 fresh pineapple, peeled, cored, chopped
2 cups sugar
Water

2 tablespoons cornstarch
2 tablespoons margarine
1 cinnamon stick

1. In a large sauce pan add pineapple, sugar, cinnamon stick and water to cover.
2. Bring to a boil, reduce heat and simmer for about 20 minutes or until pineapple is tender.
3. Remove cinnamon stick.

4. Dissolve cornstarch to 1/2 cup of water and add to the pineapple mixture, cook until thick.
5. Remove from the heat, add the margarine and cool.

PASTRY

3 cups flour
1 teaspoon salt

1 cup lard or shortening
6 tablespoons water

1. In a bowl mix flour and salt.
2. Cut in lard with a pastry cutter until fine crumbs form.
3. With a fork, stir in water, 1 tablespoon at a time.
4. Let the pastry rest for ten minutes.
5. Roll out on a floured board to about 1/8-inch thick.
6. Cut out 3-inch rounds with a biscuit cutter.

7. Place 1 tablespoon of the pineapple mixture in the center of each cut out.
8. Fold over, moisten edges with water and seal edges with a fork.
9. Brush with water and sprinkle a little sugar on the top, if desired.
10. Place on a greased and floured baking sheet.
11. Bake at 400°F for 20 minutes or until golden brown or fry in hot deep fat until golden brown.

NUTRITION FACTS per baked empanada: 160 calories, 58 calories from fat, 6.6g total fat (10%), 2.4g saturated fat (12%), 3.2mg cholesterol (1%), 67.4mg sodium (3%), 24.8g carbohydrates (8%), .5g fiber (2%), 1.3g protein (3%), 36 IU vitamin A (1%), 7mg vitamin C (11%), zero calcium and .7mg iron (4%).

GINGERBREAD WITH FILBUNKE
Makes 4 servings

Gingerbread has been popular in *Europe* since the Middle Ages and today is still enjoyed with a variety of recipes. In *France* candied fruits are often added, while in *America* it's blueberries, and the early day American colonists chose mince meat.

In *Sweden* orange marmalade and almonds are added, along with fermented cream, and the gingerbread is served with *filbunke* (fermented milk). You can top it with yogurt, if you desire.

3 tablespoons butter
2/3 cup brown sugar
2 eggs
1 cup flour
1 1/2 teaspoons baking powder

1 teaspoon cinnamon
1/2 teaspoon cloves
1 teaspoon ginger
1/2 cup fermented cream or sour cream
2 tablespoons orange marmalade

10 almonds, chopped

1. Mix butter with brown sugar until light and fluffy.
2. Add eggs and remaining ingredients until thoroughly mixed.

3. Pour into a buttered and floured 8x8-inch baking pan.
4. Bake at 325°F for about 1 hour.
5. Invert on cake rack and let stand until cold.
6. Cut into 16 squares

.

NUTRITION FACTS per square: 613 calories, 418 calories from fat, 49.4g total fat (76%), 6.1g saturated fat (30%), 33.2mg cholesterol (11%), 80.6mg sodium (3%), 32.2g carbohydrates (11%), 9.8g fiber (39%), 19.6g protein (39%), 130 IU vitamin A (3%), 1mg vitamin C (1%), 289mg calcium (29%) and 3.9mg iron (22%).

FILBUNKE

| 1 2/3 cups milk | 3 tablespoons fermented milk* | 3 tablespoons heavy cream |

1. In a saucepan, heat milk until it is just on the point to boil (this prevents the milk from curdling).
2. Cool the milk to room temperature.
3. Mix in remaining ingredients.

4. Pour into individual bowls and let set at room temperature until they have set (or overnight).
5. Place bowls in refrigerator and serve chilled with ground ginger and gingerbread

.

NUTRITION FACTS per serving: 107 calories, 70 calories from fat, 7.9g total fat (12%), 4.9g saturated (25%), 30.5mg cholesterol (10%), 59mg sodium (2%), 5.6g carbohydrates (2%), zero fiber, 4g protein (8%), 305 IU vitamin A (6%), 1mg vitamin C (2%), 141mg calcium (14%) and zero iron.

*Filbunke is basically sour milk. Sour milk or sour cream and can be used in recipes calling for filbunke.

GRANDMA HAZEL'S "SHOO, FLY" COFFEE CAKE
Makes 8 servings

Tom and Terry Rimel, the innkeepers at the *National Pike Inn* in New Market, Maryland serves this cake regularly to their guests. The name came about when Grandma Hazel would shout, "Shoo, flies!" when flies would attack her coffeecake.

4 cups flour	2 cups warm water
2 cups sugar	1 cup molasses
1 teaspoon salt	1 tablespoon baking soda
1 cup shortening	Extra crumbs

1. In a large bowl, combine flour, sugar, salt and cut in shortening.
2. Take out 1 cup of crumbs and set aside.
3. To remaining flour mixture add water, molasses and soda, mix thoroughly.

4. Pour into a greased and floured 10x13-inch baking pan.
5. Sprinkle with the set aside crumbs, or make the extra crumbs, then sprinkle over the cake.
6. Bake at 350°F for 50 to 60 minutes

.

NUTRITION FACTS with extra crumbs per serving: 885 calories, 285 calories from fat, 32.1g total fat (49%), 7.5g saturated fat (38%), zero cholesterol, 822.2mg sodium (34%), 144.6g carbohydrates (48%), .2g fiber (1%), 7.3g protein (15%), 234 IU vitamin A (5%), zero vitamin C, 101mg calcium (10%) and 5.4mg iron (30%).

EXTRA CRUMBS

| 1/2 cup flour | 1/4 cup margarine |
| 1/2 cup sugar | 1 teaspoon cinnamon |

1. Blend together and add set aside crumbs.

HONEY PECAN STICKY BUNS
Makes 12 rolls

The *National Honey Board* thinks every member of the family will enjoy these sticky buns dripping with sweetness.

3 to 3 1/2 cups flour
1 package yeast
7 tablespoons sugar, divided
1 cup warm water (120°F to 130°F)
1/2 cup butter or margarine, melted, divided

1 egg
1/3 cup honey
1/4 cup brown sugar
1 1/2 cup pecan halves, divided
1 teaspoon cinnamon

1. In a large bowl, mix thoroughly 1 cup flour, yeast, and 2 tablespoons of sugar.
2. In another bowl, beat together water, 1/3 cup butter and egg.
3. Add to yeast mixture, beat for 3 minutes.
4. With wooden spoon, mix in remaining flour, a cup at a time, until dough pulls away from the sides of the bowl.
5. Turn onto lightly floured surface; knead about 5 minutes or until smooth. If needed, sprinkle with additional flour to reduce stickiness.
6. Cover dough; let rest for 5 minutes.
7. Heat honey and brown sugar until melted; mix thoroughly.
8. Spoon evenly into 13x9-inch baking pan; sprinkle with 1 cup of pecans.

9. Roll dough to 12x10-inch rectangle; spread remaining butter over dough.
10. Combine remaining 1/4 cup sugar, 1/2 cup pecans and cinnamon; sprinkle over dough.
11. Roll dough up along 12-inch side; pinch seam to seal.
12. Cut into twelve 1-inch slices; place in pan cut-side down.
13. Cover; let rise in warm place about 25 minutes or until doubled.
14. Bake at 350°F 25 to 30 minutes or until lightly browned.
15. Immediately invert onto heat-proof serving plate. Let pan remain 2 to 3 minutes to allow honey to drizzle over rolls

NUTRITION FACTS per roll: 368 calories, 154 calories from fat, 17.5g total fat (27%), 5.6g saturated fat (28%), 38.1mg cholesterol (13%), 85.4mg sodium (4%), 48.9g carbohydrates (16%), 1.4g fiber (6%), 5.8g protein (12%), 330 IU vitamin A (7%), zero vitamin C, 21mg calcium (2%) and 2.4mg iron (13%).

LAZY DAISY COFFEE CAKE
Makes 6 servings

During World War II, butter and sugar were hard to obtain, hence this was a popular breakfast cake during the early 1940s. *Hope Abadie* of Chelan, Washington, takes you back in time so you too can enjoy this coffee cake.

1/2 cup milk
1 teaspoon butter
2 eggs

1 cup sugar
1 teaspoon vanilla
1 cup flour

1/4 teaspoon salt

1. Scald milk with butter, set aside to cool.
2. Beat eggs well, add sugar and vanilla.
3. Mix in flour and salt, alternating with milk, stirring well after each addition.

4. Pour into a greased 8x8-inch pan and bake for 25 minutes at 350°F.
5. Remove from oven and add topping.
6. Place under broiler and broil until top bubbles and is brown

NUTRITION FACTS per serving with topping: 377 Calories, 125 calories from fat, 14.2g total fat (22%), 5.2g saturated fat (26%), 86.7mg cholesterol (29%), 162.9mg sodium (7%), 56.7g carbohydrates (19%), .8g fiber (3%), 7.7g protein (15%), 336 IU vitamin A (7%), 1mg vitamin C (1%), 50mg calcium (5%) and 1.7mg iron (10%).

90

COCONUT TOPPING

5 teaspoons butter or margarine
3 tablespoons brown sugar

4 teaspoons cream
1/2 cup walnuts, chopped

1/4 cup coconut, shredded

1. Mix butter, brown sugar and cream together.
2. Sprinkle on hot cake.

3. Sprinkle with nuts on top.

QUESADILLA SALVADORENA
Makes 10 servings

This recipe comes from the small village of Rosario de La Paz in *El Salvador*. Do not confuse this recipe with the Mexican Quesadilla which are two tortillas filled with cheese and lightly grilled. The *Salvadorena* Quesadilla is more like a cheesecake. *Daisy Aguilar*, from the capitol city of San Salvador, says enjoy it with a cup of hot chocolate or coffee.

1 cup rice flour
8 ounces cream cheese, soften
3 eggs, separated
1/2 cup margarine, soften

3/4 to 1 cup sugar
1/2 cup sour cream
1/2 cup half & half cream
Dash of salt

Sesame seeds

1. In a large bowl, beat rice flour with cream cheese until well blended.
2. Beat in the 3 egg yolks, margarine, sugar, creams, and salt.
3. In another bowl, beat egg whites until firm, fold into cheese mixture.

4. Pour into an 8x11-inch greased pan.
5. Sprinkle top with sesame seeds.
6. Bake in 350°F oven for about 45 minutes or until light golden brown
7. Serve warm.

NUTRITION FACTS per serving: 350 calories, 209 calories from fat, 23.5g total fat (36%), 9.6g saturated fat (48%), 98.2mg cholesterol (33%), 204.3mg sodium (9%), 29.7g carbohydrates (10%), .4g fiber (2%), 5.8g protein (12%), 937 IU vitamin A (19%), zero vitamin C, 59mg calcium (6%) and .7mg iron (4%).

RAISIN COFFEE CAKES
Makes 8 servings

Innkeeper *Lisa Smith* from the *Country Garden Inn* in Napa, California, likes to make individual coffee cakes for her guests.

3/4 cup butter or margarine, softened
2 cups sugar, divided
2 eggs
1 teaspoon vanilla
2 1/4 cups flour
2 teaspoons baking powder

½ teaspoon baking soda
1/2 teaspoon salt
1 cup sour cream
1 1/2 cups raisins
2 teaspoons cinnamon
Powdered sugar

1. Preheat oven to 350 °F degrees.
2. In large mixer bowl cream butter and 1 1/2 cups of sugar; beat until fluffy.
3. Add eggs and vanilla; beat until light.
4. Sift flour, baking powder, soda, and salt into another bowl.

5. Add to butter mixture, one-third at a time, alternating with sour cream and beating well after each addition.
6. Fold in raisins.
7. In a small bowl mix remaining sugar with the cinnamon.
8. Grease and flour eight 2 cup oven proof molds.

9. Spread about 3/4 cup of the batter evenly in mold.
10. Sprinkle 1/3 of the cinnamon mixture equally over each mold.
11. Top with remaining batter.

12. Bake for 1 hour or until pick inserted into centers comes out clean.
13. Unmold onto racks; cool.
14. Dust with powdered sugar.

NUTRITION FACTS per serving: 625 calories, 206 calories from fat, 23.6g total fat (36%), 14.5g saturated fat (72%), 58.8mg cholesterol (20%), 496.2mg sodium (21%), 102.2g carbohydrates (34%), 1.4g fiber (6%), 5.6g protein (11%), 873 IU vitamin A (17%), 1mg vitamin C (2%), 149mg calcium (15%) and 2.6mg iron (15%).

RASPBERRY CREAM CHEESE COFFEE CAKE
Makes 8 servings

Hosts *Barbara and Marsha Stensvad* from the *Chestnut Charm Bed and Breakfast Manor* in Atlantic, Iowa, bring a bit of Victorian enchantment to their guests with recipes of yesteryear.

3 ounces cream cheese
1/4 cup margarine or butter
2 cups prepared biscuit mix
1/4 cup milk

1/2 cup raspberry preserves
1 cup powdered sugar, sifted
1 to 2 tablespoons milk
1 teaspoon vanilla

1. In a medium bowl, cut the cream cheese and margarine into the prepared biscuit mix until crumbly.
2. Stir in 1/4 cup of milk.
3. Turn onto a lightly floured surface; knead 8 to 10 strokes.
4. On waxed paper, roll dough to a 12x8-inch rectangle.
5. Invert onto a greased baking sheet; remove paper.
6. Spread preserves down center of dough.

7. Make 2 1/2 inch long cuts at 1 inch intervals on long sides.
8. Fold strips over the filling.
9. Bake at 375°F for about 20 minutes or until golden brown.
10. Let coffee cake cool 5 minutes before frosting.
11. In a small bowl, stir together powdered sugar, 1 to 2 tablespoons of milk and vanilla; drizzle over cooled coffee cake.

NUTRITION FACTS per serving: 331 calories, 128 calories from fat, 14.4g total fat (22%), 4.5g saturated fat (23%), 13.5mg cholesterol (5%), 494.5mg sodium (21%), 47.7g carbohydrates (16%), .9g fiber (4%), 3.8g protein (8%), 403 IU vitamin A (8%), 2mg vitamin C (3%), 82mg calcium (8%) and 1.1mg iron (6%).

RHUBARB-STRAWBERRY COFFEE CAKE
Makes 15 servings

From *Norway*, where rhubarb and strawberries grow in abundance, comes this favorite coffee cake by *SacoFoods, Inc.*

3 cups flour
1 cup sugar
1/2 teaspoon baking soda
1 teaspoon baking powder
1/4 cup dry cultured buttermilk powder

1 teaspoon salt
1 cup margarine (2 sticks)
1 cup water
2 eggs
1 teaspoon vanilla

1. Prepare and cool rhubarb-strawberry filling.
2. In a large bowl, sift together flour, sugar, soda, baking powder, buttermilk powder and salt.

3. Cut in margarine until mixture resembles fine crumbs.
4. Beat together water, eggs and vanilla and add to dry ingredients.

5. Stir to moisten.
6. DO NOT OVERBEAT.
7. Spread half the batter in a greased 13x9x2-inch pan.
8. Spread cooled filling over the batter.

9. Spoon remaining batter in small mounds on top of the filling.
10. Sprinkle topping over batter.
11. Bake at 350°F for 45 to 50 minutes

NUTRITION FACTS per serving: 427 Calories, 145 calories from fat, 16.4g total fat (25%), 3g saturated fat (15%), 29.7mg cholesterol (10%), 406.9mg sodium (17%), 66.2g carbohydrates (22%), 1.2g fiber (5%), 5.1g protein (10%), 701 IU vitamin A (14%), 20mg vitamin C (34%), 86mg calcium (9%) and 1.7mg iron (9%).

RHUBARB-STRAWBERRY FILLING

3 cups fresh or frozen rhubarb
16 ounce package strawberries, thawed

2 tablespoons lemon juice
1 cup sugar

1/3 cup cornstarch

1. Cut rhubarb into 1-inch pieces.
2. Slice strawberries.
3. Cook fruit, covered, 5 minutes.
4. Add lemon juice.

5. Combine sugar and cornstarch; add to rhubarb mixture.
6. Cook and stir 4 to 5 minutes or until thick and bubbly.
7. Cool before spreading on cake.

SUGAR TOPPING

3/4 cup sugar   1/2 cup flour   1/4 cup margarine (1/2 stick)

1. Combine sugar and flour.

2. Cut in margarine until it resembles fine crumbs.

BREAKFAST IN NORWAY

Norwegian cuisine embraces a multitude of traditional dishes which Norwegians regard with pride and take particular pleasure in serving on all kinds of formal and festive occasions.

At the Olympic Winter Games in Lillehammer a special menu had been developed for outdoor food-stands and takeways. Here, under the sign of *"Matklokka"* (named after the bell that was used to call farm workers to meals in days gone by), guests enjoyed a variety of breakfast treats: griddle cakes, pancakes, sour-cream porridge, sausages and grilled meats.

Most dishes are developed from the need to preserve various foods. The most common methods used are curing, salting, smoking, drying and fermenting. *Lutefisk* (dried cod soaked in lye), *rakerret* (fermented trout) and *pinnekjott* (dried, salted lamb ribs steamed over birch or juniper twigs) are examples.

Breakfast begins typically at a well-filled buffet, where guests can start the day with a wide choice of dishes. Breads have always held an important place in the hearts of Norwegians. Thin, brittle *flatbrod*, page 26 (rye crisp) has a long tradition as an accompaniment to cold, cured meats and hot dishes alike. Freshly baked rye and whole-meal breads, *lefs* (griddle cake) and waffles, served with sour cream and jam are everyday pleasures. *Blotkokt* eggs (soft boiled eggs) are served with rice porridge, rye crisp and cheese.

Julebrod, page 51 (Christmas bread) is served during the holidays and is enjoyed with butter and jam. It is fairly common to have fish, especially herring, for breakfast. Fish is served in the big resort hotels and is usually included in the breakfast smorgasbord.

Gudbrandsdalsost and *gjetost* are cheeses made from goat and cow's milk. These firm, slightly sweet brown cheeses are eaten in thin slices on bread, rye crisp and waffles.

Lamb, reindeer and elk meat are constantly used in new Norwegian dishes. Reindeer provides the basis for most *Sami* (or Lapp) dishes, which are appearing on increasing numbers in the far north.

SHAHI TUKRA

Shazia Hasan of Karachi, *Pakistan* says, *"Shahi Tukra was created for the Kings who ruled over the Indian Subcontinent several centuries ago. In those days there were no refrigerators or toasters, nor did they have any different flavor extracts. The royal cooks used rose water for flavoring and instead of toasting the bread they would fry it in butter. Shahi Tukra was left to cool overnight in dishes made of clay and was served to the Royalties the next day with red rose petals sprinkled over it. Since we're in the 21st century, it is time to bring some changes to this delicious food of the kings."*

1 cup sweetened condensed milk
8 bread slices, white or brown
1/2 teaspoon extract of your choice (banana, strawberry, orange, etc.)

1/2 teaspoon food color (optional), match the color with the chosen extract (red with strawberry, etc.)
1 1/2 cups water

1. Toast the slices of bread to a golden brown. This will harden them a little and prevent them from breaking when cooked in the milk.
2. In a big sauce pan mix the water and milk and put it on low heat.
3. Place the toasted bread slices in the milk.
4. Dip in each slice for about 5 seconds.

5. Take the slices out and spread on a jelly roll pan.
6. Continue to heat the milk until it thickens.
7. Add the flavor extract and food coloring. Pour it over the bread slices.
8. Refrigerate for at least an hour and serve cold

For best results, prepare Shahi Tukra at night and refrigerate it for breakfast the next day. Shahi Tukra is also a good dessert with any meal.

NUTRITION FACTS per slice: 189 calories, 38 calories from fat. 4.2g total fat (7%), 2.3g saturated fat (11%), 13.2mg cholesterol (4%), 183.1mg sodium (8%), 33.2g carbohydrates (11%), .6g fiber (2%), 5.1g protein (10%), vitamin A (3%), vitamin C 92%), calcium (14%) and iron (5%).

SPICED BANANA BUNDT CAKE
Makes 8 servings

Ken Torbert, the innkeeper at the *Gingerbread Mansion* in Ferndale, California, serves this tropical flavored coffee cake to his overnight guests.

3 cups flour
1 teaspoon baking soda
1 teaspoon cinnamon
2 cups sugar
1 teaspoon salt

1 1/2 cups vegetable oil
8 ounce can crushed pineapple, undrained
1 1/2 teaspoons vanilla
3 eggs
2 cups bananas, diced

1 cup pecans, chopped

1. In a large bowl, sift together dry ingredients.
2. Mix remaining ingredients by hand until just blended.

3. Pour into greased tube or bundt pan.
4. Bake 1 hour at 350°F.

NUTRITION FACTS per serving: 913 calories, 463 calories from fat, 52.7g total fat (81%), 6.2g saturated fat (31%), 79.7mg cholesterol (27%), 449.9mg sodium (19%), 106.3g carbohydrates (35%), 2.7g fiber (11%), 8.9g protein (18%), 193 IU vitamin A (4%), 8mg vitamin C (14%), 33mg calcium (3%) and 3.1mg iron (17%).

No, pineapples are not native to Hawaii, but to northern South America, where still some of the best pineapples are grown. The English gave it the name because it resembled a pine cone.. The Spanish followed suit with *piña,* a Spanish word meaning "pine cone." Spanish mariners took the pineapple to Hawaii in 1790 where today most of the world's pineapple is produced.

SWEDISH APPLECAKE WITH VANILLA SAUCE
Makes 4 servings

You will be surprised how simple it is to make this *Swedish* coffee cake. For a change of pace try replacing the rye-bread with whole wheat and other breads.

12 slices fresh rye-bread, finely chopped
1/4 cup butter

2 to 3 tablespoons brown sugar
1 cup applesauce

1. Brown the bread crumbs in butter in a frying pan.
2. Fill an ovenproof dish or frying pan with alternate layers of the bread, brown sugar and apple sauce.

3. The top layer must be bread.
4. Bake at 400°F for about 20 minutes.
5. Serve with vanilla sauce

NUTRITION FACTS per serving without the vanilla sauce: 497 calories, 230 calories from fat, 25.9g total fat (40%), 14.9g saturated fat (74%), 62.1mg cholesterol (21%), 800.2mg sodium (33%), 60.4g carbohydrates (20%), 6g fiber (24%), 7.6g protein (15%), 874 IU vitamin A (17%), 1mg vitamin C (2%), 77mg calcium (8%) and 2.8mg iron (16%).

VANILLA SAUCE

3 egg yolks
2 tablespoons sugar

1 1/2 tablespoons vanilla
1 cup whipping cream, whipped

1. Beat egg yolks with sugar and vanilla until light and fluffy.

2. Fold the egg mixture into the whipped cream.

NUTRITION FACTS per tablespoon: 28 calories, 23 calories from fat. 2.6g total fat (4%), 1.5g saturated fat (7%), 24.1mg cholesterol (8%), zero sodium, carbohydrates and fiber, .3g protein (1%), 112 IU vitamin A (2%), zero vitamin C, 6mg calcium (1%) and zero iron.

Believe it or not, the delicate sweetness of vanilla comes from an orchid, which has no odor. This tropical plant from Mexico produces a bean pod, and when dried, the pod develops a smell and taste that almost everyone is familiar with. Mostly likely it was the Aztecs who first used vanilla. They would grind the vanilla beans with cacao beans to make their chocolate drink. Spanish conquistador, Cortez, discovered its delights and carried it back to Europe. Some things are meant to be where they are, or as it is said, "Don't fool with Mother Nature," and the vanilla bean is a case in point. Once the Europeans found the orchid, they transplanted it to other tropical countries. However, the orchid produced no pods. It was found that only Mexican bees can pollinate this plant. Today, these orchids grow in other countries, but the pollination must be done by hand. Mexican vanilla is still the "queen mother" of all. Vanilla is used in almost every flour baking recipe. Pure vanilla is expensive, hence, artificial vanilla is often used. Some flavoring companies combine both pure and imitation together and generally can pass for pure vanilla. Pure vanilla will lose some of the flavor in baking, whereas artificial vanilla does not. When vanilla is added to fruit, less sugar is required, since vanilla will bring out the sweetness naturally in fruit. You can make vanilla sugar by taking a whole bean pod, split it open or break it into little pieces and mix in a cup of powdered sugar. Let it sit for a day before using. Vanilla sugar can be sprinkled on coffeecakes, breakfast cereal and fruit. Vanilla has the tendency to bring out natural flavor in foods and beverages. Add a drop or two to hot tea. You won't taste the vanilla, but it will bring out the full flavor of the tea. By using a drop or two in cream or milk used for your breakfast cereal, you will take less sugar to make the cereal enjoyable. And by all means, add it to your hot chocolate just like Montezuma did centuries ago.

CHAPTER VII

DOUGHNUTS, FRITTERS & FRIED BREADS

Fried cakes were popular in Europe and the colonists brought the recipe to America. People would complain that sometimes the center wasn't cooked. To correct the problem, the Dutch filled the center with a piece of fruit or a nut. Sometimes the filling fell out while being cooked, hence, doughnuts were then made with a hole in the middle.

When nutrition facts are given, it does not include fat absorbed from frying. Keeping the oil temperature between 350°F and 375°F, will help prevent the dough from absorbing too much fat.

Applesauce Doughnuts (*Nebraska*) 97

Baked Banana Doughnuts, with variation: Pumpkin Doughnuts (*USA)* 97

Bakes (*Trinidad & Tabago*) 98

Cassava Bread (*West Indies*) 98

Dahi Baray (*Pakistan*) 98

Dutch Fritters (*Netherlands)* 99

Floats (Trinidad *& Tabago*) 99

Hush Puppies (*Alabama*) 100

Italian Donuts (*Italy*) 100

Jellabies

with Cardamon Syrup (*Nepal*) 100

Malawach (*Israel & Yemen*) 101

Maple Potato Doughnuts (*Vermont*) 101

Mother Ada Drew Urie's Doughnuts (*Vermont*) 102

Raised Donuts 102

Cake Donuts 102

Olie Bollen (*Netherlands*) 103

Paratha (*Pakistan*) 103

Potato Stuffed Paratha (*Pakistan*) 103

Breakfast in Pakistan

Puri (*Pakistan*) 104

Roti Prata (*Singapore*) 105

Spiced Cocoa Doughnuts (*USA*) 105

Sweet Potato Fritters (*Antigua & Barbuda*) 106

Tortillas de Maiz [corn] (*Mexico*) 106

Tortillas de Harina [flour] (*Mexico*) 107

Yu't'iau (*Taiwan*) 107

APPLESAUCE DOUGHNUTS
Makes about 25 doughnuts

These spiced doughnuts are more like fritters, but with a cake taste, that are dropped by spoonfuls into the hot fat, hence have no hole. *Christie Miller* of Dunbar, Nebraska, likes to fine grind the raisins, the choice is yours.

2 eggs, beaten
3/4 cup sugar
2 tablespoons vegetable oil
1 cup applesauce
4 cups flour
1 cup raisins, grind if desired

1 teaspoon salt
2 teaspoons baking powder
1 teaspoon baking soda
1/2 teaspoon nutmeg
1 teaspoon cinnamon
1 cup milk

Sugar

1. In a large bowl, mix in order given and combine well after each addition.

2. Drop by teaspoons in hot oil, brown both sides.
3. Roll in sugar.

NUTRITION FACTS per doughnut: 143 calories, 19 calories from fat, 2.1g total fat (3%), .5g saturated fat (3%), 18.3mg cholesterol (6%), 125.6mg sodium (5%), 28.6g carbohydrates (10%), .4g fiber (2%), 3.1g protein (6%), 40 IU vitamin A (1%), zero vitamin C, 48mg calcium (5%) and 1.2mg iron (7%).

BAKED BANANA DOUGHNUTS
Makes 22 doughnuts

Not all doughnuts are fried, as you will see from this recipe by *The Sugar Association*. Also note these doughnuts are low in calories and fat. Baked doughnuts will not have quite the true shape with a hole in the middle as the fried variety.

2 ripe bananas, mashed
2 egg whites
1 tablespoon vegetable oil
1 cup brown sugar
1 1/2 cups flour

3/4 cup whole wheat flour
2 teaspoons baking powder
1/2 teaspoon baking soda
1/4 teaspoon pumpkin pie spice
1 tablespoon sugar

2 tablespoons walnuts, chopped (optional)

1. Preheat oven to 425°F.
2. Spray baking sheet with cooking spray.
3. In large mixing bowl or in food processor, beat bananas, egg whites, oil, and brown sugar.
4. Add flours, baking powder, soda and spice.
5. Mix until well blended.
6. Then let stand for 5 minutes for dough to rise.
7. Scoop out heaping tablespoon of dough onto baking sheet.

8. Using thin rubber spatula or butter knife round out doughnut hole in the center of dough (if dough sticks to knife or spatula, spray it with cooking spray).
9. Then using spatula smooth outside edges of dough into round doughnut shape.
10. Repeat until all dough is used.
11. Sprinkle with white sugar and walnuts if desired.
12. Bake 6 to 10 minutes until tops are golden.

NUTRITION FACTS per doughnut: 93 calories, 11 calories from fat, 1.2g total fat (2%), .1g saturated fat (1%), zero cholesterol, 69.7mg sodium (3%), 19.1g carbohydrates (6%), .8g fiber (3%), 2g protein (4%), zero vitamin A, 1mg vitamin C (2%), 40mg calcium (4%) and .8mg iron (4%).

PUMPKIN DOUGHNUTS

Use an 8 ounce can of pumpkin instead of bananas to make pumpkin doughnuts.

BAKES
Makes 6 servings

On the islands of *Trinidad and Tabago*, bakes were originally cooked on a hot baking stone before an open fire. Today they are fried.

2 cups flour
2 teaspoons baking powder
1 teaspoon salt

2 teaspoons sugar
2 tablespoons shortening
2/3 to 3/4 cup water

1. In a large bowl, sift together the flour, salt and baking powder.
2. Cut in the shortening.
3. In a small bowl, mix sugar and water together until the sugar dissolves.

4. Mix the water into the flour mixture, to a soft dough, knead four or five times.
5. Break off small pieces and flatten 1/4-inch thick like a pancake.
6. Fry in hot vegetable oil until golden brown and puffy.

NUTRITION FACTS per serving: 196 calories, 22% calories from fat, 4.7g total fat (7%), 1.1g saturated fat (6%), zero cholesterol, 33.6g carbohydrates (11%), 4.3g protein (9%), 479mg sodium (20%), 121mg calcium (12%), 2.1mg iron (12%).

CASSAVA BREAD

Cassava, also called *yuca*, is a popular bread in the *West Indies*. It is baked in an iron ring on a baking stone, then dried in the sun.

6 cups cassava, grated finely
Butter, melted

2 teaspoons salt

1 In a large bowl mix the cassava with the salt.
2. Take about a cupful at a time, place in a cheese cloth and squeeze out all the liquid.
3. Crumble the meal, then rub through a fine sieve.
4. Take about 1 cup of the dried meal and press into the baking ring.

5. Place on a hot stone over a glowing fire (or a hot griddle on stove top) and when steam rises, remove the ring.
6. When firm, turn over frequently until slightly brown and the bread ends are dry and stiff.
7. Spread with butter and brown in a 450°F oven before serving

NUTRITION FACTS per total recipe: 284 calories, 3% calories from fat, .9g total fat (1%), .2g saturated fat (1%), zero cholesterol, 63.7g carbohydrates ((21%), .2g fiber (1%), 7.3g protein (15%), 1085mg sodium (45%), 217mg calcium (22%), 8.5mg iron (47%), 114mg vitamin (190%) and 24 IU vitamin A.

DAHI BARAY
Makes 6 servings

The *Pakitanis* call this *"Yogurt Salad."* Your first reaction might be, "What does yogurt salad have to do with fried doughs?" Well, the first part of the recipe is deep fat fried, soften in water, then mixed with the yogurt. Give it a try, especially if you like graham crackers and yogurt.

3 cups yogurt
1/2 cup graham flour
1 teaspoon salt, divided
1/2 teaspoon cayenne pepper

¼ teaspoon black pepper
½ teaspoon cumin seeds
½ teaspoon baking powder
1/4 cup fresh green coriander leaves, chopped

3 to 4 cups water

1. In a bowl, add 1/2 teaspoon of salt, cayenne and baking powder to the graham flour.

2. Pour in just enough water to make a paste; beat well until it is smooth.
3. Let it rest for 30 minutes.

4. Pour the yogurt into a bowl and beat in the remaining salt, black pepper, cumin and coriander.
5. Heat oil for deep frying in a pan.
6. Drop 1 tablespoon of graham batter at a time.
7. The batter will look like a little golden balloon.

8. Remove from the oil and drop in a bowl of water at room temperature.
9. Let them absorb the water.
10. It will soften them.
11. Add the graham balls to the yogurt.
12. The yogurt salad can be served at room temperature or chilled.

NUTRITION FACTS per serving: 104 calories, 40 calories from fat, 4.5g total fat (7%), 2.6g saturated fat (13%), 14.4mg cholesterol (5%), 483.5mg sodium (20%), 11.6g carbohydrates (4%), .4g fiber (2%), 4.7g protein (9%), 203 IU vitamin A (4%), 8mg vitamin C (13%), 184mg calcium (18%) and 1mg iron (6%).

DUTCH FRITTERS

Traditionally these are served as part of the New Year's Eve celebration. *Margaret Klyn* of Pella, Iowa, suggests to try them for breakfast anytime you like.

2 cups lukewarm water or milk
1/2 cup sugar
2 teaspoons salt
2 cakes compressed yeast
2 eggs, beaten

1/2 cup shortening, softened
4 cups apples, chopped
1 cup raisins
1 cup currants
7 to 7 1/2 cups flour

1. Mix water, sugar, salt, and yeast in a large bowl.
2. When yeast is dissolved, beat in eggs, shortening and 1 cup of flour.
3. Stir in apples, raisins and currants.
4. Stir in flour until it leaves the sides of the bowl.

5. Turn dough out on a flour board and kneed in remaining flour.
6. Cover, let rise in a warm place until doubled in bulk.
7. Break off by spoonfuls and fry in deep oil at 375°F until golden brown.
8. Roll in powdered sugar.

FLOATS
Makes 6 servings

In *Trinidad and Tobago*, floats are similar to bakes, except yeast is used for leavening, rather then baking powder.

1/2 package yeast
1/2 cup water, lukewarm, divided
1 teaspoon sugar

1 teaspoon salt
2 1/2 cups flour
3 tablespoons shortening

1. Pour 1 tablespoon of warmed water in a small bowl and add the yeast.
2. In a large bowl, add sugar, salt and shortening.
3. Heat remaining water and pour over sugar mixture.
4. Cool to lukewarm and add yeast.
5. With a wooden spoon mix in flour.
6. Knead for 15 to 20 minutes.

7. Place in a greased bowl, cover and let rise until double, about 2 hours.
8. Punch down, shape into small balls, cover and let rise again.
9. With rolling pin, roll out thin and fry in oil in a skillet until brown on both sides.
10. Drain on paper towels and serve hot.

NUTRITION FACTS per serving: 252 calories, 25% calories from fat, 7g total fat (11%), 1.7g saturated fat (8%), zero cholesterol, 41g carbohydrates (14%), .3g fiber (1%), 5.8g protein (12%), 357mg sodium (15%), 9mg calcium (1%), 2.6mg iron (14%).

HUSH PUPPIES
Makes about 36 hush puppies

Throughout America's south, hush puppies are standard fare for breakfast. According to the *Alabama Bureau of Tourism*, hush puppies are served in place of hash brown potatoes, grits or corn bread. When red pepper flakes are added, they are called firecracker sticks.

2 cups cornmeal
1 tablespoon flour
1/2 teaspoon baking soda
1 teaspoon baking powder
1 teaspoon salt
1 egg, beaten
3 teaspoons onion, chopped
1 cup buttermilk
2 teaspoons red pepper flakes, crushed (optional)

1. In a large bowl, mix dry ingredients.
2. Add onion, milk, and egg until well mixed. Add red pepper, if desired.

3. Drop by tablespoons in deep hot fat and fry until golden brown.

NUTRITION FACTS per hush puppy: 34 calories, 3 calories from fat, .3g total fat (1%), .1g saturated fat (1%), 6.1mg cholesterol (2%), 99mg sodium (4%), 6.5g carbohydrates (2%), .6g fiber (2%), 1.1g protein (2%), 43 IU vitamin A (1%), zero vitamin C, 19mg calcium (2%) and .4mg iron (2%).

ITALIAN DONUTS
Makes about 24 doughnuts

All doughnuts do not have holes, as you will see with this yeast dough. *Danna Bransky* of Bensenville, Illinois says the pepper makes the taste unique.

2 cups milk
2 tablespoons vegetable oil
Pinch of salt
2 eggs, beaten
1 package dry yeast
Pinch of pepper

Flour

1. In a large bowl, combine milk, oil, salt, eggs, yeast and pepper.
2. Add enough flour as needed to make a dough; mix well.
3. Dough should be soft and sticky.
4. Do not add too much flour.
5. Let stand in mixing bowl until it rises, about 2 hours.

6. Stir with fork.
7. Fill large frying pan half full with oil; let it get very hot.
8. Drop large tablespoons of dough into oil; turn over when one side is golden brown.
9. While still warm, coat with honey or sugar-cinnamon

NUTRITION FACTS per doughnut: 68 calories, 21 calories from fat, 2.4g total fat (4%), .7g saturated fat (4%), 20.5mg cholesterol (7%), 15.7mg sodium (1%), 9.1g carbohydrates (3%), .1g fiber (1%), 2.5g protein (5%), 52 IU vitamin A (1%), zero vitamin C, 28mg calcium (3%) and .6mg iron (4%).

JELLABIES WITH CARDAMON SYRUP
Makes 8 servings

When you went to the fair, did you have a "*funnel cake*" covered with powdered sugar? If you answered, "*yes,*" well then, you have had *Nepal* jellabies. Instead of the messy powdered sugar dropping down your front, you will end up with sticky fingers.

1 package yeast   1 3/4 cups water, warmed   2 2/3 cups flour

1. In a bowl, soften yeast in warm water and let it rest for 10 minutes.

2. Add flour and beat until smooth.

100

3. Cover and leave it for 24 hours in a warm place to ferment.
4. Heat 2 inches of vegetable oil to 350°F in a deep frying pan.
5. Put batter in a funnel, with your finger over the outlet.
6. Let the batter run into the hot fat in continuous circles or figure eights.
7. Cook on each side until golden brown.
8. Remove and drain on paper towels.
9. Dip in cardamon syrup and drain

NUTRITION FACTS per serving: 287 calories, 5 calories from fat, .5g total fat (1%), zero saturated fat, cholesterol and sodium, 66g carbohydrates (22%), .4g fiber (2%), zero vitamins A and C, 9mg calcium (1%) and 2.3mg iron (13%).

CARDAMON SYRUP

1 1/3 cups sugar
1/2 cup water

2 cardamon seeds, cracked
Pinch of saffron for coloring (optional)

1. Boil above ingredients and keep warm in a double boiler for dipping.

MALAWACH
Makes 8 servings

Malawach is a recipe brought to *Israel* by the Jews from *Yemen*. The popularity of this versatile dish, which may be served with a variety of fillings and toppings, testifies to the love for *Yemenite* food which *Israelis* have acquired.

4 cups flour
1 1/4 cups water
1/2 teaspoon salt

1/4 pound margarine
Tomato sauce (optional)
Sour cream (optional)

1. In a bowl, mix flour, water and salt until dough becomes soft.
2. Add more flour if dough is sticky.
3. Cut dough into two sections.
4. Knead and roll each section into a 20x20 inch sheet.
5. Spread margarine on the sheets.
6. Fold each sheet like an envelope with ends meetings at center.
7. Repeat folding process to get two layers of folds.
8. Cover with a paper towel, let sit for 30 minutes.
9. Cut each sheet into 10 parts.
10. Form each piece of dough to the shape of your frying pan and fry until golden brown on both sides.
11. Serve with tomato sauce or sour cream, if desired.

NUTRITION FACTS per serving without sauce or cream: 329 calories, 109 calories from fat, 12g total fat (19%), 2.1g saturated fat (10%), zero cholesterol, 268.3mg sodium (11%), 47.8g carbohydrates (16%), zero fiber, 6.6g protein (13%), 469 IU vitamin A (9%), zero vitamin C, 14mg calcium (1%) and 2.9mg iron (16%).

MAPLE POTATO DOUGHNUTS

Jeanette Auger from *The Sugarmill Farm* in Barton, Vermont, keeps busy making various maple products for her family and guests.

2 cups mashed potatoes
1 cup sour milk (if not sour, add 1 teaspoon vinegar)
3 eggs
1/2 cup sugar
1/4 cup maple syrup

3 tablespoons margarine
5 teaspoons baking soda
1 teaspoon salt
2 teaspoons nutmeg
5 cups flour (more if needed)

1. In a large bowl, combine eggs, sugar, maple syrup and margarine; beat well.
2. Add milk, potatoes and remaining ingredients.
3. Let the mixture set overnight in the refrigerator.
4. Roll out on a floured board and cut with a doughnut cutter.
5. Fry in hot vegetable oil.
6. The key to making these doughnuts perfect, immediately after frying, dip in hot maple syrup, slightly diluted with water

NUTRITION FACTS per doughnut (doesn't include amount of maple syrup absorbed): 188 calories, 24% calories from fat, 5g total fat (8%), 1.4g saturated fat (7%), 128mg cholesterol (43%), 28g carbohydrates (9%), .1g fiber (0%), 6.9g protein (14%), 411mg sodium (17%), 3% calcium, 10% iron, 2% vitamin C and 5% vitamin A.

MOTHER ADA DREW URIE'S DOUGHNUTS

Fay U. Valley of Barton, Vermont talks about her mother: *"My mother was born in Glover, just south of Barton, in 1901. Being of Scottish decent, Mom always started out breakfast with oatmeal steamed overnight. Mom baked many items for the Summer People who vacationed at our lakes. These are two of her favorite doughnut recipes."*

RAISED DONUTS
Makes 1 dozen

1 cup milk	Sprinkle of nutmeg	1/3 cup warm water
1/3 cup + 1 teaspoon sugar	2 to 3 tablespoons butter	1 package yeast
1 teaspoon salt	2 1/2 cups flour, sifted	1 egg, beaten

1. Scald the milk, add 1/3 cup sugar, salt, butter and nutmeg.
2. Pour milk into a large bowl; cool to lukewarm.
3. In a small bowl, soften yeast in water with 1 teaspoon of sugar.
4. Add yeast to the milk mixture, with egg and 1 1/2 cups flour; beat well.
5. Add more flour to make a soft dough.
6. Knead 3 to 4 minutes, cover and let rise about 1 hour.
7. Knead again for a minute or two.
8. Roll dough, cut into strips and form a figure 8 or cut with a doughnut cutter.
9. Let rise again and fry at 350°F

NUTRITION FACTS per doughnut: 164 calories, 38 calories from fat, 4.3g total fat (7%), 2.4g saturated fat (12%), 28mg cholesterol (9%), 223mg sodium (9%), 27.2g carbohydrates (9%), .3g fiber (1%), 4.3g protein (9%), 159 IU vitamin A (3%), zero vitamin C, 32mg calcium (3%) and 1.5mg iron (8%).

CAKE DONUTS
Makes 1 dozen

3/4 cup sour milk	3/4 teaspoon baking soda
1/4 cup sour cream	1/2 teaspoon baking powder
1 tablespoon sugar	2 tablespoons butter, melted
1/2 teaspoon salt	1 1/2 to 2 cups flour

1. In a large bowl, combine all ingredients; chill for 1 to 2 hours.
2. Roll out on a floured board and cut into strips .

To make into a figure 8 or cut with doughnut cutter,
3. Fry at about 375°F

Delicious with maple syrup.

NUTRITION FACTS per doughnut: 116 calories, 33 calories from fat, 3.6g total fat (6%), 2.2g saturated fat (11%), 9.3mg cholesterol (3%), 124mg sodium (5%0, 18g carbohydrates (6%), zero fiber, 2.8g protein (6%), 128 IU vitamin A (3%), zero vitamin C, 42mg calcium (4%) and 1mg iron (6%).

OLIE BOLLEN
Makes about 30 dumplings

This fried dumpling is a *Dutch* treat made with baking powder and is similar to a large doughnut hole with fruit added. This recipe is by *Mina Baker-Roelofs* of Pella, Iowa and is found in the *A Taste of the World Cookbook*

3/4 cup milk
4 tablespoons vegetable oil
2 eggs, beaten
1/2 cup sugar

2 1/2 cups flour
1 tablespoon baking powder
1/2 teaspoon salt
1 teaspoon nutmeg

1/2 to 3/4 cup raisins, citron or apples, chopped

1. In a large bowl, combine liquid ingredients, add sifted dry ingredients, and raisins.
2. Mix thoroughly.
3. Drop by teaspoonfuls into hot vegetable oil at 375°F.

4. Fry until golden brown.
5. Drain on absorbent paper and roll in cinnamon-sugar mix or powdered sugar.

PARATHA
Makes 4 parathas

Shazia Hasan, from Karachi, *Pakistan*, says, *"Over the last 20 years, we Pakistanis have turned quite modern to our grandmothers' dislike. We now gulp down a glass of orange juice or a cup of tea with biscuits or cup cakes. But once in a while we enjoy going back to our traditional breakfast. Paratha is my favorite bread."*

2 cups flour

1/2 cup butter, melted or vegetable oil

Water

1. In a large bowl, mix the flour with enough water to make a soft dough.
2. Knead well.
3. Divide the dough into 4 pieces and make each into a ball.
4. With a rolling pin, roll out thin on a floured board.
5. Brush it with butter and fold it to make a square not letting the butter come out.

6. Roll again, this time it will look like a big square.
7. Place the paratha on a hot griddle.
8. Turn it after 5 seconds.
9. When tiny blisters appear on the under side, pour a tablespoon of vegetable oil around it.
10. Turn it over again.
11. When the other side gets big blisters, the paratha is ready.

Serve with the small blisters on top. Top with sugar and yogurt, if desired. Great with a cup of tea and scrambled eggs.

NUTRITION FACTS per serving without toppings: 285 calories, 140 calories from fat, 15.6g total fat (24%), 9.5g saturated fat (47%), 40.9mg cholesterol (14%), 155.1mg sodium (6%), 31.8g carbohydrates (11%), zero fiber, 4.5g protein (9%), 571 IU vitamin A (11%), zero vitamin C, 11mg calcium (1%) and 2mg iron (11%).

POTATO STUFFED PARATHA
Makes 3 stuffed parathas

Did you enjoy making and eating *paratha*? If so, go one step further and stuff them with potatoes, peppers, and onions. *Shazia Hasan* says, *"I serve them with ketchup and pickles. They're tasty!"*

2 cups flour, white or whole wheat
1/2 cup vegetable oil

Water
2 potatoes, boiled, mashed

1 green pepper, chopped
1/3 cup fresh green coriander leaves, chopped
1 onion, chopped

1 tablespoon lemon juice
½ teaspoon salt
½ teaspoon cayenne pepper

1. In a bowl, mix the flour with enough water to make a soft dough.
2. Knead well; set aside.
3. In a bowl, combine potatoes, salt, cayenne, green pepper, coriander leaves, onions and lemon juice; mix well.
4. Divide the flour dough into 6 pieces, and shape into a ball.
5. On a floured surface, roll into a thin circle.
6. Take 1/3 of the potato mixture and spread on the dough.

7. Cover it with another rolled out circle, like a sandwich.
8. Press the sides together so they are joined.
9. Place the stuffed paratha on a hot griddle.
10. Carefully turn it over after 5 seconds.
11. When tiny blisters appear on the underside, pour a tablespoon of vegetable oil around it.
12. Turn over again.
13. When big blisters form on the underside, the stuffed paratha is ready to eat.
14. Serve with the small blisters up.

NUTRITION FACTS per parahta: 707 calories, 335 calories from fat, 37.5g total fat (58%), 4.4g saturated fat (22%), zero cholesterol, 549.1mg sodium (23%), 82.2g carbohydrates (27%), 2.6g fiber (10%), 11.3g protein (23%), 279 IU vitamin A (6%), 52mg vitamin C (87%), 67mg calcium (7%) and 5.4mg iron (30%).

BREAKFAST IN PASKISTAN

Puri, Cholay and *Halwa* is a favorite breakfast of Pakistanis. Many restaurants open specially on weekends very early in the morning and the only menu is *Puri, Cholay* and *Halwa*. Some enterprising folk bring out their stoves on the footpaths each morning just to serve this delicious breakfast to the people who come and sit at the tables by the road side. The poor and homeless too come with plates in their hands asking the people at the tables to treat them to a free breakfast and not many refuse since this breakfast is very cheap. Usually one *Puri* which resembles a pan cake costs Rs. 2.00, which means you can buy 16 for a dollar and usually a person is full after having three or four. *Cholay* is a curry made of chickpeas and it is free. But you have to buy *Puri* to get *Cholay*. The *Halwa* is a dessert made with Semolina. Some people spread it over their Puri and have it at the end of their breakfast. *Halwa* is not free, but also not very expensive. *Choley* is in the "Vegetable" chapter on page 233 and *Halwa* is in the "Hot Cereals" chapter on page 67.

PURI
Makes 20 puri

2 cups flour
1/2 teaspoon baking powder

Water (about 1/4 cup)
1/4 cup butter, melted

1. Sift flour and baking powder in a large bowl.
2. Make a well in the center, add the butter and mix.
3. Slowly add enough water to make a soft dough.

4. Divide the dough into 20 parts and roll into small balls.
5. Roll each ball on a floured board as thin as possible.
6. Deep fat fry in vegetable oil for about 10 seconds until the cakes turn golden.

NUTRITION FACTS per puri: 66 calories, 22 calories from fat, 2.4g total fat (4%), 1.4g saturated fat (7%), 6.1mg cholesterol (2%), 32.5mg sodium (1%), 9.6g carbohydrates (3%), zero fiber, 1.3g protein (350, 86 IU vitamin A (2%), zero vitamin C, 11mg calcium (1%) and .6mg iron (3%).

ROTI PRATA
Makes 8 roti pratas

Indian griddled bread comes from *India* by the early traders. In *Singapore* it is made by the *prata man* (see back cover photo), as he is called by the locals. He flips the dough into the air like pizza dough and stretches it paper thin. He then folds in several layers and fries it on a griddle. *Roti prata* comes out chewy and flaky in texture.

3 1/2 cups flour
1 teaspoon salt

3/4 cup butter or margarine, melted, divided
1 1/4 cups milk, warmed

1. Sift the flour and salt into a large bowl. Add 5 tablespoons of butter, stir until the mixture looks crumbly.
2. Slowly pour in the milk and mix with your hands.
3. The dough will feel soft, spongy and sticky.
4. Knead the dough without adding extra flour until it pulls away from the bowl and forms a smooth ball.
5. Continue kneading until the dough feels just slightly sticky, about 10 minutes.
6. Cut the dough into 8 pieces.
7. Roll each piece into a ball, flatten it lightly, and rub it with butter.
8. Cover the balls with a damp cloth and let the dough rest for at least 5 hours.
9. Lightly butter a rolling pin and roll out one ball, stretching the dough into about a 9-inch circle.
10. Brush lightly with butter and sprinkle lightly with flour.
11. Starting at the edge, roll up the dough into a rope.

12. Gently pull on the ends and stretch it an inch longer.
13. Take one end and roll it clockwise into a coil until it reaches the center of the rope.
14. Roll the opposite end clockwise until the two coils meet in the middle.
15. Fold one coil over on top of the other.
16. Press the two coils gently together into one thick round.
17. Wrap it with plastic wrap; set aside for 1 hour.
18. Repeat with remaining balls.
19. On a lightly floured surface, roll out one round into a 6 to 7-inch circle.
20. In a skillet pour 1 teaspoon of vegetable oil and 1 teaspoon of butter and fry the dough over medium heat about 2 minutes.
21. Add 1 teaspoon each of oil and butter, turn over and fry 1 minute more or until brown, speckled and puffy.
22. Drain on a paper towel and eat immediately.

NUTRITION FACTS per roti prata: 373 calories, 170 calories from fat, 18.9g total fat (29%), 11.5g saturated fat (57%), 51.2mg cholesterol (17%), 459.8mg sodium (19%), 43.5g carbohydrates (15%), zero fiber, 7.1g protein (14%), 690 IU vitamin A (14%), zero vitamin C, 59mg calcium (6%) and 2.6mg iron (14%).

SPICED COCOA DOUGHNUTS
Makes about 2 dozen doughnuts

Say thanks to the *Aztecs* of *Mexico* for giving the world the cocoa bean to make this cocoa cake doughnut and enjoy it with a cup of hot chocolate.

2 1/4 cups flour
1/2 cup HERSHEY'S® cocoa
2 1/2 teaspoons baking powder
1/2 teaspoon baking soda
1/4 teaspoon cinnamon

1/4 teaspoon mace
1/4 teaspoon salt
1 1/2 tablespoons butter, softened
3/4 cup sugar
1 egg

1/2 cup milk

1. In medium bowl, stir together flour, cocoa, baking powder, soda, spices and salt.

2. In large bowl, beat butter and sugar until creamy.

3. Add egg; beat well.
4. Add flour mixture alternately with milk, mixing until well blended; shape into a ball.
5. On lightly floured surface, roll dough to 1/4-inch thickness.
6. With floured 2 1/2-inch doughnut cutter, cut into rings.

7. Fry two or three doughnuts at a time in 375°F deep fat about 30 seconds, turning once with slotted spoon.
8. Drain on paper towels.
9. Sprinkle powdered sugar and cinnamon over top of warm doughnuts (1/4 cup powdered sugar and a dash of cinnamon).

NUTRITION FACTS per doughnut: 84 calories, 13 calories from fat, 1.5g total fat (2%), .8g saturated fat (4%), 11.5mg cholesterol (4%), 99.3mg sodium (4%), 16.6g carbohydrates (6%), .6g fiber (2%), 2g protein (4%), 47 IU vitamin A (1%), zero vitamin C, 47mg calcium (5%) and .9mg iron (5%).

HERSHEY'S is a registered trademark. Recipe courtesy of Hershey Kitchens, and reprinted with permission of Hershey Foods Corporation.

Did you know that the cocoa tree originated in South America? The cocoa word comes from the Mexican word *cacahuatl*, which describes the flavoring. Today most cocoa comes from Brazil, Dominican Republic and Ecuador. Cocoa trees are also found throughout the tropics, including the African countries of Ghana, Nigeria, Cameroon and the Ivory Coast. The main use for the cocoa bean is cocoa powder to make chocolate. The beans are fried, roasted, ground, and the cocoa butter removed. The beans are ground again into cocoa powder. The Dutch treat the cocoa with an alkali, thus providing a richer flavor and a darker color. In the supermarket cocoa powder is sometimes blended with sugar to make an instant beverage that can be added to hot or cold milk. Cocoa needs to be stored in a cool, dry place (the refrigerator is my choice). If the cocoa powder is stored in a high temperature, or even in a moist location, it will lose its brown color and becomes lumpy. The cocoa butter is used to make chocolate, candy (such as white chocolate) and pharmaceutical products. For information log on: www.sacofoods.com or www.nestleusa.com

---

SWEET POTATO FRITTERS
Makes 4 servings

In the *Caribbean* islands, *Victoria Lake* from the *Consulate General of Antigua and Barbuda* says these fritters are enjoyed at almost every meal.

2 cups flour
Salt to taste
1 egg
2 cups milk

1/2 cup sugar
1 cup sweet potato, grated
1/4 teaspoon cinnamon
1/4 teaspoon nutmeg

1. Sift flour, salt and spices into a large bowl.
2. Break an egg in the center.
3. Mix with 1 cup of milk.
4. Beat well with the back of a spoon.

5. Set aside for 10 minutes.
6. Add remaining milk; beat well.
7. Add sweet potato; mix well.
8. Fry as fritters in hot oil.

NUTRITION FACTS per serving: 453 calories, 55 calories from fat, 6.1g total fat (9%), 3.1g saturated fat (15%), 69.7mg cholesterol (23%), 81.3mg sodium (3%), 86.6g carbohydrates (29%), 1.1g fiber (4%), 12.6g protein (25%), 6754 IU vitamin A (135%), 9mg vitamin C (14%), 171mg calcium (17%) and 3.4mg iron (19%).

TORTILLAS DE MAIZ (*CORN*)

Breakfast in *Mexico*, isn't breakfast unless it includes tortillas. And you have a choice of this flat bread, made with either corn or flour.

2 cups masa harina

1 1/2 cups warm water

1. In a medium bowl, mix the two ingredients together and form a ball.
2. Pinch off about 3 tablespoons and form a small ball.
3. Do like the Mexicans, pat the masa flat with the palms of your hands (might need to wet your hands with water, to prevent sticking). If that doesn't work, place the ball between to sheets of plastic wrap and roll out thin with a rolling pin (or use a tortilla press).
4. The tortilla will be about 6-inches in diameter.
5. Cook on a medium hot griddle, maybe with just a little oil, turning frequently until flecked with brown spots and very dry.

Tortillas can be reheated in the oven, microwave or on the griddle.

NUTRITION FACTS per tortilla: 56 calories, 5 calories from fat, .6g total fat (1%), zero saturated fat and cholesterol, 40.3mg sodium (2%), 11.7g carbohydrates (4%), 1.3g fiber (5%), 1.4g fiber (3%), 61 IU vitamin A (1%), zero vitamin C, 44mg calcium (4%) and .4mg iron (2%).

Did you know that the tortilla is Mexico's most famous bread? This flat bread is similar to other flat bread made around the world. The corn tortilla is made with *masa harina*. The word "masa" refers to both dough and a farmhouse. And "harina" refers to either corn or wheat flour. *Masa harina* is corn that has been treated with lime water and ground into flour. This flour is also used to make tamales. Corn tortillas are generally made into a round, thin, flat cake and cooked on a griddle. They can be eaten as is, stuffed and rolled with meat, cheese, topped with a sauce and made into enchiladas, When folded and filled with meat, cheese, lettuce and other ingredients, they are called "tacos." Note the name "tortillas de maiz." The word *maiz* is corn and this tortilla is made from *masa harina* or treated corn flour. When they are called "tortillas de harina," they are made from wheat flour.

TORTILLAS DE HARINA (*FLOUR*)

Flour tortillas are made in many sizes from 6 to 18- inches. Mexican women pat them out with their hands, with the large 18-inch ones extended up the arm as the tortilla is patted and pulled into shape.

4 cups all-purpose flour
2 teaspoons salt

1/2 cup lard
1 cup warm water

1. In a large bowl, combine flour and salt.
2. Cut in the lard, best with your fingertips.
3. Stir in a little water at a time to form a firm ball.
4. Knead on a lightly floured board for a minute or two.
5. Cover and let rest for 15 to 20 minutes.
6. Pinch off about 4 tablespoons and roll out until about 7-inches in diameter.
7. Flour tortillas are cooked the same as corn tortillas, turning often, about a total of 3 minutes.

Flour tortillas can be thin or thick. The thicker ones are called "gorditas," and can be split open and stuffed with cheese. The larger tortillas need to be thin, as most are used to make burritos.

NUTRITION FACTS per tortilla: 114 calories, 23 calories from fat, 2.5g total fat (4%), .4g saturated fat (2%), zero cholesterol, 167.3mg sodium (7%), 19.5g carbohydrates (6%), 1.1g fiber (4%), 3.1g protein (6%), zero vitamins A and C, 44mg calcium (4%) and 1.2mg iron (6%).

YU'T'IAU

Linda Sherwood from West Jordon, Utah, was a missionary in *Taiwan* from 1977-1979. She reported, "Breakfast in *Taiwan* usually consisted of a bowl of rice and leftovers from the previous day's meals. *Yu'T'iau* was a very popular breakfast. It was similar to a deep fried breadstick. The *Yu'T'iau* dough is made from rice flour and powdered ammonia. The *Yu'T'iau* was eaten hot and dipped in soy milk. Because of the powdered ammonia, the *Chinese* people warned us not to eat this on a regular basis.

CHAPTER VIII

DUMPLINGS & DOUGHS THAT ARE STEAMED OR BOILED

Dumplings for breakfast? Yes, and they are great! Dumplings were probably invented by the *Scandinavians*, but are found throughout *Europe*. The colonists bought recipes to the *New World* and added American ingredients. Most of these recipes not only make a great breakfast, but can also be served as dessert. When serving dumplings, don't waste one drop of the sauce, spoon all on top of the dumplings.

Apricot Dumplings (*Austria*) 109

Blueberry Slump (*New England, USA*) 109

Caramel Dumplings (*New England, USA*) 110

Cheese Dumplings (*Hungary*) 110

Breakfast in Singapore

Chwee Kuey (*Singapore*) 111

Cottage Cheese Dumplings (*Austria*) 112

Ducknoor (*British Virgin Islands*) 112

Eskimo Dumplings (*Alaska*) 113

Fruit Dumplings (*USA*) 113

Germknodel (*Austria*) 114

Honey Yogurt Dumplings with Apples (*USA*) 114

Matzo Balls (*Israel*) 115

Plum Ravioli (*Hungary*) 115

Steamed Bread Dumplings (*Amish & Minnonite, (USA*) 116

Sweet Tamales (*Mexico & Central America*) 116

APRICOT DUMPLINGS
Makes 10 servings

In this chapter you will find several dumpling recipes from *Austria*, all a little different, you will want to try them all.

2 1/4 pounds potatoes
3 cups flour
1 tablespoon butter
1 egg, beaten
Pinch of salt

Apricots, pitted
Sugar cubes
Breadcrumbs
Butter
Sugar

1. In a large pot, boil potatoes whole.
2. Remove the peeling; than sieve.
3. Place the potatoes on a board, add the flour, salt and egg and work into a dough.
4. Form the dough into a long roll, cut out egg-sized pieces and flatten.
5. Place an apricot with a cube of sugar in place of the seed.

6. Wrap the dough around the apricot and form a ball.
7. Drop dumplings in boiling salted water and cook until dumplings rise to the top, about 10 minutes.
8. Roll in breadcrumbs and fried in butter.
9. Sprinkle with sugar and serve.

NUTRITION FACTS per serving: 350 calories, 61 calories from fat, 6.9g total fat (11%), 3.8g saturated fat (19%), 36.6mg cholesterol (12%), 72mg sodium (3%), 66.2g carbohydrates (22%), 3.3g fiber (13%), 7.3g protein (15%), 2092 IU vitamin A (42%), 27mg vitamin C (45%), 26mg calcium (3%) and 2.8mg iron (16%).

Did you know that the apricot tree originated in Asia, where it still grows wild? The apricot is related to the peach. The Chinese have cultivated apricots for more than 4,000 years. The first apricots were bought to California by the Spanish in the 1770s

---

BLUEBERRY SLUMP
Makes 8 servings

According to the *North American Blueberry Council*, this is a take-off of a recipe made during colonial times. Since baking powder wasn't invented until the 1880s, the colonists probably used an egg for leavening. You will enjoy this modern version.

30 ounce canned blueberries
1/2 cup sugar
1 1/2 cups flour
2 teaspoons baking powder

2 teaspoons orange rind, grated
1/4 teaspoon nutmeg
1/4 teaspoon salt
3/4 cup milk

1. In 10-inch skillet over medium heat, mix blueberries and their juice with sugar.
2. Cook until juice starts to boil.
3. Reduce heat to low; simmer.
4. In medium bowl, mix flour, baking powder, orange rind, nutmeg and salt.
5. Stir in milk until dry particles are just moistened.

6. Drop dough by heaping tablespoons on top of simmering blueberries.
7. Cover skillet and cook 15 minutes or until dough is puffed.
8. Serve dumplings with the blueberry sauce from the skillet.

NUTRITION FACTS per serving: 208 calories, 12 calories from fat, 1.4g total fat (2%), .5g saturated fat (3%), 3.1mg cholesterol (1%), 175.6mg sodium (7%), 46.9g carbohydrates (16%), 2.9g fiber (12%), 3.9g protein (8%), 137 IU vitamin A (3%), 15mg vitamin C (25%), 123mg calcium (12%) and 1.4mg iron (8%).

CARAMEL DUMPLINGS
Makes 4 servings

The *New Englanders* liked the flavor from the maple trees, so added maple syrup to their dumpling recipes. These dumplings are baked, rather than steamed.

1/2 cup brown sugar
1 cup water

1 cup maple syrup
2 teaspoons vanilla

1. In an iron skillet, cook brown sugar with low heat until it starts to melt.
2. Slowly add water and syrup; boil for 2 minutes.
3. Remove the skillet from heat, stir in vanilla.

4. Drop dumpling batter by tablespoons into the sugar mixture.
5. Bake in a 425°F oven for about 15 minutes.
6. Cool in the skillet for a couple of minutes.
7. Best served hot, but are good cold.

NUTRITION FACTS per serving: 646 calories, 41 calories from fat, 4.6g total fat (7%), 2.5g saturated fat (13%), 11.8mg cholesterol (4%), 241.1mg sodium (10%), 145.4g carbohydrates (48%), zero fiber, 7.5g protein (15%), 145 IU vitamin A (3%), zero vitamin C, 284mg calcium (28%) and 4.4mg iron (25%).

DUMPLING BATTER

2 cups flour
1/2 cup sugar

2 teaspoons baking powder
1 tablespoon butter, melted

1/2 cup milk

1. Combine dry ingredients in a large bowl.
2. Mix butter and milk together, quickly mix into dry ingredients until ingredients are moistened.

3. Do not beat

CHEESE DUMPLINGS
Makes 5 servings

Early day dumplings used eggs for leavening, as in this recipe from *Hungary*.

1 pound cottage cheese, drained
2 3/4 ounces semolina
Pinch of salt

3 eggs, separated
3 1/3 tablespoons butter
4 1/2 ounces breadcrumbs

Sour cream

1. Rub the curds through a sieve into a medium bowl.
2. Sprinkle with semolina, salt and beaten egg yolks; blend thoroughly.
3. Beat the egg white until stiff and mix with the curd mixture.

4. With wet hands make walnut size balls and drop in boiling water.
5. Boil for 10 to 15 minutes.
6. Heat the butter and the breadcrumbs in a fry pan until golden brown, stirring continuously.
7. Drain the dumplings, arrange on a serving plate, top with breadcrumbs and sour cream.

NUTRITION FACTS per serving: 371 calories, 146 calories from fat, 16g total fat (25%), 8.3g saturated fat (42%), 159.4mg cholesterol (53%), 666.4mg sodium (28%), 34.2g carbohydrates (11%), 1.9g fiber (8%), 21.6g protein (43%), 608 IU vitamin A (12%), zero vitamin C, 111mg calcium (11%) and 2.3mg iron (13%).

BREAKFAST IN SINGAPORE

Food is a national passion among Singaporeans. The secret is that migrants down the ages have imported their favorite dishes from every province in China, most of the Indian states, Malaysia, Indonesia, the Middle East and a wide variety of Western countries including the Americas. Visitors to Singapore can enjoy a variety of eating establishments.

Hawker food is the most popular cuisine in Singapore. These are little stalls that operate almost around the clock. They offer a feast of Chinese, Malay and Indian dishes, along with fresh tropical fruit to be eaten sliced or passed through a juicer for drinking. Many of the Hawker stalls are attached to fresh produce markets. Many people walking through the stalls with the sights, sounds and smells find it exciting. Just imagine the sizzling of charcoal fires, the bubbling of cauldrons, the frantic tossing of noodles inside giant woks, the whirring of tropical fruit in juice blenders and the calls of the hawkers as they summon their assistants. Some of the Hawkers have moved into shopping complexes and offer air conditioning, which is often a welcome during the heat of the day.

Some of the dishes found in Singapore, include: *Bak Kut Teh* (pork bone tea), a popular breakfast soup that has been simmered with spices and soy sauce; *Chye Tow Kway* a solid cake made with grated radish steamed with rice flour and water, which is then fried with fish sauce and eggs to form an omelet; and *Kai Chok,* (chicken rice porridge, page 176), a porridge seasoned with sesame oil, pepper and salted radish along with bits of chicken and fish. All are popular breakfast dishes.

Many of the finest restaurants are found in hotels, but there are a growing number of independent restaurants springing up all over the city. Visitors to Singapore will never run out of things to eat for breakfast.

CHWEE KUEY

In *Singapore* steamed rice cakes are served with preserved, salted radish, as well as with sweet chili sauce.

2 1/2 cups water, divided
5 ounces rice flour
1 heaped tablespoon sago flour
1/2 teaspoon salt
2 tablespoons vegetable oil

3/4 cup suet
2 garlic cloves, lightly bashed
4 ounces preserved, salted radish, chopped
1/2 teaspoon MSG (optional)
Dash of pepper

1. Mix well 1 cup of the water with the two flours and salt in a bowl.
2. Add the oil and beat well with a fork until well blended; set aside.
3. In a saucepan, bring the remaining 1 1/2 cups of water to the boil.
4. Pour gradually into the rice mixture, stirring all the time to prevent lumps forming.
5. Arrange the moulds on a steamer tray and steam empty moulds over boiling water for 5 minutes.
6. Pour rice mixture into each mould.
7. Steam for 10 to 15 minutes or until well cooked.

8. Remove the rice cakes from steamer and allow to cool for about 10 minutes, before taking them out of the moulds.
9. Dice the suet, wash and drain.
10. Cook suet and garlic in a small saucepan until suet turns light brown.
11. Discard garlic and suet, leaving oil to cook radish, msg and pepper, over low heat for 1/2 hour.
12. Stir occasionally to prevent burning.
13. Place a spoonful of cooked radish on top of the steamed rice cakes and serve.

Monosodium glutamate (MSG) enhances the flavor and color in meats and vegetables. Originally made from seaweed, now is made from wheat and sugar beets. Some people are allergic to MSG, which can cause headaches, dizziness, and other sensations. MSG is widely used on salad bars and by Chinese chefs. If you are allergic, be sure to requests your Chinese food prepared without MSG.

COTTAGE CHEESE DUMPLINGS
Makes 4 servings

In *Austria*, dumplings find their way to the breakfast table in several forms as you will see in this chapter.

1/4 cup butter, unsalted, soften
2 eggs, separated
2/3 cup cottage cheese, 2% butterfat content
7 slices white bread, diced

1/2 cup light cream
2/3 cup cake flour
1/3 cup wheat semolina
Pinch of salt

1. In a bowl, pour cream over white bread, allow to soak in, stir until smooth.
2. In another bowl, beat together butter, yolks until foamy.
3. Add cottage cheese and salt.
4. Fold in bread mixture.
5. Whip egg whites, add to the bread mixture.

6. Carefully fold in flour and semolina.
7. Let mixture rest in refrigerator for about 1 hour.
8. Form small round dumplings.
9. Drop them into simmering salted water, turn off heat, let dumpling cook for about 12 minutes.

Toss dumplings in buttered bread crumbs and serve with a fruit sauce (strawberry, raspberry, apricot, etc.), if desired.

NUTRITION FACTS per serving: 505 calories, 231 calories from fat, 26.5g total fat (41%), 15g saturated fat (75%), 171.9mg cholesterol (57%), 946.5mg sodium (39%), 52.9g carbohydrates (18%), 6g fiber (24%), 17.6g protein (35%), 993 IU vitamin A (20%), zero vitamin C, 131mg calcium (13%) and 4.2mg iron (24%).

FRUIT SAUCE

You can make an easy fruit sauce by mixing 1 cup of jam with ¼ cup of water, rind and juice from 1 lemon and cook over low heat just until it simmers.

DUCKNOOR
Makes 4 servings

When the Europeans arrived to the *British Virgin Islands*, they added local ingredients to their recipes, many of these new ingredients were introduced to them by the *Arawak* and *Carib* natives. *Docknoor* looks like a tamale.

1 1/2 cups fresh corn, grated from the cob
3/4 cup sugar
1/2 teaspoon allspice
1/2 cup flour
1 coconut, grated

4 tablespoons margarine, melted
1/2 teaspoon nutmeg
Milk
Salt & pepper to taste
Banana leaves

1. In a large bowl, mix corn, sugar, allspice, flour, coconut, margarine, nutmeg, salt and pepper.
2. Mix in enough milk to make a batter of dropping consistency.
3. Pour about 2 tablespoons of batter on a piece of steamed banana leaf and tie securely. If banana leaves are not available, soaked corn husks or plastic wrap could be used, but the docknoor will not have the same flavor.
4. Put in boiling water and cook for 30 minutes or until corn mixture is firm.

NUTRITION FACTS per serving: 440 calories, 167 calories from fat, 19.3g total fat (30%), 8.4g saturated fat (42%), 2.1mg cholesterol (1%) 147.3mg sodium (6%), 66.4g carbohydrates (22%), 3.4g fiber (14%), 4.8g protein (10%), 567 IU vitamin A (11%), 5mg vitamin C (8%), 33mg calcium (3%) and 1.5mg iron (9%).

ESKIMO DUMPLINGS
Makes 4 servings

When the missionaries arrived in *Alaska,* they introduced dumplings to the *Eskimos*, which were added to a walrus stew called *kyusolik* (se MEATS), page 193).

2 cups flour
4 teaspoons baking powder
1 tablespoon fat, melted
1 teaspoon salt
1 cup milk

1. In a large bow, mix flour, baking powder and salt.
2. Make a well and pour milk and fat into center of flour mixture.
3. Mix just until flour is dampened.

4. Do not over mix.
5. Drop by tablespoons on top of kyusolik.
6. Cover and do not lift the lid for at least 12 minutes.
7. Cooking times is from 12 to 15 minutes

.

NUTRITION FACTS per serving without kyusolik: 292 calories, 50 calories from fat, 5.5g total fat (8%), 3.1g saturated fat (16%), 16mg cholesterol (5%), 956.1mg sodium (40%), 51.7g carbohydrates (17%), zero fiber, 8.5g protein (17%), 184 IU vitamin A (4%), 1mg vitamin C (15), 422mg calcium (42%), and 3.5mg iron (19%).

FRUIT DUMPLINGS
Makes 4 servings

These breakfast dumplings can be made with any one fruit, or a combination of fruits. Great served in a bowl, topped with milk or cream.

4 cups fresh or canned, drained, fruit, chopped
(apricots, fruit cocktail, pears, peaches, or plums)
1 cup sugar
2 cups water

1. In a deep, wide sauce pan, mix fruit, sugar and water.
2. Bring to a boil.
3. Cook until fruit is almost tender.

4. Drop batter by tablespoons on top of the fruit.
5. Cover, reduce heat to simmer and cook about 10 minutes.

NUTRITION FACTS per serving made with fresh apricots: 431 calories, 28 calories from fat, 3.2g total fat (5%), 1.1g saturated fat (6%), 57.3mg cholesterol (19%), 124.2mg sodium (5%), 95.9g carbohydrates (32%), 3.7g fiber (15%), 7.9g protein (16%), 4130 IU vitamin A (83%), 16mg vitamin C (26%), 154mg calcium (15%) and 2.6mg iron (15%).

DUMPLING BATTER

1 cup flour
1 teaspoon baking powder
1/2 cup milk
1 tablespoons sugar
1 egg, beaten

1. In a medium bowl, mix all ingredients together until dry ingredients are moistened.

2. Do not over mix.

Did you know that the pear is a member of the rose family and was native from central Europe to western Asia? There are more than 5,000 varieties of pears, making at least one variety fresh off the tree during most months. Pears are one of the few fruits where the flavor improves as it ripens, even after it is picked. Most pears become soft when ripe, but at least one small green variety remains firm and crunchy when ripe and sweet. You just have to cut one to taste and see. Pears are available fresh, canned and dried.

GERMKNODEL
Makes 10 servings

This yeast dumpling from *Austria* is filled with plum preserves, gently boiled, then topped with poppy seeds and butter.

4 1/2 cups flour	Milk, lukewarm
2 packages yeast	3/4 cup plum preserves
Pinch of salt	Poppy seeds
2 eggs, beaten	Butter, melted
1/4 cup butter	Sugar

1. I a large bowl, mix flour, yeast and salt.
2. Work in eggs, butter and milk to form a very firm dough.
3. Knead until smooth.
4. Cover with a towel and let the dough rest for an hour.
5. Form a long roll and cut into egg-size pieces.
6. Flatten and add 1 teaspoon of plum preserves.
7. Carefully wrap the preserves with the dough.

8. Cover and let rest for 1/2 hour.
9. Bring salted water to a boil in a large pot.
10. Drop in gently the dumplings and cook for about 6 minutes.
11. Remove from the water, rip open dumpling with two forks, top with poppy seeds, melted butter and some sugar.
12. Serve immediately

NUTRITION FACTS per serving: 317 calories, 54 calories from fat, 6.1g total fat (9%), 3.2g saturated fat (16%), 55mg cholesterol (18%), 72.7mg sodium (3%), 58.4g carbohydrates (19%), .7g fiber (3%), 7.7g protein (15%), 234 IU vitamin A (5%), 3mg vitamin C (4%), 35mg calcium (3%) and 2.9mg iron (16%)

HONEY YOGURT DUMPLINGS WITH APPLES
Makes 8 servings

Prior to refined sugar, honey was the choice as a sweetener. This healthy recipe by the *National Honey Board* is filled with goodness, low calories and fat, and high in vitamin C and calcium.

4 cups apple slices	1/3 to 1/2 cup honey
2 cups cranberry juice	1 cinnamon stick

1/4 teaspoon nutmeg

1. Combine apples, juice, honey, cinnamon and nutmeg in heavy skillet.
2. Mix well and bring to a boil.
3. Reduce to simmer, drop tablespoons of

dumpling batter over hot apple mixture.
4. Cover and simmer 15 to 20 minutes or until dumplings are cooked throughout and a wooden tooth pick inserted in center comes out clean

NUTRITION FACTS per serving: 217 calories, 13 calories from fat, 1.5g total fat (2%), .5g saturated fat, 28.2mg cholesterol (9%), 464.4mg sodium (19%), 50.6g carbohydrates (17%), 1.7g fiber (7%), 3g protein (6%), 89 IU vitamin A (2%), 26mg vitamin C (44%), 201mg calcium (20%) and 1.5mg iron (8%).

DUMPLING BATTER

1 cup flour	1 egg
4 teaspoons baking powder	6 tablespoons plain yogurt
1 teaspoon cinnamon	1 tablespoon honey
1 teaspoon salt	1 tablespoon milk

1 teaspoon orange peel, grated

1. In a medium, combine flour, baking powder, cinnamon and salt.

2. In another bowl, combine eggs, yogurt, honey, milk and orange peel.

3. Stir into flour mixture to form moist batter.

MATZO BALLS
Makes 4 servings

One might not think of this *Jewish* recipe from *Aron Streit, Inc. Matzo Bakers,* as dumplings, but that's exactly what they are. These dumplings are usually cooked in chicken soup during *Passover*; but since they are so good, enjoy them in place of potato hash browns.

1 cup matzo meal
1/2 cup water
4 eggs, beaten

1/3 cup shortening, melted
1 teaspoon salt
Dash of pepper

1. In a medium bowl, combine water, eggs, shortening, salt and pepper.
2. Add matzo meal, stir thoroughly.
3. Refrigerate 1 hour.

4. Form into balls and drop into 1 1/2 quarts of boiling salted water.
5. Cook uncovered for 20 minutes or until cooked

NUTRITION FACTS per serving: 459 calories, 208 calories from fat, 22.9g total fat (35%), 6g saturated fat (30%), 212.5mg cholesterol (71%), 597.1mg sodium (25%), 50.1g carbohydrates (17%), 1.8g fiber (7%), 12.2g protein (24%), 317 IU vitamin A (6%), zero vitamin C, 33mg calcium (3%), and 2.6mg iron (14%).

PLUM RAVIOLI
Makes 4 servings

Ravioli for breakfast! Sure why not, they are made of the same ingredients as bread, and these ravioli from *Hungary* are stuffed with plum preserves.

About 2 1/2 cups flour
3 eggs, beaten
Pinch of salt
Water

Vegetable oil
Cinnamon
Lemon rind, grated
Plum preserves

Egg whites, beaten slightly
Butter
Breadcrumbs
Powdered sugar

1. In a large bowl, mix flour, salt, eggs and enough water to make a dough, but not too stiff.
2. Divide into 3 loaves, brush with vegetable oil and let rest for an hour.
3. Roll out each loaf to the thickness of a noodle.
4. By rounded teaspoons, fill half the dough with a mixture of preserves, cinnamon and lemon rind, spaced out at intervals. If you have a ravioli mold, use it.

5. Brush egg white over the other half, fold over and press the edges and in between the fillings to seal.
6. Cut the dough with a ravioli cutter and cook in some boiling water.
7. Roll the cooked ravioli in breadcrumbs and fry in some butter.
8. Put on a serving plate and sprinkle with powdered sugar

NUTRITION FACTS per serving: 951 calories, 188 calories from fat, 21g total fat (32%),, 9.1g saturated fat (45%), 190mg cholesterol (63%), 292mg sodium (12%), 170.2g carbohydrates (57%), 1.6g fiber (6%), 21.6g protein (43%), 676 IU vitamin A (14%), 7mg vitamin C (12%), 69mg calcium (7%) and 8.1mg iron (45%).

Did you know that the plum is in the same family as almonds, apricots, cherries and peaches. Also, did you know that native plums have been found in Europe, Asia and North America? Plums are both sweet and tart, with a thick, juicy flesh. Plums are eaten fresh, stewed, dried (formerly called prunes), and made into desserts. Plums are available fresh and canned, or as preserves. Fresh plums are available in early summer to mid fall, and from Chile arrive in January and last until April.

STEAMED BREAD DUMPLINGS

Many cultures around the world steam their breads. Some are quite spicy and sweetened with molasses, others filled with meat and other ingredients like in China, while other steamed breads are really puddings. *Hope Irvin Marston* from Black River, New York offers this easy to make *Amish and Mennonite* recipe you can make from almost any bread dough.

1. Make your favorite white bread dough. (Frozen dough, thawed, can also be used.)
2. Let it rise until double.
3. Punch down and let it rise a second time.
4. Divide dough into bun size balls.

5. Place the balls in a buttered dish about 2 inches deep.
6. Steam over boiling water for 30 minutes.
7. Serve hot with fruit or milk.

NUTRITION FACTS per bun using FRENCH BREAD recipe: 123 calories, 20 calories from fat, 2.2g total fat (3%), .5g saturated fat (3%), zero cholesterol, 240.8mg sodium (10%), 21.6g carbohydrates (7%), zero fiber, 3.7g protein (7%), zero vitamins A and C, 60mg calcium 6% and 1.4mg iron (8%).

SWEET TAMALES
Makes about 20 sweet tamales.

In *Mexico* and *Central America* these sweet tamales are often found on the breakfast table. Some stuffed with meat or poultry and fruit such as pineapple. I have made this recipe easy, instead of being stuffed, all ingredients are mixed together, much like *Cuban* tamales. Tamales can be wrapped in green or dried corn husks or banana leaves. If using dried corn husks, soak for about an hour in hot water to soften them.

2 cups masa corn flour	1 teaspoon salt
1/2 cup rice flour	1 1/2 cups water
3 tablespoons brown sugar	1 cup lard or shortening
2 teaspoons cinnamon	1/2 cup butter, soften
1/2 teaspoon nutmeg	1 1/2 cups pecans or pine nuts
1 teaspoon baking powder	1 1/2 cups dried or candied fruit

(apples, apricots dates, mango, papaya, peaches, pears, pineapple, raisins or mixed)

1. If using dried fruit, plump in hot water for 15 minutes; drain before adding to dough.
2. Mix flours, spices, sugar, salt and baking powder in a large bowl.
3. Slowly add water and knead to form a dough.
4. Blend lard and butter together in another bowl.
5. Add flour mixture, 1/2 cup at a time until thoroughly combined.

6. Fold in nuts and fruit.
7. Place 1/4 cup of the dough on a corn husk, fold over to seal.
8. With string, tie both ends to hold in the dough.
9. Place on a rack in a large kettle and steam over boiling water for about 45 minutes
10. Serve warm.

NUTRITION FACTS per tamale with raisins: 280 calories, 181 calories from fat, 20.8g total fat (32%), 7.5g saturated fat (38%), 18mg cholesterol (6%), 173.5mg sodium (7%), 23.3g carbohydrates (8%), 2.2g fiber (9%), 2.3g protein (5%), 182 IU vitamin A (4%), 1mg vitamin C (1%), 44mg calcium (4%), and 1.3mg iron (7%).

Pine nuts are small oblong seeds extracted from certain pine cones. In the United States they are found in the Rocky mountains and along the Pacific coast. In Europe they are found in the Mediterranean. Pine nuts are used in many recipes in the Near East countries, especially in Arab lands. Pine nuts are also sold as *piñons* in the United States. When pine nuts are labeled *pignolias* they have been imported from Italy. Pine nuts are eaten fresh, added to meat recipes, and make wonderful cookies.

CHAPTER IX

EGGS

There's a great deal of confusion about eggs. Some nutritionists present serious health claims about cholesterol and fat. However, at the same time other nutritionists claim eggs provide the highest quality of protein in nature. It's the yolk that contains the fat and cholesterol, while the white has no fat or cholesterol and is higher in protein than the yolk.

For those concerned about fat and cholesterol in your diet, two egg whites can replace one whole egg in most recipes. Moderation is the key when it comes to any kind of fat. You can enjoy an egg or two in the morning, then limit other fats later in the day.

Almost every culture around the world eats eggs in one form or another. While chicken eggs are the most popular, duck and other eggs are also consumed.

Eggs Arnold (*USA*) 119

Eggs Benedictine (*cruise ship*) 119

Florentine Baked Eggs (*USA*) 120

Florentine Benedict (*Iowa*) 120

Fried Eggs with Creole Sauce (*Nicaragua*) 121

Garden Patch Scramble (*USA*) 122

Goldenrod Eggs (*Mississippi*) 122

Ham & Eggs Pesto (*California*) 123

Haystack Eggs (*Missouri*) 124

Huevos A La Mexicana (Mexico) 124

Huevos Casas (*Southwest, USA*) 124

Huevos Rancheros (*Mexico*) 125

Matzo Breil (*Israel*) 125

Orange Eggs Benedict with Orange Hollandaise (*Oregon*) 126

Poached Eggs with Hollandaise a l'Orange (*France*) 126

Scotch Eggs (*Nebraska & Louisiana*) 127

Shirred Eggs (*Mississippi*) 127

Smoked Salmon Tortilla (*Alaska*) 128

Son-in-Law Eggs (*Thailand*) 128

Yesterday's Dinner, Today's Breakfast (*18th Century, USA*) 128

CASSEROLES

Biscuit Egg Scramble (*Kansas*) 129

Creole Eggs Grinalds (*Kansas*) 129

French Country Strata with Zesty Cheese Sauce (*Kansas*) 130

Grace Eggs (*Louisiana*) 131

Hot Deviled Eggs (Ohio) 131

Morning Mexican Fiesta (*Illinois*) 132

Saucy Mediterranean Frittata (*Kansas 132*)

Sausage Cheese Strata (*Indiana*) 133

OMELETS

Banana Omelet (*USA*) 133

Breakfast in Austria

Bohemian Omelets with Prune Mix
(*Austria*) 124

Cheesy Chive Blossom Omelet
(*California*) 135

Chili Egg Puff (*Southwest, USA*) 135

Crayfish Omelet (*Louisiana*) 135

Dutch Omelet (*Netherlands*) 136

Frittata Omelet (*Italy*) 136

Ham Omelet (*USA*) 137

Ijja (*Egypt*) 137

Little Korean Omelets (*Korea*) 138

Low-Calorie Irish Mushroom Omelet
(*Ireland*) 138

Strawberry Omelet (*North Carolina*) 139

QUICHE

Quiche Pastry Crust 139

Apple Raisin Quiche (*Washington*) 140

Apricot Frittata (*Italy*) 140

Arizona Breakfast Pie,

(*Southwest, USA*) 141

Fiesta Quiche Ole (*Mexico*) 141

Florentine Cheese Tarts (

Pennsylvania) 142

Italiano Eggs Florentine (*Italy*) 142

Quiche Alsace (*Germany*) 143

Quiche Italiano (*Italy*) 143

Quiche Lorraine (*France*) 144

POPULAR QUICHE CHEESES

CHEDDAR CHEESE: Made from whole milk, cheddar cheese is generally colored a deep orange, but is available white. Cheddar is eaten fresh or used for cooking. Cheddar is mild when fresh, but made sharp by aging. Originating in Cheddar, England, the English Cheddar is drier and milder than American Cheddar.

COTTAGE CHEESE: It's the fresh curd from either whole or nonfat milk, with cream added, and is available salted or unsalted. Cottage cheese can be eaten cold or used for cooking.

MONTEREY JACK CHEESE: Made with whole, low-fat, or nonfat milk, Monterey Jack cheese has a mild flavor. An aged, dry Jack for grating is also produced. Monterey Jack cheese is also available flavored with jalapeño peppers, garlic, pesto and many other flavors.

MOZZARELLA CHEESE: Originally made in Italy from buffalo milk, today mozzarella is made with cow's whole milk, but it doesn't have quite the same flavor. Mozzarella cheese is white, semisoft, and mild. It is used for eating and cooking.

SWISS CHEESE: Known as "emmentaler" cheese in Switzerland, Swiss cheese is available both imported and American made. Swiss cheese has a mild, nutty flavor, is generally light yellow in color, has holes when cured, and is made from whole milk.

EGGS ARNOLD

Makes 4 servings

The *American Egg Board* realizing that many are concerned about eggs, created this recipe that is similar to *Eggs Benedict*, but contains 30 grams less fat. Muffins are not buttered, turkey ham has replaced fried Canadian bacon, and a mustard sauce has substituted for the hollandaise sauce. Compare the nutrition facts of this recipe with the following recipe Eggs Benedictine.

4 eggs
2 English muffins, split, toasted

8 slices ready-to-eat smoked turkey ham
Mustard sauce

1. In a skillet or saucepan, bring 2 to 3 inches of water to boiling.
2. Reduce heat to keep water gently simmering.
3. Break eggs, one at a time, into a saucer.
4. Holding dish close to water's surface, slip eggs, one by one, into water.

5. Cook until whites are completely set and yolks begin to thicken, but are not hard, about 3 to 5 minutes.
6. With slotted spoon, lift eggs and drain in the spoon.
7. Top each muffin half with 2 slices of the turkey ham, one of the poached eggs and top with 2 tablespoons of the mustard sauce

NUTRITION FACTS per serving: 226 calories, 76 calories from fat, 8.4g total fat (13%), 2.5g saturated fat (13%), 281.5mg cholesterol (94%), 540.5mg sodium (23%), 21.4g carbohydrates (7%), zero fiber, 15.6g protein (31%), 397 IU vitamin A (8%), zero vitamin C, 87mg calcium (9%) and 2.6mg iron (14%).

MUSTARD SAUCE

1 egg
1/4 cup water

1/4 cup vinegar
2 tablespoons sugar

1 to 1 1/2 tablespoons prepared mustard

1. In a small pan sauce, stir together all ingredients until well blended.
2. Cook over low heat, stirring constantly, until mixture thickens and starts to simmer.

3. Remove from heat.
4. Refrigerate any leftover sauce.

EGGS BENEDICTINE

Makes 4 servings

If you like eggs, then you will want to try this recipe from the chefs aboard *Royal Caribbean Cruise Line* ships. If fat and cholesterol is a problem, skip this recipe and try Eggs Arnold.

8 eggs, poached

4 English muffins, split, toasted

8 slices ham

HOLLANDAISE SAUCE

3 egg yolks
3/4 cup butter, melted

1/2 teaspoon lemon juice
Cayenne pepper to taste

Salt to taste
Parsley, chopped

1. Whip the egg yolks in a stainless steel bowl over steam or in a double boiler over boiling water.

2. Gradually add the melted butter, lemon juice and seasonings.
3. Cook only until thicken.

4. Do not over cook.
5. Fry the sliced ham in butter on both sides, then place on top of a toasted English muffin half.

6. Put a drained poached egg on top of the ham and cover all with Hollandaise sauce.
7. Garnish with chopped parsley

NUTRITION FACTS per serving: 720 calories, 478 calories from fat, 53g total fat (82%), 26.9g saturated fat (135%), 704.8mg cholesterol (235%), 1546.3mg sodium (64%), 29.2g carbohydrates (10%), zero fiber, 31.3g protein (63%), 2389 IU vitamin A (48%), 14mg vitamin C (23%), 194mg calcium (19%) and 4.7mg iron (26%).

FLORENTINE BAKED EGGS
Makes 4 servings

When the word "florentine" is used in a recipe, there will always be spinach as one of the ingredients. Cookbook authors *Renee Shepherd* and *Fran Raboff (Recipes from a Kitchen Garden)* says, *"Baked eggs make a wonderful breakfast or a Sunday brunch."*

1 cup spinach, chopped, cooked & well drained
1/8 teaspoon nutmeg
Salt & pepper to taste
1/2 cup heavy cream
3 tablespoons fresh basil, minced

8 drops Tabasco sauce
White pepper
4 eggs
1/2 cup Swiss cheese, grated
Parmesan cheese

1. Preheat oven to 375°F.
2. Mix spinach with nutmeg, salt and pepper.
3. Butter 4 large custard cups.
4. Line each with a nest of 1/4 cup of spinach.
5. Mix together the cream, basil and Tabasco.
6. Pour 1 tablespoon of cream mixture into the center of each spinach nest.
7. Break an egg into each cup and top with

another tablespoon of the cream mixture.
8. Sprinkle with white pepper and cheeses over the tops.
9, Place cups in a baking pan and pour boiling water into pan to come halfway up the side of the cups.
10. Bake eggs 10 to 12 minutes or set to your liking..

Serve with toasted English muffins.

NUTRITION FACTS per serving: 256 calories, 182 calories from fat, 20.7g total fat (32% DV), 11.2g saturated fat (566%), 267.3mg cholesterol (89%), 322.1mg sodium (13%), 5.8g carbohydrates (2%), 1.9g fiber (8%), 13.1g protein (26%), 4963 IU vitamin A (99%), 10mg vitamin C (17%), 317mg calcium (32%) and 3.1mg iron (17%).

VARIATION:

Cooked chopped Canadian bacon can be added on top of spinach.

FLORENTINE BENEDICT
Makes 4 servings

Barbara and Narsha Stensvad are the hosts at their *Chestnut Charm Bed & Breakfast Manor* at Atlantic, Iowa and serve their guests this benedict delight.

4 potatoes, washed, pierce several times with a fork

1. Bake unpeeled potatoes about 15 minutes in microwave.
2. Set aside to cool slightly.
3. Dice in medium cubes, fry in vegetable oil until brown.

4. Remove from pan, drain on paper towel; keep warm.
5. While potatoes are cooking make a sauce.

1 tablespoon butter or margarine
1 1/2 to 2 tablespoons flour
1/2 cup cheddar cheese, shredded

1/4 teaspoon dry mustard
1/8 teaspoon white pepper
1 tablespoon chives

1 1/4 cups skim milk

1. Melt butter in a sauté pan over very low heat.
2. Stir in flour, mustard, pepper, chives and mix until smooth
3. Add milk gradually; stir constantly.
4. Add cheese and continue to stir until mixture is thick.

5. If mixture is too thick, add a little more milk.
6. If mixture is not thick enough, mix a little flour with a little milk and stir into mixture.
7. Keep warm.

1 pound fresh young spinach leaves, washed, torn into small pieces
1/4 pound mushrooms, cleaned, trim bottom, sliced
8 slices bacon, cooked, drained on paper towel, broken into small pieces
4 red onion thin slices
8 eggs, poached

1. Divide browned potatoes into four equal portions and place on dinner plates.
2. Place spinach on top of hot potatoes.

3. Sprinkle on bacon, mushrooms and red onion slices.
4. Put two poached eggs per plate.
5. Add sauce and serve immediately. with toast

NUTRITION FACTS per serving: 515 calories, 241 calories from fat, 27.2g total fat (42%), 11.8g saturated fat (59%), 468.7mg cholesterol (156%), 1129.2mg sodium (47%), 39.5g carbohydrates (13%), 7.2g fiber (29%), 30.3g protein (61%), 8643 IU vitamin A (173%), 67mg vitamin C (111%), 435mg calcium (43%) and 6.5mg iron (36%).

FRIED EGGS WITH CREOLE SAUCE
Makes 2 servings

"If you like ketchup on your eggs," says *Margarita Aguilar* from Leon, *Nicaragua, "you will like this sauce even better."* The red pepper can be quite hot. If you like the sauce not too spicy, substitute the pepper of your choice.

1 onion, finely chopped
1 tomato, finely chopped
1 small red pepper, seeded, finely chopped
(optional)

1 teaspoon vegetable oil, lard or butter
1/4 teaspoon salt
1/4 teaspoon sugar

1 teaspoon vinegar

1. Sauté onion, tomato and red pepper in vegetable oil until tender.

2. Add remaining ingredients; simmer for 3 minutes.

4 eggs

Vegetable oil, lard or butter

3. Fry eggs until desired doneness.

4. Top eggs with sauce and serve immediately

NUTRITION FACTS per serving: 208 calories, 113 calories from fat, 12.6g total fat (19%), 3.4g saturated fat (17%), 425mg cholesterol (142%), 673.3mg sodium (28%), 10.1g carbohydrates (3%), 2.5g fiber (10%), 14g protein (28%), 3127 IU vitamin A (63%), 85mg vitamin C (142%), 89mg calcium (9%) and 2mg iron (11%).

GARDEN PATCH SCRAMBLE
Makes 2 servings

Garden vegetables add extra vitamins and minerals to these scrambled eggs. Recipe courtesy *American Egg Board.*

1 teaspoon butter or cooking oil
1/2 cup whole kernel corn (cut fresh from cobs, frozen or canned, drained)
2 tablespoons sweet red pepper, chopped
2 tablespoons green onions with tops, chopped

1 tablespoon water
4 eggs
1 teaspoon lemon juice
1/2 teaspoon basil leaves, crushed
2 tablespoons low-fat Swiss cheese, shredded (optional)

1. In 10-inch omelet pan or skillet over medium heat, melt butter.
2. Add vegetables and water.
3. Cover and cook just until peppers are tender, about 2 to 3 minutes.
4. In small bowl, beat together eggs, lemon juice and basil until blended.
5. Pour over vegetables.
6. As mixture begins to set, gently draw an inverted pancake turner completely across bottom and sides of pan, forming large soft curds.
7. Continue until eggs are thickened and no visible liquid egg remains.
8. DO NOT STIR.
9. Sprinkle with cheese, if desired.

NUTRITION FACTS per serving: 219 calories, 112 calories from fat, 12.6g total fat (19%), 4.6g saturated fat (23%), 432.6mg cholesterol (144%), 166.1mg sodium (7%), 11.1g carbohydrates (4%), 2.3g fiber (5%), 16g protein (32%),1190 IU vitamin A (24%), 17mg vitamin C (28%), 126mg calcium (13%) and 1.8mg iron (10%).

GOLDENROD EGGS
Makes 6 servings

At the *Corners Mansion* in Vicksburg, Mississippi, hosts *Bettye and Cliff Whitney* stuff popovers with these eggs. You can also enjoy them topped on an English muffin.

4 eggs
1 cup white sauce

Salt & pepper to taste
1/2 cup cooked corned beef or chipped beef

1. Cover eggs with cold water and bring to a boil.
2. Turn off heat, cover and let stand until water cools and eggs are hard cooked.
3. Reserve one yolk for garnish.
4. Chop eggs, add white sauce and season to taste.
5. Sauté corned beef is small amount of butter.
6. Add to egg mixture.
7. Split open the hot popovers and fill with creamed egg mixture or eat on top of an English muffin.
8. Force egg yolk through a sieve and sprinkle yolk on top of each.

WHITE SAUCE

1 tablespoon butter
1 tablespoon flour

1 1/4 cups milk
1/4 teaspoon salt

3 tablespoons half & half cream

1. In a sauce pan, melt butter.
2. Add flour and stir for 2 minutes.
3. Add milk, salt and half and half.
4. Simmer for 10 minutes.

POPOVERS

1 egg
1/2 cup milk

1/2 cup flour
1/8 teaspoon salt

1. Pout all ingredients in a blender and blend until smooth.
2. Grease 6 deep muffin tins.
3. Pour batter into muffin tins until about half full.

4. Bake in a preheated 450°F for 10 minutes. Reduce heat to 350°F and continue to bake another 35 minutes.
5. Remove from oven, run a knife around the edge of the cup, and remove

NUTRITION FACTS per serving (eggs only): 104 calories, 65 calories from fat, 7.1g total fat (11%), 2.2g saturated fat (11%), 152.2mg cholesterol (51%), 178.3mg sodium (7%), 2.1g carbohydrates (1%), zero fiber, 7.4g protein (15%), 212 IU vitamin A (4%), 5mg vitamin C (9%), 40mg calcium (4%) and .8mg iron (5%).

HAM & EGGS PESTO
Makes 4 servings

It's the pesto that makes this recipe special. It is served to guests at *Scott Courtyard* in Calistoga, California by *Lauren and Joe Scott*

6 eggs
1 teaspoon butter

1/4 cup ham, cubed or bacon, fried, drained
1/8 cup Parmesan cheese, grated

1/4 cup cream

1. Beat eggs and cream in a medium bowl.
2. Brown butter with ham in a small skillet.
3. Add egg mixture and scramble.

4. Place in four dishes, top with cheese and pesto.

NUTRITION FACTS per serving without pesto: 184 calories, 127 calories from fat, 13.9g total fat (21%), 6g saturated fat (30%), 341.3mg cholesterol (114%), 271.5mg sodium (11%), 1.8g carbohydrates (1%), zero fiber, 12.3g protein (25%), 670 IU vitamin A (13%), 3mg vitamin C (4%), 86mg calcium (9%) and 1.2mg iron (7%).

PESTO

Use leftover pesto with pasta, as a dip for chips, or topping for vegetables and baked potatoes.

5 cups fresh basil, stems removed
1 cup extra virgin olive oil
1 teaspoon salt

1 teaspoon pepper
1 cup walnuts
1 cup Parmesan cheese, grated

1. Mix all ingredients a blender except cheese.
2. Stir in cheese by hand.

3. Freeze leftovers in small containers

NUTRITION FACTS per tablespoon: 32 calories, 28 calories from fat, 3.3g total fat (5%), .5g saturated fat (3%), zero cholesterol, 37.8mg sodium (2%), zero carbohydrates and fiber, .7g protein (15), 95 IU vitamin A (2%), zero vitamin C, 16mg calcium (2%) and .1mg iron (1%).

BEATING EGGS; Eggs beat best to full volume at room temperature, whether it is the whole egg, the yolks or the whites. If recipe requires the egg to be slightly beaten, best only until frothy or foamy with large air bubbles. When beating only the yolk, use a narrow diameter bowl and beat until thick and lemon-yellow in color.

HAYSTACK EGGS
Makes 4 servings

This recipe has it all, bacon, eggs and potatoes. This dish is served by *Irv and Diane Feinberg* to guests at their *Garth Woodside Mansion* at Hannibal, Missouri.

1 3/4 ounce canned shoestring potatoes
4 eggs
1 tablespoon fresh parsley, chopped
1 cup Cheddar cheese, shredded
6 slices bacon, cooked, crumbled

1. Heat oven to 350°F.
2. Butter a pie pan and spread the shoestring potatoes evenly over bottom.
3. Make four indentations into potatoes down to the bottom of the dish, about 1 1/2 inches apart.
4. Carefully break one egg into each indentation.
5. Bake for 8 to 10 minutes or until eggs are almost set.
6. Top with cheese, bacon and parsley.
7. Return to oven and bake until cheese melts and eggs are set.
8. Cut into four wedges.

NUTRITION FACTS per serving: 312 calories, 211 calories from fat, 23.4g total fat (36%), 10.6g saturated fat (53%), 250.3 cholesterol (83%), 468.4mg sodium (20%), 8.1g carbohydrates (3%), .7g fiber (3%), 17.3g protein (35%), 837 IU vitamin A (17), 9mg vitamin C (14%), 247mg calcium (25%) and 2.2mg iron (12%).

HUEVOS A LA MEXICANA
Makes 1 serving

These eggs have much the same seasonings as *huevos rancheros*. However, these are mixed into the eggs, rather than topping the eggs.

1 tablespoon vegetable oil
1 tablespoon onion, chopped
1 tomato, chopped
1 chili serrano, chopped
1/8 teaspoon salt
2 eggs

1. Heat the oil in a skillet.
2. Add the onion and sauté until transparent.
3. Add the tomato, chili and salt and sauté over medium heat for 5 minutes (for a quick breakfast use 1 cup of salsa, mild or hot, in place of onion, tomato and chili).
4. Lightly beat the eggs, add to the tomato sauce and stir gently.
5. Cover and cook over medium heat for 2 to 3 minutes or until the eggs are set.

Serve with hot corn tortillas.

NUTRITION FACTS per serving: 357 calories, 211 calories from fat, 24.4g total fat (37%), 4.8g saturated fat (24%), 425mg cholesterol (142%), 451.1mg sodium (19%), 21.5g carbohydrates (7%), 3.7g fiber (15%), 16.6g protein (33%), 2556 IU vitamin A (51%), 388mg vitamin C (646%), 87mg calcium (9%) and 3.8mg iron (21%).

HUEVOS CASAS
Makes 1 serving

Huevos Rancheros are very popular in *America's Southwest, Mexico* and other Spanish speaking countries. This version by the *American Egg Board* contains 15 grams less fat then some recipes. A corn tortilla has replaced the flour tortilla, lettuce replaces the avocado, and mozzarella cheese for cheddar.

1 egg
1 teaspoon water
1 tablespoon part-skim mozzarella cheese
1 corn tortilla
2 tablespoons prepared salsa or taco sauce
Shredded lettuce

1. Spray an 8-inch skillet or omelet pan with a light coating of vegetable oil spray.
2. Over medium-high heat, heat coated pan until just hot enough to sizzle a drop of water.
3. Break and slip an egg into the pan.

4. Immediately reduce heat to low.
5. Cook until edges turn white, about 1 minute.
6. Add water, cover pan tightly to hold in steam, cook 3 minutes.
7. Sprinkle with cheese.
8. Recover pan and continue cooking until white is completely set and yolk begins to thicken, but Is not hard.
9. On a plate, place cooked egg on tortilla.
10. Top with salsa and lettuce.
11. For ease in eating, lap edges of tortilla over egg to form a roll.

NUTRITION FACTS per serving: 166 calories, 72 calories from fat, 8.1g total fat (12%), 2.6g saturated fat (13%), 216.6mg cholesterol (72%), 166mg sodium (7%), 13.6g carbohydrates (5%), 1.7g fiber (7%), 9.9g protein (20%), 898 IU vitamin A (18%), 4mg vitamin C (6%), 132mg calcium (13%) and 1.4mg iron (8%).

HUEVOS RANCHEROS
Makes 1 serving

In days gone by, two breakfasts were served in *Mexico*. The first coffee and pan dulce (sweet bread) in the early hours, and mid-morning the popular ranch-style eggs were eaten for a late breakfast. They would be served with *frijoles refritos* (fried beans) and tortillas.

1/4 cup vegetable oil, divided
1 tablespoon onion, finely chopped
1/2 garlic clove, finely chopped
1 tomato, chopped

1 chile serrano, finely chopped
1/8 teaspoon salt
1/8 teaspoon pepper
1 corn tortilla

2 eggs

1. Heat 1 tablespoon of oil in a saucepan, add onion and garlic and sauté until transparent.
2. Add the tomato and cook for 2 minutes.
3. Add the chili (remove the seeds and membranes for a less picante taste or leave them it for those who need a fiery breakfast to bring them awake), salt and pepper and cook another 3 minutes.
4. Taste to see if the seasonings are right for your taste.
5. Heat the remaining oil in a skillet, add the tortilla, fry for 30 seconds; drain.
6. Pour off the oil, add the eggs and fry until set.
7. Place the tortilla on a plate, top with the fried eggs and cover with the sauce.
8. Serve immediately

NUTRITION FACTS per serving: 777 calories, 575 calories from fat, 65.9g total fat (101%), 9.6g saturated fat (48%), 425mg cholesterol (142%), 491.8mg sodium (20%), 33.8g carbohydrates (11%), 5.1g fiber (21%), 18.2g protein (36%), 2617 IU vitamin A (52%), 388mg vitamin C (647%), 135mg calcium (13%) and 4.3mg iron (24%).

MATZO BREIL
Makes 2 servings

Jewish food laws state that dairy dishes must be cooked and eaten separately from meat dishes. Hence, milk and meat are never eaten together. However, eggs can be eaten with milk as in this recipe from *Manischewitz*.

3 matzos
2 tablespoons butter or pareve margarine
2 eggs

2 tablespoons water or milk
1/4 teaspoon salt
Dash of pepper

1. In a bowl, break matzos into pieces.
2. Cover with water and then pour water off immediately.
3. Press excess water out of matzos.
4. Melt butter in a skillet; add matzos and fry until lightly toasted.
5. Beat eggs with remaining ingredients.
6. Pour egg mixture over matzos and fry, stirring frequently, until eggs are set.

ORANGE EGGS BENEDICT WITH ORANGE HOLLANDAISE
Makes 4 servings

Peggy Kuan, innkeeper at *Chanticleet Inn* at Ashland, Oregon serves this recipe to her guests, especially during the Oregon Shakespeare Festival.

8 eggs
8 slices Canadian style bacon
4 orange scones (see BISCUITS & SCONES, page 33)

2 cups Hollandaise sauce
1 tablespoon fresh mint leaves, chopped

1. Sauté bacon until slightly crisp.
2. Drain on paper towel.
3. Slice scones in half, toast lightly; set aside.
4. Poach eggs.

5. Place 2 scone halves on plates.
6. Top each with a slice of bacon, a poached egg, and hollandaise sauce.
7. Garnish with mint and serve immediately

NUTRITION FACTS per serving with scones and sauce: 1219 calories, 801 calories from fat, 89.2g total fat (137%), 47.6g saturated fat (238%), 1059mg cholesterol (353%), 1813.4mg sodium (76%), 64.7g carbohydrates (22%), .3g fiber (1%), 39.8g protein (80%), 3958 IU vitamin A (79%), 75mg vitamin C (124%), 322mg calcium (33%) and 6.6mg iron (37%).

ORANGE HOLLANDAISE
Makes 2 cups

The name suggests this sauce originated in Holland, sorry, the sauce came from the *French*.

2 cups fresh orange juice
1 cup unsalted butter

6 egg yolks
1/2 teaspoon salt

1. Place orange juice in heavy saucepan, bring to a boil.
2. Reduce heat and simmer until thick and syrupy, about 10 to 12 minutes.
3. Should yield about 1/4 cup of syrup.
4. Set aside.

5. In another saucepan, melt butter and heat until bubbling.
6. Place egg yolks in food processor and process a few seconds while adding orange juice and salt.
7. Slowly add butter in a running stream.
8. Process a few more seconds, until thick.
9. Serve immediately

NUTRITION FACTS per half cup: 575 calories, 501 calories from fat, 56.7g total fat (87%), 32.7g saturated fat (163%), 450.4mg cholesterol (150%), 285mg sodium (12%), 13.4g carbohydrates (4%), .3g fiber (1%), 5.5g protein (11%), 2567 IU vitamin A (51%), 62mg vitamin C (103%), 62mg calcium (6%) and 1.3mg iron (7%).

POACHED EGGS WITH HOLLANDAISE A L'ORANGE
Makes 2 servings

While this recipe from *Grand Marnier Liqueurs* is similar to the above recipe, the preparation is different, as is the taste.

2 tablespoons lemon juice
2 tablespoons orange juice
1/4 teaspoon salt
1 tablespoon cold water
4 egg yolks

1 cup chilled unsalted butter, cut into tablespoons
2 tablespoons Grand Marnier
2 croissants, split lengthwise, heated
4 slices Canadian bacon, heated

4 poached eggs, freshly cooked

1. In a small sauce pan, cook lemon and orange juices with salt over high heat until reduced to 1 tablespoon.
2. Beat in the water.
3. In a medium unheated saucepan, whisk egg yolks until thickened and creamy.
4. Beat in the reduced juice.
5. Over very low heat, whisk in the butter, 1 piece at a time, adding additional butter before the previous butter melts completely.

6. Whisk in the Grand Marnier.
7. Keep the sauce warm.
8. Place the two halves of the croissant on each plate, top with Canadian bacon and the poached egg.
9. Divide the sauce between the servings, spooning over the eggs.
10. Serve immediately.

NUTRITION FACTS per serving (without croissant nutrition facts): 1457 calories, 1161 calories from fat, 127.1g total fat (196%), 70.8g saturated fat (354%), 1166.6mg cholesterol (389%), 1642.4mg sodium (68%), 37.4g carbohydrates (12%), 1.7g fiber (7%), 35.6g protein (71%), 5047 IU vitamin A (101%), 27mg vitamin C (46%), 150mg calcium (15%) and 4.4mg iron (24%).

SCOTCH EGGS
Makes 6 servings

The name suggests the recipe came from *Scotland*, but is actually an *English* invention. It was given the name because the *Scots* were known for being thrifty and finding ways to stretch the meat bill. There are two ways to make these eggs, either deep fat fried or baked. It's your choice. *Christie Miller* from Dunbar, Nebraska deep fat fries her scotch eggs.

1 pound pork, ground, divided into 6 portions
6 eggs, hard boiled, cooled, shelled

2 eggs (for coating)
Bread crumbs

1. Completely cover each boiled egg with a portion of the ground pork.
2. Beat 2 eggs lightly.
3. Coat each egg with the egg.

4. Roll in bread crumbs.
5. Fry in 350°F deep fat fryer until golden brown.

Pat Robertson from Transylvania, Louisiana prefers to roll them in crushed corn flakes and baked them in a 375°F oven until brown, about 30 minutes.

SHIRRED EGGS

Some cooks like to butter a small baking dish, then line it with dried bread crumbs, then drop two eggs in it and baked until done. At the *Corners Mansion* in Vicksburg, Mississippi, *Bettye and Cliff Whitney* make shirred eggs this way for their guests.

2 eggs
1/4 cup grated cheese, Swiss or haveriti
Salt & pepper to taste
1/8 teaspoon dry mustard

2 tablespoons cream
1 tablespoon dry bread crumbs
1 teaspoon butter
Paprika

1. Use one ramkin or individual baking dish per serving.
2. Spray ramkin with non-stick oil or grease lightly with butter.
3. Sprinkle grated cheese in the bottom of dish.

4. Break two eggs in each ramkin and season to taste with salt, pepper and mustard.
5. Top with cream, bread crumbs and butter.
6. Bake at 350°F for 15-20 minutes.
7. Sprinkle with paprika

NUTRITION FACTS per serving: 390 calories, 268 calories from fat, 29.6g total fat (45%), 15.3g saturated fat (76%), 487.4mg cholesterol (162%), 296.5mg sodium (12%), 8.2g carbohydrates (3%), .3g fiber (1%), 22.2g protein (44%), 1299 IU vitamin A 26%, zero vitamin C, 355mg calcium (36%) and 1.8mg iron (10%).

SMOKED SALMON TORTILLA
Makes 8 servings

Aboard *Carnival Cruise Lines* this recipe is served to passengers, especially in Alaskan waters.

10 eggs, beaten
3 or 4 potatoes, sliced thin, fried

1 onion, finely chopped
9 ounces smoked salmon, minced

Salt & pepper to taste

1. In a 12-inch oven-proof frying pan, arrange cooked potatoes, onions and salmon.
2. Season to taste.
3. Pour eggs over potato mixture until pan is about 3/4 full.

4. Cook on top of the stove until egg begins to set on the sides.
5. Transfer to 350°F oven and finish cooking until eggs are firm.
6. Divide into 8 wedges and serve with slices of smoked salmon

NUTRITION FACTS per serving: 178 calories, 71 calories from fat, 7.7g total fat (12%), 2.3g saturated fat (11%), 273mg cholesterol (91%), 400.8mg sodium (17%), 11.6g carbohydrates (4%), 1.1g fiber (5%), 15g protein (30%), 425 IU vitamin A (8%), 12mg vitamin C (20%), 46mg calcium (5%) and 1.6mg iron (9%).

SON-IN-LAW EGGS
Makes 2 servings

In *Thailand* this dish is usually served with steamed rice for breakfast.

3 tablespoons lard, butter or vegetable oil
5 eggs, hard boiled, shelled
1 tablespoon onion, minced
3 tablespoons sugar

2 tablespoons white vinegar
1 tablespoon cornstarch
1 cup cold water
1 teaspoon salt

1. Heat lard in a frying pan.
2. Drop in whole eggs and fry until golden brown.
3. Place eggs on a serving plate and slice into quarters.
4. Fry the onion in the same pan with vinegar, salt, and sugar, stir until it boils.

5. Dissolve the corn starch with the water and stir into the pan.
6. Cook until thick.
7. Pour sauce on top of the eggs.
8. Serve hot

NUTRITION FACTS per serving: 450 calories, 287 calories from fat, 31.8g total fat (49%), 11.6g saturated fat (58%), 542mg cholesterol (181%), 1242.6mg sodium (52%). 25g carbohydrates (8%), zero fiber, 15.7g protein (31%), 794 IU vitamin A (16%), zero vitamin C, 66mg calcium (7%) and 1.9mg iron (11%).

YESTERDAY'S DINNER, TODAY'S BREAKFAST
Makes 4 servings

Boo Heisey of San Diego, California, says, *"Back in the 18th century, breakfast was generally dinner's leftovers. In fact, leftovers were left on the table to savor or spoil as the case might be. About the only thing fresh were the eggs."* If you don't have leftovers, make up the sausage and potatoes fresh.

1/2 pound sausage, mild, hot or spicy
6 eggs

1 cup cheddar cheese, shredded
Salt & pepper to taste

1 pound potatoes, cooked, cubed, sliced, grated, or mashed

1. Cook sausage in frying pan until done.

2. Crumble the sausage with a spatula as you cook.

3. Drain off grease.
4. Add potatoes and heat.
5. In a bowl, beat the eggs, add cheese.

6. Pour into frying pan with sausage and potatoes and cook until eggs are set, stirring frequency.
7. Season to taste

NUTRITION FACTS per serving: 552 calories, 362 calories from fat, 39.9g total fat (61%), 16.6g saturated fat (83%), 387.1mg cholesterol (129%), 744.6mg sodium (31%), 22.3g carbohydrates (7%), 1.8g fiber (7%), 25.4g protein (51%), 777 IU vitamin A (16%), 23mg vitamin C (39%), 260mg calcium (26%) and 2.7mg iron (15%).

CASEROLES

By combining a number of ingredients with eggs, some interesting and tasty casseroles can be obtained. Many casserole recipes can be assembled the night before, covered and refrigerated, and baked in the morning. Here are a few examples.

BISCUIT EGG SCRAMBLE
Makes 5 servings

This recipe won first prize for *Tamara Datson* of Coffeyville, Kansas at the First Annual Kansas Egg Recipe Contest in 1985

2 tablespoons butter
8 eggs, beaten
5 ounces evaporated milk
2 cups American cheese, cubed

1 teaspoon prepared mustard
1/2 cup frozen peas, thawed, drained
3/4 cup cooked ham, cubed
10 ounce can refrigerated biscuits

1. In large skillet, melt butter.
2. Add eggs, scramble just until set; set aside.
3. Combine milk, cheese and mustard in a saucepan.
4.. Cook over low heat, stirring until cheese is melted.
5. Stir in peas and ham.
6. Pour cheese sauce over the eggs, stirring until combined.

7. Pour into an ungreased 8x8-inch baking dish.
8. Separate dough into 10 biscuits; cut each in half.
9. Place biscuit pieces, rounded edge up, in a single row around edge of dish.
10. Bake 375°F for 15 to 20 minutes or until biscuits are golden brown

NUTRITION FACTS per serving: 598 calories, 350 calories from fat, 38.8g total fat (60%), 18.2g saturated fat (91%), 415.4mg cholesterol (138%), 1404.2mg sodium (59%), 32g carbohydrates (11%), .7g fiber (3%), 30g protein (60%), 1445 IU vitamin A (29%), 9mg vitamin C (15%), 410mg calcium (41%) and 3.2mg iron (18%).

CREOLE EGGS GRINALDS
Makes 6 servings

Caren Rowland makes this New Orleans classic recipe for her family in Endora, Kansas. She assembles the recipe the night before and bakes it in the morning. Generally, *Creole* food is less spicy than most *Cajun* recipes.

1 onion, finely chopped
2 tablespoons bacon drippings
16 ounces can tomatoes
Salt & pepper to taste

1/2 cup butter, divided
3 tablespoons flour
1 cup milk
8 eggs, hard cooked, sliced

1 cup bread crumbs, toasted

1. In a skillet, brown onion in drippings.

2. Add tomatoes, salt and pepper; and simmer until onion is tender.

3. In another skillet, melt 1/4 cup butter; stir in flour.
4. Add milk and cook stirring until thickened.
5. Add tomato mixture and stir well.
6. Layer tomato mixture, eggs and bread crumbs in greased casserole.

7. Dot with the remaining butter (at this point, casserole dish can be covered and refrigerated until the next morning).
8. Bake at 400°F for 25 minutes

NUTRITION FACTS per serving: 405 calories, 260 calories from fat, 29g total fat (45%), 14.7g saturated fat (73%), 334.2mg cholesterol (111%), 622.5mg sodium (26%), 23.2g carbohydrates (8%), 2g fiber (8%), 13.3g protein (27%), 1502 IU vitamin A (30%), 13mg vitamin C (21%), 131mg calcium (13%) and 2.4mg iron (13%).

FRENCH COUNTRY STRATA
Makes 8 servings

Robert Logan of Garnett, Kansas won first place in the 1992 Eighth Annual Kansas Egg Recipe Contest with this recipe.

1 1/2 cups fresh vegetables, diced
(asparagus, green beans, snow peas, carrots or a combination)
1/4 cup fresh herbs, chopped
(chives, oregano, tarragon, parsley or a combination)

6 cups day old French bread, cubed
1 1/2 cups cooked meat, diced
(smoked turkey, ham, chicken or any combination)
6 eggs
2 1/2 cups milk

White pepper to taste

1. Blanch vegetables briefly in boiling water; drain well.
2. In a bowl, mix herbs with bread.
3. Spread 1 1/2 cups of bread cubes into the bottom of a well buttered 2-quart ovenproof casserole.
4. Scatter 1 cup of vegetables over bread cubes.
5. Top with another 1 1/2 cups of bread.
6. Cover with meat.
7. Add another 1 1/2 cups of bread.
8. Top with remaining vegetables.

9. Cover with remaining bread cubes.
10. In a bowl, combine the eggs, milk and white pepper.
11. Pour the egg mixture over bread cubes.
12. Cover and chill for at least 4 hours or overnight.
13. Bake uncovered at 350°F for 1 hour.
14. Let stand 15 minutes before serving. Serve with Zesty Cheese Sauce, if desired

NUTRITION FACTS per serving without sauce: 237 calories, 91 calories from fat, 10g total fat (15% DV), 3.7g saturated fat (19%), 200mg cholesterol (67%), 225.1mg sodium (9%), 15g carbohydrates (5%), 1.1g fiber (4%), 21.2g protein (42%), 546 IU vitamin A (11%), 5mg vitamin C (8%), 139mg calcium (14%) and 1.9mg iron (10%).

ZESTY CHEESE SAUCE

3 tablespoons butter
3 tablespoons flour
1/2 teaspoon dry mustard

Hot pepper sauce to taste
2 cups milk
1 cup sharp Cheddar cheese, shredded

1/4 teaspoon white pepper

1. Melt butter in a saucepan.
2. Stir in flour.
3. Stir in mustard and pepper.
4. Cook, stirring for about 1 minute. Do not brown.

5. Add milk and cook, stirring until mixture comes to a boil.
6. Add cheese.
7. Continue stirring until cheese is melted.
8. Season with hot pepper sauce.

Can be made ahead and reheated slowly.

GRACE EGGS
Makes 10 servings

This southern dish is served to guests at the *Bosobel Cottage Bed and Breakfast* in Monroe, Louisiana by hosts *Kay and Cliff LaFrance.*

2 1/2 cups seasoned croutons
2 cups sharp cheddar cheese, shredded
2 pounds sausage

8 eggs
3/4 teaspoons dry mustard
2 1/2 cups milk

1 can cream of mushroom or celery soup

1. Place croutons in greased 9x13-inch dish.
2. Top with cheese.
3. Cook sausage in a skillet until brown; drain well.

4. Place cooked sausage over cheese
5. In a bowl, beat eggs, mustard, milk and soup.
6. Pour over sausage.
7. Bake 1 1/2 hours at 300°F

May be refrigerated uncooked overnight. Also may be reheated.

NUTRITION FACTS per serving: 608 calories, 464 calories from fat, 51.2g total fat (79% DV), 20.6g saturated fat (103%), 264mg cholesterol (88%), 981 sodium (41%), 11.2g carbohydrates (4%), .5g fiber (2%), 572 IU vitamin A (11%), 2mg vitamin C (4%), 285mg calcium (19%) and 1.9mg iron (11%).

HOT DEVILED EGGS
Makes 4 servings

A visit to Kelleys Island, Ohio is a step back in time where *Bev and Paul Johnson* of the *Sweet Valley Inn* greet their guests in a 1892 Victorian home. This egg dish is on the breakfast menu, usually served with popovers (for popover recipe, see GOLDENROD EGGS, page 123).

6 eggs, hard boiled

1/4 cup mayonnaise
1 tablespoon cider vinegar
1/2 teaspoon dry mustard
1/2 teaspoon salt
1 tablespoon butter

1/3 cup onion, chopped
1/3 cup green pepper, chopped
8 ounces sour cream
1 can cream of mushroom soup

1 cup fresh mushrooms, sliced

1. Slice hard boiled eggs in half.
2. Separate the yolks from the whites.
3. In a bowl. blend mayonnaise, vinegar, mustard and salt and mix with the yolks.
4. Fill the whites with the yolk mixture and place in a buttered baking dish.
5. In a skillet, sauté the onion and green pepper in a little butter.

6. Add sour cream and soup.
7. Stir and simmer for a few minutes.
8. Spoon sauce carefully over deviled eggs.
9. Chop fresh mushrooms and sprinkle over top.
10. Bake 350°F for 15 minutes or until bubbly. Can be made and refrigerated overnight. Serve with popovers or biscuits

NUTRITION FACTS per serving: 387 calories, 308 calories from fat, 34.5g total fat (53% DV), 13.3g saturated fat (67%), 359.7mg cholesterol (120%), 803mg sodium (33%), 7.8g carbohydrates (3%), .5g fiber (2%), 12.1g protein (24%), 1124 IU vitamin A (22%), 9mg vitamin C (15%), 130mg calcium (13%) and 1.4mg iron (8%).

THE EGG: IS IT RAW OR COOKED? Suppose you have hard cooked some eggs and by mistake placed them in the carton with raw eggs. How can you tell which is which? No you don't need to crack the shell to tell. Just spin the eggs, and they will tell you. On a dinner plate spin each egg. The eggs that spin the longest are hard cooked. Now spin a hard cooked egg with a raw egg, and you will see the raw egg stop first., while the cooked egg will continue spinning

---

MORNING MEXICAN FIESTA
Makes 6 servings

Ingredients from *Mexico* has inspired many American cooks, like *Karen Barnett-Woods* of Naperville, Illinois, to include them in recipes.

4 cups corn or flour tortilla chips
1/2 cup mozzarella cheese, shredded
1/2 cup mild cheddar cheese, shredded
1 tomato, chopped
6 slices bacon, cooked
1/2 cup ham, cooked, chopped (optional)
1/2 teaspoon butter or margarine

1/4 cup mild salsa (optional)
1/2 cup canned corn, drained
1/2 cup chicken, cooked, chopped
1/4 cup milk
6 eggs
1/4 teaspoon salt

1. Grease the bottom and sides of an 8x8-inch baking dish with butter.
2. In a large bowl, beat eggs on high speed with milkand salt until mixture is fluffy.
3. Layer the greased baking dish with 1/2 of the tortilla chips, cheeses, bacon, chicken, tomato, corn, ham and salsa.

4. Repeat the process and then pour the fluffy egg mixture over the layers.
5. Cover the dish and place in microwave for about 5 to 6 minutes on high.
6. Remove cover and bake in the oven at 350°F for about 10 minutes or until center rises

NUTRITION FACTS per serving with ham and salsa: 1048 calories, 519 calories from fat, 58.9g total fat (91%), 15.3g saturated fat (77%), 255.3mg cholesterol (85%), 1365.6mg sodium (57%), 105g carbohydrates (35%), 11g fiber (44%), 29.9g protein (60%), 1064 vitamin A (21%), 11mg vitamin C (18%), 408mg calcium (41%) and 3.7mg iron (21%).

SAUCY MEDITERRANEAN FRITTATA
Makes 4 servings

Charlotte Altenbernd of Lawrence, Kansas, has combined ingredients from the America's with those of the *Mediterranean* to create this recipe with *Italian* flavors.

8 ounces canned tomato sauce
1/4 teaspoon dried basil
1/2 teaspoon dried oregano, divided
1/8 teaspoons dried garlic, minced
1 teaspoon dried onion, minced
1/4 teaspoon pepper, divided
1 tablespoon olive oil
1/3 cup onion, chopped

1 tomato, chopped
1 tablespoon fresh basil, finely chopped
1/3 cup orzo, cooked, drained
1/3 cup black olives, pitted, chopped
8 eggs
1/2 teaspoon salt
2 tablespoons butter
1/2 cup mozzarella cheese, shredded

1. Combine tomato sauce, dried basil, 1/4 teaspoon oregano, garlic, dried onion and 1/8 teaspoon pepper in a sauce pan; cook, stirring for 5 minutes.
2. Set the sauce aside and keep warm.
3. Heat olive oil over medium heat in ovenproof 10-inch skillet.
4. Add onion; cook 5 minutes or until tender.
5. Add tomato, fresh basil and 1/4 teaspoon oregano, stirring for 3 minutes.
6. Stir in orzo and olives. Remove from heat.

7. In a large bowl, beat eggs with salt and pepper.
8. Stir in tomato mixture; set aside.
9. Melt butter in skillet.
10. Add egg mixture; sprinkle with cheese.
11. Cook over low heat for 8 to 10 minutes until bottom and most of middle is set.
12. Place under broiler 1 to 2 minutes or until top is browned.
13. Serve with warm sauce.

SAUSAGE CHEESE STRATA
Makes 10 servings

This strata is somewhat related to *French* toast, because of the eggs and the bread. *Carol G. Traub* of South Bend, Indiana, services this recipe on special occasions.

1 pound bulk sausage, mild
10 slices white bread
8 eggs
3 cups milk

2 tablespoons parsley
1/2 teaspoon salt
1 teaspoon mustard
1 cup sharp cheddar cheese, grated

2 tablespoons onions or chives, chopped
2 tablespoons green pepper, chopped (optional), and/or 2 tablespoons green olives, chopped (optional)

1. Break up sausage and brown in skillet.
2. Drain on paper towel.
3. Remove crusts and break bread into small cubes; set aside.
4. In a large bowl, beat eggs, add milk, parsley and seasonings.
5. Stir in sausage, cheese and onion into egg mixture.

6. Add bread cubes.
7. Add green pepper and/or olives, if desired.
8. Turn into greased 9x13-inch casserole.
9. Bake uncovered in preheated 350°F oven for 40 minutes or until set and browned.
10. Cut into squares.

NUTRITION FACTS per serving with options: 411 calories, 269 calories from fat, 29.6g total fat (46%), 11.9g saturated fat (60%), 223mg cholesterol (74%), 732.2mg sodium (31%), 17.6g carbohydrates (6%), .7g fiber (3%), 17.8g protein (36%), 656 IU vitamin A (13%), 4mg vitamin C (6%), 238mg calcium (24%) and 2.7mg iron (15%).

OMELETS

Omelets need to be eaten fresh from the skillet or omelet pan to be good. It is best and easier to make small omelets, 1 or 2 servings, then a large omelet. Most recipes can be cut in half, thirds or quarters.

BANANA OMELET
Makes 2 servings

The American Egg Board created a natural breakfast that almost every kid will like, and its loaded with vitamins and minerals.

1 cup plain yogurt, divided
2 tablespoons light brown sugar
1 banana, sliced
4 eggs

2 tablespoons water
1 tablespoon wheat germ (optional)
1/4 teaspoon salt
2 tablespoons butter, divided

1/2 cup granola, divided (optional)

1. In a bowl, blend 3/4 cup of the yogurt with the brown sugar.
2. Stir in banana slices; reserve.
3. In another bowl mix eggs, remaining yogurt, water, wheat germ and salt with a fork.
4. Heat 1 tablespoon butter in an 8-inch skillet over medium high heat until just hot enough to sizzle a drop of water.
5. Pour in half of the egg mixture (about 1/2 cup).

6. Mixture should set at edges at once.
7. With pancake turner, carefully push cooked portions at edges toward center, so uncooked portions flow to bottom.
8. Tilt pan as necessary so uncooked eggs can flow.
9. While top is still moist and creamy-looking, fill with half of the banana-yogurt mixture.
10. Sprinkle 1/4 cup granola over filling, if desired.

11. With the pancake turner, fold omelet in half and turn out onto a plate.

12. Repeat procedure with second omelet.

BREAKFAST IN AUSTRIA

Austria was a melting pot of nationalities. The Germans contributed smoked pork, sausages and sauerkraut. From Bohemia and Moravia came dumplings and yeast pastries. Hungary introduced strudels (strudels originally came from Turkey). Switzerland was responsible for butter and cheeses. Poland for poppy seed pastries. And the coffee arrived from Turkey.

Some 16th century cookbooks have been found, with recipes starting out with "Take two eagles,". or a handful of lard with cooking instructions odd to today's standards. Like many other countries, Austria still uses the "weight system" for measuring ingredients, and is actually more accurate than using spoons and cups (spoons and cup measurements listed are approximate).

An Austrian breakfast today consists of fresh bread, butter, marmalade, cold meats, cheese and maybe some yogurt with fresh fruits and cereal.

BOHEMIAN OMELETS
Makes 2 servings

It is said, an *Austrian* artist created this simple omelet, which today is enjoy by many in *Austria*.

3 eggs, separated
3 tablespoons sugar
2 tablespoons flour
Prune mix
Powdered sugar

1. In a bowl, whip egg whites with sugar to an oily consistency.
2. In another bowl, beat yolks until smooth, add to whisked egg whites.
3. Carefully fold in flour.
4, Heat two 5 1/2 inch omelet pans and grease with butter, pour in batter, carefully bake on low heat for about 3 minutes.
5. Turn omelets, slowly bake other side.
6. Coat omelets with desired amount of the prune mix, fold, serve on plates, dusted with powdered sugar

PRUNE MIX

15 prunes
1/2 cup sugar
Water
Dark rum, to taste
3 tablespoons cream

1. Mix prunes, sugar and small amount of water in a baking pan.
2. Slowly roast in a 300°F oven.
3. Place in a blender, puree and flavor to taste with rum.
4. Add cream to make a smooth paste

While the recipe calls for prunes, most packages are now labeled "dried plums"

CHEESY CHIVE BLOSSOM OMELET
Makes 2 servings

Chives were part of Charlemagne's herb garden and the use of the flowers date back to Roman cooks. *Renee Shepherd* from Felton, California says *"Flowers are generally not available in the market, but are easy to grow at home."*

4 eggs
1 teaspoon water
1/4 teaspoon salt
1/8 teaspoon white pepper

1 tablespoon fresh parsley, chopped
1 tablespoon butter
3 chive blossoms, broken into individual florets
3 tablespoons Swiss cheese, grated

Garnish with whole chive blossoms

1. In a bowl, whisk together eggs, water, salt, pepper and parsley.
2. Melt butter in a 10-inch omelet pan just until butter sizzles (don't let it brown).
3. Pour in egg mixture, shaking pan immediately.
4. With the flat side of a fork, stir eggs and move and tilt pan in a circular motion until eggs begin to set.
5. Sprinkle chive florets and cheese down the center; allow cheese to melt slightly, then fold omelet over and serve immediately.
6. Garnish with chive blossoms

NUTRITION FACTS per serving: 245 calories, 170 calories from fat, 18.7g total fat (29%), 8.5g saturated fat (43%), 450.1mg cholesterol (150%), 486.5mg sodium (20%), 2.7g carbohydrates (1%), .2g fiber (1%), 16.1g protein (32%), 1442 IU vitamin A (29%), 3mg vitamin C (5%), 182mg calcium (18%) and 3.4mg iron (19%)

CHILI EGG PUFF
Makes 8 servings

It's the green chilies that give this baked omelet a south of the border flavor. *Barbara O'Neill* from Cypress, California, likes to make this recipe for a crowd.

10 eggs
1/2 cup flour
1 teaspoon baking powder
1/3 teaspoon salt

1 pint cottage cheese
1 pound Monterrey Jack cheese, grated
1/2 cup butter, melted
8 ounces green chilies, mild or hot, diced

1. Beat eggs in a bowl.
2. Add remaining ingredients, except chilies, beat slightly.
3. Stir in chilies.
4. Pour into a 9x13-inch butter baking dish.
5. Bake at 350°F for 35 minutes.
6. Serve with fresh tortillas and fresh fruit. Salsa is nice too

NUTRITION FACTS per serving: 496 calories, 324 calories from fat, 36g total fat (55%), 20.5g saturated fat (103%), 351.5mg cholesterol (117%), 864.5mg sodium (36%), 12g carbohydrates (4%), .4g fiber (2%), 31g protein (62%), 1622 IU vitamin A (32%), 69mg vitamin C (115%), 545mg calcium (54%) and 2.2mg iron (12%).

CRAYFISH OMELET
Makes 8 servings

In Louisiana, crayfish are affectionately known as mudbugs. In other parts of the world, they are often called fresh water shrimp. Even though crayfish are a member of the crustacean family, they are related to the lobster, not the shrimp. *James Provost,* with his wife *Betty*, of *Wildlife Gardens* in Gibson, Louisiana, prepares this recipe for their guests.

2 pounds raw crayfish, peeled
12 eggs, beaten

1 onion, diced
1/2 cup cheese (your choice)

1/2 cup margarine
Salt to taste

1. In a large iron skillet, cook crawfish and onions in margarine for about 10 minutes.

2. Gradually add beaten egg and scramble into the crayfish mixture.

3. Fold over and cover with cheese

NUTRITION FACTS per serving: 333 calories, 205 calories from fat, 22.2g total fat (34), 6.1g saturated fat (31%), 455.7mg cholesterol (152%), 405mg sodium (17%), 1.9g carbohydrates (1%), .2g fiber (1%), 29.5g protein (59%), 1077 IU vitamin A (22%), 2mg vitamin C (4%), 131mg calcium (13%) and 2.2mg iron (12%).

DUTCH OMELET
Makes 3 servings

Mina Baker-Roelofs of Pella, Iowa, says, "At the Eethuis Taverne in Amsterdam, Holland, the omelet includes cooked rice, applesauce and lettuce with strips of pimiento. The Dutch also would use potatoes. An omelet served with vegetables, ground meat or mushrooms would be known as a farmer's omelet."

6 eggs
1/3 cup milk or light cream
1/2 teaspoon salt

Dash of pepper
3 tablespoons butter or margarine
Vegetables, your choice, sautéed or cooked meat

1. In a bowl, beat slightly the eggs, milk, and seasonings.
2. Melt butter in a skillet.
3. Add egg mixture.

4. Run spatula around edge, lifting to allow uncooked portion underneath.
5. Brown bottom slightly.
6. Add vegetables or meat to half and fold in pan

NUTRITION FACTS per serving without vegetable or meat filling: 266 calories, 202 calories from fat, 22.3g total fat (34%), 10.7g saturated fat (54%), 459.3mg cholesterol (153%), 610.3mg sodium (25%), 2.5g carbohydrates (1%), zero fiber, 13.5g protein (27%), 1097 IU vitamin A (22%), zero vitamin C, 85mg calcium (9%) and 1.5mg iron (8%).

FRITTATA OMELET
Makes 2 servings

The American Egg Board says this *Italian*-style omelet goes together in minutes. Variations are only limited to your imagination or what ever might be leftover in the refrigerator (vegetables, meat, fish, chicken, herbs, etc.).

1 1/2 cup O'Brien frozen potatoes
1 tablespoon butter
4 eggs
1/4 cup cheese, shredded (cheddar, American, or Monterey Jack)

1/4 cup water
1/2 teaspoon dried Italian herbs (your choice)
1/4 teaspoon salt

1. In an 8-inch ovenproof skillet, cook potatoes oven medium heat in butter, stirring occasionally, until lightly browned, about 5 minutes.
2. In a bowl, beat together eggs, water, herbs and salt.
3. Pour into pan over potatoes.

4. Cover and cook over low heat until eggs are almost set, about 5 minutes.
5. Sprinkle with cheese.
6. Broil about 6 inches from heat until eggs are completely set and cheese melts, about 3 minutes.
7. Cut in half and serve.

NUTRITION FACTS per serving: 366 calories, 185 calories from fat, 20.6g total fat (32%), 9.7g saturated fat (48%), 455.2mg cholesterol (152%), 572.7mg sodium (24%), 26.1g carbohydrates (9%), 4.1g fiber (16%), 19.5g protein (39%), 1078 IU vitamin A (22%), 31mg vitamin C (51%), 165mg calcium (17%) and 3mg iron (17%).

HAM OMELET
Makes 6 servings

In the Montana mountains at Big Fork, *Natalie and BJ Burggraf* serve a hearty breakfast to their guests at their *Countryland Bed & Breakfast Resort* which includes this omelet.

4 eggs
1/2 cup prepared biscuit baking mix
1/2 cup skim milk
1 teaspoon salt

1 tablespoon Worcestershire sauce
2 tablespoons prepared mustard
1 teaspoon garlic powder
1 cup cheddar cheese, shredded

1/2 teaspoon cayenne pepper
2 zucchinis, chopped
2 tomatoes, chopped
1 onion, chopped
1 cup ham, cooked, cut up

1. Heat oven to 325°F.
2. In a bowl, beat eggs slightly.
3. Beat in baking mix, milk, salt, Worcestershire, and seasonings.
4. In an ungreased 8x8-inch baking dish, layer vegetables and ham.

5. Pour egg mixture on top.
6. Sprinkle with cheese.
7. Bake uncovered 40 to 50 minutes or until knife inserted comes out clean.
8. Let stand 12 minutes before serving

NUTRITION FACTS per serving: 245 calories, 126 calories from fat, 14.1g total fat (22%), 6.2g saturated fat (31%), 175.3mg cholesterol (58%), 1147mg sodium (48%), 14.1g carbohydrates (5%), 1.7g fiber (7%), 15.9g protein (32%), 921 IU vitamin A (18%), 20mg vitamin C (33%), 225mg calcium (23%) and 1.8mg iron (10%).

IJJA

There's just a hint of cinnamon, but it's the cinnamon, the parsley and the mint that makes this omelet unique from *Egypt*.

4 eggs
1/2 cup milk
1/8 teaspoon cinnamon
Salt & pepper to taste
1 teaspoon onion flakes

1/2 cup parsley, finely chopped
2 green onions, chopped
1/4 cup green mint, chopped (optional)
4 tablespoons vegetable oil

1. In a bowl, beat the eggs.
2. Add the milk and beat well.
3. In a small bowl add the onion flakes and work the seasoning in with your fingers.
4. Add to the eggs along with parsley, green onions and mint; mix well.
5. In a 400°F oven, heat the oil in an 8-inch square pan.

6. Pour the egg mixture into the pan and bake until done. The mixture can be tested with a toothpick, like a cake.
7. Cut into 4 squares and serve. This can be prepared on top of the stove like a regular omelet, turning once during cooking.

NUTRITION FACTS per square with mint: 260 calories, 175 calories from fat, 20.2g total fat (31%), 3.8g saturated fat (19%), 216.7mg cholesterol (72%), 124.2mg sodium (5%), 11.8g carbohydrates (4%), 2.8g fiber (11%), 10.4g protein (21%), 2397 IU vitamin A (48%), 24mg vitamin C (40%), 230mg calcium (23%) and 0.4mg iron (52%).

PREPARING EGGS: How many ways of preparing eggs can you think of? You can fry, scramble, poach, shirr, boil, stir omelets, and bake quiches. Do you know eggs will stay fresh for a long period of time if stored properly? Store with the large end up in the carton, and keep at a temperature just above freezing. That way they will keep for months.

LITTLE KOREAN OMELETS
Makes 6 servings

A meat ball wrapped with cooked egg, the flavor of sesame seeds and a dipping sauce makes this recipe from *Korea* a bit different. *Barbara Hobson* from Arkansas City, Kansas, says these little omelets also make nice appetizers.

1/4 pound lean ground round
1 green onion, finely chopped
1 garlic clove, minced
2 tablespoons white sesame seed
1/4 teaspoon salt
2 tablespoons soy sauce

Peanut oil
6 eggs, beaten
1/2 cup soy sauce
1/2 cup cider vinegar
1/4 cup sugar
1 tablespoon pine nuts, finely chopped (optional)

1. Mix the meat, onion and garlic in a small bowl; set aside.
2. Cook the sesame seed in a skillet over medium heat until golden brown.
3. Place the seeds in a bowl along with the salt and crush them with the back of a tablespoon.
4. Add the seeds and 2 tablespoons of soy sauce to the meat mixture; mix well.
5. Form the meat into 1/2 inch balls.
6. In a skillet, sauté in peanut oil over medium heat.
7. Place some peanut oil in another skillet over medium heat.
8. Place 1 tablespoon of the beaten eggs on the heated surface and allow it to spread in a circle about 2 ½ inches in diameter.

9. As soon as the edges become firm, place a meatball on one half the circle.
10. Using a spatula, turn the other half of the egg circle over the meatball.
11. Press edges slightly so that the runny portion of the circle completely seals the meatball.
12. Continue to sauté for a few seconds longer until the omelets are firm and golden brown.
13. Place the omelets in an oven proof platter in a 250°F oven until you have used all of the egg and meatballs.
14. For the dipping sauce, mix 1/2 cup soy sauce, vinegar and sugar together.
15. Place sauce in serving dish. Sprinkle with pine nuts. Serve as a dip with the little omelets

NUTRITION FACTS per serving: 206 calories, 102 calories from fat, 11.6g total fat (18%), 3.5g saturated fat (18%), 226.7mg cholesterol (76%), 1275.5mg sodium (53%), 14.3g carbohydrates (5%), .9g fiber (4%), 12.3g protein (25%), 417 IU vitamin A (8%), 5mg vitamin C (8%), 54mg calcium (5%) and 2.3mg iron (13%).

LOW-CALORIE IRISH MUSHROOM OMELET
Makes 4 omelets

Okay, you've searched through the egg recipes and many contain too much fat for your diet. If that is the case try this recipe by *The Limerick Bacon Company*.

2 cups egg substitute
4 teaspoons skim milk

Salt & pepper to taste
Mushroom filling

1. Spray an 8-inch non-stick skillet with vegetable cooking spray; set over medium heat.
2. For each omelet, in a small bowl, beat 1/2 cup egg substitute with 1 teaspoon milk and salt and pepper to taste.
3. Pour into skillet.

4. Cook, lifting edges to allow uncooked portion to flow underneath.
5. When almost set, spoon 1/4 of the mushroom filling over half of the omelet.
6. With a spatula, fold other half over filling; slide onto a plate.
7. Serve immediately

NUTRITION FACTS per omelet: 148 calories, 55 calories from fat, 6.1g total fat (9%), 1.4g saturated (7%), 4g cholesterol (1%), 287.9mg sodium (12%), 5.4g carbohydrates (2%), 1.2g fiber (5%), 18g protein (36%), 3207 IU vitamin A (64%), 8mg vitamin C (13%), 112mg calcium (11%) and 5.4mg iron (30%).

MUSHROOM FILLING

4 slices Irish bacon, diced 1/2 cup scallions, chopped	3 cups fresh mushrooms, sliced	2 tablespoons parsley, minced

Salt & pepper to taste

1. In non-stick skillet cook bacon and scallions over medium heat until bacon begins to brown and onions are tender.
2. Increase heat to medium-high; add mushrooms.
3. Cook, stirring frequently, until mushrooms begin to brown.
4. Stir in salt and pepper to taste.
5. Remove from heat.
6. Stir in parsley.

STRAWBERRY OMELET
Makes 4 servings

A delightful southern breakfast is served to guests at the *Buttonwood Inn*, Franklin, North Carolina, by *Liz Oehser*, which includes this delicious strawberry omelet.

1/2 cup butter (unsalted), soften	3 tablespoons sugar, divided
1/2 cup strawberry jam	1 tablespoon rum
2 teaspoons lemon juice	Pinch of salt
3 eggs, separated (at room temperature)	2 tablespoons sour cream

8 fresh strawberries, sliced

1. In a bowl, whip butter, jam and juice until smooth; set aside.
2. Butter 10-inch oven proof skillet or omelet pan.
3. Preheat oven to 350°F.
4. In a second bowl, beat yolks with 1 tablespoon of sugar and rum.
5. In a third bowl, add pinch of salt to whites and beat until frothy.
6. Gradually add remaining sugar to the whites and beat until peaks form.
7. Fold whites into yolks.
8. Pour into skillet.
9. Bake 20 minutes.
10. Remove from oven and spread strawberry butter (reserving 2 tablespoons) on half of the omelet and fold over.
11. Top with remaining 2 tablespoons strawberry butter, sour cream, and sliced strawberries

NUTRITION FACTS per serving: 502 calories, 254 calories from fat, 29.2g total fat (45%), 16.3g saturated fat (81%), 223.9mg cholesterol (75%), 73.3mg sodium (3%), 56.8g carbohydrates (19%), 7.3g fiber (29%), 7.3g protein (15%), 1236 IU vitamin A (25%), 173mg vitamin C (288%), 83mg calcium (8%) and 1.9mg iron (11%).

QUICHE

It has been said, *Real Men Don't Eat Quiche.* Nonsense! A quiche can be a hearty breakfast that anyone can enjoy. Basically, a quiche is a custard pie filled with all kinds of goodies. Originally, this *French* pie from the province of Lorraine was made with eggs, cheese, cream and bacon, seasoned with a little salt and pepper. The quiche has been Americanized and hardly resembles the early recipe from Lorraine, France. Quiche also makes wonderful appetizers. Just cut into 12 wedges, instead of 6.

QUICHE PASTRY CRUST

If a quiche recipe calls for a pastry crust, this recipe works well with a 9-inch pie tin.

1 ½ cups flour	½ cup shortening
¾ teaspoon salt	3 tablespoons water (about)

1. Mix flour and salt.
2. Cut in the shortening until mixture resembles coarse bread crumbs.
3. Do not over mix.
4. Sprinkle with water, a few drops at a time, and mix lightly with a fork until all dry ingredients are moistened.

5. Knead two or three times and press into a ball.
6. Do not handle anymore than necessary.
7. Chill for about 20 minutes.
8. Roll out to fit pie tin.
9. Fold crust in half and in half again.
10. Place in pie tin with the point in the middle of the plate; unfold and flute the edges

YES, YOU CAN MICROWAVE YOUR QUICHE

Most quiche recipes can be microwaved, if in a glass or other microwave safe baking container. Cook on full power, rotating dish ½ turn once or twice for 5 minutes. Continue cooking on 50% power, rotating dish ¼ turn 2 to 3 times, until puffed in center and knife inserted near center comes out clean, about 8 to 12 minutes. Best to let the quiche stand for about 10 minutes to complete the cooking process.

APPLE RAISIN QUICHE
Makes 6 servings

This quiche is served at the *Chambered Nautilus Inn* in Seattle Washington and is almost like an apple pie. Try it for breakfast or for a late night snack.

Pastry for a 9-inch pie crust (page 139)
3 3/4 cups Granny Smith apples, peeled, cored, thinly sliced
1/2 cup raisins
1 cup whipping cream
1/4 cup light brown sugar
2 teaspoons cinnamon
3 cups Monterey Jack cheese, shredded
3 eggs

1. Preheat oven to 400°F.
2. Line 9-inch pie tin with pastry.
3. Crimp edge and prick bottom and sides with a fork at 1/2-inch intervals.
4. To prevent shrinkage, set 8-inch round cake pan into pie shell; bake for 6 minutes.
5. Remove cake pan and continue to bake shell until lightly browned, about 10 minutes.
6. Remove from oven.
7. Layer half the apples, raisins, sugar and
cinnamon in pie shell; repeat layers.
8. Cover completely with cheese.
9. Beat eggs with cream.
10. Make a small hole in cheese; pour egg mixture into hole.
11. Cover hole with cheese.
12. Bake about 1 hour until top is browned and apples are tender when tested with a pick.
13. Cool 10 to 15 minutes before cutting into wedges

NUTRITION FACTS per serving: 740 calories, 459 calories from fat, 51.7g total fat (80%), 24.9g saturated fat (125%), 210.5mg cholesterol (70%), 619.2mg sodium (26%), 49.5g carbohydrates (17%), 2.2g fiber (9%), 21.5g protein (43%), 1277 IU vitamin A (26%), 4mg vitamin C (6%), 484mg calcium (48%) and 3mg iron (16%).

APRICOT FRITTATA
Makes 6 servings

This *Italian*-style quiche has no crust. *The California Apricot Advisory Board* says this quiche is a snap to prepare. The curry and apricots are a pleasing complement that makes this a sensation for that special breakfast.

17 ounce canned apricot halves in syrup
1 onion, sliced
2 tablespoons vegetable oil
1 teaspoon garlic, minced
1 teaspoon curry powder
10 eggs, beaten with a fork
1/2 teaspoon salt
1/4 teaspoon pepper

1. Drain apricots, reserving syrup.
2. In a 10-inch oven safe skillet, sauté onion in the oil until golden.
3. Add garlic and curry and sauté briefly.
4. Add eggs, salt, pepper and 1/4 cup reserved apricot syrup to the skillet.

5. Stir and place in 400°F oven for 10 to 12 minutes or until mostly set.
6. Arrange drained apricots in a ring on top.
7. Return to the oven and bake 5 to 6 minutes until set.

NUTRITION FACTS per serving: 238 calories, 116 calories from fat, 13g total fat (20%), 3.1g saturated fat (16%), 354.2mg cholesterol (118%), 377.7mg sodium (16%), 19.7g carbohydrates (7%), 1.5g fiber (6%), 11.1g protein (22%), 1521 IU vitamin A (30%), 4mg vitamin C (6%), 62mg calcium (6%) and 1.6mg iron (9%).

ARIZONA BREAKFAST PIE
Makes 6 servings

Carol Salazar from Florence, Arizona, says the local cowboys enjoy this quiche, just as long as you don't call it a quiche.

1 pound bulk pork sausage
1 9-inch unbaked pie shell (page139)
1 1/2 cups Jack cheese, shredded
2 tablespoons pimento, diced

1/3 cup green chili, hot or mild, cut into strips
3 tablespoons onions
4 eggs, beaten
1 cup cream

1. Prepare sausage, breaking up pieces, cook until done; drain.
2. In the unbaked pie shell, sprinkle the cooked sausage, top with cheese, pimento, chili and onion.
3. Mix eggs and cream, pour over ingredients in pie shell.

4. Bake at 375°F for 40 to 45 minutes or until eggs are set.
5. Cool for about 10 minutes, slice and serve.
6. Can be prepared the night before and refrigerated (add 5-minutes to baking time).

NUTRITION FACTS per serving: 835 calories, 628 calories from fat, 69.7g total fat (107%), 27.8g saturated fat (139%), 252.9mg cholesterol (84%), 997.9mg sodium (42%), 27.4g carbohydrates (9%), .2g fiber (1%), 24.2g protein (48%), 994 IU vitamin A (20%), 10mg vitamin C (17%), 283mg calcium (28%) and 3mg iron (16%).

FIESTA QUICHE OLÉ
Makes 6 servings

Charlotte Altenbernd of Lawrence, Kansas says you don't need to go south of the border to enjoy the flavors of *Mexico*.

Pastry for 9-inch pie (page 139)
6 eggs, beaten
2 avocados, peeled, seeded, finely chopped
1/4 cup onion, finely chopped
2 tablespoons lemon juice
1 tablespoon canned green chilies, chopped
1 garlic clove, minced
1 green or red bell pepper, chopped

1 onion, chopped
1 tablespoon vegetable oil
1/2 pound ground beef
1 1/4 ounce package taco seasoning mix
8 ounce canned tomato sauce
1 1/4 cups Cheddar cheese, grated, divided
1/2 milk
1/4 cup black olives, pitted, thinly sliced

1 tomato, chopped

1. Prepare pastry for 9-inch pie tin.
2. Brush inside of pie crust with small amount of beaten eggs.

3. Bake pie crust, uncovered, in 425°F oven for 5 minutes; remove.
4. Combine avocados, 1/4 cup onion, lemon juice, chilies and garlic in blender container.

141

5. Blend until smooth; cover and refrigerate.
6. In a skillet, sauté pepper and onion in oil until crisp-tender.
7. Remove to a small bowl; set aside.
8. In same skillet, brown ground beef until crumbly; drain.
9. Add taco mix, tomato sauce to the cooked hamburger; blend well.
10. Bring to a boil; reduce heat and simmer, uncovered 15 minutes.
11. Stir in onion and peppers.
12. Combine eggs, 3/4 cup of cheese and milk; stir in meat mixture.
13. Pour into pie crust.
14. Bake uncovered at 350 F for 40 minutes.
15. Sprinkle top with 1/4 cup of cheese and bake 5 minutes longer.
16. Let stand 5 minutes.
17. Before serving, surround outer edges of quiche with avocado mixture, sprinkling with olives, tomatoes and remaining cheese.

NUTRITION FACTS per serving: 733 calories, 482 calories from fat, 54.3g total fat (84%), 17.3g saturated fat (87%), 272.2mg cholesterol (91%), 1168.6mg sodium (49%), 39g carbohydrates (13%), 5.4g fiber (22%), 24.9g protein (50%), 1615 IU vitamin A (32%), 33mg vitamin C (55%), 263mg calcium (26%) and 4.4mg iron (24%).

FLORENTINE CHEESE TARTS
Makes about 30 tarts

Innkeepers *Susan and William Day* serve these tarts to guests at their *Beechmont Bed and Breakfast Inn*, in Hanover, Pennsylvania.

18 eggs
1/2 cup flour
2 tablespoons sugar
1 pound cheddar cheese, shredded
1 pound cottage cheese, large curd
1/2 cup butter
1 onion, minced
12 ounce canned evaporated milk

10 ounce package frozen spinach, thawed
1 pound low fat turkey sausage, ground or ham, diced
1/2 teaspoon celery seed
1/2 teaspoon dry mustard
1/2 teaspoon Bon Appetit seasoning
1/2 teaspoon nutmeg
2 tablespoons flour

1. Sauté together sausage, butter, onion, spinach, spices and 2 tablespoons of flour; set aside.
2. In a large bowl, whisk eggs, sugar, 1/2 cup of flour, and cheeses.
3. Add sausage mixture.
4. Ladle into greased muffin cups.
5. Bake for 30 minutes at 325°F.
6. Cool completely.
7. Slide knife around each tart to loosen and remove from pans.
8. Reheat on baking sheet at 325°F for 15 minutes.

NUTRITION FACTS per tart: 205 calories, 61% calories from fat, 14g total fat (21%), 5g saturated fat (36%), 165mg cholesterol (55%), 6g carbohydrates, .4g fiber, 14g protein (27%), 461mg sodium (19%), 180mg calcium (17%), 7mg vitamin C (11%), 1,254 IU vitamin A (25%) and 1mg iron (5%)

ITALIANO EGGS FLORENTINE
Makes 6 servings

Sallie and Welling Clark from the *Holden House* in Colorado Springs, Colorado, have bought a little bit of *Italy* to their overnight guests.

2 pie crusts, ready made
4 eggs
2 cups milk
4 tablespoons flour
16 ounces frozen spinach, thawed
1 cup cheese (Swiss, jack or mozzarella), shredded

8 slices turkey bacon, sliced in half
Italian seasoning
Nutmeg
Marinara sauce, small jar
Parsley
Parmesan cheese, shredded

1. Divide each pie crust into four sections and place one piece of the cut crust in eight 12-ounce size quiche dishes (will form a triangular shaped crust in each of the 8 dishes).
2. In a bowl, beat eggs, milk and flour; set aside.
3. Evenly divide spinach into the quiche dishes on top of the crust.
4. Pour egg mixture equally on top of the spinach, top with cheese and 2 half slices of bacon over cheese.
5. Sprinkle with Italian seasonings and nutmeg.
6. Bake in a 375°F oven for 30 to 40 minutes or until eggs are firm and slightly brown on top.
7. Garnish with 3 tablespoons of marinara sauce, parmesan cheese and parsley

NUTRITION FACTS per serving: 411 calories, 209 calories from fat, 23.4g total fat (36%), 8.6g saturated fat (43%),144.3mg cholesterol (48%), 809.1mg sodium (34%), 30.6g carbohydrates (10%), 1.7g fiber (7%), 20.3g protein (41%), 4560 IU vitamin A (91%), 19mg vitamin C (32%), 352mg calcium (35%) and 4.9mg iron (27%).

QUICHE ALSACE
Makes 6 servings

The *Germans* in the Alsace province claim they invented the quiche, not the *French*. This recipe from the *American Egg Board* is similar to *"Quiche Lorraine,"* but contains 22 grams less fat. A noodle crust has been substituted for a pastry crust, buttermilk for half and half, turkey ham for bacon, and 50% less cheese, as well as reduced fat cheese.

6 eggs, divided
2 cups fine egg noodles, cooked
1 cup buttermilk
1/4 teaspoon nutmeg
8 ounce canned sauerkraut, washed, drained

1/2 cup reduce-fat Swiss cheese, shredded
2 slices ready-to-eat smoked turkey ham, chopped
2 tablespoons green onions with tops, finely chopped

1. In medium bowl, beat 1 egg.
2. Stir in noodles until well blended.
3. To form crust, press noodles over bottom and up sides of lightly greased 9-inch quiche dish.
4. Beat together remaining 5 eggs, buttermilk and nutmeg until well blended.
5. Stir in remaining ingredients until well combined.
6. Pour into prepared crust.
7. Bake in preheated oven at 375°F until puffed in center and knife inserted near center comes out clean, about 30 to 40 minutes.

NUTRITION FACTS per serving: 209 calories, 75 calories from fat, 8.3g total fat (13%), 2.8g saturated fat (14%), 248.9mg cholesterol (83%), 731.9mg sodium (30%), 13.9g carbohydrates (5%), 1.4g fiber (5%), 19.1g protein (38%), 379 IU vitamin A (8%), 6mg vitamin C (11%), 183mg calcium (18%) and 2.9mg iron (16%).

QUICHE ITALIANO
Makes 6 servings

These *Italian* ingredients gives a new twist to the original recipe.

6 eggs, divided
1/4 cup Parmesan cheese, grated
2/3 cup orzo (rice-shaped pasta) cooked, drained
1/2 cup skim milk
1/2 cup mozzarella cheese, shredded

3/4 teaspoons Italian seasoning, crushed
2 cups zucchini, sliced, cooked, drained
1/2 cup cured prosciutto (Italian ham) or cooked ham, chopped

1. In medium bowl, beat together 1 egg and the Parmesan cheese.
2. Stir in orzo until well blended.
3. To form crust, spread orzo mixture over bottom and up sides of lightly greased deep 9-inch quiche dish or pie tin.

4. Beat together remaining eggs, milk and seasoning until well blended.
5. Stir in remaining ingredients until well combined.
6. Pour into prepared crust.

.

7. Bake in preheated 375°F oven until puffed in center and knife inserted near center comes out clean, about 30 to 40 minutes.
8. Let stand 5 minutes before serving

NOTE: *The American Egg Board* says that the quiche can take on many other international flavors. In *Spain*, mashed beans could be used to make a crust and fish for the meat. In the *Orient,* let the cooked rice from the crust, with oriental vegetables and pork in place of the bacon. In the *Southern United States*, you will find that grits make a great crust. And in the *Western United States*, hash browns are favored for the crust.

QUICHE LORRAINE
Makes 6 servings

The original quiche from the Lorraine province of *France* is made with cream, bacon and Swiss cheese.

1 9-inch pastry shell
1/2 pound bacon, cooked crisp, drained, crumbled
1/2 onion, sliced thinly
4 eggs

1 cup milk
1 cup cream
1 teaspoon salt
Pinch white pepper
Pinch cayenne

1/2 pound Swiss cheese, grated

1. Preheat oven to 400°F.
2. 9-inch pie tin with pastry.
3. Flute the edges for a standing rim.
4. Chill while preparing filling.
5. In a bowl mix eggs, milk, cream, salt, peppers and beat thoroughly with rotary beater until foamy.

6. Arrange bacon and onion in pastry-lined pie tin.
7. Add cheese to form next layer.
8. Pour egg mixture over the cheese.
9. Bake for 35 to 40 minutes, or until a knife comes out clean from the center of the mixture.
10. Remove from oven and cool for 10 minutes before serving.

SEPERATING EGGS: It's best to separate eggs when they are cold, since the yolks are less likely to break. Carefully crack the egg in the center, pull apart over a bowl and let the whites pour into the bowl. Pour the remaining yolk into the other half of the shell to remove the remaining whites. If the yolk breaks, even a little yolk in the whites will prevent the whites from beating to full volume. Best to separate the egg in a small bowl, then add the separated whites to a larger bowl with the other whites, thus preventing any yolk to contaminating a whole bowl of whites. If a small bit of yolk falls into the whites, it generally can be removed with the corner of a paper towel.

CHAPTER X

FRENCH TOAST

Have you ever wondered where recipes originated? Take French toast for an example. Do the French eat French toast for breakfast? Maybe, but not like the recipes in this chapter, since most of these recipes have been Americanized.

In France, as in New Orleans, they call it *pain perdu*, which means "lost bread." This is dried out, leftover, day old bread. The French leave this bread out overnight to dry out even more, and that is correct; stale bread makes better French toast.

To those who claim they do not like French toast, you will change your mind when you sample just one of these recipes. They are not like some you have had in the past, which I like to call, *Fried Milk Toast*. Most of these recipes can be made the night before, refrigerated, and cooked in the morning. A great, hearty breakfast for those on-the-go.

Once the French toast is cooked, it should be golden brown and crisp on the outside, and light and puffy on the inside.

Baked Islander French Toast (*Colorado*) 146

Blueberry-Stuffed French Toast with Blueberry Sauce (*Maine*) 146

Buttermilk French Toast with variations & Orange Syrup (*California*) 147

Cinnamon Logs (*California*) 148

French Custard Toast (*California*) 148

Breakfast in France

French Toast (*France*) 149

Oven Baked Maple French Toast (*Texas*) 150

Smoked Turkey Stuffed French Toast with Orange Sauce (*France*) 150

Stuffed French Toast with Apple-Raisin Sauté (*California*) 151

NOTE: French toast can be high in calories, fat and cholesterol. If this is a problem, substitute butter with margarine, eggs with egg substitute (1/4 cup of egg substitute per egg), and cream with skim milk. This will cut calories about 20%, fats by almost 50%, with a slight increase in sodium, and there will be zero cholesterol.

BAKED ISLANDER FRENCH TOAST
Makes 8 servings

The title will tell you this recipe is not served in *France,* probably more like something you would find in the *South Pacific. Sallie and Welling Clark* are the innkeepers at *Holden House,* in Colorado Springs, Colorado, this is served to their guests on special occasions.

9 slices potato bread
6 eggs
1 1/2 cups milk
1/2 teaspoon pineapple extract
1/2 teaspoon coconut extract
1/2 teaspoon banana extract
Dash nutmeg

6 rings canned pineapple
1 cup brown sugar
2 tablespoons corn syrup
1/2 cup butter
1/2 cup coconut, flaked
1/2 cup almonds, slivered
2 bananas, sliced

Whipped cream (optional)

1. Melt brown sugar, butter and corn syrup in a microwave or in a sauce pan on top of stove.
2. Grease a 9x13-inch pan and pour melted sugar mixture in bottom of pan.
3. Sprinkle coconut, almonds and banana slices over sugar mixture.
4. Place the pineapple rings over the nuts and bananas.
5. Place bread slices over sugar mixture.

6. Whip eggs, milk and extracts and pour over bread.
7. Refrigerate overnight.
8. Bake at 400°F for 20 to 30 minutes.
9. When serving, turn over on plates with the sugar mixture on top (like an upon side down cake).
10. Top with whipped cream, more pineapple, coconut and nutmeg, if desired

NUTRITION FACTS per serving: 685 calories, 272 calories from fat, 31.5g total fat (48%), 14.8g saturated fat (74%), 261.8mg cholesterol (31%), 376.6mg sodium (16%), 93.8g carbohydrates (31%), 4.1g fiber (16%), 13.9g protein (28%), 1091 IU vitamin A (22%), 28mg vitamin C (46%), 210mg calcium (21%) and 3.1mg iron (17%)

BLUEBERRY-STUFFED FRENCH TOAST
WITH BLUEBERRY SAUCE
Makes 8 servings

In Maine, especially in season, blueberries will make their way to the breakfast table. Hosts *Ellen and Paul Morissette* from the *Five Gables Inn* in East Boothbay, Maine make good use of blueberries in this strata recipe.

12 slices of homemade white bread, crust discarded, cut into 1-inch cubes
16 ounces cream cheese, cut into 1-inch cubes

1 cup blueberries
12 eggs
1/3 cup maple syrup

2 cups milk

1. Arrange half the bread cubes in a buttered 13x9-inch glass baking dish.
2. Scatter the cream cheese over the bread and sprinkle the blueberries over the cream cheese.
3. Arrange remaining bread over the blueberries.
4. In a large bowl whisk together the eggs, syrup and milk.

5. Pour the egg mixture evenly over bread mixture, cover and refrigerate overnight.
6. Bake covered with foil, in the middle of preheated 350°F oven for 30 minutes.
7. Remove foil and bake for another 30 minutes or until puffed and golden.
8. Serve with Blueberry Sauce.

NUTRITION FACTS per serving: 492 calories, 276 calories from fat, 30.8g total fat (47%), 16.4g saturated fat (82%), 390mg cholesterol (130%), 496mg sodium (21%), 35.2g carbohydrates (12%), 1.4g fiber (5%), 19g protein (38%), 1380 IU vitamin A (28%), 3mg vitamin C (5%), 205mg calcium (21%) and 3.1mg iron (17%).

BLUEBERRY SAUCE
Makes 2 cups

Best made fresh and served warm. Can be made several days earlier and refrigerated.

1 cup sugar
2 tablespoons cornstarch

1 cup water
1 cup blueberries

1 tablespoon unsalted butter

1. In a small saucepan stir together sugar, cornstarch and water.
2. Cook over medium-high heat, stirring occasionally, until thickened.

3. Stir in blueberries and simmer, stirring occasionally, until berries burst.
4. Add butter and stir until butter is melted

NUTRITION FACTS per tablespoon: 32 calories, 3 calories from fat, .4g total fat (1%), .2g saturated fat (1%), zero cholesterol and sodium, 7.3g carbohydrates (2%), (zero fiber, protein, vitamin A and C, calcium and iron).

BUTTERMILK FRENCH TOAST WITH ORANGE SYRUP
Makes about 28 slices

Lisa Smith, innkeeper at the *Country Garden Inn* in Napa, California says, *"Soaking overnight is the secret to French toast. It makes the finished dish rich and moist. After it is soaked, the bread can be frozen, then thawed before cooking."*

9 eggs
3/4 cup buttermilk

1 1/2 teaspoons vanilla
1/2 teaspoon cinnamon

2 loaves unsliced day-old French bread

1. Beat together first 4 ingredients.
2. Cut bread into 3/4-inch slices.
3. Dip both sides of slices into egg mixture, turning with tongs.

4. Cover cookie sheets with plastic wrap and place dipped slices on top of plastic wrap.
5. Wrap and refrigerate overnight.
6. Cook on medium griddle until golden brown.

Great with orange syrup!

NUTRITION FACTS per slice: 103 calories, 25 calories from fat, 2.7g total fat (4%), .8g saturated fat (4%), 68.8mg cholesterol (23%), 180.9mg sodium (8%), 14.7g carbohydrates (5%), .7g fiber (3%), 4.6g protein (9%), 104 IU vitamin A (2%), zero vitamin C, 47mg calcium (5%) and 1.1mg iron (6%).

VARIATIONS

This is an excellent recipe to add various flavors for a change of pace.

MOLASSES FRENCH TOAST: Add 1/4 cup of molasses to the egg/milk mixture.

MAPLE FRENCH TOAST: Add 1/4 cup of maple syrup to the egg/milk mixture.

SPICED FRENCH TOAST: Add up to 1/2 teaspoon of your flavor spice, such as cloves, nutmeg, etc.

ORANGE FRENCH TOAST: Add 1 tablespoon of orange zest to the egg/milk mixture. Lemon zest can also be added.

These recipes can also be baked or broiled. Place on a greased cookie sheet and bake at 450°F until golden brown and puffy. To broil, place about 4-inches from the heat source and cook about 4 minutes on each side until golden brown.

ORANGE SYRUP

3 cups brown sugar
6 ounces concentrated frozen orange juice
1 cup honey

1 pound butter
2 tablespoons maple flavoring
Grated peel from 2 or 3 oranges

1. In a large pot melt and blend sugar, honey and undiluted orange juice.
2. In a separate pot melt butter and blend in maple and orange peel.

3. Blend all together in 1 pot, simmer very slowly 5 minutes.
4. Pour into jars and refrigerate up to 2 weeks.

NUTRITION FACTS per 1/4 cup: 258 calories, 133 calories from fat, 15.4g total fat (24%), 9.6g saturated fat (48%), 41.4mg cholesterol (14%) and 164.2mg sodium (7%).

CINNAMON LOGS
Makes 6 servings

Kids love finger foods, and this recipe by *Cecile and Moye Stephens,* proprietors of the *Wine Way Inn* of Calistoga, California fits the bill perfectly.

1 loaf unsliced bread
2 cups milk
5 eggs, beaten

2 tablespoons sugar
1 teaspoon cinnamon
1/2 teaspoon vanilla

Pinch of nutmeg

1. Trim the crusts off the bread. Slice bread 3/4-inch thick, cut each slice in half to form a log.
2. Blend milk, eggs, sugar, cinnamon, nutmeg and vanilla in the blender.
3. Pour into a shallow pan.
4. Arrange bread slices in this mixture turning to coat all sides.

5. Chill until all the mixture has been absorbed or overnight.
6. Fry logs in deep oil at 360°F until golden brown on all sides, about 3 to 4 minutes.
7. Drain briefly on paper towel.
8. Serve immediately with butter and maple syrup.

NUTRITION FACTS per serving: 291 calories, 85 calories from fat, 9.3g total fat (14%), 3.5g saturated fat (18%), 188.8mg cholesterol (63%), 451.mg sodium (19%), 37.7g carbohydrates (13%), 1.8g fiber (7%), 13.4g protein (27%), 368 IU vitamin A (7%), 1mg vitamin C (1%), 194mg calcium (19%) and 16mg iron (16%).

FRENCH CUSTARD TOAST
Makes 8 servings

Just wait until you savor this recipe by *Trish Kasper* of San Jose, California. These little fluffy pillows will melt into your mouth.

6 eggs
2 tablespoons flour
1 tablespoon sugar
1 teaspoon cinnamon
1 teaspoon salt
1 teaspoon baking powder

1/4 teaspoon nutmeg
2 cups milk
1 teaspoon vanilla
1 pound loaf French bread, cut into 1 1/2-inch thick slices

1. With a wire whisk, slightly beat the eggs.
2. Add the flour, sugar and other dry ingredients.
3. Beat until it's a smooth, thin batter.
4. Gradually beat in milk and vanilla.
5. Pour the mixture into a 9x13-inch baking dish.

6. Dip one side of each slice into the batter; turn the slices over and place them in a single layer in the batter.
7. Push the slices together to make them fit.
8. Cover the dish and refrigerate overnight.

9. About 30 minutes before ready to cook, turn the slices over to soak the other side.
10. Heat a large frying pan or griddle over medium heat.
11. Melt a small amount of butter or margarine in the pan and add as many bread slices as will fit.
12. Pour any of the extra batter over the tops of the slices.
13. Cook for 8 to 10 minutes on each side or until the slices are golden.

NUTRITION FACTS per serving: 264 calories, 69 calories from fat, 7.6g total fat (12%), 2.8g saturated fat (14%), 167.7mg cholesterol (56%), 734.7mg sodium (31%), 36.3g carbohydrates (12%), 1.8g fiber (7%), 11.9g protein (24%), 316 IU vitamin A (6%), 1mg vitamin C (1%), 180mg calcium (18%) and 2.3mg iron (13%).

BREAKFAST IN FRANCE

"Avoir un oeuf ... peler ensemble," roughly translates, *"To have an egg to peel together,"* or in this case means, *"To set the record straight,"* and to set the record straight, breakfast is relatively new in France.

Previously people did not eat just after waking, but after having begun their work. This was called *"casse-croute"* (meaning *"break crust"*) and is quite varied by regions. Many French still do not eat breakfast because of lack of time or appetite. Some do have fruit juice and coffee or tea with or without bread. Some will have coffee, crepes and butter. In Paris, many have *"panade,"* which is bread broken into the previous dinner's leftover soup.

Breakfast is called *"petit d,jeuner"* and is served at the noon hour and can consist of grilled meats, sausages, omelets, pastries, croissants, French toast, fresh fruit, *cafe au lai,t* page 18 (coffee with milk) and a glass of Burgundy wine and is more like the Sunday brunch in the United States. Croissants are made with butter and some are filled with almond paste, chocolate, apple, blueberry, cherry, raisin, strawberry, cinnamon or cream cheese. The traditional butter croissants can be topped with eggs, sausage and cheese for a breakfast sandwich. A dairy product called *"Le Slim Cow"* is often used as a replacement for butter and margarine. It is made from buttermilk, milk fat and soybean oil and is low in cholesterol and sodium, high in calcium and protein, and can be used in baking as well as a spread. It is available in many supermarkets in the United States.

A country breakfast, again served near the noon hour, could consist of ham, French toast, eggs, muffins, croissants, coffee and hot chocolate.

FRENCH TOAST FROM FRANCE
Makes 6 servings

While searching for *French toast* recipes around the world, only *France* would admit they eat *French toast*. This recipe courtesy of *Grand Marnier Liqueurs* is seldom eaten at breakfast, but is often served during the noon hour.

3 eggs
3 tablespoons Grand Marnier
1 tablespoons sugar
1 tablespoon vanilla

1 cup milk
12 slices French baguettes, cut diagonally, 2-inches thick
1/4 cup butter

1. In a bowl, beat eggs, Grand Marnier, sugar, vanilla and milk until smooth and well blended.
2. Place baguette slices into the egg mixture and let stand until liquid is absorbed, turning once.

3. Heat butter in large skillet and fry slices until golden brown on both sides.
4. Serve with fresh berries and preserves.

NUTRITION FACTS per serving: 374 calories, 130 calories from fat, 13.7g total fat (21%), 6.8g saturated fat (34%), 132.2mg cholesterol (44%), 589mg sodium (25%), 46.5g carbohydrates (16%), 2.1g fiber (8%), 11.2g protein (22%), 495 IU vitamin A (10%), zero vitamin C, 120mg calcium (12%) and 2.3mg iron (13%).

OVEN BAKED MAPLE FRENCH TOAST
Makes 6 servings

I found this recipe in Texas. It makes its own syrup while it bakes and the toast melts in your mouth. Delicious!

1/2 cup butter
1 cup brown sugar
3 tablespoons corn syrup
1/2 cup pecans or walnuts, chopped
1 loaf soft crust French bread

6 eggs
1 3/4 cups 1/2 & 1/2 cream
1 teaspoon vanilla
1 teaspoon maple extract
1 teaspoon cinnamon

1/2 teaspoon nutmeg

1. Cut off ends of bread and slice into 6 equal pieces, about 1 3/4-inches thick.
2. Leave the crusts on.
3. Set sliced bread on a plate and let it get staled for several hours.
4. Melt butter in a small sauce pan with the brown sugar, corn syrup, and pecans.
5. Pour butter mixture into a 9x13-inch oven proof pan.

6. Place the bread slices on top of the butter mixture.
7. In a bowl, beat the eggs with remaining ingredients and pour about 2/3 cup of the egg mixture on top of each slice of bread.
8. Cover with plastic wrap and refrigerate overnight.
9. Remove plastic wrap and bake in a 350°F oven for 30 minutes. Remove slices with a spatula and invert on to a serving plate.

NUTRITION FACTS per serving: 618 calories, 273 calories from fat, 30.6g total fat (47%), 16.5g saturated fat (83%), 273.4mg cholesterol (93%), 724.1mg sodium (30%), 71.7g carbohydrates (24%), 2.1g fiber (8%), 15.2g protein (30%), 1195 IU vitamin A (24%), 1mg vitamin C (1%), 180mg calcium (18%), and 3.2mg iron (18%).

SMOKED TURKEY STUFFED FRENCH TOAST WITH ORANGE SAUCE
Makes 4 servings

If you have enjoyed a *Monte Cristo* sandwich for lunch, then you will enjoy this breakfast recipe by *Grand Marnier Liqueurs*. Breakfast sandwiches are popular in Europe and are generally eaten with a knife and fork.

1 cup cream or milk
2 eggs
2 tablespoons Grand Marnier

8 slices smoked turkey
8 slices French bread
1 tablespoon butter

1 tablespoon vegetable oil

1. In a medium bowl beat cream, eggs and Grand Marnier until well combined.
2. Make 4 sandwiches, using 2 slices each of bread and turkey.
3. Dip the sandwiches in the batter and let the excess drip off.
4. These sandwiches can be made up to 8 hours ahead of time, wrap the sandwiches in plastic wrap and refrigerate.
5. In a large skillet, heat the butter and oil over moderate heat.

6. Place the sandwich in the skillet and cook until the underside is golden brown, about 3 minutes.
7. Adjust the heat as necessary so as not to burn.
8. Turn over and cook the other side until golden, about another 3 minutes.
9. Continue with other sandwiches, adding more butter as necessary.
10. Serve hot, with orange sauce.

NUTRITION FACTS per serving: 452 calories, 254 calories from fat, 27.1g total fat (42%), 13.1g saturated fat (66%), 185.5mg cholesterol (62%), 403.5mg sodium (17%), 31.1g carbohydrates (10%), 1.4g fiber (6%), 16.5g protein (33%), 829 IU vitamin A (17%), zero vitamin C, 110mg calcium (11%) and 2mg iron (11%).

ORANGE SAUCE
Makes 4 servings

1 1/2 cups orange juice

2 tablespoons cornstarch

6 tablespoons Grand Marnier

1. In a medium saucepan, bring the orange juice to a simmer over moderate heat.
2. In a small bowl, dissolve the cornstarch in the Grand Marnier.

3. Stir the dissolved cornstarch into the orange juice and simmer just until thickened.
4. Serve hot.
5. Can be refrigerated for up to 2 days in a covered container

NUTRITION FACTS per serving: 140 calories, zero fats, cholesterol and sodium, 21.6g carbohydrates (7%), .2g fiber (1%), .7g protein (1%), 47 IU vitamin A (4%), 47mg vitamin C (78%), 10mg calcium (1%) and .2mg iron (1%).

STUFFED FRENCH TOAST WITH APPLE-RAISIN SAUTÉ
Makes 12 servings

Ken Torbert from the *Gingerbread Mansion* in Ferndale, California serves this delicious recipe to his overnight guests. This is a great recipe for those who do not have time in the morning to fix breakfast, as it can be baked while dressing.

12 slices of bread without the crusts, or cinnamon-raisin bread
16 ounces cream cheese

12 eggs
2 cups milk
1/3 cup maple syrup

Cinnamon or nutmeg, to taste

1. Cube bread; spread half in greased 9x13-inch baking dish.
2. Cube cream cheese and place on bread cubes.
3. Top with remaining bread cubes.
4. Combine eggs, milk, and syrup, mixing well.
5. Pour egg mixture over bread in baking dish.

6. Top with cinnamon or nutmeg.
7. Refrigerated (covered) overnight.
8. In morning, bake at 375°F for 45-50 minutes (uncovered), or until done.
9. Serve warm with apple-raisin sauté, syrup, or fresh fruit.

NUTRITION FACTS per serving with apple-raisin sauté: 388 calories, 188 calories from fat, 21.2g total fat (33%), 11.3g saturated fat (57%), 261.5mg cholesterol (87%), 341.8mg sodium (14%), 37.8g carbohydrates (13%), 1.4g fiber (6%), 13g protein (26%), 972 IU vitamin A (19%), 8mg vitamin C (13%), 145mg calcium (14%) and 2.4mg iron (13%).

APPLE-RAISIN SAUTÉ

2 teaspoons butter
2 golden delicious apples, cored, cut into 1/3 inch slices
3/4 cup raisins

1/2 cup orange juice
1/3 cup apricot jam
1 teaspoon grated orange peel
1/2 teaspoon cinnamon

1/8 teaspoon allspice

1. Melt butter over medium heat in large non-stick skillet.
2. Add apple slices.
3. Cook, tossing occasionally, about 10 minutes, or until golden brown.

4. Stir in remaining ingredients; cook about 3 minutes, stirring constantly, until sauce thickens slightly.
5. Pour over baked Stuffed French Toast.

Did you know that when grapes are dried and made into raisins, they have a higher sugar content and a completely different flavor from grapes? The darker raisins are usually made from muscats and are best sun dried. Golden variety are made from sultanas and are dehydrated indoors.

CHAPTER XI

FRUIT

Do you prefer fruit over juice? If you like fruit for breakfast, it's okay to use fruit in place of juice, or serve it with juice as the second course. Many of these fruit recipes also make excellent desserts.

Ambrosia, Food of the Gods (*tropics*) 153

Baked Nutty Apples (*Missouri*) 153

Breakfast Fruit Salad (*Oregon*) 153

Broiled Grapefruit (*Missouri*) 154

Cantaloupe Mousse (*North Carolina*) 154

Fruit Kabobs (*Mississippi*) 154

Honeyed Fruit (*China*) 155

Hot Banana & Grapefruit Cups (*tropics*) 155

Maduro en Gloria (*Nicaragua*) 156

Maple Baked Apples (*Maine*) 156

Poached Pears with Vanilla Yogurt Sauce (*California*) 157

Spring Tonic Compote (*New Jersey*) 157

Strawberry Mango Tofu Frappe (*Canada 158*)

Stuffed Plantains (*Antigua & Barbuda*) 158

Breakfast in Antigua & Barbuda

FRUIT TOPPINGS

Blackberry Delight 159
Cream Sauce 159
Honey Cream Fruit Sauce 159
Quark 159

AMBROSIA, FOOD OF THE GODS
Makes 6 servings

Everyone who enjoys fruit will be delighted with this recipe from *Del Monte Tropical Fruit Company*.

1 large orange, peeled, seeded, sliced
3 cups fresh or canned pineapple, cubed
2 bananas, sliced

16 strawberries, stems removed
1/4 cup powdered sugar
1/4 cup coconut, flaked

1/2 cup pineapple juice

1. Cut orange slices into quarters.
2. Arrange fruit in serving bowl.
3. Combine sugar and coconut; sprinkle over fruit.

4. Add pineapple juice.
5. Cover and chill at least 1 hour or overnight

NUTRITION FACTS per serving: 245 calories, 26 calories from fat, 3.2g total fat (5%), 1.2g saturated fat (6%), zero cholesterol and sodium, 57.3g carbohydrates (19%), 11.8g fiber (47%), 3.5g protein (7%), 202 IU vitamin A (4%), 260mg vitamin C (434%), 76mg calcium (8%) and iron 2.1mg (12%).

BAKED NUTTY APPLES
Makes 6 servings

Irv and Diane Feinber at their famous *Garth Woodside Mansion Bed and Breakfast County Inn* in Hannibal, Missouri always have these baked apples on their menu. Bake apples can be made ahead of time, refrigerated and reheated in the microwave.

6 apples, Rome or McIntosh, cored
1/3 cup walnuts, chopped

1/3 cup brown sugar
2 teaspoons butter, softened

1 teaspoon lemon rind, grated

1. Remove about 1 1/2 inches of peel around stem end.
2. Arrange in a buttered shallow baking dish that is large enough to hold apples.

3. Mix nuts, brown sugar, butter and lemon rind and divide mixture among apples.
4. Add water to the dish to a depth of 1/4 inch.
5. Bake uncovered at 350°F for 40 to 45 minutes.
6. Baste as needed

NUTRITION FACTS per serving: 165 calories, 47 calories from fat, 5.7g total fat (9%), 1.1g saturated fat (6%), 3.4mg cholesterol (1%), 16.1mg sodium (1%), 29.8g carbohydrates (10%), 4.1g fiber (16%), 2g protein (4%), 141mg vitamin A (3%), 9mg vitamin C (14%), 21mg calcium (2%) and .6mg iron (3%).

BREAKFAST FRUIT SALAD
Makes 6 servings

Teresa and Harry Pastorious at the *Klamath Manor* in Klamath Falls, Oregon, offer their guests both a cold glass of orange juice and this fruit salad.

2 apples, chopped
1/2 cup mandarin oranges, sectioned
3 bananas, sliced

1 cup canned pineapple chunks, drained
1 cup fresh strawberries, sliced
1/4 cup golden raisins

1/2 cup strawberry/banana yogurt

1. In a large bowl toss fruit with yogurt.

2. Chill about 30 minutes before serving.

BROILED GRAPEFRUIT
Makes 2 servings

On request, guests can enjoy this recipe at the *Garth Woodside Mansion* in Hannibal, Missouri.

1 grapefruit
Cinnamon

2 tablespoons maple syrup
2 grapes

1. Cut grapefruit in half.
2. Loosen sections with paring knife, but leave section in peel.

3. Sprinkle with cinnamon and pour 1 tablespoon of maple syrup over top on each half.
4. Broil 5 minutes or until bubbly.
5. Garnish with grape in center

NUTRITION FACTS per serving: 93 calories, 2 calories from fat, zero fat, cholesterol and sodium, 23.6g carbohydrates (8%), 1.4g fiber (5%), .8g protein (2%), 151 IU vitamin A (3%), 41mg vitamin C (68%), 2.8mg calcium (3%) and .4mg iron (2%).

CANTALOUPE MOUSSE
Makes 8 servings

You will think you are in heaven when you savor the first sip of this famous recipe that is served to guests by innkeeper *Liz Oehser* at her *Buttonwood Inn* in Franklin, North Carolina.

1/2 cantaloupe, seeded, pared & pureed
2 tablespoons unflavored gelatin (2 envelopes)
1/4 cup cold water

2 cups heavy cream
2 egg whites (room temperature)
2 cups sugar, divided

1. Sprinkle gelatin over cold water to soften. Stir in top of a double boiler over hot water to dissolve.
2. Cool and add to the melon.
3. Beat cream until soft peaks form, gradually adding 1 cup sugar.

4. Beat whites until fluffy, gradually add remaining sugar.
5. Fold whipped cream and egg whites together, and fold into melon.
6. Chill 1 hour.

NUTRITION FACTS per serving: 357 calories, 131 calories from fat, 15g total fat (23%), 9.3g saturated fat (47%), 52.3mg cholesterol (17%), 40.3mg sodium (2%), 55.2g carbohydrates (18%), .3g fiber (1%), 2.8g protein (6%), 1639 IU vitamin A (33%), 16mg vitamin C (27%), 59mg calcium (6%) and .1mg iron (1%).

FRUIT KABOBS
Makes 2 servings

Harry Sharp and his wife makes these kabobs for guests at *The Duff Mansion* on the banks of the Mississippi River in Vicksburg, Mississippi.

8 (12-inch) wooden skewers
16 slices bacon
1 fresh pineapple, peeled, cored

2 Granny Smith apples, cored
2 Rome apples, cored
6 ounce can pineapple juice

1/3 cup brown sugar

1. Soak wooden skewers in water and set aside.
2. Cook bacon until limp, but not crisp, drain and set aside.
3. Cut pineapple and apples into 1-inch chucks.
4. Combine fruit chucks and juice, tossing to coat fruit.

5. Thread end with a piece of bacon on skewer, alternate pieces of apple and pineapple, weaving a piece of bacon around each piece of fruit.
6. Add another slice of bacon when needed.
7. Sprinkle each kabob with brown sugar.

8. Broil 6-inches from heat for 6-minutes, turning once or until fruit begins to brown around the edges.

NUTRITION FACTS per serving: 243 calories, 62 calories from fat, 7.3g total fat (11%), 2.3g saturated fat (12%), 10.8mg cholesterol (4%), 206.7mg sodium (9%), 43.3g carbohydrates (14%), 4.2g fiber (17%), 4.8g protein (10%), 82 IU vitamin A (2%), 46mg vitamin C (77%), 29mg calcium (3%) and 1.2mg iron (77%).

HONEYED FRUIT
Makes 4 servings

From *China* comes an extra special treat that's not only easy to make, but fun to eat. The recipe was included in the *Cuisine Internationale Cookbook of the 1965 International Festival* in Eugene, Oregon.

2 apples, peeled, cored, sliced
or 2 bananas, sliced
1/2 cup egg whites, DO NOT BEAT
3 tablespoons cornstarch
3 tablespoons flour

1/4 cup vegetable oil
1 cup water
2 cups sugar
1 tablespoon corn syrup
1 tablespoon sesame seeds or walnuts, chopped

1. Mix together egg whites, cornstarch and flour.
2. Add apples to the batter and coat.
3. Deep fat fry the coated apple slices until light brown; drain on paper towels.
4. Make a syrup with fresh vegetable oil (not the deep fry oil), water, sugar and corn syrup.
5. Boil it to 240°F (firm soft ball).
6. Add the fried fruit and cook until the syrup turns brown and starts to caramelize, about 3 to 4

minutes. Continually stir the fruit gently. Do not let the syrup burn.
7. During the last minute of cooking add sesame seeds.
8. Pour syrup and fruit onto a greased platter.
9. To serve, quickly pick up a fruit slice with chopsticks or toothpicks, dip it into cold water, and eat

NUTRITION FACTS per serving: 636 calories, 133 calories from fat, 15.2g total fat (23%), 1.8g saturated fat (9%), zero cholesterol, 58.6mg sodium (2%), 124.8g carbohydrates (42%), 1.9g fiber (8%), 4.6g protein (9%), 38 IU vitamin A (1%), 4mg vitamin C (7%), 12mg calcium (1%) and .7mg iron (4%).

HOT BANANA & GRAPEFRUIT CUPS
Makes 4 servings

If you enjoy chilled grapefruit, maybe with a touch of sweetener, try this hot version for a change of pace.

2 grapefruits
2 tablespoons honey

1 tablespoon fresh mint, chopped
1/4 teaspoon cinnamon

3 bananas, sliced

1. Cut grapefruit in half.
2. With a grapefruit knife cut out the grapefruit.
3. With a sharp knife, remove the membranes from the grapefruit sections.
4. In a bowl stir honey, mint and cinnamon.
5. Add the grapefruit sections and bananas.

6. Fill the grapefruit shells with the grapefruit mixture.
7. Place under a boiler for 2 minutes or until warmed through.
8. Serve immediately.

NUTRITION FACTS per serving: 151 calories, 5 calories from fat, .6g total fat (1%), .2g saturated fat (1%), zero cholesterol and sodium, 38.6g carbohydrates (13%), 3.5g fiber (14%), 1.8g protein (4%), 216 IU vitamin A (4%), 50mg vitamin C (83%), 29mg calcium (3%) and .8mg iron (5%).

MADURO EN GLORIA
Makes 8 servings

Odilia Aguilar from Leon, *Nicaragua* says a lot of breakfast recipes can be made with plantains. This is her favorite plantain recipe. Plantains look like large bananas and are available in many supermarkets.

2 plantains, ripe and very soft
2 cups milk
1/4 cup sugar
4 cups casique cheese or Monterey Jack, grated

1 tablespoon cornstarch
1 teaspoon cinnamon
1/2 teaspoon vanilla
1 tablespoon butter, divided

1. Slice the plantains into 1/2-inch cubes.
2. Fry in vegetable oil until brown; set aside.
3. In a bowl combine sugar with cornstarch, cinnamon, milk, cheese and vanilla.
4. Grease a 6x9-inch casserole with 1/2 tablespoon of butter.

5. Pour half of the cheese mixture in the casserole, top with plantains and top with remaining cheese mixture.
6. Top with remaining butter cut into pieces.
7. Bake in a 350°F for about 30 minutes or until cheese mixture is set

NUTRITION FACTS per serving: 343 calories, 181 calories from fat, 20.6 total fat (32%), 12.8g saturated fat (64%), 62mg cholesterol (21%), 346.7mg sodium (14%), 24.9g carbohydrates (8%), 1.2g fiber (5%), 16.3g protein (33%), 1167 IU vitamin A (23%), 9mg vitamin C (15%), 496mg calcium (50%) and .8mg iron (5%).

MAPLE BAKED APPLES
Makes 6 servings

Ellen and Paul Morissette are the hosts at the *Five Gables Inn* at East Boothbay, Maine. Ellen says, *"You can bake these apples ahead of time and warmed in the oven at 350°F for 15 minutes, leave out at room temperature for 30 minutes or warm in your microwave per instructions."*

6 McIntosh apples, uniform in size
1/2 cup raisins
6 tablespoons brown sugar

1/2 cup maple syrup
1/2 cup orange juice
1 tablespoon sugar

1 teaspoon cinnamon

1. Core apples from stem ends, leaving bottoms intact.
2. Place in shallow baking dish.
3. Mix raisins and brown sugar; pack into apple cavities.
4. Pour syrup over apples.
5. Pour juice into bottom of dish.

6. Mix sugar and cinnamon; sprinkle over apples.
7. Bake in 350°F oven, basting 2 or 3 times, until apples are tender, 30 minutes to 1 hour, depending on size of apples.
8. Serve warm or at room temperature, with cream

NUTRITION FACTS per serving: 238 calories, 2.3% calories from fat, .7g total fat (1%), .1g saturated fat (1%), 130mg cholesterol (43%), 15g carbohydrates (5%), .8g fiber (3%), 12g protein (24%), 318mg sodium, 214mg calcium (24%), 1.5mg iron (8%), 24mg vitamin C (40%) and 616 IU vitamin A (12%)

"An apple a day will keep the doctor away." There's more truth than fiction to that old saying. Here's why. Take a look at the nutrition facts for an apple. It has only 81 calories, 4 calories from fat, .5g total fat (1%), zero saturated fat, zero cholesterol, zero sodium, 2.1g carbohydrates (7%) 3.7g fiber (15%0, .3g protein (1), 73 IU vitamin A (1%), 8mg vitamin C (13%), 10mg calcium (1%), .3mg iron (1%), and 159mg potassium .For more information log on: www.usapple.org

---

POACHED PEARS
Makes 1 serving

In Santa Barbara, California, Innkeeper *Susan Brown* of the century old *Bath Street Inn* offers these wonderful poached pears with vanilla yogurt sauce to her guests. This can be made ahead of time and refrigerated.

Fresh pears (1 pear per serving)
Apple juice

4 to 5 whole cloves
Vanilla yogurt sauce

1. Peel, core and halve pears.
2. Simmer in the apple juice with cloves until tender.

3. Remove from liquid and cool.
4. Service at room temperature or chilled

NUTRITION FACTS per pear without sauce: 158 calories, 8 calories from fat, .9g total fat (1%), zero saturated fat, cholesterol, and sodium, 39.9g carbohydrates (13%), 4.3g fiber (17%), .8g protein (2%), 37 IU vitamin A (1%), 8mg vitamin C (14%), 30mg calcium (3%) and .9mg iron (5%).

VANILLA YOGURT SAUCE

1 cup vanilla yogurt
1/2 teaspoon cinnamon

1 teaspoon vanilla
Fresh spearmint leaves (optional)

1. Thoroughly mix above ingredients.
2. Pour 1 to 2 tablespoons of vanilla sauce over the cooled poached pears.

3. Garnish with spearmint, if desired

NUTRITION FACTS per tablespoon: 9 calories, 4 calories from fat, .5g total fat (15%), .3g saturated fat (2%), 1.8mg cholesterol (1%), zero sodium, carbohydrates and fiber, .5g protein (1%), zero vitamin A and C, 18mg calcium (2%) and zero iron.

SPRING TONIC COMPOTE
Makes 8 servings

Ashing Cottage in Spring Lake, New Jersey have been welcoming visitors since 1877. Hosts *goodie and Jack Stewart* serve this fruit compote to present day guests.

1 quart strawberries, hulled, sliced
2 cups rhubarb, cut into 1-inch chunks

8 ounces canned crushed pineapple, undrained
1/4 cup brown sugar

1 envelope unflavored gelatin, softened in a little warm water

1. Cook rhubarb slowly with sugar until fruit starts to soften.
2. Add berries and continue cooking until both are soft.

3. Add pineapple, cook 1-minute more.
4. Add gelatin, continue cooking another minute.
5. Cool and serve

NUTRITION FACTS per serving: 97 calories, 4 calories from fat, total fat .5g (1%), zero saturated fat, zero cholesterol, 25mg sodium (1%), 15g carbohydrates (5%), 2.6g fiber (11%), 10g protein (20%), 58 IU vitamin A (1%), 49mg vitamin C (82%), 49mg calcium (5%), and .7mg iron (4%).

> **Did you know** the rhubarb is also known as "pieplant?" Rhubarb originated in Mongolia, but today it is grown in Europe and America. Rhubarb belongs to the buckwheat family. Although rhubarb is technically a vegetable, it is used as a fruit. Early varieties were green with red in the stems. Today's varieties are bright red with a much sweeter taste.

STRAWBERRY MANGO TOFU FRAPPE
Makes 6 servings

Chef Bernard Casavant of the *Chateau Whistler Resort* in Whistler, British Columbia, Canada serves his frappe in the resort's Wildflower Cafe. It is delicious served chilled with a slice of warm zucchini lemon thyme bread (see TEA BREADS, page 42).

4 cups strawberries, fresh or frozen
1 cup fresh mango
1 1/2 cups soft tofu

1 tablespoon sugar
1/4 cup yogurt
1/4 cup granola

Yogurt and sliced strawberries for garnish

1. Puree half of the strawberries and mango until smooth.
2. Add the tofu and blend until smooth.
3. Add the rest of the fruit and continue to puree.
4. Add sugar to taste.

5. Pour mixture into 6 tall glasses and garnish with sliced strawberries, a dollop of yogurt and a sprinkle of granola, if desired.
6. Served chilled.

NUTRITION FACTS per serving: 124 calories, 37 calories from fat, 4.5g total fat (7%), .8g saturated fat (4%), zero cholesterol and sodium, 17.9g carbohydrates (6%), 3.9g fiber (16%), 5.7g protein (11%), 1154 IU vitamin A (23%), 64mg vitamin C (107%), 83mg calcium (8%) and 3.3mg iron (18%).

BREAKFAST IN ANTIGUA & BARBUDA

In a chain of magical islands strung like pearls down the Eastern Caribbean, Antigua and Barbuda stands out as special gems -- ringed with palm lined golden beaches, uninhabited islands and coral reefs, and low mountains all cooled by the constant trade winds.

It is said that Columbus discovered these islands on his second voyage. That might be true in European eyes, but to the Carib natives, they discovered them first and really were not too happy about being colonized.

The people of these islands have learned to use local grown foods, as the cost of importing from other lands is quite expensive. Fruit, fish and sweet potatoes are usually part of the breakfast table. The islands grow a variety of fruits such as oranges, limes, lemons, mangoes, bananas, soursops, sugar-apples, marmee-apples, guavas, cherries, dumps, gooseberries, tamarinds, ginnips, pineapples, custard apple, tangerines, cashews, grapefruits, pawpaw, watermelon, muskmelon, coconuts, sea-side-grapes, garden-grapes and sapodilla. These fruits add minerals and vitamins, as well as color and flavor to the menu.

STUFFED PLANTAINS
Makes 16 servings

Plantain recipes are found throughout the *Caribbean* and *Latin America*. This delicious recipe is from *Antigua and Barbuda*. A bit unusual for American tastes, however, if you like the ingredients, you will enjoy this dish.

8 ripe plantains
1 pound hamburger
2 tablespoons margarine
1 onion, chopped
2 tablespoons ketchup
1/4 teaspoon cloves

1/2 teaspoon garlic, minced
1 1/2 teaspoons flour
4 tablespoons water or meat stock
1 egg
Milk
1 cup bread crumbs

1. Slice plantains into about 2 inch chunks, fry lightly in oil; set aside.

2. Mix hamburger, margarine, onion, ketchup, cloves, garlic, flour and water.
3. Fry this mixture in a hot pan; set aside.

4. Flatten fried plantain slices with a rolling pin.
5. Fill with meat mixture.
6. Fold over and fasten with a toothpick.

7. Dip in beaten egg with a little milk and coat with the breadcrumbs.
8. Fry in hot oil until golden brown.

NUTRITION FACTS per serving: 249 calories, 55 calories from fat, 6.4 total fat (10%), 1.9g saturated fat (9%), 24.9mg cholesterol (8%), 251.8mg sodium (10%), 44.8g carbohydrates (15%), 2.6g fiber (10%), 6.6g protein (13%), 1111 IU vitamin A (22%), 17mg vitamin C (29%), 39mg calcium (4%) and 1.7mg iron (9%).

FRUIT TOPPINGS

BLACKBERRY DELIGHT
Makes 3 cups

A great topping for fruit, and a spread for toast and muffins.

10 ounces seedless blackberry or raspberry jam

1 pound cream cheese, softened

1. At a medium speed with an electric mixer, blend jam and cream cheese until smooth.

CREAM SAUCE

This cream sauce can be used over fresh fruit, mixed with fruit or as a dip for fresh fruit.

1 cup sour cream

1/2 cup powdered sugar, sifted

4 tablespoons lemon juice

1. In a bowl, stir all ingredients together.

2. Cover and chill in refrigerator.

Fresh berries, jellies, fresh or dried fruits or nuts can be added. Adjust sugar for sweetness to taste.

HONEY CREAM FRUIT SAUCE
Makes 3 cups

A good sauce for topping fresh fruit. Also try using it as a topping for granola.

1 pint sour cream

1/2 cup honey

1/4 cup orange juice

1. Mix all ingredients thoroughly and chill.

QUARK
Makes 2 1/2 cups

A great topping for fruit and granola.

2 cups plain yogurt
1/2 cup sour cream

1/4 cup sugar
1 1/2 teaspoons vanilla

1 1/2 teaspoons cinnamon
1/2 teaspoon nutmeg

1. Combine all ingredients until smooth.

2. Refrigerate only as quark does not freeze well.

Makes 2 1/2 cups.

CHAPTER XII

MEAT AND SEAFOOD

A century ago, meat was the main course for breakfast. Today, meat is a side dish, usually with eggs. In the work world, such as a lumber camp or a cattle ranch, beef steaks, pork chops, bacon, ham, and sausage are usually served piled high on a large platter. This is generally not the case at home or even in breakfast restaurants, since today, meat is served as a side with the main course. As you will note, fish and seafood recipes are mainly in coastal areas. If meat or seafood is not part of your morning diet, take a look at the following recipes and add some variety to your breakfast.

BEEF

Carne Asada (*Mexico*) 162

Corned Beef Hash (*Ireland*) 162

Cowboy Steaks (*Southwest, USA*) 163

Creamed Chipped Beef (*Maryland*) 163

Breakfast in Egypt

Egyptian Meatballs (*Egypt*) 164

Grandma's Goulash (*Maryland*) 164

Green Chile Stew (*New Mexico*) 165

Mexican Steaks (*Mississippi*) 165

Tourtiere Meat Pie (*Canada*) 166

PORK

Bacon (*information*) 166

Ham (*information*) 167

Country Sausage (*USA*) 167

A French Breakfast (*France*) 167

The Irish "Fry" (*Ireland*) 168

Mardi Gras Canadian Bacon Brunch (*Louisiana*) 168

Minorcan Pork Cake (*Minorca*) 169

Orange Glazed Ham (*France*) 169

Oxford Sausage (*England*) 170

Pastel de Maleta (*Nicaragua*) 170

Pork Chops (*USA*) 171

Pork Porridge (*Singapore*) 171

Posole Ortize (*New Mexico*) 171

Savory Green Onion Bacon (*USA*), with Black Pepper and Green Chile Salsa variations 172

Savory Sausage Casserole (*Delaware*) 173

Southern Virginia Ham with Red Eye Gravy (*West Virginia*) 173

POULTRY

Chicken Breast Dijon (*France*) 174

Chicken Enchiladas with Green Chile Sauce (*New Mexico*) 174

Chicken Scaloppini Palermo (*Italy*) 175

Chicken Pilau with Bottled Hell (*Minorca*) and Shrimp variation 175

Chicken Porridge (Singapore) 176

Chicken with Figs (*Mediterranean*) 177

Cornish Hens Stuffed with Bulgur (*Egypt*) 177

Creole Turkey Pastrami Surprise (*Creole, USA*) 178

Karahi Chicken (*Pakistan*) 178

Mexican Chicken (*Mexico*) 179

Moroccan Chicken (*Morocco*) 179

Pollo en Cacahuate (*Mexico*) with Mole-Style variation179

Ptarmigan (*Alaska*) 180

Red Eye Chicken (*Cajun, USA*) 180

FISH & SHELLFISH

Accra (*Trindad & Tobago*) 181

Baked Fish with Tomato Sauce (*Antigua & Barbuda*) 181

Barbecued Shrimp (*Louisiana*) 182

Batter Fried Shrimp (*Louisiana)* 183

Boiled Fish (*Antigua & Barbuda*) 183

Conch (*British Virgin Islands*) 183

Crawfish Louise (*Louisiana*) 184

Double Salmon Pate (*Canada*) 184

Fish Croquettes (*France*) 184

Fried Fish Cutlets with Lemon Sauce (*Antigua & Barbuda*) 185

Grilled Halibut with Pesto Sauce (*Alaska*) 185

Huachinango al Perejil (*Mexico*) 186

Oyster Pie (*Virginia*) 186

Salmon Nuggets (*Alaska*) 187

Salt Fish Cundy (*British Virgin Islands*) 187

Salt Fish Pie (*Antigua & Barbuda*) 188

Salt Fish with& Rice (*British Virgin Islands*) 188

Scalloped Oysters (*Virginia*) 189

Steamed Fish with Cucumber Sauce (*Antigua & Barbuda*) 189

Teochew Fish Porridge (*Singapore*) 190

OTHER MEATS

Alligator a la James (*Louisiana*) 190

Greek Lamb Skillet (*Greece*) 191

Grillades with Vegetables & Gravy (Louisiana) 191

Seal & Seal Liver (*Alaska*) 192

Walrus (*Alaska*) 192

Walrus Kyusolik (*Alaska*) 192

Walrus Meat Loaf (*Alaska*) 193

Walrus Steak with Gravy (*Alaska)* 194

MEAT SEASONINGS

Home Made Chile Powder (*New Mexico*) 193

Red Chile Sauce (*New Mexico)* 194

West Indian Seasonings (*British Virgin Islands*) 194

BEEF

Beef is not the first choice for breakfast, pork is number one for most diners. Try one of these recipes for a change of pace.

CARNE ASADA
Makes 4 servings

In America's southwest, *Mexico* and most *Latin American* countries, *carne asada* is normally barbecued over coals. The *National Live Stock and Meat Board*, suggests that in your busy world, with no time to prepare a barbecue before breakfast, the steaks can be made in the broiler, but could lack some of the flavor of the meat juice smoke from the hot coals.

4 beef rib eye steaks, cut 3/4 inch thick
2 tablespoons fresh lime juice
8 flour tortillas, warmed

1/4 cup Colby cheese, shredded
1/4 cup Monterey Jack cheese, shredded
Prepared salsa

1. Place steaks in a dish; sprinkle both sides with lime juice, rubbing into surface.
2. Cover and refrigerate about 15 minutes while preparing coals.
3. Place steaks over medium coals (to check temperature, cautiously hold hand about 4-inches above coals; medium coals will force removal of hand in 4 seconds).
4. Grill steaks 7 to 9 minutes for rare to medium, turning once.

5. In a bowl, combine the cheeses and top each steak with an equal amount of cheese 1 minute before the end of cooking time.
6. Trim excess fat from steak; carve into slices.
7. Serve with salsa and tortillas.
8. Tortillas can be warmed over the coals by securely wrapping tortillas in heavy-duty aluminum foil and placed on outer edge of grill for about 5 minutes, turning once

NUTRITION FACTS per serving: 592 calories, 313 calories from fat, 34.3g total fat (53%), 13.5g saturated fat (68%), 87.3mg cholesterol (29%), 494.1mg sodium (21%), 40.3g carbohydrates (13%), 2.3g fiber (9%), 28.7g protein (57%), 295 IU vitamin A (6%), 3mg vitamin C (5%), 201mg calcium (20%) and 4.5mg iron (25%).

CORNED BEEF HASH
Makes 4 servings

It has been said, on *Saint Patrick's Day*, everyone is *Irish,* so what is a better *Irish* breakfast than corned beef and potatoes made into a hash?

12 ounces corned beef, cooked,
cut into 1/2-inch cubes
Water
1 pound potatoes, cut into 1/2-inch cubes
1 teaspoon salt (optional)
2 tablespoons butter, divided

1 onion, coarsely chopped
1 cup bell pepper, red, yellow or green, chopped
3 tablespoons parsley, chopped
1/4 cup half & half
3 tablespoon dry white wine
1/2 teaspoon dry mustard

Pepper to taste

1. Bring water to a boil in large saucepan; add potatoes and salt.
2. Return to boil and cook 5 minutes; drain well.

3. Melt 1 tablespoon butter in large heavy skillet over medium-high heat; add onion and bell pepper.
4. Cook 2 minutes or until crisp-tender, remove to medium bowl.

5. Add corned beef, potatoes and parsley to onion mixture; mix lightly.
6. Combine half and half, wine, mustard and pepper; add to corned beef mixture and mix well.
7. Wipe out skillet with paper towel.

8. Place over medium heat until hot; add remaining butter.
9. Add corned beef mixture, pressing down firmly.
10. Cook 15 minutes or until browned, turning with flat spatula several times

NUTRITION FACTS per serving: 363 calories, 185 calories from fat, 20.4g total fat (31%), 8.7g saturated fat (43%), 66.4mg cholesterol (22%), 858.1mg sodium (36%), 27.5g carbohydrates (9%), 3.5g fiber (14%), 16.7g protein (33%), 1243 IU vitamin A (25%), 94mg vitamin C (156%), 96mg calcium (10%) and 5.4mg iron (30%).

COWBOY STEAKS
Makes 4 servings

Herding cattle, mending fences, and cleaning out the barn requires a hearty breakfast. These steaks with eggs and hash brown potatoes makes a great breakfast for anyone needing get-up-and-go energy.

4 onions, sliced
3 tablespoons olive oil, divided
1 teaspoon pepper
1 teaspoon oregano

1 teaspoon thyme
1 teaspoon Cajun seasoning
2 garlic cloves, minced
4 beef tenderloin steaks, about 4 ounces each

1. Pour 2 tablespoons of olive oil into a preheated skillet and sauté onions until tender; set aside.
2. In a small bowl, combine 1 tablespoon olive oil with seasonings and garlic.

3. Rub mixture on both sides of steak.
4. Place steaks under broiler, cooked as desired.
5. Serve steaks on a bed of onions

NUTRITION FACTS per serving: 448 calories, 329 calories from fat, 36.5g total fat (56%), 12g saturated fat (60%), 80.6mg cholesterol (27%), 658.2mg sodium (27%), 8g carbohydrates (3%), 2.4g fiber (9%), 21.8g protein (44%), 41 IU vitamin A (1%), 7mg vitamin C (12%), 94mg calcium (9%) and 3.6mg iron (20%).

Did you know the average American eats more than sixty-five pounds of beef a year? And that's down from a decade ago. Europeans eat about half that amount, and the Japanese eat only about ten percent.

CREAMED CHIPPED BEEF
Makes 4 servings

Prior to refrigeration, beef was salted and dried to preserve for future use. Our early pioneers depended on this beef, called "chipped Beef," to survive during the lean months. Chipped beef can be a little salty for the average taste. If salt is a problem, cover with boiling water for about a minute, drain and use in this recipe from *Tom and Terry Rimel* of the *National Pike Inn* in New Market, Maryland.

5 tablespoons butter   1/3 cup flour   1 1/2 cups milk
3 ounces dried chipped beef, cut into small pieces, fat removed

1. In a skillet, melt butter over low heat.
2. Add chipped beef and sauté over low heat 5 minutes.
3. Turn heat up to medium high and slowly add flour, stirring constantly.

4. Add milk pouring in slowly a small amount at a time.
5. When mixture is thick, remove and serve

Makes a great topping for biscuits

NUTRITION FACTS per serving: 246 calories, 162 calories from fat, 18.3g total fat (28%), 11.2g saturated fat (56%), 60.5mg cholesterol (20%), 457.2mg sodium (19%), 12.6g carbohydrates (4%), zero fiber, 8.5g protein (17%), 650 IU vitamin A (13%), 5mg vitamin C (9%), 117mg calcium (12%) and 1.2mg iron (7%).

BREAKFAST IN EGYPT

Egypt began around 4,000 B.C. when nomadic hunters settled in the Nile Valley. However, it was a thousand years later that Egypt crowned her first Pharaoh. The pyramids, tombs and temples were started about 2700 B.C. and are one of the remaining Seven Wonders of the World.

The Nile Valley is Egypt's main inhabited area. This fertile strip of land is about 8 miles wide and 900 miles long. The main agricultural products are rice, wheat, millet, barley, onions, sugar cane, various vegetables, citrus, mangoes, dates, figs, and grapes. Within this area, farm livestock include cattle, sheep and chickens. Fish from the Mediterranean and the Red Sea also adds to Egyptian diet.

As in many countries of the Mediterranean, there have been ethnic cultures presenting various types of cuisine. Hence, Middle Eastern dishes may have originated anywhere from Morocco to India with delights and samplings from a number of European countries as well. Visitors to Cairo can find many inexpensive cafes serving Egyptian specialties.

EGYPTIAN MEATBALLS
Makes 6 servings

It's the herbs and spices that make these meatballs great! *Egyptians* serve these breakfast meatballs with rice.

1 1/2 pounds lean ground round or sirloin
1/2 cup onion, finely minced
2 garlic cloves, minced
1/4 cup fresh parsley, minced
1/4 cup fresh dill, minced or 1 teaspoon dried dill
1/2 teaspoon cumin

1/4 teaspoon allspice
Salt & pepper to taste
3 tablespoons clarified butter
1 garlic clove, whole
1 tablespoon butter
2 cups tomato juice

1. In a large bowl, combine meat, onion, minced garlic, parsley, dill, cumin, allspice, salt and pepper.
2. Shape into meatballs and fry in clarified butter until browned.
3. Drain and wipe skillet dry.

4. Fry remaining garlic clove in 1 tablespoon of butter.
5. Stir in tomato juice.
6. Add meatballs, stirring to coat with sauce; bring to a boil.
7. Reduce heat and simmer, uncovered, for 10 to 15 minutes

NUTRITION FACTS per serving: 403 calories, 292 calories from fat, 32.4g total fat (50%), 14.8g saturated fat (74%), 107.7mg cholesterol (36%), 449.6mg sodium (19%), 6.2g carbohydrates (2%), .7g fiber (3%), 21.6g protein (43%), 984 IU vitamin A (20%), 17mg vitamin C (28%), 78mg calcium (8%) and 4.5mg iron (25%).

GRANDMA'S GOULASH
Makes 6 servings

Hungarians have many versions of this hearty stew. This American version by *Virginia Hammett* of Mount Airy, Maryland makes an excellent breakfast during the cold winter months.

1 pound hamburger or bacon, crumbled
32 ounce can tomatoes
30 ounce can kidney beans
1/3 cup macaroni or other pasta

1 onion, chopped
1 tablespoon Worcestershire sauce
Dash of pepper

1. In a large Dutch Oven, sizzle the hamburger with the onion.
2. Drain off the fat; discard.

3. In blender chop tomatoes and pour into Dutch Oven.

4. Add kidney beans, Worcestershire, and pepper.
5. In a separate pan cook the macaroni.

6. When tender, add to mixture in Dutch Oven and simmer 30 minutes

NUTRITION FACTS per serving: 404 calories, 95 calories from fat, 10.9g total fat (17%), 3.6g saturated fat (18%), 29.5mg cholesterol (10%), 1183.4mg sodium (49%), 59.1g carbohydrates (20%), 2g fiber (8%), 20.1g protein (40%), 916 IU vitamin A (18%), 26mg vitamin C (43%), 146mg calcium (15%) and 5.1mg iron (28%).

GREEN CHILE STEW
Makes 6 servings

Rosella Frederick of Cochiti, New Mexico is known for her good cooking. One of her specialties is her green chile stew. She has cut her recipe down for *The Best of New Mexico Kitchens* cookbook to family size. This stew should be eaten with a spoon.

2 pounds lean beef chuck, 1/2 inch cubes
Lard or vegetable oil
1/2 onion, chopped
4 potatoes, peeled, diced (optional)
4 zucchini, diced (optional)

12 green chilies, roasted, peeled, chopped or
8 ounce can green chile, chopped
1 teaspoon garlic salt
1 teaspoon salt
6 to 7 cups water

1. Brown the meat in a little lard in a heavy pan.
2. Add the onions, potatoes and cook until browned.
3. Add the zucchini, chilies, garlic salt, salt and water.

4. Bring to a boil, reduce to simmer for at least 30 minutes.
5. Ladle into bowls and serve with homemade bread

NUTRITION FACTS per serving: 463 calories, 252 calories from fat, 28.3g total fat (43%), 11.4g saturated fat (57%), 89.9mg cholesterol (30%), 138.4mg sodium (6%), 25g carbohydrates (8%), 3.8g fiber (15%), 28.3g protein (57%), 988mg vitamin A (20%), 241mg vitamin C (402%), 49mg calcium (5%) and 4.8mg iron (26%).

MEXICAN STEAKS
Makes 4 servings

The taste of *Mexico* comes out in this recipe. *Carolyn M. Kilgore* of Vicksburg, Mississippi likes to serve these steaks with grits.

3/4 cup flour
1/4 teaspoon salt
1/4 teaspoon pepper
4 beef steaks, cubed, about 1/4 pound each
3 tablespoons vegetable oil

1/2 cup onion, chopped
1/2 cup green pepper, hot or mild, chopped
1 tablespoon margarine
10 ounce can tomatoes with green chili peppers, undrained

1 cup Jack cheese, grated

1. Blend flour, salt and pepper.
2. Dip meat in flour mixture.
3. Heat oil in large skillet.
4. Cook meat over medium heat for 8 to 10 minutes on each side.
5. Remove to platter.

6. Cook onion and green pepper in margarine until tender.
7. Add tomatoes; heat thoroughly.
8. Add cheese and stir until melted.
9. Pour sauce over steaks

NUTRITION FACTS per serving: 554 calories, 330 calories from fat, 36.4g (56%), 12.7g saturated fat (64%), 96.4mg cholesterol (32%), 736mg sodium (31%), 22.4g carbohydrates (7%), .5g fiber (2%), 738 IU vitamin A (15%), 16mg vitamin C (27%), 243mg calcium (24% and 3.9mg iron (21%).

TOURTIERE MEAT PIE
Makes 6 servings

Connie Vatthauer from Grand Forks, North Dakota says, "My *French Canadian* grandmother often made this breakfast pie. It is still a family favorite." Connie serves this meat pie with cranberry relish.

1/2 garlic clove, mashed	1/4 teaspoon nutmeg	1 cup water
1 teaspoon salt	1/4 teaspoon mace	1 pound beef, ground
1/4 teaspoon pepper	1 tablespoon corn starch	Double crust pastry

1. In a sauce pan, mix spices, cornstarch and water.
2. Add the meat and heat to boiling.
3. Reduce heat to simmer and cook for 30 minutes.

4. Pour mixture into unbaked pie crust and cover with second crust.
5. Cut in steam vents.
6. Bake for 30 minutes in a 425°F oven.

NUTRITION FACTS per serving with 1/4 cup of relish: 779 calories, 399 calories from fat, 44.7g total fat (69%), 12.1g saturated fat (61%), 29.5mg cholesterol (10%), 682.2mg sodium (28%), 79.8g carbohydrates (27%), 1.3g fiber (5%), 53 IU vitamin A (1%), 14mg vitamin C (23%), 72mg calcium (7%) and 4.6mg iron (25%).

VARIATION

Use sausage or a mixture of sausage and ground beef or shredded roast beef or pork.

CRANBERRY RELISH

Cranberries, chopped	Oranges, chopped	Sugar

1. Mix cranberries and oranges.

2. Add sugar to taste.

Relish should be tart.

RICH MEAT CRUST

2 1/2 cups flour	1 cup shortening	3 to 4 tablespoons water

1. In a medium bowl, cut shortening into flour with a pastry blender until the mixture looks like course cornmeal.

2. Sprinkle with water, a few drops at a time and mix with a fork until all dry ingredients are moistened.

3. Make into a ball and chill 20 minutes before rolling out.

PORK

Pork is the number one red meat consumed during the breakfast meal in America. Pork is also a breakfast treat in other countries as well. Pork might be in the form of bacon, sausage, ham, pork chops, or as an ingredient in a recipe.

BACON

Slab bacon is probably the most consumed of the pork products. But have you heard the expression, *"Eating high on the hog?"* This refers to Arkansas bacon. This bacon comes from the upper part of the pork shoulder (where's there's more lean meat and less fat), in front of the loin (*Canadian bacon*) and above the sides (*slab bacon*). It is dry-rubbed with sugar and deep hickory smoked with no added water.

Irish bacon is similar to Arkansas bacon. Arkansas bacon is cooked like any other bacon, either fried or broiled. It is important that Arkansas bacon be fried very slowly over low heat and turned frequently to prevent burning. The drippings make excellent gravy.

HAM

Generally the ham you purchase at the supermarket has been brine cured. The meat is injected with a solution of water, salt, sodium nitrate, and sugar or honey. Some of these hams are smoked, many are injected with smoky flavor, and all lack the flavor of a dry-cured ham.

Specialty hams are cured in a variety of ways. Most are dry-cured, some aged, others smoked with a number of different kinds of woods, and some are coated with beef blood, black pepper, or honey.

Country hams are the most popular specialty hams in America. They are dry-cured with salt and brown sugar, slow smoked with green hickory and aged for about a year. These hams will continue to age, but will stop the aging process once refrigerated, and freezing will destroy some of the flavor.

COUNTRY SAUSAGE
Makes 4 servings

There are as many recipes for making sausage as there are recipes for eggs. The supermarket has a dozen different kinds of sausage, the best is made from the whole-hog. This produces a leaner sausage, with full flavor.

You can prepare and season your own homemade fresh sausage. If ground pork and ham is not available in the supermarket, chop it up in a food processor. Best if aged overnight before cooking.

3/4 pound ground fresh pork (not sausage)
1/4 pound ground ham
1/2 teaspoon salt (optional)
1/2 teaspoon dried thyme

1/2 teaspoon dried red pepper flakes (hot or mild)
1/2 teaspoon black pepper
1 1/2 teaspoons dried sage

1. Combine all ingredients and wrap in plastic wrap until ready for use.

Keeps 2 to 3 days in the refrigerator. Can be made into individual patties and frozen.

NUTRITION FACTS per serving: 306 calories, 191 calories from fat, 20.7g total fat (32%), 7.6g saturated fat (38%), 96.2mg cholesterol (32%), 702.6mg sodium (29%), zero carbohydrates, .2g fiber (1%), 26.9g protein (54%), 42 IU vitamin A (1%), 9mg vitamin C (15%), 30mg calcium (3%) and 1.8mg iron (10%).

A FRENCH BREAKFAST
Makes 6 servings

It's the smoked sausage that makes this recipe special. Best when made the night before, refrigerated, and baked in the morning.

12 slices bread with crusts removed
6 slices Swiss cheese
1/4 cup green onion, chopped
1/4 cup green pepper, chopped
3/4 pound smoked sausage, chopped

3 eggs
2 cups milk
1/2 teaspoon salt
1/8 teaspoon pepper
1 cup corn flakes, crushed (optional)

1. Place 6 slices of bread across the bottom of a 2- quart oblong casserole.
2. Cover each with a slice of cheese.
3. Cover the cheese with green onion, green pepper and sausage.

4. Top with remaining slices of bread and cut each sandwich in half diagonally.
5. In a bowl, combine eggs and milk thoroughly and season with salt and pepper.
6. Pour over the sandwiches.

7. Cover with foil and let stand several hours or overnight in the refrigerator.
8. Remove cover, sprinkle with cornflakes, if desired.

9. Bake at 350ºF for 40 to 45 minutes or until puffed and set.
10. Let stand 5 to 10 minutes before serving.

NUTRITION FACTS per serving: 539 calories, 301 calories from fat, 33.1g total fat (51%), 14.5g saturated fat (72%), 184.9mg cholesterol (62%), 1287.1mg sodium (54%), 34.8g carbohydrates (12%), 1.5g fiber (6%), 24.3g protein (49%), vitamin A (17%), vitamin C (31%), calcium (35%) and iron (18%).

THE IRISH "FRY"
Makes 4 servings

In *Ireland*, a large bowl of oatmeal is usually followed by the traditional Irish Fry (front cover photo). Irish bacon is cured pork loin. Irish bacon has two-thirds less fat than regular bacon. Breakfast white pudding is made with pork, rusk, onion and spices, while black pudding has the addition of barley and dried pork blood. Often this breakfast includes smoked cheese and/or smoked salmon and is served with brown bread, preserves and tea.

Irish bacon and the breakfast puddings are imported from Ireland by the *Limerick Bacon Company* and is available in many of the larger supermarkets or by mail order (see MAIL ORDER SOURCES, Dairygold USA Inc.)

8 slices Irish bacon
4 Irish sausages (bangers)
4 slices, each, black & white breakfast pudding

4 eggs
4 tomatoes
Freshly ground pepper

1. Over low heat, fry bacon, turning frequently until done to taste. It is important to note that Irish bacon is not cooked crispy hard.
2. Remove from pan and drain on paper towels; keep hot.
3. Place sausage in pan and cook until brown on all sides.

4. Cut tomatoes in half and fry with slices of white and black breakfast pudding in the bacon fat.
5. Remove and keep hot. All the above items can be broiled instead of being fried, if desire.
6. Cook eggs to order, fried, poached, scrambled, etc.

MARDI GRAS CANADIAN BACON BRUNCH
Makes 5 servings

If you can't make the Mardi Gras celebration in New Orleans, have your own Mardi Gras breakfast at home.

12 ounces Canadian-style bacon, cut 1/8-inch thick
1 onion, finely chopped
7 tablespoons butter or margarine, divided
2 cups okra, sliced
3 tomatoes, peeled, seeded, chopped

3/4 cup bread crumbs, dried, divided
3 tablespoons flour
1 1/3 cups milk
¼ teaspoon salt
¼ teaspoon hot pepper sauce
¾ cup Colby cheese, shredded

1. Reserve 12 slices of the Canadian bacon; cut remaining slices into 1x1-inch pieces; set aside.
2. Heat 3 tablespoons butter in large skillet.
3. Add onion; cook until transparent.
4. Add okra; cook slowly 8 to 10 minutes or until okra is tender, stirring occasionally.
5. In a bowl, combine bacon pieces, onion mixture and tomatoes.

6. Melt 2 tablespoons butter in small saucepan; add bread crumbs, stirring lightly to coat.
7. Place 1/4 cup crumbs evenly over bottom of 11 3/4 x 7 1/2-inch baking dish.
8. Place half of the bacon mixture over crumbs; sprinkle with additional 1/4 cup crumbs.
9. Top with remaining bacon mixture.
10 Heat remaining butter in saucepan; add flour, stirring until smooth.

11. Gradually add milk, salt and hot pepper sauce; cook until thickened, stirring constantly.
12. Add cheese; stir until melted.
13. Pour sauce evenly over bacon mixture, sprinkle with remaining crumbs.
14. Bake in 350ºF oven 30 minutes.
15. Arrange reserved bacon slices on top; continue baking 5 minutes.

NUTRITION FACTS per serving: 474 calories, 266 calories from fat, 29.7g total fat (46%), 16.5g saturated fat (83%), 101.9mg cholesterol (34%), 1594.8mg sodium (66%), 27.8g carbohydrates (9%), 3.1g fiber (12%), 24.5g protein (49%), 1582 vitamin A (32%), 39mg vitamin C (66%), 267mg calcium (27%) and 2.2mg iron (12%).

MINORCAN PORK CAKE
Makes 48 slices

On the island of *Minorca* in the Mediterranean Sea, the *Minocans* make this delicious fruit cake. The pork cake is equally enjoyed at breakfast and for dessert. This recipe is from the collection of the late *Helen E. Becker* of Saint Augustine, Florida.

1 pound fat salt pork, finely ground
2 cups hot coffee
2 cups brown sugar
2 eggs, well beaten
2 teaspoons baking soda
1 cup molasses
1 pound raisins

1 pound currants
1/2 pound citron, chopped
1 cup walnuts, chopped
1 tablespoon cloves
1 teaspoon nutmeg
6 cups flour
1 apple, sliced

1. In a medium bowl, mix salt pork, coffee, brown sugar and eggs.
2. Stir in soda and molasses.
3. In a large bowl combine raisins, currants, citron, walnuts, cloves and flour.
4. Add the pork mixture and beat well.
5. Line 3 bread pans with waxed paper and grease well.
6. Divide batter evenly in the 3 pans.
7. Bake in a 375ºF oven for about 2 hours.
8. When cool, wrap in plastic wrap with apple and place in a covered container and age for at least 1 week.

NUTRITION FACTS per slice: 260 calories, 89 calories from fat, 9.6g total fat (15%), 3g saturated fat (15%), 20.9mg cholesterol (7%), 211.3mg sodium (9%), 37.9g carbohydrates (13%), 1.3g fiber (5%), 3.7g protein (7%), 21 IU vitamin A (1%), 1mg vitamin C (2%), 43mg calcium (4%) and 1.9mg iron (10%).

ORANGE GLAZED HAM STEAKS
Makes 4 servings

For an elegant *French* breakfast, add a little *Grand Marnier* to these ham steaks. Grand Marnier is made in the small French town of Neauphle-le-chateau from oranges that have been distilled and blended and aged with cognac. This recipe can also be made with cherry preserves and Cherry Marnier.

1 tablespoon cornstarch
5 tablespoons Grand Marnier

1/2 cup orange marmalade
4 ham steaks, about 8 ounces each

1. In a small bowl, dissolve the cornstarch in the Grand Marnier.
2. In a small sauce pan bring the marmalade to a simmer over low heat, stirring often.
3. Stir in the dissolved cornstarch and simmer just until slightly thickened.
4. Broil the ham steaks just until they begin to brown, turn over and boil about 1 minute longer,
5. Brush the ham steaks with the orange glaze and continue to broil about 1 minute more or until the glaze bubbles.

OXFORD SAUSAGE

This *English* sausage is similar to Ireland's white breakfast pudding. This recipe comes from *John Adams Wickham's* book, Food Favorites of Saint Augustine (Florida).

2 pounds fresh lean pork, coarsely ground
1/2 pound beef suet, finely diced
1 cup bread crumbs, dried
1 lemon rind, grated

1 1/2 teaspoons thyme or sage
Dash of cayenne pepper
3/4 teaspoon black pepper
1 teaspoon salt

1. In a large bow, mix well all ingredients with your hands.
2. Divide in half and shape into two sausage rolls, wrapping each securely in foil.

3. Put in the refrigerator to blend flavors for at least 24 hours.
4. Cut off slices and fry in butter until brown on both sides and well done.

Sausage will keep for several weeks under refrigeration or can be frozen.

NUTRITION FACTS per serving: 556 calories, 422 calories from fat, 46.3g total fat (71%), 21.6g saturated fat (108%), 97.6mg cholesterol (33%), 424.3mg sodium (18%), 10.3g carbohydrates (3%), .9g fiber (3%), 22.8g protein (46%), zero vitamin A, 2mg vitamin C (3%), 35mg calcium (4%) and 2mg iron (11%).

PASTEL DE MALETA

Margarita Aguilar from Leon, Nicaragua serves this pork pastry for special occasions.

PASTRY

4 cups flour
1 teaspoon salt

2 teaspoons sugar
1/2 cup butter, chilled
Cold water

1/4 cup vegetable oil
2 eggs. beaten

1. Combine flour, salt and sugar in a large bowl.
2. Cut in butter with a pasty cutter until fine crumbs form.
3. In a small bowl combine eggs and oil.

4. Add egg mixture to flour mixture.
5. Add just enough water, a few drops at a time until mixture forms into a ball.
6. Refrigerate while making the filling.

FILLING

1 1/2 pounds pork, chunks
Water
2 onions, chopped, divided
3 garlic cloves
2 green bell peppers, chopped, divided
Salt and pepper to taste
2 red bell peppers, chopped

1/3 cup butter
3 eggs, hard boiled, sliced
1/3 cup raisins
1/3 cup capers
2 tablespoons Worcestershire sauce
1 1/2 teaspoons sugar
1/4 teaspoon nutmeg

Cayenne pepper to taste

1. Pour 4 cups of water in a sauce pan.
2. Add pork, 1 onion, garlic, 1 green pepper, salt and pepper to taste.
3. Cook until tender, adding more water if necessary.
4. Drain liquid and reserve.
5. Grind the cooled pork mixture in a food processor; set aside.

6. In a frying pan sauté remaining bell peppers and onion in butter for about 2 minutes.
7. Add the meat mixture and remaining ingredients.
8. Add salt and pepper to taste, if required.
9. If mixture is too dry add a little of the reserved liquid as needed.

10. Roll out the pastry to rectangle on floured board to about 1/4-inch thick.
11. Add the filling on top of the pastry.
12. Fold the pastry over the filling.
13. Brush edges with water and seal with a fork.
14. Place on a aluminum foil lined cookie sheet.
15. Brush pastry top with beaten egg yolk, if desired.
16. Bake at 350°F for 1 hour or until golden brown.
17. Cool.
18. Cut into 10 slices.
19. Serve hot or cold.

NUTRITION FACTS per slice: 594 calories, 316 calories from fat, 35g total fat (54%), 14.9g saturated fat (74%), 194.1mg cholesterol (65%), 622.5mg sodium (26%), 47.7g carbohydrates (16%), 1.1g fiber (5%), 21.6g protein (43%), 926 IU vitamin A (19%), 29mg vitamin C (48%), 58mg calcium (6%) and 3.8mg iron (21%).

PORK CHOPS
Makes 4 servings

Pork chops have been a breakfast favorite since pigs were brought to America. They are still found on tables across the country. Did you know that pork contains less calories and fat than most beef recipes?

4 pork chops, 1/2 thick

Salt and pepper to taste

1. Season pork chops to taste.

2. Place chops in a cold skillet and cook on medium heat, about 5 to 7 minutes per side, or until brown on both sides

NUTRITION FACTS per chop: 232 calories, 136 calories from fat, 14.7g total fat (23%), 5.1g saturated fat (25%), 73.7mg cholesterol (25%), 58.5mg sodium (2%), zero carbohydrates and fiber, 23.1g protein (46%), zero vitamin A, 1mg vitamin C (1%), 21mg calcium (2%) and .9mg iron (5%).

PORK PORRIDGE
Makes 12 servings

Do you have some leftover pork? If so, add it to this rice porridge like they do in *Singapore*.

6 1/2 quarts water
3 cups rice
10 dried scallops (optional)
3 tablespoons sesame oil

1 pound pork, cooked, minced
2 teaspoons salt
2 tablespoons fish sauce
4 tablespoons green onions, chopped

2 teaspoons pepper

1. In a large pot, put rice in the water with scallops; bring to a boil.
2. Simmer for 1 1/2 hours.
3. Add salt and fish sauce.
4. Add pork and simmer for 10 minutes.
5. Add sesame oil, onions and pepper and serve immediately.

NUTRITION FACTS per serving: 299 calories, 96 calories from fat, 10.4g total fat (16%), 2.9g saturated fat (14%), 29.2mg cholesterol (10%), 392mg sodium (16%), 38.2g carbohydrates (13%), .7g fiber (3%), 11.7g protein (23%), zero vitamin A, 1mg vitamin C (2%), 24mg calcium (2%) and 2.5mg iron (14%).

POSOLE ORTIZ
Makes 4 servings

Everyone has his own special recipe for posole. This is the way *Willie and June Ortiz* prepare it at *La Tertulia* in Santa Fe, New Mexico.

2 cups frozen white posole (hominy)
1 quart water

1 pound pork shoulder, cut up
1/8 teaspoon oregano

1 teaspoon whole black peppercorns   4 dried red chile peppers, crumbled
1/3 cup onion, chopped   Salt to taste

1. Mix all ingredients in a large, heavy pot.
2. Bring to a boil and simmer, covered, for about 2 ½ hours or until the kernels are soft, but not mushy.

NUTRITION FACTS per serving: 282 calories, 147 calories from fat, 16.2g total fat (25%), 5.4g saturated fat (27%), 60.4mg cholesterol (20%), 274.4mg sodium (11%), 16.8g carbohydrates (6%), 3.9g fiber (16%), 16.6g protein (33%), 4227 IU vitamin A (85%), 142mg vitamin C (236%), 35mg calcium (3%) and 1.8mg iron (10%).

SAVORY GREEN ONION BACON

Are you tired of eating just plain fried bacon? If so, try this recipe and/or a couple of the variations, or make up your own bacon flavoring creations.

1 pound bacon, sliced   1/4 cup green onions with tops, chopped
1/2 to 1 teaspoon hot pepper sauce

1. Heat oven to 375°F.
2. Arrange bacon slices on a jelly roll pan or on a rack in broiler pan.
3. In a small bowl, combine onions and pepper sauce.
4. Sprinkle evenly over bacon slices.
5. Bake for 17 to 20 minutes to desired crispness.
6. For thick-sliced bacon, increase cooking time to 22 to 26 minutes.
7. Drain on paper towels.

NUTRITION FACTS per slice based on 22 slices to the pound: 119 calories, 93 calories from fat, 10.2g total fat (16%), 3.6g saturated fat (18%), 17.5mg cholesterol (6%), 329.6mg sodium (14%), zero carbohydrates and fiber, 6.3g protein (13%), zero vitamin A, 7mg vitamin C (12%), zero calcium and .4mg iron (2%)

BLACK PEPPER VARIATION

Black pepper is a favorite of *Europeans* and is gaining in popularity in America. For a *Cajun* taste, replace black pepper with desired amount of Louisiana seasonings (red pepper, hot sauce, etc.)

1. Substitute 1 tablespoon coarse grind black pepper for onion and sauce.
2. Sprinkle pepper over bacon.
3. Bake as directed above

GREEN CHILE SALSA VARIATION

For the taste of *Mexico,* make this recipe. Red chile salsa works well with this recipe also.

1. Substitute 1/4 cup drained green chili salsa for onions and sauce.
2. Lightly brush salsa over bacon slices.
3. Bake as directed above

What other international bacon creations can you make? Maybe curry from *India?* Ginger from *China?* Ground caraway seeds from *Austria?* Along with a variety of herbs, spices and sauces, the possibilities are endless.

Do you know where the word "bacon" comes from? It comes from the French. It originally referred to "the meat on a pig's back." Later, in England, it meant, "a side of pig's meat." It used to mean pork of any kind but today it means certain cuts cured and smoked. Do you know that bacon was first sold by cheesemongers instead of the butchers? That's true! Bacon is cured to prevent bacteria. Preserving is done by drying and smoking with salt, brown sugar, and saltpeter.

SAVORY SAUSAGE CASSEROLE
Makes 8 servings

Valarie L.V. Stewart from Newark, Delaware says, "*Mother would make this dish the day before Easter, then reheat and serve when we returned from Easter Sunday church services. It's quick, easy and delicious!*"

1 pound sausage
2 1/2 cups crisp rice cereal
1 cup rice, cooked

8 ounces cheddar cheese, shredded
1 can mushroom soup
1/4 cup milk

3 eggs, beaten

1. Fry sausage; drain.
2. Cover bottom of rectangular casserole dish (glass works best) with rice cereal.
3. Spread sausage over cereal.
4. Spread rice over sausage.
5. Sprinkle cheese over rice.

6. In a bowl, mix mushroom soup, milk and eggs until creamy; pour over cheese.
7. Bake in preheated 350°F oven for 35 to 45 minutes, until top is a deep golden color with a hint of brown.

NUTRITION FACTS per serving: 465 calories, 320 calories from fat, 35.2g total fat (54%), 15.1g saturated fat (75%), 149.1mg cholesterol (50%), 831.6mg sodium (35%), 18g carbohydrates (6%), .3g fiber (1%), 17.9g protein (36%), 821 IU vitamin A (16%), 6mg vitamin C (10%), 246mg calcium (25%) and 1.7mg iron (9%).

SOUTHERN VIRGINIA HAM WITH RED EYE GRAVY

This cookbook wouldn't be complete without a Virginia baked ham. *Carol Salvati* from Summersville, West Virginia presents her version she calls, *Flossie.* Carol always serves buttermilk biscuits (page 24) with ham and red eye gravy.

8 to 10 pound ham   7 cups water   ¼ cup vinegar

1. Place the ham, skin side down in a roaster pan with water and vinegar.
2. Cover pan.
3. In preheated 500°F oven, place ham and cook for 15 minutes.
4. Turn off heat.
5. Do not open oven door.

6. After 3 hours, turn on oven again to 500 F and cook 20 minutes.
7. Turn off and leave in oven overnight.
8. Do not open oven door.
9. Slice ham for breakfast, heat in frying pan and serve with Red Eye Gravy.

NUTRITION FACTS per 4 ounce serving without gravy; 207 calories, 111 calories from fat, 12g total fat (18%), 3.9g saturated fat (19%), 64.7mg cholesterol (22%), 1495mg sodium (62%), 3.5g carbohydrates (1%), zero fiber, 19.9g protein (40%), zero vitamin A, 31mg vitamin C (52%), 8mg calcium (1%) and 1.1mg iron (6%).

RED EYE GRAVY

Pan drippings from fried ham slice   1 cup coffee

1. Pour coffee into pan drippings.
2. Boil down to about ¼ cup of gravy.

3. Top fried ham with red eye gravy.

Red eye gravy is also great on grits!

POULTRY

It's rare to find any kind of poultry recipes for breakfast in cookbooks. Poultry meat for breakfast is no different than a beef steak or a slice of ham, it all reverts back, *"you-eat-what-you-got."* Our early pioneers ate a lot of poultry for breakfast. They enjoyed it, so will you.

CHICKEN BREAST DIJON
Makes 4 servings

Amanda Beth Wilson of Greenfield, Wisconsin says, "About the only *French* thing about this recipe is the Dijon mustard, from Dijon France." This recipe can be doubled.

2 whole chicken breasts, cut in half
2 teaspoons Dijon-type mustard
1 teaspoon lemon juice

1/4 teaspoon pepper
2 green onions, finely chopped
1/2 cup soft white bread crumbs

1. Preheat broiler and lightly grease rack.
2. Broil chicken breasts 5 to 6 inches from heat for 5 minutes.
3. Turn and repeat.
4. In a small bowl, combine mustard, juice, pepper and onions.

5. On the rack coat one side of the breasts with mixture and sprinkle with half of the bread crumbs.
6. Broil 2 minutes.
7. Turn breasts over and repeat the process with other half of mustard mixture and bread crumbs.

NUTRITION FACTS per serving: 379 calories, 139 calories from fat, 15.3g total fat (24%), 4.3g saturated fat (22%), 92.7mg cholesterol (31%), 311.8mg sodium (13%), 24.6g carbohydrates (8%), 3.4g fiber (14%), 34.7g protein (69%), 411 IU vitamin A (8%), 16mg vitamin C (27%), 92mg calcium (9%) and 3.3mg iron (18%).

CHICKEN ENCHILADAS
Makes 6 servings

When Americans discovered the *Mexican* enchilada, it was Americanized along the Mexican border. This version is from New Mexico and is featured in *The Best of New Mexico Kitchens* cookbook. You can use commercially made green chili sauce or you can make your own.

12 corn tortillas
4 cups green chili sauce

3 cups chicken, cooked, minced
1 pound Jack cheese, grated
1 pint sour cream

1/4 cup onion, minced (optional)
Salt to taste

1. Heat tortillas on a hot griddle and keep warm under a dish towel (can also be heated in oil and drained on paper towels).
2. In a bowl, mix 1 cup of the sauce with the chicken.
3. Put 1/4 cup of the chicken mixture on each tortilla and roll it up.

4. Place in an oblong baking dish.
5. Cover the enchiladas with the cheese, onion, salt and remaining chili sauce.
6. Bake at 350°F for about 20 minutes.
7. Smother with sour cream and return to the oven for 10 minutes more.
8. Serve immediately.

NUTRITION FACTS per serving made with commercial made green sauce: 442 calories, 267 calories from fat, 30.1g total fat (46%), 16.2g saturated fat (81%), 100.4mg cholesterol (33%), 430.1mg sodium (18%), 19.4g carbohydrates (6%), 2.1g fiber (9%), 24.9g protein (50%), 2218 IU vitamin A (44%), 32mg vitamin C (53%), 403mg calcium (40%) and 1.6mg iron (9%).

GREEN CHILE SAUCE
Makes 1 1/2 cups

1/4 cup vegetable or olive oil
1 garlic clove
1/2 cup onion, minced
1 tablespoon flour

1 cup water
1 cup green chile, diced (hot or mild)
Salt to taste

1. In the oil sauté garlic and onion in heavy saucepan.
2. Blend in flour with wooden spoon.

3. Add water and chile.
4. Bring to a boil and simmer, stirring frequently for 5 minutes.
5. Add salt to taste.

CHICKEN SCALOPPINI PALERMO
Makes 6 servings

Holland American Line presents international cuisine to their passengers. This famous *Italian* recipe has replaced veal with chicken served in a raspberry sauce, rather than a wine gravy. And look at the nutrition facts, low in calories and fat, and it tastes great!

1 1/2 pounds chicken breast, cut into 6 pieces, pounded to 1/4-inch thick
3 egg whites mixed with 2 tablespoons cold water
3/4 cup whole wheat bread crumbs

1 teaspoon garlic powder
1/4 cup raspberry vinegar
2 tablespoons sugarless raspberry fruit conserve
3/4 cup fresh or frozen raspberries, thawed
1 tablespoon Dijon-style mustard

Raspberry for garnish

1. Preheat oven to 350°F.
2. Spray baking sheet with non-stick vegetable oil.
3. In a bowl, mix bread crumbs with garlic powder.
4. Dip chicken in egg white mixture, coat chicken with bread crumbs and arrange chicken on the baking sheet.

5. Bake about 25 minutes or until golden brown.
6. Combine vinegar and conserve in a sauce pan, bring to a boil.
7. Add raspberries and mustard, simmer 10 minutes.
8. Spoon about 3 tablespoons of the raspberry sauce on each chicken breast and top with 4 raspberries.

NUTRITION FACTS per serving: 244 calories, 79 calories from fat, 8.9g total fat (14%), 2.5g saturated fat (12%), 58.1mg cholesterol (19%), 119.5mg sodium (5%), 18.2g carbohydrates (6%), 3g fiber (12%), 23.2g protein (46%), 96 IU vitamin A (2%), 5mg vitamin C (9%), 24mg calcium (2%) and 1.5mg iron (8%).

CHICKEN PILAU
Makes 6 servings

In 1934 *Clara Lopez de Mier* opened up the *El Patio Restaurant* in Saint Augustine, Florida and the most asked breakfast dish was her chicken pilau. This *Minorcan* recipe can be made with fish, beef, pork or eggs (see recipe in HOT CEREALS for EGG PILAU, page 66) Serve with "bottled Hell.".

1/4 cup lard
3 onions, chopped
28 ounce can of tomatoes, mashed
1 teaspoon salt
1 teaspoon sugar

1/4 teaspoon thyme
1/4 teaspoon cayenne pepper
1 chicken, cut into 8 pieces
2 cups chicken broth
1 cup rice

1. Put the lard in a large, heavy pot.
2. When the lard is hot, but not smoking, add the onions.
3. Simmer over low heat for 10 minutes.
4. Add the tomatoes, salt, sugar, thyme and pepper.
5. Simmer down until thick.
6. Add the chicken, stir into the sauce, simmer for 20 minutes.
7. Add the broth and rice; cover, simmer for 1 hour over low heat, stirring occasionally.

NUTRITION FACTS per serving: 553 calories, 201 calories from fat, 22g total fat (34%), 7g saturated fat (35%), 129mg cholesterol (43%), 1487mg sodium (62%), 38.7g carbohydrates (13%), 3.4g fiber (13%), 47.9g protein (96%), 909 IU vitamin A (18%), 23mg vitamin C (39%), 98mg calcium (10%) and 4.5mg iron (25%).

SHRIMP VARIATION

Replace chicken with 2 pounds raw shrimp and cook only until rice is fluffy, about 40 minutes.

BOTTLED HELL
Use with caution, those tiny peppers are atomic!

Datil pepper seeds were bought to Saint Augustine by the *Minorcan* women in 1777. They are used in local cuisine, as well as making this hot sauce.

2 cups datil peppers	3 cups vinegar, divided	2 large bottles catsup

1. In a blender, put peppers and 1/2 cup of vinegar, blend for 5 minutes.
2. Put mixture into a saucepan; add the catsup and the remaining vinegar.
3. Bring to a boil and simmer for 10 minutes.

CHICKEN PORRIDGE
Makes 6 servings

Street hawkers in *Singapore* offer a variety of rice porridges. Chicken porridge is second only to fish porridge (page 190) for breakfast.

4 cups water	3 1/2 quarts water	4 tablespoons ginger, shredded
2 pounds chicken	1 chicken bouillon cube	2 scallions, chopped
2 teaspoons salt	2 teaspoons fish sauce	Pepper to taste
1 1/4 cups rice (broken grains)	4 tablespoons vegetable oil	2 tablespoons sesame oil
	10 shallots, sliced	

1. Wash and clean the chicken and put to boil with the 4 cups of water.
2. Boil for 30 minutes and turn off heat.
3. Lift out chicken and allow to cool, then remove meat from the bones.
4. Wash rice in several changes of water and put to boil with bouillon, fish sauce and chicken broth (water from the boiled chicken).
5. Simmer for 20 minutes.
6. Add shredded chicken meat.
7. In a skillet, fry shallots in oil.
8. Stir sesame oil into the porridge and serve.
9. Garnished with scallions, fried shallots, ginger and pepper.

NUTRITION FACTS per serving: 491 calories, 203 calories from fat, 22.2g total fat (34%), 4g saturated fat (20%), 82.9mg cholesterol (28%), 990mg sodium (41%), 40.6g carbohydrates (14%), .7g fiber (3%), 30.9g protein (62%), 5365 IU vitamin A (107%), 4mg vitamin C (7%), 45mg calcium (4%) and 3.4mg iron (19%).

CHICKEN WITH FIGS
Makes 6 servings

In the Bible, Adam and Eve used fig leaves to cover up their privates. With that information, we know that figs have been around since the beginning of time. The *Spaniards* bought ginger to the Mediterranean from *Asia* in the 16th century and it didn't take long before figs and ginger were mixed with chicken. Enjoy this recipe from *Sun-Diamond of California* for that special breakfast.

12 ounce package dried figs
2 teaspoons vegetable oil
2 teaspoons butter
1 onion, cut into thin wedges

4 teaspoons fresh ginger, minced
1/2 teaspoon pepper
3 pounds chicken breasts
1/4 teaspoon salt

1 1/2 cups apple cider
1/2 teaspoon dried thyme or
1 teaspoon fresh thyme
1 tablespoon lemon juice

1. Cut stems from figs, cut each fig in half; set aside.
2. In a large non-stick skillet, heat oil and butter.
3. Add onions, ginger and pepper.
4. Cook over medium-low heat, stirring occasionally until onions are dark golden brown, about 15 minutes; remove, set aside.
5. Add chicken to the skillet, sprinkle with salt.
6. Cook turning occasionally until golden on all sides.
7. Add onion mixture, figs, apple cider and thyme; cover.
8. Simmer until chicken is tender, 20 to 30 minutes.
9. Turn once during cooking.
10. Remove chicken, onions and figs to a serving platter.
11. Over medium heat, add lemon juice to pan.
12. Cook and stir until sauce thickens slightly, about 30 seconds; spoon over chicken.

NUTRITION FACTS per serving: 517 calories, 180 calories from fat, 20.4g total fat (32%), 5.9g saturated fat (40%), 119.6mg cholesterol (40%), 315.9mg sodium (13%), 45.8g carbohydrates (15%), 5.7g fiber (23%), 39.9g protein (80%), 280 IU vitamin A (6%), 5mg vitamin C (8%), 121mg calcium (12%), and 3.1mg iron (17%).

CORNISH HENS STUFFED WITH BULGUR
Makes 4 servings

Wheat is one of the chief agriculture products in *Egypt* and is used in many of *Egyptian* recipes. Bulgur is cooked cracked wheat that has been steamed. It is also known as *ala*.

2 cornish hens
1/2 cup bulgur

1 onion, minced
Salt & pepper to taste

2 tablespoons butter
Parsley

1. Wash hens and wipe dry.
2. Wash the bulgur and squeeze dry.
3. In a bowl, combine bulgur, onion, salt, pepper and butter.
4. Stuff each hen with half the mixture.
5. Use a trussing needle and thread to sew each hen closed.
6. Boil hens in about 7 cups of water.
7. Skim off froth, reduce heat and simmer gently for 45 minutes to one hour.
8. Remove hens from the water and fry in butter to brown them.
9. Split in half.
10. Garnish with parsley.

NUTRITION FACTS per serving: 796 calories, 406 calories from fat, 44.4g total fat (68%), 14.3mg saturated fat (71%), 263.3mg cholesterol (88%), 1093mg sodium (46%), 15.7g carbohydrates (5%), 3.9g fiber (15%), 79.9g protein (160%), 1105 IU vitamin A (22%), 4mg vitamin C (6%), 95mg calcium (9%) and 5.9mg iron (33%).

NOTE: Save the liquid, cool, skim off fat and refrigerate. Use when recipe calls for chicken broth. This broth is far superior than any broth found in a can.

CREOLE TURKEY PASTRAMI SURPRISE
Makes 4 servings

This recipe by the *National Turkey Federation* is sort of a take-off of eggs benedict, but with ,out the eggs, there are less calories, fat and cholesterol

1/2 cup egg substitute, room temperature
2 tablespoons lemon juice
1/8 teaspoon creole seasoning
1/3 cup margarine, melted

2 whole wheat English muffins, split, toasted
1/2 pound turkey pastrami, cut into 4 slices
14 ounce can artichoke hearts,
drained, cut in half

1 tomato, cut into 4 slices

1. In blender combine egg substitute, lemon juice and seasoning.
2. While the blender is running, slowly add the margarine in a steady stream, until blended.
3. Pour mixture into a 1 cup glass measure and microwave on 30% power (defrost setting) for 1 minute.

4. Stir mixture and microwave an additional 30 seconds.
5. Allow mixture to stand 1 minute.
6. Spoon 2 tablespoons of sauce over each muffin half.
7. Top with pastrami slice, tomato and 2 artichoke heart halves.
8. Top with 2 more tablespoons of sauce.

NUTRITION FACTS per serving: 367 calories, 179 calories from fat, 20.6g total fat (32%), 4.1g saturated fat (20%), 31mg cholesterol (10%), 1140mg sodium (47%), 27.9g carbohydrates (9%), 7.8g fiber (31%), 21g protein (42%), 1668 IU vitamin A (33%), 19mg vitamin C (32%), 162mg calcium (16%) and 3.8mg iron (21%).

KARAHI CHICKEN
Makes 6 servings

Shazia Hasan of Karachi, Pakistan, says, "We like this chicken dish so much that we eat it for breakfast, lunch and dinner. I generally serve karchi with warm croissants or toasted bread."

1 chicken, skinned, cut up into 12 pieces
2 tomatoes, chopped
6 green chilies, cut length wise, seeds removed
Handful fresh green coriander leaves
1-inch piece of fresh ginger, shredded

3 garlic cloves, minced
1 1/4 teaspoons salt
1 teaspoon cayenne pepper
1 teaspoon cumin seeds
3 cups water

1/2 cup vegetable oil

1. In a wok or big sauce pan, pour in the water.
2. Put in the chicken, salt, cayenne and cumin.
3. Cook over medium heat for about 20 to 30 minutes, until the water is almost gone.
4. Put in tomatoes, chilies, coriander, ginger, garlic and oil.

5. Carefully mix it with the chicken.
6. Simmer until almost all the liquid is gone.
7. It will be necessary to stir once in awhile, so the chicken does not stick.
8. When the tomatoes start to disappear and the chicken is tender, it is ready

NUTRITION FACTS per serving: 483 calories, 275 calories from fat, 30.6g total fat (47%), 5.4g saturated fat (27%), 123.4mg cholesterol (41%), 573.9mg sodium (24%), 9.9g carbohydrates (3%), q.5g fiber (6%), 41.9g protein (84%), 806 IU vitamin A (16%), 125mg vitamin C (208%), 54mg calcium (5%) and 3.3mg iron (18%).

Did you know that chickens originated in the jungles of southeastern Asia and have been domesticated for more than 4,000 years? It was the European explorers who found them tasty and brought them to Europe in the 3rd century B.C. Chickens came to America in the early 1600s. At that time chickens were raised mainly for their eggs and feathers. The feathers were, and still are, prized as pillow stuffing.

MEXICAN CHICKEN
Makes 4 servings

Perdue Farms, Inc., presents the flavor of *Mexico* in this easy stir-fry recipe. Serve with warmed corn tortillas.

1 pound chicken meat, cut up to stir-fry-size
1 teaspoon chili powder
1/2 teaspoon cumin
1/4 teaspoon oregano

2 tablespoons olive oil, divided
2 green onions, chopped
1 garlic clove, minced
4 ounces can mild green chilies, chopped

19 ounces can black beans, drained and rinsed.

1. In a bowl, place chicken, chili powder, cumin, oregano and 1 tablespoon of oil; toss well.
2. Heat a wok or large, non-stick skillet over medium- high heat.
3. When hot, coat with remaining oil.

4. Add chicken mixture; stir-fry 4 to 5 minutes until barely cooked through.
5. Add remaining ingredients and stir-fry 2 to 3 minutes longer until heated through.

NUTRITION FACTS per serving: 488 calories, 181 calories from fat 20.5g total fat (31%), 4.7g saturated fat (24%), 76.1mg cholesterol (25%), 96.1mg sodium (4%), 40.9g carbohydrates (14%), 14.4g fiber (58%), 37.1g protein (74%), 857 IU vitamin A (17%), 85mg vitamin C (141%), 115mg calcium (12%) and 5.5mg iron (31%).

MOROCCAN HONEY CHICKEN
Makes 6 servings

ConAgra Poultry Company offers a spicy chicken for your breakfast meal. Enjoy it with warm pita bread.

1 pound boneless chicken breast
1/4 cup honey, divided
1 tablespoon water
1 1/2 teaspoons curry powder
1 teaspoon salt

1/2 teaspoon pepper
Dash of allspice (optional)
2 tablespoons butter or margarine
1/2 cup chicken bouillon or water
1/4 cup raisins

1 lemon, thinly sliced

1. In a large bowl mix well 2 tablespoons honey, 1 tablespoon water, curry, salt, pepper and allspice.
2. Add chicken; turn to coat.
3. Let stand at least 20 minutes or refrigerate overnight, turning occasionally.

4. In a 12-inch skillet over medium heat add butter, remaining honey and brown the chicken.
5. Add remaining marinade and remaining ingredients.
6. Bring to a boil.
7. Reduce heat; cover and cook 30 minutes or until chicken is done.

NUTRITION FACTS per serving: 242 calories, 107 calories from fat, 12.4g total fat (19%), 4.8g saturated fat (24%), 61mg cholesterol (20%), 573.2mg sodium (24%), 18.9g carbohydrates (6%), .5g fiber (2%), 16g protein (32%), 230 IU vitamin A (5%), 15mg vitamin C (25%), 29mg calcium (3%) and 1.2mg iron (6%).

POLLO EN CACAHUATE
Makes 6 servings

In *Spain* the Spanish would cook this chicken in an almond sauce. This *Mexican* version is made with peanuts. In *Mexico* cocoa is sometimes added and is called "*mole*" and is served during special holidays. If you like it more picante, add some hot chilies.

1/4 cup vegetable oil
3 pounds chicken, cut into serving pieces

2 cups chicken stock
1 onion, cut into chunks

1 garlic clove, chopped	3 tomatoes, peeled, seeded, quartered
1 cinnamon stick	1/2 cup peanuts, shelled
2 whole allspice	1/2 cup dry sherry

Salt to taste

1. Heat oil in a skillet.
2. Add the chicken and sauté until golden brown.
3. Transfer the chicken to a large pot, add the stock and cook until the chicken is tender, about 30 minutes.
4. Drain and reserve the stock.
5. In the drippings remaining in the skillet, sauté the onion, garlic, cinnamon and allspice.
6. Remove with a slotted spoon and transfer to a blender.

7. Add the tomatoes, peanuts and 1/2 cup of the reserved stock.
8. Blend until the sauce is very smooth (more stock might be required), add the sherry and pour into the pot containing the chicken (if you want it mole-style, add ½ cup of cocoa).
9. Cook, covered, over low heat until the sauce thickens slightly.
10. Add salt to taste

NUTRITION FACTS per serving: 492 calories, 262 calories from fat, 27.8g total fat (43%), 5.3g saturated fat (26%), 123.8mg cholesterol (41%), 657.4mg sodium (27%), 8.8g carbohydrates (3%), 2.2g fiber (9%), 45.8g protein (92%), 461 IU vitamin A (9%), 13mg vitamin C (22%), 53mg calcium (5%) and 2.9mg iron (16%).

PTARMIGAN

When I lived in Alaska, my good friend Benny and I would go ptarmigan hunting. This chicken-like bird is related to the grouse, is brown during the summer and white in the winter. For some reason we only hunted during the winter and to find the white bird against the snow was difficult. We would shot at what we thought was a ptarmigan, and if we saw blood on the snow, we knew we had a hit. Most of the time we just shot at snow. In any event, ptarmigan is good eating, Here's how I made it.

1. I cut the ptarmigan in individual pieces.
2. Skin on or off is your choice, I left them on.
3. I rolled the pieces in flour, seasoned them with salt and pepper to taste.

4. In a deep pan, I next browned them in hot fat.
5. Once brown, I poured in enough tomato juice to cover, along with 3 cloves of sliced garlic, covered the pan and simmered them until tender.

Cooking time varies, as old ptarmigans take longer. If it takes more than 30 minutes, the bird is probably too old to enjoy.

RED EYE CHICKEN
Makes 4 servings

If you like your chicken hot and spicy, then try this Cajun specialty by *Perdue Farms, Inc.*

1 pound boneless, skinless chicken breasts	1/2 teaspoon paprika, divided
2 tablespoons vegetable oil, divided	Salt to taste
1/2 teaspoon white pepper, divided	13 ounces can reduced sodium chicken broth
1/2 teaspoon black pepper, divided	3 tablespoons unsalted tomato sauce
1/8 to 1/4 teaspoon cayenne red pepper, divided	2 tablespoons flour

1. Trim off and discard visible fat from chicken.
2. In a large skillet over medium-high heat, heat 1 tablespoon oil.
3. Add chicken.
4. In a small bowl, combine peppers and paprika; mixing well.
5. Sprinkle half of the seasonings on top of the chicken.

6. Salt to taste.
7. Brown for 2 to 4 minutes.
8. Turn chicken over and sprinkle remaining seasonings.
9. Continue pan frying until chicken is cooked through.
10. Remove from skillet and keep warm.
11. To skillet, add remaining oil and flour.

12. Continue to cook and stir for about 4 minutes until flour is well combined and brown.
13. Gradually add broth and tomato sauce, continue to cook and stir until sauce is smooth and thickened.

14. Season with salt and cayenne to taste.
15. Spoon sauce over chicken and serve.

NUTRITION FACTS per serving: 216 calories, 77 calories from fat, 8.8g total fat (14%), 1.3g saturated fat (7%), 65.8mg cholesterol (22%), 337.9mg sodium (14%), 5.1g carbohydrates (2%), .3g fiber (1%), 31.1g protein (62%), 342 IU vitamin A (7%), 3mg vitamin C (5%), 24mg calcium (2%) and 1.7mg iron (9%).

FISH AND SHELLFISH

Fish for breakfast is not very popular in America, and even might sound a bit strange to you. However, fish is prized as a breakfast food in many countries, and even along America's waterways. One of my cherished memories happened in the 1960s. I went trout fishing in the High Sierra with my friend Ray "Crash" Corrigan (a western movie star of the 1930s) in his camper. We awoke early and caught a dozen trout and Ray showed me how he cooked them. Without removing the innards or the head, Ray fried them in butter until crisp like bacon. They were delicious, head, innards and all!

ACCRA
Makes 6 servings

Fish for breakfast is an everyday treat in the Caribbean country of *Trinidad and Tobago*.

1/4 pound salt fish
1/2 cup onion, chopped
2 chive blades
1 fresh thyme sprig
1/4 teaspoon pepper

1/4 cup green pepper, chopped
2 cups flour
1/2 teaspoon salt
1/2 package yeast
1 1/2 cups water, lukewarm

1. Scald the fish with boiling water twice.
2. Remove bones and skin.
3. Pound the fish, vegetables and herbs until fine.
4. Add the yeast to the warm water; let it sit for 10 minutes.
5. Add the flour, salt and pepper.

6. Add the fish mixture, beat smooth.
7. Put in a greased bowl, cover and let rise for about 2 hours.
8. Heat vegetable oil in a skillet, drop fish mixture by tablespoonfuls and fry until brown.
9. Drain on power towels

Serve with floats (see FRIED DOUGHS, page 99).

NUTRITION FACTS per serving: 176 calories, 3.5% calories from fat, .7g total fat (1%), .1g saturated fat (1%), 8mg cholesterol (3%), 34g carbohydrates (11%), .7g fiber (3%), 8.3g protein (17%), 241mg sodium (10%), calcium (3%), 3.2mg iron (18%), 5mg vitamin c 98%) and 105 IU vitamin A (2%).

BAKED FISH WITH TOMATO SAUCE
Makes 4 servings

On the islands of *Antigua and Barbuda* fish is enjoyed at every meal.

1 whole fish (1 1/2 to 2 pounds,
    allow 6 ounces per person)
Salt & pepper to taste
2 cups soft bread crumbs

5 tablespoons margarine, divided
2 tablespoons onion, chopped
1 tablespoon lime juice
1 teaspoon garlic, minced

1 tablespoon ketchup
1 tablespoon fresh chives, pounded

1 tablespoon fresh thyme, pounded
1 teaspoon cloves

Fat pork or bacon

1. Prepare fish for cooking.
2. Sprinkle outside with salt and pepper.
3. Rub inside of fish with 1 tablespoon of margarine.
4. In a bowl, mix 4 tablespoons margarine, onion, lime juice, garlic, ketchup, herbs, cloves and salt and pepper to taste.
5. Fry mixture lightly.
6. Add crumbs; stir.
7. Moisten with water if too dry.

8. Pack mixture inside the fish.
9. Sew up the opening.
10. Place fish in a greased dish.
11. Lay slices of fat pork or bacon on fish.
12. Add a little water to the baking dish.
13. Bake in 350ºF oven for 20 minutes for the first pound and add 10 minutes per pound thereafter.
14. Baste every 10 minutes.
15. Serve with tomato sauce

NUTRITION FACTS per serving based on 1 1/2 pounds of fish: 660 calories, 302 calories from fat, 33.1g total fat (51%), 8.5g saturated fat (43%), 97.3mg cholesterol (32%), 1152.8mg sodium (48%), 42.6g carbohydrates (14%), 3.2g fiber (13%), 45.8g protein (92%), 749 IU vitamin A (15%), 14mg vitamin C (24%), 98mg calcium (10%) and 4.2mg iron (23%).

TOMATO SAUCE
Makes 4 servings

1 pound tomatoes
3 whole cloves
1 garlic clove, minced
1 tablespoon chives
1 tablespoon thyme

1 onion, chopped
Salt & pepper to taste
4 tablespoons vegetable oil
1 tablespoon margarine
2 cups water

1. In a large sauce pan, heat oil and margarine.
2. Add tomatoes; stir.

3. Add the rest of the ingredients; simmer until thick.
5. Strain, if desired.

NUTRITION FACTS per serving: 197 calories, 150 calories from fat, 18g total fat (28%), 2.4g saturated fat (12%), zero cholesterol, 193.5mg sodium (8%), 10.8g carbohydrates (4%), 3.7g fiber (15%), 1.8g protein (4%), 923 IU vitamin A (18%), 28mg vitamin C (47%), 78mg calcium (8%) and 2.3mg iron (13%).

BARBECUED SHRIMP
Makes 4 servings

One of the great traditions of New Orleans *Creole* cooking is its flair for creativity. Often complex, this creative urge occasionally take a turn toward absolute simplicity. Here's one of the best originals from the *Court of Two Sisters* restaurant. You will need plenty of napkins for this hands on dish!

48 large shrimp, heads on
4 tablespoons black pepper
1/2 teaspoon cayenne red pepper

1 pound butter, melted, divided
1 cup water
French bread

Absolutely no salt

1. Select 48 (about 2 1/2-pounds) 16-20 count shrimp with heads on.
2. Place in a shallow baking dish large enough to contain shrimp in a double layer.
3. Add water and half of the butter.

4. Sprinkle shrimp with peppers and cover with remaining butter.
5. Place in a 375ºF oven and roast for 10 minutes.
6. Turn with a large spoon and roast for another 10 minutes until shrimp are an even robust pink.

Serve with French bread to mop up the delicious liquor created by the butter and roasted shrimp.

BATTER FRIED SHRIMP
Makes 3 servings

In Burnside, Louisiana, *The Cabin Restaurant* serves these shrimps to their guests.

1 pound shrimp, peeled, deveined
1 cup flour
1 egg, beaten

1/2 cup buttermilk
Salt to taste
Cayenne pepper to taste

1. Shrimp need to be dried with a paper towel to be coated.
2. Season with salt and pepper.
3. Mix flour, egg and buttermilk until smooth.

4. For a thin batter add just a little more buttermilk.
5. For a thick batter has a little more flour.
6. Heat oil to 365°F and deep fat fry the batter coated shrimp

NUTRITION FACTS per serving: 353 calories, 47 calories from fat, 5g total fat (8%), 1.3g saturated fat (6%), 302.3mg cholesterol (101%), 288.6mg sodium (12%), 35.4g carbohydrates (12%), zero fiber, 38.5g protein (77%), 392 IU vitamin A (8%), 3mg vitamin C (6%), 141mg calcium (14%) and 5.8mg iron (32%).

BOILED FISH
Makes 4 servings

Have you eaten boiled fish? If not, try this recipe from the country of *Antigua and Barbuda*. Use any firm fish, red snapper is a good choice.

1 pound fish, scaled, cleaned
1 onion, sliced
4 carrots, sliced
2 summer-type squash
Chives

Thyme
2 tablespoons ketchup
2 tablespoons margarine
Salt & pepper to taste
1 tablespoon lime juice

1. Place fish in a saucepan.
2. Add vegetables in layers.
3. Dot with margarine and ketchup.
4. Season to taste and add lime juice.

5. Pour in enough water to about 2 inches above the vegetables.
6. Cook on a low heat until fish and vegetables are cooked.

NUTRITION FACTS per serving: 204 calories, 60 calories from fat, 6.8g total fat (10%), 1.2g saturated fat (6%), 48.8mg cholesterol (16%), 380.4mg sodium (16%), 14.1g carbohydrates (5%), 4g fiber (16%), 22.3g protein (45%), 20528 IU vitamin A (411%), 21mg vitamin C (36%), 75mg calcium (7%) and 1.4mg iron (8%).

CONCH FRITTERS
Makes 4 servings

In the *British Virgin Islands* shellfish are used to make delicious recipes. Conch meat can be sautéed in butter, ground into patties, but one of the best ways is to make fritters.

2 cups conch, sliced very thin
1 1/2 cups flour

1 teaspoon baking powder
1 egg, beaten

1 cup milk
1/2 teaspoon salt

1. In a bowl, sift flour, baking powder and salt.
2. Make a well in the center and pour the egg into it.

3. Gradually add the milk.
4. Beat mixture into a smooth batter.
5. Dip the conch in the batter and fry in deep fat.

NUTRITION FACTS per serving: 287 calories, 42 calories from fat, 4.6g total fat (7%), 1.8g saturated fat (9%), 88.6mg cholesterol (30%), 448.6mg sodium (19%), 41.1g carbohydrates (14%), zero fiber, 18.7g protein (37%), 396 IU vitamin A (8%), 11mg vitamin C (18%), 208mg calcium (21%) and 13.7mg iron (76%).

CRAWFISH LOUISE
Makes 2 servings

Crawfish may look like shrimp, however, these fresh water crustaceans have a taste of their own. With shrimp, you only eat the tails. With crawfish you not only eat the tails, but eat the fat out of the body. Here's how first time guests at *The Court of Two Sisters* in New Orleans, Louisiana are told to eat them: Remove the tail and squeeze the tail to crack the shell. Remove the meat, discard the black vein, eat and enjoy. With your little finger, remove the golden fat from the body or suck the fat out with your mouth.

1 pound crawfish tails & fat*
1 tablespoon butter
3 tablespoons olive oil
1 bunch green onions

1/2 pound mushrooms, sliced
1 tablespoon garlic, pureed
1 tomato, peeled, chopped
1/2 cup Italian bread crumbs

1/2 cup Parmesan cheese

1. Heat crawfish and fat (*the fat is the body portion between the tail and the head).
2. Melt butter, add oil, sauté green onions, garlic and mushrooms.

3. Add tomato.
4. Add crawfish.
5. Add bread crumbs and cheese.
6. Heat thoroughly and serve immediately.

NUTRITION FACTS per serving: 677 calories, 327 calories from fat, 36.6g total fat (56%), 11.3g saturated fat (56%), 290.1mg cholesterol (97%), 773.1mg sodium (32%), 35.8g carbohydrates (12%), 5.5g fiber (22%), 52.2g protein (104%), 1146 IU vitamin A (23%), 34mg vitamin C (57%), 430mg calcium (43%) and 6.3mg iron (35%).

DOUBLE SALMON PATE

If you stop by *Sonia's Bed and Breakfast By the Sea* in Victoria, British Columbia, *Canada*, changes are *Sonia and Brian McMillan* will serve you this delicious pate,.

14 ounce canned salmon, drained
1/2 pound smoked salmon, diced very fine
2 tablespoons fresh parsley, chopped
3 green onions, finely chopped
1 teaspoon dried tarragon

1/2 cup butter, softened
1/2 cup mayonnaise
1 tablespoon Dijon mustard
1 tablespoon lemon juice
1/2 teaspoon pepper

1. In a bowl, flake salmon and combine with herbs and onions.
2. In separate bowl, cream butter, mayonnaise, mustard, lemon juice and pepper.

3. Add salmon mixture and gently combine.
4. Refrigerate a few hours until firm.

NUTRITION FACTS per tablespoon: 54 calories, 40 calories from fat, 4.5g total fat (7%), 1.6g saturated fat (8%), 12.1mg cholesterol (4%), 121.4mg sodium (5%), zero carbohydrates, .3g fiber (1%), 2.8g protein (6%), 161 IU vitamin A (3%), 2mg vitamin C (4%), 29mg calcium (3%) and .4mg iron (2%).

FISH CROQUETTES
Makes 4 servings

The *French* came up with the this recipe and from their word *croquer,* meaning "to crunch," and gave the recipe the name of croquette. This is only one of many versions, as croquettes are also made with chicken, rice, sweet potatoes, and eggs.

2 cups salmon or tuna,
cooked or canned, flaked
1/2 cup rice, cooked
Salt & pepper to taste

1 teaspoon lemon juice
1 teaspoon onion, minced
1 egg, beaten
Bread crumbs

1. In a bowl, mix fish, rice, lemon juice and onion together.
2. Chill for 30 minutes.

3. Form 1 inch balls, dip in egg, roll in the bread crumbs.
4. Fry in deep fat until golden and well crusted.

NUTRITION FACTS per serving: 244 calories, 59 calories from fat, 6.3g total fat (10%), 1.3g saturated fat (6%), 114.6mg cholesterol (38%), 192.9mg sodium (8%), 17.4g carbohydrates (6%), .8g fiber (3%), 27.5g protein (55%), 219 IU vitamin A (4%), 1mg vitamin C (1%), 35mg calcium (4%) and 1.7mg iron (9%).

FRIED FISH CUTLETS WITH LEMON SAUCE
Makes 4 servings

Rhona Baptiste from the Caribbean island of *Antigua* says the people enjoy all kinds of fish for breakfast, and this is one of their favorites.

1 pound fish fillets
1/2 onion, grated

1 garlic clove, minced
Salt & pepper to taste
2 cups bread crumbs

1 teaspoon lime juice
2 eggs, beaten

1. In a bowl, mix onion, garlic, salt, pepper and lime juice.
2. Season the fish with this mixture for 30 minutes; drain.

3. Dip fish in egg and then crumbs.
4. Fry in hot oil until golden brown.
5. Serve with Lemon Sauce.

NUTRITION FACTS per serving: 355 calories, 63 calories from fat, 6.9g total fat (11%), 1.8g saturated fat (9%), 155.1mg cholesterol (52%), 544.1mg sodium (23%), 41.2g carbohydrates (14%), 3.1g fiber (12%), 30g protein (60%), 204 IU vitamin A (4%), 3mg vitamin C (4%), 82mg calcium (8%) and 3mg iron (17%).

LEMON SAUCE
Makes 4 servings

This sauce goes well with any fish. Also makes a great topping for eggs or vegetables.

1/4 cup butter
2/3 cup sugar
2 egg yolks, beaten

1/4 teaspoon lemon rind, grated
2 tablespoons milk
2 egg whites, beaten

1 tablespoon lemon juice

1. In a bowl, cream the butter, add the sugar and yolks.
2. Cook in a double boiler until thick.

3. Add rind, milk and juice.
4. Fold in egg whites.
5. Serve at once.

NUTRITION FACTS per serving: 272 calories, 124 calories from fat, 14.1g total fat (22%), 8g saturated fat (40%), 137.9mg cholesterol (46%), 151.3mg sodium (6%), 34.3g carbohydrates, zero fiber, 3.5g protein (7%), 597 IU vitamin A (12%), 2mg vitamin C (3%), 25mg calcium (3%) and .4mg iron (2%).

GRILLED HALIBUT WITH PESTO SAUCE
Makes 4 servings

This delicious halibut recipe is served aboard *Holland America Line* ships on a bed of pasta.

4 halibut fillets, about 3 1/2 ounces each
1 cup chicken broth
2 teaspoons cornstarch
2 tablespoons fresh basil
2 teaspoons extra virgin olive oil

6 garlic cloves, diced
1/2 teaspoon oregano
2 tablespoons onion, finely diced
2 cups whole wheat pasta, cooked
1 tablespoon Parmesan cheese, grated

1. Grill or broil halibut fillets for 4 to 6 minutes on each side until just done.
2. To make pesto sauce, mix cornstarch with chicken broth, pour into blender, add basil and puree until smooth, about 2 minutes.
3. Heat oil in a small sauce pan, add garlic, oregano and onion; sauté until onions are translucent.
4. Add basil mixture and bring to a boil over medium heat, stirring often.
5. Place 1/2 cup of cooked pasta in the center of a dinner plate.
6. Arrange a halibut fillet on top of the pasta, spoon about 1/3 cup of cooked pesto sauce over fish.
7. Sprinkle 1/2 teaspoon of Parmesan cheese over sauce.

NUTRITION FACTS per serving: 387 calories, 82 calories from fat, 9.2g total fat (14%), 1.1g saturated fat (6%), 37.9mg cholesterol (13%), 496.4mg sodium (21%), 43.6g carbohydrates (15%), 3.2g fiber (13%), 33.4g protein (67%), 249 IU vitamin A (5%), 2mg vitamin C (3%), 102mg calcium (10%) and 2.2mg iron (12%).

HUACHINANGO AL PEREJIL
Makes 4 servings

In *Mexico*, flat-leafed Italian parsley is preferred for this sauce, accenting the fresh, light taste of the fish. If a whole fish is not available, any fish with firm white flesh can be substituted.

1 red snapper, about 3 pounds, head and tail on
2 tablespoons lime juice
1 garlic clove, finely chopped
Salt and pepper to taste, divided
2 cups light cream or half and half
1 cup fresh parsley, chopped

1. Preheat the oven to 325°F.
2. Rinse the fish and pat dry with paper towel.
3. In a small bowl, combine the lime juice, garlic, salt and pepper.
4. Rub the entire fish, inside and out, with this mixture and let it marinate for 20 minutes.
5. Put the cream and parsley in a blender until smooth.
6. Add salt and pepper to taste.
7. Place the fish in a greased baking dish.
8. Cover with the parsley cream and bake for about 30 minutes or until the fish is cooked, the time will vary depending on the thickness of the fish.

NUTRITION FACTS per serving: 593 calories, 257 calories from fat, 28g total fat (43%), 15.4g saturated fat (77%), 205.3mg cholesterol (68%), 289.1mg sodium (12%), 8g carbohydrates (3%), .6g fiber (2%), 74.3g protein (149%), 2419 IU vitamin A (48%), 15mg vitamin C (25%), 303mg calcium (30%) and 5.7mg iron (32%).

OYSTER PIE
Makes 6 servings

Jackie Russell of Chincoteague Island, Virginia, says, *"This was my Grandfather's favorite breakfast. Many of the seniors on Chincoteague Island still enjoy this for breakfast. There are several recipes for this oyster pie. Some have bacon, more vegetables and a biscuit top."*

1 pint oysters
1/2 cup green pepper, diced
5 tablespoons flour
1 teaspoon salt
1/2 cup celery, diced
4 tablespoons butter
2 cups milk
1/8 teaspoon pepper
2 tablespoons pimientos, chopped
Pie pastry

1. In a saucepan, cook oysters in their liquid about 5 minutes or until edges begin to curl; drain.
2. Sauté celery and green pepper in butter until tender.
3. Blend in flour, add milk and cook until thick, stirring constantly.
4. Add oysters and seasonings.
5. Pour in a casserole and top with pastry.
6. Bake at 425°F about 15 minutes or until crust is brown.

PIE PASTRY

1 1/2 cups flour
3/4 teaspoon salt

1/2 cup shortening
3 tablespoons water (about)

1. In a bowl, mix flour and salt.
2. Cut in shortening until mixture resembles coarse bread crumbs.
3. Do not over mix.
4. Sprinkle with water, a few drops at a time, and mix lightly with a fork until all dry ingredients are moistened.
5. Knead 2 or 3 times and press into a ball.
6. Don not handle anymore than necessary.
7. Chill in the refrigerator about 20 minutes.
8. Roll out to fit casserole dish.

NUTRITION FACTS per serving: 313 calories, 19g total fat (30%), 11g saturated fat (55%), 91mg cholesterol (30%), 24g carbohydrates (8%), 11g protein (22%), 698mg sodium (29%), 147mg calcium (14%), 7mg iron (37%), 15mg vitamin C (25%) and 847 IU vitamin A (16%).

SALMON NUGGETS
Makes 4 servings

When I lived in Alaska, I would go down to the fish house after the king salmon were split. I would take a teaspoon and scrap off the meat from the back bones. This rich meat was perfect for making breakfast salmon nuggets.

1 pound salmon, fresh or canned, drained
1 tablespoon onion, grated
1/4 teaspoon salt
1/4 teaspoon pepper
1/4 teaspoon celery seed
1 teaspoon Worcestershire sauce

1/4 pound sharp cheddar cheese, cut into 3/8-inch cubes
1/2 cup cooked mashed potatoes
1 tablespoon butter
1 egg, beaten
1 cup dry bread crumbs

1. Flake the salmon.
2. Combine all ingredients, except cheese and crumbs, mix thoroughly.
3. Shape into balls the size of walnuts.
4. Insert a cheese cube into the center of each fish ball and reshape.
5. Roll in bread crumbs.
6. Fry in deep fat, 375°F for 3 to 4 minutes or until golden brown.

SALT FISH CUNDY
Makes 8 servings

One way to preserve fish is by salting. Today, salt fish, as it is called, is generally made with cod. While salt fish is not that popular in America, it is found in many countries. The salt preserves the fish and in a sense cooks the fish. You can if you wish pre-cook the salt fish. Salt fish must be soaked and washed in several changes of water. This recipe from the *British Virgin Islands* is basically a salad. In some of the Caribbean islands, other vegetables are added, such as avocado and tomatoes, and usually lime juice is used as a dressing. The salad is enjoyed either hot or chilled.

2 pounds salt fish
1 sweet pepper
1/2 piece of hot pepper (optional)
1 onion

3 sprigs parsley
2 tablespoons prepared mustard
1/2 cup stuffed olives
1 cup vegetable oil

1. Soak salt fish overnight.
2. Remove fish and wash in fresh water, removing bones and skin.
3. Break into small pieces.
4. Put fish, pepper, onion, parsley and olives through a grinder.
5. Whip mustard into salad oil.
6. Mix thoroughly with salt fish mixture.

7. Garnish with onion rings and wedges of hard boiled eggs, if desired.

NUTRITION FACTS per serving: 356 calories, 261 calories from fat, 29.1g total fat (45%), 3.4g saturated fat (17%), 48.8mg cholesterol (16%), 252.3mg sodium (11%), 2.9g carbohydrates (1%), .7g fiber (3%), 20.9g protein (42%), 290 IU vitamin A (6%), 24mg vitamin C (41%), 46mg calcium (5%) and 1.4mg iron (8%).

SALT FISH PIE
Makes 8 servings

Salt fish is popular in *Antigua and Barbuda* and other Caribbean Islands, as well along the European coast, especially *Spain* (where it is called *bacalao*), *Portugal* (called *bacalhau*), and France (called *morue*).

2 pounds salt fish, soaked, boiled, bones removed
2 1/2 pounds yams, skinned, quartered, cooked, divided
1/4 cup milk
1 tablespoon butter

1 onion, thinly sliced
3 tomatoes, sliced
4 tablespoons margarine
4 tablespoons mayonnaise
2 eggs, hard cooked, sliced
Salt & pepper to taste

1/2 cup ketchup

1. Mash 1 3/4 pounds of the yams with a little milk and butter.
2. Slice the remaining yams.
3. Grease a pie dish and line with half of the mashed yams.
4. Place alternately layers of sliced yam, salt fish, onions, tomatoes in the dish.
5. Top with ketchup, salt, pepper, mayonnaise, eggs and dots of margarine.
6. Flour a board, roll out the remaining yams (if too soft, knead in a little flour).
7. Cover the dish carefully with the rolled out yams.
8. Dot with butter and bake in a 375°F oven until brown.

NUTRITION FACTS per serving: 425 calories, 137 calories from fat, 15.3g total fat (24%), 3.5g saturated fat (17%), 110.9mg cholesterol (37%), 642mg sodium (27%), 47.4g carbohydrates (16%), 6.8g fiber (27%), 25.2g protein (50%), 880 IU vitamin A (18%), 37mg vitamin C (62%), 75mg calcium (8%) and 1.8mg iron (10%).

SALT FISH & RICE
Makes 6 servings

Like many in the Caribbean, the citizens of the *British Virgin Islands* like salt fish prepared in many ways.

1 pound salt fish
1 cup tomatoes, canned or fresh
1 sprig thyme
1 garlic clove, chopped
3 cups boiling water

1/2 cup shortening
1 sprig parsley
1 tablespoon green pepper, chopped
2 cups rice
1 onion, chopped

1. Soak fish, remove bones and skin.
2. In a frying pan, sauté onion, tomatoes, green pepper, thyme, garlic and parsley in the shortening.
3. Pick salt fish in fine pieces.
4. Add to the vegetable mixture and sauté.
5. Add the boiling water, boil rapidly.
6. Add the rice, slowly cook uncovered until water disappears.
7. Cover and steam on low heat until rice is tender.

NUTRITION FACTS per serving: 451 calories, 165 calories from fat, 18.2g total fat (28%), 4.5g saturated fat (23%), 32.5mg cholesterol (11%), 139.3mg sodium (6%), 52.2g carbohydrates (17%), 1.5g fiber (6%), 18.5g protein (37%), 282 IU vitamin A (6%), 9mg vitamin C (15%), 51mg calcium (5%) and 3.6mg iron (20%),

SCALLOPED OYSTERS
Makes 4 servings

Chincoteague, Virginia is world famous for its oyster beds. Like most shellfish, oysters can be prepared in many ways. One of the favorite ways on Chincoteague Island is this recipe.

1 pint oysters
4 tablespoons oyster liquor, divided
2 tablespoons milk, cream or sherry wine, divided

1/2 cup stale bread crumbs
1 cup cracker crumbs
1/2 cup butter, melted
Salt & pepper to taste

Mace or nutmeg (optional)

1. In a bowl, mix crumbs and stir in butter.
2. Put a thin layer in bottom of a buttered shallow baking dish.
3. Cover with oysters.
4. Sprinkle with salt, pepper and mace.
5. Add one half each of oyster liquor and milk.
6. Repeat with more crumbs and oysters, top with remaining crumbs and liquids.

7. IMPORTANT: Never allow more than two layers of oysters. If three layers are used, the middle layer will be underdone.
8. Bake 30 minutes in a 400°F oven.
9. A sprinkling of mace or nutmeg to each layer is considered by many an improvement.

NUTRITION FACTS per serving made with milk: 480 calories, 27g total fat (42%), 15g saturated fat (77%), 128mg cholesterol (43%), 44g carbohydrate (15%), .7g fiber (3%), 14g protein (29%), 872mg sodium (36%), 106mg calcium (10%), 11mg iron (59%), 5mg vitamin C (7%) and 984 IU vitamin A (19%).

STEAMED FISH WITH CUCUMBER SAUCE
Makes 2 servings

In this chapter I have showed you many ways the people of *Antigua and Barbuda* cook fish. You will find these recipes similar to many countries. About the only difference are the local ingredients that might be used, as well as spices and herbs.

1/2 pound whole fish, scaled, cleaned
1 onion, sliced
Salt & pepper to taste

1 tablespoon lime juice
Sprig of parsley or thyme
2 tablespoons margarine

1. Wrap fish in aluminum foil or heavy brown paper with all the ingredients.
2. Place in the top of a steamer, covered tightly.

3. Steam for 6 to 8 minutes.
4. Serve with Cucumber Sauce.

NUTRITION FACTS per serving: 212 calories, 111 calories from fat, 12.2g total fat (19%), 2.1g saturated fat (11%), 48.8mg cholesterol (16%), 471.8mg sodium (20%), 4.1g carbohydrates (1%), 1.1g fiber (4%), 21.1g protein (42%), 658 IU vitamin A (13%), 7mg vitamin C (12%), 66mg calcium (7%) and 1.1mg iron (6%).

CUCUMBER SAUCE
Makes 2 servings

1 cup cucumber, chopped
1 teaspoon sweet pepper, chopped
Salt & pepper to taste

1 teaspoon lemon juice
Dash of vinegar
Dash of cayenne pepper

1. Combine all ingredients.

2. Chill for 1 hour.

NUTRITION FACTS per serving: 4 calories, zero fats, cholesterol, sodium and carbohydrates, .2g fiber (1%), zero protein, 63 IU vitamin A (1%), 3mg vitamin C (6%), zero calcium and iron.

TEOCHEW FISH PORRIDGE
Makes 6 servings

In *Singapore* this is a very special dish served during the festival months by hawker stalls on the streets leading up to the Wayang Stages.

1 cup rice
4 1/2 quarts water
1 pound mackerel, sliced into small pieces
6 tablespoons vegetable oil
3 dried sole or any unsalted dried fish

10 shallots, sliced
3/4 cup dried shrimps
2 tablespoons light soy sauce or fish sauce
1 teaspoon pepper
2 tablespoons salted winter vegetables (optional)

4 scallions

1. Wash rice in several changes of water and put to boil with water.
2. Heat oil and fry dried fish until brown.
3. Remove and drain.
4. When cool to the touch crush with a rolling pin coarsely.
5. In the remaining oil fry shallots until brown and crisp.

6. When rice grains are cooked, but still whole, add mackerel, shrimps, soy sauce, pepper and simmer for 3 minutes.
7. Serve garnished with salted winter vegetables, scallions, fried fish, shallots and a side dish of cut red chilies for those with a taste for it.

NUTRITION FACTS per serving: 383 calories, 144 calories from fat, 15.9g total fat (24%), 2g saturated fat (10%), 73.9mg cholesterol (25%), 324.4mg sodium 14%), 33.8g carbohydrates (11%), .9g fiber (4%), 25.4g protein (51%), 6025 IU vitamin A (121%), 8mg vitamin C (13%), 72mg calcium (7%) and 4.1mg iron (23%).

OTHER MEATS

Except for lamb, these other meats are generally not available, except in regions where they are accessible.

ALLIGATOR A LA JAMES
Makes 4 servings

Strange as it might seem, alligators are only found in the rivers, swamps, and lakes of southern United States; and in the Yangtze River basin of China. Here's how *James Provost* of *Wildlife Gardens* in Gibson, Louisiana makes alligator for guests that overnight in his cabins.

1 pound alligator meat, sliced into 1 inch cubes
7-UP®
Mustard
Lemon juice

Tony Chachere's Creole Seasoning*
Hot sauce
4 onions, diced
Butter

1. Make a marinate to suit your taste with 7-UP, mustard, lemon juice, Tony's seasoning and hot sauce to cover the meat.
2. Marinate meat in the refrigerator for 3 days.
3. Drain marinate; reserve.

4. Sauté the onions in butter until brown.
5. Pile the alligator meat in the middle of a skillet and top with the cooked onions.
6. Pour the marinate on top and cook over medium-high heat until all the sauce is gone.

*If not available, make a mixture of salt, cayenne pepper and garlic powder to taste

GREEK LAMB SKILLET BREAKFAST
Makes 4 servings

Lamb is not the most popular meat in America, however, in some countries, especially in the Mediterranean regions, lamb is the first choice. This recipe from *Greece* is from the *National Live Stock and Meat Board*.

1 pound ground lamb
1 teaspoon garlic salt
1 teaspoon Italian seasoning, crushed
15 ounce can great northern beans, drained

2 tomatoes, chopped
1 cup dry white wine
1 tablespoon fresh parsley, chopped
1 teaspoon lemon peel, grated

1. In a bowl, combine lamb and seasonings; mix lightly but thoroughly.
2. Pinch off 1 1/2 inch pieces of lamb mixture to make approximately 16 meatballs.
3. Brown meatballs in a large skillet over medium heat.

4. Pour off drippings; discard.
5. Add beans, tomatoes and wine; cook, uncovered, over medium heat 15 minutes, stirring occasionally.
6. Sprinkle with parsley and lemon peel

NUTRITION FACTS per serving: 735 calories, 264 calories from fat, 28g total fat (43%), 12g saturated fat (60%), 82.9mg cholesterol (28%), 96mg sodium (4%), 70g carbohydrates (23%), .8g fiber (3%), 42.7g protein (85%), 434 IU vitamin A (9%), 19mg vitamin C (32%), 215mg calcium (21%) and 8.1mg iron (45%).

GRILLADES WITH VEGETABLES AND GRAVY
Makes 6 servings

When in New Orleans, stop by *The Court of Two Sisters* for one of my favorite breakfast meat and vegetable dishes. I enjoy it so much, not only do I have it for breakfast, but it also makes the dinner scene on occasions.

1 pound veal cutlets, trimmed
1 cup flour
1 1/2 teaspoon cayenne red pepper

1 tablespoon black pepper
1 tablespoon white pepper
1 tablespoon garlic salt

1/4 cup vegetable oil

1. Prepare vegetables and gravy; set aside.
2. Cut cutlets into medallions and flatten with a mallet between sheets of wax paper to avoid tearing.
3. Mix flour and spices and dredge the cutlets in the mixture.

4. Brown both sides in oil, about 2-minutes each.
5. Place in heavy skillet and simmer covered with gravy and vegetables about one-half hour or until tender.

VEGETABLES AND GRAVY

1/4 cup bacon grease
1/4 cup flour
1 quart water
1 teaspoon white pepper
1 teaspoon black pepper
1 teaspoon cayenne red pepper
1 1/2 teaspoon salt

1 tablespoon garlic, minced
3 tablespoons butter
1 bell pepper, julienne
3 tablespoons celery, sliced
1 cup onions, diced
3/4 cup mushrooms, sliced
2 tomatoes, peeled, diced

1. In an iron skillet, create a roux with bacon grease and flour, heating until dark chocolate brown, stirring continuously, being careful not to burn.

2. Add seasonings and spoon into heated water in a large saucepan.
3. Cook over moderate heat for 1 hour.

4. Sauté pepper, celery and onions, then add mushrooms and finally tomatoes, cooking to reduce slightly.
5. Add to the gravy and simmer for 15 minutes.
6. Add to grillades as described.

SEAL

In Alaska, the Eskimos and other native Alaskans enjoy seal meat, as well as the liver. If seal meal is not available, substitute beef pot roast. Here's how some Alaskans cook seal.

Seal meat
Salt to taste
Macaroni
Willow leaves
Onions, chopped

1. Place desired amount of seal meat in a pot.
2. Add salt to taste.
3. Add some willow leaves.
4. Add some chopped onions.

5. Cover with water and boil until almost done.
6. Add some macaroni.
7. Continue to cook until meat is tender.
8. Serve with raw onions and seal oil.

SEAL LIVER

Calves liver can be substituted for seal liver.

Seal liver   Flour   Salt and pepper to taste

1. Slice liver about 1/3-inch thick.
2. Wash thoroughly in water.
3. Coat with flour.

4. Fry in fat.
5. Season to taste

WALRUS

Tired of eating boiled walrus for breakfast? There are other ways that are just as good. To destroy some of the strong odor of walrus, mix 1/4 cup vinegar with 1 gallon of water and soak the walrus meat for 10 minutes. Walrus meat grinds easier if the white connective tissue is removed from the meat before grinding. Since walrus meat is rather tough, it can be made tender by the use of tomato juice, milk or meat tenderizer. If walrus is not available, use round steak for a substitute.

WALRUS KYUSOLIK

1 pound walrus, cut into small chunks
4 cups water
1 tablespoon vinegar
1/4 teaspoon salt
1/4 teaspoon pepper
1 teaspoon dry mustard
2 tablespoons catsup
1/2 teaspoon meat tenderizer (optional)
Flour
2 tablespoons fat
1 tablespoon onion flakes
1 cup water
1/2 cup dry milk powder

1. In a bowl, mix water and vinegar and soak meat for 10 minutes; drain.
2. Sprinkle seasonings and tenderizer over the meat and refrigerate for 2 hours.

3. Coat meat in flour.
4. Heat fat in skillet with onion flakes, brown all sides of the meat.

5. Remove meat from pan and add a little more flour to the fat and stir.
6. Add water, milk powder and stir until gravy is smooth.
7. Put meat in the gravy.

8. Add the catsup.
9. Cover and cook very slowly until the meat is tender.
10. Check it once in a while and if it begins to get dry, add a little more water.

Kyusolik is good served over cooked rice or with Eskimo dumplings (page 113).

WALRUS MEAT LOAF
If walrus is not available, substitute ground beef.

2 pounds ground walrus
1/4 cup fat or vegetable oil
1/2 cup catsup
1 egg
2 cups milk

1 cup rolled oats
1 bay leaf, broken into pieces
1/2 teaspoon pepper
1/2 teaspoon salt
1 tablespoons soy sauce (optional)

1. In a bowl, mix all ingredients and place in a greased loaf pan.
2. Cover it with foil.

3. Bake at 300°F for 1 1/2 to 2 hours.
4. Check the meat loaf every once in a while. If it seems to dry, add a little water.

WALRUS STEAK WITH GRAVY
Makes 4 servings

From the shoulder of a young walrus cut some steaks.

4 walrus steaks, cut 1/2-inch thick
Flour
2 tablespoons onion flakes

1/4 cup catsup
1 cup water
Salt & pepper to taste

1
. On a floured board, pound the steak with a meat tenderizer, turning steaks often so flour is cut into meat on both sides.
2. Season the walrus steak with salt and pepper to taste.
3. Brown the meat on both sides in a well greased skillet.
4. Add onion flakes, catsup and water.

5. Cover skillet and cook slowly over low heat until tender.
6. Add a little water once in a while so the pan does not get dry.
7. Cooking time will be from 1 to 2 hours, depending on how tender the meat was before cooking.

MEAT SEASONINGS

HOME MADE CHILE POWDER

Commercial chile powder is a blend of chile and herbs, which could included garlic, cumin, oregano, allspice, and cloves. Don't be fooled by those imitations. This is the way New Mexicans make it.

Dried chile pods (the only ingredient)

1. Wash the pods well.
2. The pod can be toasted in a warm oven first, if desired, but don't let them burn.
3. Remove seeds and veins.

4. Put the chilies into an electric blender and grind to a powder.
5. For hot chile, throw in a few of the seeds, more seeds for very hot chile powder.

RED CHILE SAUCE
Makes 2 cups

Use this sauce not only to top meats, but for most recipes calling for chile sauce. Also makes a great topping for eggs.

3 tablespoons olive oil or lard
1 garlic clove, minced
2 tablespoons flour

1/2 cup home made chile powder
2 cups water
Salt to taste

1. In a saucepan, sauté garlic in oil.
2. Blend in flour with a wooden spoon.
3. Add chile powder and blend in.
4. Don't let pan get too hot, as chile will burn easily.

5. Blend in water and cook to desired consistency.
6. Add salt to taste.

WEST INDIAN SEASONING

In the *British Virgin Islands* this seasoning is used to flavor all types of meat, fish, and poultry. In *Jamaica* a similar seasoning called *"jerk"* is made. Jerk is much hotter as it contains jalapeño peppers, ginger, cinnamon and other spices.

1 cup rock salt, pounded
4 teaspoons black or cayenne pepper
1/2 teaspoon cloves
1 celery rib

1 sprig parsley
1 teaspoon mace
1 teaspoon nutmeg
5 garlic cloves

1. Combine all ingredients by putting in a mortar and pounding with a pestle until well mixed.

2. Store in a jar for future use.

NUTRITION FACTS per teaspoon: 1 calorie, zero fats and cholesterol, 1504.8mg sodium (63%), all other facts are zero.

HERBS AND SPICES FOR COOKING

Adding an herb and/or spice or two can bring additional life to your breakfast recipes. However, be careful. Adding too many can spoil the end result. Generally one or two, maybe three at the most can be added. Also some herbs and spices will intensify as it cooks, such as pepper. To be on the safe side, if possible, add toward the end of the cooking time.

Beef: Bay leaf, chives, cloves, cumin, garlic powder, black and white pepper, red pepper, marjoram, rosemary, savory, onion powder, tarragon, basil, anise, burnet, caraway, chervil, fenugreek, lovage, mustard, oregano, parsley, thyme, chili powder, mace, paprika, and curry.

Beverages: Burnet, fennel, cinnamon, nutmeg, and mint.

Bread: Caraway, marjoram, oregano, poppy seed, rosemary, thyme, sesame seed, cardamon, savory, anise, basil, celery seed, sage, mint, parsley, allspice, cinnamon, cloves, ginger, mace, nutmeg, saffron, turmeric, and dill.

Eggs: Basil, caraway, chevil, sage, chives, fennel, marjoram, mustard, oregano, parsley, rosemary, savory, tarragon, allspice, nutmeg, paprika, black and white pepper, red pepper, turmeric, and thyme.

Fruit: Allspice, anise, basil, cinnamon, coriander, cloves, ginger, mint, and nutmeg.

Pork: Coriander, cumin, garlic powder, black and white pepper, red pepper, cloves, cinnamon, sage, savory, ginger, and thyme.

CHAPTER XIII

MUFFINS

Muffins are fairly new and have not been well received in many other countries. Some bakeries and restaurants in a few countries now offer muffins, but they are still not as popular as in the United States. One of the reasons is that baking powder is a fairly new invention, and while baking powder is now used in many countries for pancakes and other baked goods, muffins still haven't caught on.

Washington's Muffins (*muffin history*) 196

Banana Pecan Muffins (*Southern USA*) 196

Berry Streusel Muffins (*Iowa*) 196

Blueberry Muffins (*USA*) 197

Breakfast Puffs I (*West Virginia*) 197

Breakfast Puffs II (*Iowa*) 198

Corny Corn Muffins (*Vermont*) 198

Cranberry Muffins (*USA*) 199

Crunchy Bacon & Green Chile Muffins (*New Mexico*) 199

English Muffins (*England*) 200

Marmalade Filled Muffins (*Nebraska*) 200

Mincemeat Muffins (*Canada*) 20`

Oatmeal Muffins (*USA*) 201

Orange Walnut Muffins (*Missouri*) 202

Pineapple Carrot Muffins (*Missouri*) 202

Pumpkin Spice Muffins (*Massachusetts*) 203

Rhubarb Muffins (*Indiana*) 203

Spicy Bean Muffins (*USA*) 204

Grains (*information*)

WASHINGTON'S MUFFINS

The earliest muffin recipe I have found came from George Washington's home. The recipe might sound a bit strange. Can you make it?

4 Cups of flour, one of butter - one of Cream - two of Sugar, and Tea spoonful of Pearlash; spice to taste – bake it gently in Tins or Saucers.

You are probably asking, what is Pearlash? Pearlash is made from potash, and potash is made from wood ashes. Sounds yucky doesn't it? But it did work, sort of. How about baking a muffin in a saucer? Not a bad idea, as they would be flat and leftovers could be heated in a toaster. Saucer muffins are still found in some homes and bakeries.

BANANA PECAN MUFFINS
Makes 12 muffins

A very popular muffin, especially in the southern United States.

1/3 cup shortening	2 cups flour	1 cup bananas, mashed
2/3 cup sugar	1 tablespoon baking powder	1 teaspoon vanilla
2 eggs, slightly beaten	1/2 teaspoon salt	1/2 cup pecans, chopped

1. In a large bowl cream shortening with sugar until very light and fluffy, about 2 minutes.
2. Beat in eggs and vanilla until mixture is thick.
3. Sift flour, baking powder and salt together and blend into mixture.
4. Fold in the bananas and pecans.
5. Spoon batter in greased muffin cups.
6. Bake in preheated 350°F oven for about 20 minutes

NUTRITION FACTS per muffin: 230 calories, 87 calories from fat, 9.9g total fat (15%), 2g saturated fat (10%), 35.4mg cholesterol (12%), 190.9mg sodium (8%), 32.6g carbohydrates (11%), .8g fiber (3%), 3.7g protein (7%), 74 IU vitamin A (1%), 2mg vitamin C (3%), 95mg calcium (9%) and 1.4mg iron (8%).

BERRY STREUSEL MUFFINS
Makes 12 muffins

This mid-west favorite is served to guests at *Chestnut Charm Bed and Breakfast* located in Atlantic, Iowa by *Barbara and Marsha Stensvad*.

1 cup fresh or frozen strawberries	1/2 cup milk
1 3/4 cup flour, divided	1/2 cup, plus 2 tablespoons butter or margarine, melted
1/2 cup sugar	1/4 cup pecans, chopped
2 teaspoons baking powder	1/2 cup brown sugar
1 egg, beaten	

1. Preheat oven to 375°F.
2. Grease 12 muffin tins.
3. In a bowl, prepare streusel topping by combining pecans, brown sugar and 1/4 cup flour.
4. Stir in 2 tablespoons of melted butter until mixture looks like moist crumbs; set aside topping.
5. In a large bowl stir together 1 1/2 cups of flour, sugar and baking powder.
6. In a small bowl, combine milk, 1/2 cup of butter and egg.
7. Stir milk mixture into dry ingredients just until moistened.
8. Do not beat.
9. Fill muffin tins 2/3 full.
10. Add berries on top of filled muffin cups.
11. Sprinkle pecan streusel topping over berries.

BLUEBERRY MUFFINS
Makes 18 muffins

Since the days when the colonist first landed in America, wild native blueberries has been a choice baking ingredient. These old-fashioned blueberry muffins are hard to beat!

2 cups flour
2 teaspoons baking powder
1 teaspoon cinnamon
1/4 teaspoon salt

2 eggs
1 cup milk
3/4 cup sugar
1/2 cup vegetable oil

1 cup fresh or frozen blueberries, thawed

1. In a bowl, combine flour, baking powder, cinnamon and salt; mix well.
2. In another bowl, beat eggs lightly; stir in milk, sugar and oil.
3. Quickly stir egg mixture into dry ingredients.
4. Carefully fold in blueberries.
5. Spoon into greased muffin cups, about 2/3 full.
6. Bake at 400ºF for 15 to 17 minutes.

NUTRITION FACTS per muffin: 158 calories, 65 calories from fat, 7.2g total fat (11%), 1.2g saturated fat (6%), 25.5mg cholesterol (8%), 84.5mg sodium (4%), 21g carbohydrates (7%), .3g fiber (1%), 2.6g protein (5%), 61 IU vitamin A (1%), 1mg vitamin C (2%), 61mg calcium (6%) and .9mg iron (5%).

BREAKFAST PUFFS I
Makes 15 puffs

There are two kinds of "puffs," one made with baking powder, as this recipe from *Laura Amick* from Summerville, West Virginia, to those made with yeast (see following recipe).

1/3 cup shortening
1/2 cup sugar
1 egg
1 1/2 cups flour

1 1/2 teaspoons baking powder
1/2 teaspoon salt
1/4 teaspoon nutmeg
1/2 cup milk

1. Preheat oven to 350ºF.
2. Grease 15 muffin cups.
3. In a bowl, mix thoroughly shortening, sugar and egg.
4. Combine all other dry ingredients in a separate bowl.
5. Add milk and dry mixture alternately to egg mixture.
6. Fill muffin cups 2/3 full.
7. Bake about 15 to 20 minutes.
8. Coat baked puffs by rolling in butter and then the cinnamon sugar mixture.

NUTRITION FACTS per puff without coating: 122 calories, 47 calories from fat, 5.3g total fat (8%), 1.4g saturated fat (7%), 15.3mg cholesterol (5%), 116mg sodium (5%), 16.8g carbohydrates (6%), zero fiber, 2g protein (4%), 31 IU vitamin A (1%), zero vitamin C, 47mg calcium (5%) and .7mg iron (4%).

PUFF COATING

1/2 cup butter or margarine melted
1/2 cup sugar
1 teaspoon cinnamon

1. In small bowl, mix the sugar and cinnamon together.

Makes enough for 15 coastings

NUTRITION FACTS per coating: 80 calories, 53 calories from fat, 6.1g total fat (9%), 3.8g saturated fat (19%), 16.4mg cholesterol (5%), 61.8mg sodium (3%), 6.8g carbohydrates (2%), zero fiber and protein, 229 IU vitamin A (5%), and zero vitamin C, calcium and iron.

BREAKFAST PUFFS II
Makes 12 puffs

Barbara and Marsha Stensvad served this old world recipe to their guests at their *Chestnut Charm Bed and Breakfast* in Atlantic, Iowa. Even though they have the same name as the baking powder variety, they are closer to a roll, than a muffin.

2 cups bread flour
2 tablespoons sugar
1 package fast-rising dry yeast
1/2 teaspoon salt
1 egg, beaten

3/4 cup water
1/4 cup vegetable oil
Fresh or frozen fruit
1/4 cup powdered sugar
1/4 cup margarine or butter, melted

1. Combine 1 cup of flour and yeast in a bowl.
2. In a pan heat water, salt, sugar and oil until just warm (stir and test with a finger).
3. Pour over flour and beat well with a mixer.
4. Add egg and mix well.
5. Using a wooden spoon, mix in enough additional flour until dough makes a ball and leaves the sides of the bowl.
6. Place on a floured surface and knead in just enough flour until it is not longer sticky.
7. Place dough in a greased bowl and let it rise in a warm place until doubled, about an hour.
8. Cut into 12 equal balls.

9. Put a small piece fruit in the middle of each ball and enclosed the fruit in the dough (sweeten fruit if necessary with sugar).
10. Place each filled dough ball in a greased muffin tin, seam side down.
11. Cover and let it rise in a warm place until almost doubled. about 45 minutes.
12. Bake at 350°F for about 20 minutes.
13. Remove and cool on wire rack for a short while.
14. Dip into melted margarine, than into powdered sugar.

NUTRITION FACTS per puff using unsweetened apples as the fruit: 197 calories, 83 calories from fat, 9.3g total fat (14%), 1.4g saturated fat (7%), 17.7mg cholesterol (6%), 139.4mg sodium (6%), 25.1g carbohydrates (8%), 1.5g fiber (6%), 3.7g protein (7%), 194 IU vitamin A (4%), 1mg vitamin C (2%), 9mg calcium (1%) and 1.3mg iron (7%).

CORNY CORN MUFFINS
Makes 12 muffins

What could be more American, than these cornmeal muffins filled with corn kernels? *Paul and Lois Dansereau* served these to their guests at *Silas Griffith Inn* at Darby, Vermont.

1 cup flour
1/2 cup cornmeal
1/2 cup sugar
1 tablespoon baking powder
1/2 teaspoon salt

1 cup canned corn, drained or frozen corn, thawed
2 eggs
1/2 cup milk
1/2 cup margarine, melted

1. In a large bowl, mix flour, cornmeal, sugar, baking powder, and salt.
2. Add corn, toss to coat.
3. In small bowl beat eggs, add milk and melted margarine, beat well.

4. Add to flour mixture, stir until blended.
5. Fill greased muffin pan 2/3 full.
6. Bake in preheated 400°F oven for 15 to 20 minutes.

NUTRITION FACTS per muffin: 190 calories, 80 calories from fat, 9.1g total fat (14%), 1.8g saturated fat (9%), 36.8mg cholesterol (12%), 285mg sodium (12%), 24.5g carbohydrates (8%), .8g fiber (3%), 3.4g protein (7%), 418 IU vitamin A (8%), 1mg vitamin C (2%), 106mg calcium (11%) and 1.1mg iron (6%).

Did you know that corn grow wild as Mexican grass? It was under Aztez cultivation that made corn possible. It was Columbus and his men who were the first Europeans to eat corn. As a curiosity, the explorers took some seeds back to the Old World.

CRANBERRY MUFFINS
Makes 12 large or 24 mini muffins. The smaller muffins rise better

From the test kitchen of *Arrowhead Mills* brings an American favorite with the goodness of cranberries and maple syrup.

1/2 cup cranberries, chopped
1/4 cup maple syrup or honey
2 tablespoons vegetable oil

3/4 cup orange juice
1 cup oat bran
1 cup whole wheat flour

1 tablespoon baking powder

1. Place berries, maple syrup, oil, orange juice in blender and blend slightly.
2. Mix together dry ingredients in a bowl.
3. Add liquid to the dry ingredients and mix well.

4. Fill greased muffin tins.
5. Bake at 400°F for 20 to 25 minutes or until nicely browned.

NUTRITION FACTS per muffin: 106 calories, 24 calories from fat, 3.1g total fat (5%), .4g saturated fat (2%), zero cholesterol, 92.1mg sodium (4%), 21.2g carbohydrates (7%), 2.8g fiber (11%), 3g protein (6%), 33 IU vitamin A (1%), 8mg vitamin C (14%), 96mg calcium (10%) and 1.1mg iron (6%).

Did you know that cranberries were first known as "crane berries?" These red berries were found wild in boggy parts of the northern United States. Most of the cranberry crop comes from Massachusetts, the rest are cultivated in Rhode Island, New Jersey, Wisconsin, Oregon, and Washington. In Sweden, their cranberries are called "lingonberries" and are much spicier than ours. There are more than a hundred known varieties of cranberries, many with interesting names such as: Potter's Favorite, Budd's Blues, Centennial and Aviator, which can conjure up fascinating pictures of earlier days.

CRUNCHY BACON & GREEN CHILI MUFFINS
Makes 18 muffins

Laura Parker from Los Alamos, New Mexico presents the exciting taste of the old southwest.

½ pound bacon
2 cups flour
¼ cup sugar
1 tablespoon baking powder

Vegetable oil
1 egg, beaten
¾ cup milk
1 ½ cups cheddar cheese, shredded

¼ to ½ cup green chili, mild or hot, diced

1. In a skillet cook bacon until crispy; drain, reserve the drippings.
2. Crumble the bacon; set aside.
3. In a medium bowl stir together the flour, sugar and baking powder.
4. Make a well in the center.
5. Measure the drippings, add vegetable oil, if necessary to measure 1/3 cup.
6. In a bowl, combine the drippings with the egg and milk.

7. Add to the flour mixture and stir until moist.
8. Batter will be lumpy. Carefully fold in the bacon, cheese and green chili. Use amount of green chili to suit your taste.
9. Grease muffin tins and fill about ¾ full.
10. Bake in a 400 F oven for 15 to 20 minutes or until golden brown.
11. Remove muffins from pans and cool completely on a wire rack.

NUTRITION FACTS per muffin: 184 calories, 92 calories from fat, 10.1g total fat (16%), 4.5g saturated fat (23%), 33.8mg cholesterol (11%), 329.5mg sodium (14%), 14.6mg carbohydrates (5%), zero fiber, 8.4g protein (17%), 163 IU vitamin A (3%), 14mg vitamin C (24%), 142mg calcium (14%) and 1.1mg iron (6%).

ENGLISH MUFFINS

Not really a true muffin in the American sense. These yeast flat-type rolls originated in *England*. During the Edwardian era, wandering muffin men sold these fresh muffins door to door to households in the English towns. This Americanized version came from the test kitchens of *SACO Foods, Inc.*

1 package dry yeast
6 tablespoons cultured buttermilk powder
1 tablespoon sugar
½ teaspoon baking soda

1 ½ teaspoons salt
3 tablespoons shortening, soften
4 ½ to 5 ½ cups flour
2 cups water (120 F to 130 F)

Cornmeal

1. In large mixing bowl thoroughly mix yeast, buttermilk powder, sugar, soda, shortening and 2 cups flour.
2. Gradually blend in warm water and beat at low speed until moistened.
3. Beat on medium speed for 2 minutes.
4. By hand, add enough remaining flour to make a moderately stiff dough.
5. Cover and let rise until double, about 1 hour.
6. Turn dough out on well floured board and knead 3 to 4 times.
7. Let rest 5 minutes.

8. Lightly roll about ½ inch thick.
9. Cut into 3-inch rounds with floured cutter.
10. Carefully place on cookie sheet that is lightly covered with cornmeal.
11. Cover and let rise 30 minutes.
12. Heat griddle over medium heat (electric griddle 350°F).
13. Sprinkle with corn meal.
14. Carefully transfer muffins to griddle.
15. Bake 7 to 10 minutes.
16. Turn, bake 7 to 10 minutes on second side.

To serve, split horizontally with fork. Toast and serve with butter and jam.

NUTRITION FACTS per muffin: 160 calories, 24 calories from fat, 2.7g total fat (4%), .7g saturated fat (3%), 1.7mg cholesterol (1%), 226.6mg sodium (9%), 28.7g carbohydrates (10%), .2g fiber (1%), 4.7g protein (9%), zero vitamin A and C, 35mg calcium (4%) and 1.7mg iron (10%).

MARMALADE FILLED MUFFINS
Makes 12 muffins

Great Britain gave us marmalade made from Spain's Seville oranges, and *Christie Miller* of Dunbar, Nebraska presents her version of these delicious muffins.

3 cups flour
2 teaspoons baking powder
1/4 teaspoon baking soda

1 1/2 teaspoons salt
1/3 cup sugar
3/4 cup buttermilk

1/4 cup shortening, melted
1 egg, beaten
3/4 cup marmalade

1. In a bowl, sift together flour, baking powder, soda, salt and sugar.
2. In another bowl, combine buttermilk and shortening, and beat in egg.
3. Stir into dry ingredients mixing just enough to moisten.

4. Place half the mixture in 12 greased 2-inch muffin tins.
5. Put 1 tablespoon of marmalade on top of batter in each muffin cup.
6. Cover with remaining batter.
7. Bake in 400°F oven for 20 minutes.

NUTRITION FACTS per muffin: 197 calories, 44 calories from fat, 5g total fat (8%), 1.3g saturated fat (7%), 18.3mg cholesterol (6%), 386.2mg sodium (16%), 35.7g carbohydrates (12%), zero fiber, 3.2g protein (6%), 41 IU vitamin A (1%), 1mg vitamin C (2%), 87mg calcium (9%) and 1.2mg iron (6%).

Marmalade is a preserve made with sweet or bitter citrus peels and sugar. Marmalade can also be made with peaches, quince, blueberries and other fruits.

MINCEMEAT MUFFINS
Makes 24 muffins

Mincemeat was a way of preserving meat in 18th century Europe. Now mincemeat is used in many recipes from pies to gingerbread. *Sonia and Brian McMillan*, hosts of *Sonia's Bed and Breakfast by the Sea*, in Victoria, British Columbia, *Canada*, have incorporated mincemeat in their muffins for their guests. If you like mincemeat, you will love these muffins!

2 eggs, well beaten
1 cup sugar
1 cup bran cereal
2 cups milk
3/4 cup vegetable oil

2 cups flour
2 teaspoons baking soda
1/2 teaspoon salt
2 teaspoons baking powder
1 cup mincemeat

1. In a bowl, combine eggs, sugar, bran, milk and oil: beat well.
2. In a large bowl mix flour, soda, salt and baking powder.
3. Add the egg mixture to the flour mixture, mixing until dry ingredients are moistened.

4. Fold in mincemeat.
5. Mixture will be thin.
6. Fill each muffin tin 2/3 full.
7. Bake at 375ºF for 15 to 20 minutes

NUTRITION FACTS per muffin: 187 calories, 73 calories from fat, 8.6g total fat (13%), 1.4g saturated fat (7%), 20.5mg cholesterol (7%), 233.7mg sodium (10%), 27.7g carbohydrates (9%), 1.7g fiber (7%), 2.8g protein (6%), 206 IU vitamin A (4%), 2mg vitamin C (3%), 62mg calcium (6%) and 1.3mg iron (7%).

OATMEAL MUFFINS
Makes 12 muffins

Oatmeal muffins are a real back-to-basics treat. The recipe is from *The King Arthur Flour 200th Anniversary Cookbook.*

1 1/2 cups flour
1/2 cup rolled oats
1/2 cup dark brown sugar
1/2 teaspoon salt
1 tablespoon baking powder

1 cup milk
1/4 cup vegetable oil, butter or margarine, softened
2 eggs
1 teaspoon vanilla

Cinnamon-sugar topping (optional)

1. Preheat oven to 500ºF.
2. In a large bowl, stir together flour, oats, sugar, salt and baking powder.
3. In a separate bowl, beat together milk, oil, eggs and vanilla.
4. Gently stir wet ingredients into dry ingredients, mixing only enough to blend.
5. Spoon equally into 12 muffin cups.

6. Sprinkle with cinnamon-sugar, if desired.
7. Place muffins in oven, and immediately reduce heat to 400ºF.
8. Bake muffins for 20 minutes, or until golden brown.
9. Remove muffins from pan and cool completely on wire rack.

NUTRITION FACTS per muffin: 147 calories, 58 calories from fat, 6.4g total fat (1%), 1.3g saturated fat (6%), 38.2mg cholesterol (13%), 200.5mg sodium (8%), 18.2g carbohydrates (6%), .4g fiber (1%), 3.9g protein (8%), 82 IU vitamin A (2%), zero vitamin C, 117mg calcium (12%) and 1.1mg iron (6%).

Cinnamon sugar is a mixture of 1/3 cup of sugar and 1 teaspoon cinnamon. Other spice sugars can be made with cloves, nutmeg, allspice or ginger. Adjust spice amounts to suit your tastes

ORANGE WALNUT MUFFINS
Makes 12 muffins

Did you say there's no time to fix breakfast? With this recipe from *Teri and Jim Murguia* of The *Branson Hotel* in Branson. Missouri, you can prepare the batter the night before and bake in the morning.

1/2 cup butter at room temperature
2/3 cup brown sugar
1 teaspoon baking soda
1/2 cup sour cream

2 eggs, beaten
1 1/2 cups flour
1 cup walnuts, chopped
1 teaspoon vanilla

1 tablespoon orange zest

1. In a bowl, cream butter and sugar.
2. In a separate bowl, mix soda with sour cream.
3. Add the eggs and sour cream mixture to the butter mixture.

4. Fold in the flour, nuts, vanilla, and orange zest.
5. Fill greased muffin tins 2/3 full.
6. Bake at 350°F for 25 minutes or until the tops are lightly browned.

Batter may be refrigerated overnight and baked in the morning.

NUTRITION FACTS per muffin: 251 calories, 144 calories from fat, 16.5g total fat (25%), 6.6g saturated (33%), 60.1mg cholesterol (20%), 201.2mg sodium (8%), carbohydrates (7%), .5g fiber (2%), 5.6g protein (11%), 447 IU vitamin A (9%), 1mg vitamin C (2%), 33mg calcium (3%) and 1.3mg iron (7%).

Did you know it is believed that walnuts originated in Persia? In the Mediterranean region, English walnuts are known as Persia walnuts. The walnut name comes from the Welsh word *wealhhnutu* that meant "foreign nut." In America, there were native black walnuts and these trees because root stock for the English walnut. Black walnuts are quite rich with oil and are seldom eaten out of hand but used for cakes, candy and ice cream.

PINEAPPLE CARROT MUFFINS
Makes 30 muffings

In the 19th century, John and Helen Garth welcomed guests to their home, which included the noted author Mark Twain. Today, *Irv and Diane Feinberg* welcome guests to their *Garth Woodside Mansion Bed and Breakfast Country Inn,* located in Hannibal, Missouri where guests savor these muffins.

1 1/2 cups flour, sifted
1 cup sugar
1 teaspoon baking powder
1 teaspoon baking soda
1 teaspoon cinnamon

1 teaspoon vanilla
2/3 cup vegetable oil
2 eggs
1 cup carrots, finely shredded
1/2 cup pineapple, crushed with syrup

1/2 cup walnuts, chopped

1. In large mixing bowl, mix together first 5 ingredients.
2. Add oil, eggs, carrot, pineapple and vanilla.
3. Mix until moist.

4. Beat two minutes at medium speed.
5. Add walnuts.
7. Bake at 350°F for 15 to 20 minutes.

NUTRITION FACTS per muffin: 114 calories, 57 calories from fat, 6.4g total fat (10%), .8g saturated fat (4%), 14.2mg cholesterol (5%), 61mg sodium (3%), 12.9g carbohydrates (4%), .4g fiber (2%), 1.7g protein (3%), 2002 IU vitamin A (40%), 1mg vitamin C (2%), 18mg calcium (2%) and .5mg iron (3%).

PUMPKIN SPICE MUFFINS
Makes 24 muffins

Ebenezer Crafts in 1771 offered Yankee soldiers a hearty breakfast at his *Publick House Historic Inn,* which included a similar muffin to this recipe. Could it be, since baking powder had not been invented, these muffins were baked in a saucer? The Inn is located in Sturbridge, Massachusetts and still offers a hearty breakfast to their guests.

2 cups sugar
1/3 cup vegetable oil
3 eggs
1 1/2 cups canned pumpkin
1/2 cup water
3 cups bread flour
1 1/2 teaspoons baking powder

1 teaspoon baking soda
1 teaspoon salt
3/4 teaspoon cinnamon
1/2 teaspoon nutmeg
1/2 teaspoon cloves
1 1/2 cups raisins
1 cup walnuts, coarsely chopped

1. In a large bowl, mix sugar, oil, eggs, pumpkin and water to blend thoroughly.
2. Mix to blend thoroughly.
3. Fold in raisins and walnuts.
4. Let stand 1 hour at room temperature.

5. With 1/3 cup measure, portion mixture into greased muffin cups.
6. Bake in a preheated 400°F oven 15 to 20 minutes until springy to the touch.
7. Cool slightly on racks.
8. Serve warm.

NUTRITION FACTS per muffin: 227 calories, 61 calories from fat, 7g total fat (11%), .8g saturated fat (4%), 27mg cholesterol (9%), 38.4g carbohydrates (13%), 1.5g fiber (6%), 4.6g protein (9%), 174mg sodium (7%), 40mg calcium (4%), 1.5mg iron (8%), 1mg vitamin C (2%) and 3434 IU vitamin A (69%).

RHUBARB MUFFINS
Makes 18 muffins

People line up at *The Nut Tree* mornings in the Swiss community of Berne, Indiana for *Tammy Nussbaum and Brenda Huey's* rhubarb muffins.

1 cup rhubarb, diced
3/4 cup sugar, divided
3 cups flour
3 1/2 teaspoons baking powder
1/2 teaspoon salt

1/4 teaspoon baking soda
1/2 cup butter
1 egg
1 1/2 cups buttermilk
2 tablespoons orange juice

1. In a bowl, combine rhubarb and 1/4 cup sugar; set aside.
2. In another bowl, mix remaining sugar and the rest of the dry ingredients.
3. Cut in butter.

4. Add rhubarb and remaining ingredients and mix well.
5. Pour into greased muffin cups and sprinkle with streusel topping.
6. Bake at 325°F for about 20 minutes or until tested done.

NUTRITION FACTS per muffin with topping: 221 calories, 82 calories from fat, 9.1g total fat (14%), 4g saturated fat (20%), 26.2mg cholesterol (9%), 264 sodium (11%), 31.4g carbohydrates (10%), zero fiber, 3.7g protein (7%), 363 IU vitamin A (7%), 2mg vitamin C (3%), 104mg calcium (10%) and 1/3mg iron (7%).

STREUSEL TOPPING

1/2 cup flour   1/4 cup sugar   1/3 cup margarine

1. Mix all ingredients together with a fork.

Did you know that beans are one of the world's oldest cultivated plants? They are known to have grown more than 5,000 years ago in Europe. Beans are a member of the legume family with peas, lentils and peanuts (yes, peanuts are beans, not nuts). Only the kidney bean and the lima bean are native to the Americas. It is believed these two bean types originated in Peru, since they were first cultivated by the Incas. Most other varieties originated in Africa, Asia and the Middle East. Beans are best known for their protein and are prized as an energy food.

SPICY BEAN MUFFINS

Wow! Muffins made with beans! What will they think of next? Actually beans have been used for centuries to make bread in England as the poor couldn't afford flour. *The Idaho Bean Commission* sums it up best: *"Move over bran! Share the healthy spotlight with high fiber, no cholesterol beans that are also packed with extra protein and taste great."* So, don't knock it until you've tried them!

1 cup pinto beans, cooked
3/4 cup milk
2 egg whites
1/4 cup vegetable oil
1/2 cup brown sugar
3/4 cup flour
3/4 cup whole wheat flour

2 teaspoons baking powder
1/2 teaspoon baking soda
1/2 teaspoon salt
1/2 teaspoon cinnamon
1/4 teaspoon nutmeg
1/4 teaspoon cloves
1/2 cup raisins, dates or apples, chopped

1. Puree beans with milk in blender or food processor until smooth.
2. Transfer to a bowl.
3. Beat in egg whites, oil and brown sugar.
4. In another bowl, combine remaining ingredients.

5. Fold into bean mixture, mixing just until dry ingredients are moistened.
6. Spoon into greased muffin cups.
7. Bake in preheated 400°F oven for 15 to 18 minutes or until golden brown

NUTRITION FACTS per muffin: 135 calories, 32 calories from fat. 3.7g total fat (6%), .6g saturated fat (3%), zero cholesterol, 149.2mg sodium (6%), 22.2g carbohydrates (7%), 3.4g fiber (14%), 4.3g protein (9%), zero vitamin A, 1mg vitamin C (2%), 72mg calcium (7%) and 1.3mg iron (7%).

GRAINS

All grains are grasses, which include: amaranth (high in protein with a nutty flavor), barley (one of the earliest known cultivated grasses), buckwheat (not a true grain, but a grass), millet (rich in iron and amino acids), oats, quinoa (a supergrain from the Incan Empire, as it supplies all the nutrients to sustain life), rice, rye (high in protein, with a sour flavor), sorghum (mostly used for animal feed and molasses), triticale (a combination of rye and wheat), and wheat (more than 30,000 different varieties).

All edible grains have four basic features:

1. The hull, which is generally not eaten but removed;
2. The bran, which is the layer that is rich in vitamins and minerals, as well as fiber;
3. The germ, or the embryo that contains enzymes, minerals, and vitamins; and
4. The endosperm, the starchy center, rich in carbohydrates.

NUTRITION FACTS: When the whole grain is used, it will contain the most nutrients. When the grain is refined to only the starchy center, most of the nutrients are lost. White flour, unless it has been enriched, is made from the endosperm, and contains almost no nutrients. Bulgur, also called ala, is whole wheat which has been steamed, hull removed, and cracked, retaining all the nutrients.

CHAPTER XIV

PANCAKES & CREPES

The pancake is the oldest form of bread. Ancient civilizations made pancake batters with pounded grains and mixed with water. They were then spread out on a hot rock to sun dry. Those pancakes were not light and fluffy like the ones made today, since soda and other leavening agents hadn't bee discovered. Those early pancakes would be similar to a tortilla, but not as tasty.

Home Made Prepared Pancake Mix 206

Banana Pancakes (*Malaysia*) 207

Apricot Harvest Pancakes (*Canada*) 206

Blintzes (*Israel*) 207

Blueberry Banana Pancakes (*cruise ship*) 208

Cilantro Corn Pancakes (*California*) 208

Crepe a L'Orange with Orange Yogurt Sauce (*France*) 209

Breakfast in Denmark

Danish Pancake Balls (*Denmark*) 209

Flensjes met Applen (*Netherlands*) 211

Dutch Baby (*Netherlands*) 210

Fried Matzoh (*Israel*} 211

German Apple Pancakes with 3 variations (*Germany*) 212-213

Ginger Spiced Pancakes with Lemon Pear Sauce (*Amish*) 213

Honey-Butter Blintzes (*Passover, Israel*) 214

Hungarian Pancakes (*Hungry*) 214

Kartoffelpuffer (*Germany*) 215

Latkes (*Israel*) 215

Oatmeal Blinis (*Ireland & Scotland*) 216

Odyssey Tropical Crepes with Low Calorie variation (*tropics*) 216-217

Old Fashioned Buckwheat Cakes (*Russia & Poland*) 217

Palatschinken (*Austria*) 218

with 2 variations

Emperor's Omelet and Curd Pancakes 218

Ruffled Crepes Isabel with Egg Filling (*Colorado*) 219

Saucijze Broodjes (*Holland*) 219

Sourdough Hot Cakes (*Alaska*) 220

Viees Pannekorken (*Holland*) 221

HOME-MADE PREPARED PANCAKE MIX
Makes about 24 4-inch pancakes

Some recipes require prepared pancake mix. This can be purchased at the supermarket or you can make your own without preservatives and other ingredients with funny sounding names that few of us can pronounce.

1/2 cup buttermilk powder
1 1/3 cups all-purpose flour
2/3 cup whole wheat flour

1/4 cup sugar
1/2 teaspoon salt
2 teaspoons baking powder

1 teaspoon baking soda

1. Mix all ingredients and store in an airtight container, in a dry, cool place.

The recipe can be doubled, tripled, etc.

When it is time to make the pancake, all that is required are the following liquid ingredients (or measure out dry ingredients per recipe and use liquid ingredients as listed in recipe):

2 eggs, slightly beaten

2 cup water

5 tablespoons vegetable oil

1. In a bowl, add one recipe of dry ingredients.
2. In another, combine liquid ingredients.
3. Add liquid ingredients to dry ingredients.
4. Stir only until all dry ingredients are moistened.
5. Batter will be lumpy.

APRICOT HARVEST PANCAKES
Makes 4 servings

A great time to celebrate the fruit harvest is with these pancakes that are served to guests at *Chalet Luise* in Whistler, British Columbia, *Canada* by *Luise and Eric Zinsli.*

2 cups prepared pancake mix
1 1/4 cups water
2 eggs
Butter or margarine

Fresh apricots, peaches or plums
Powdered sugar
1 teaspoon cinnamon
2 tablespoons sugar

Whipping cream, whipped (optional)

1. In large bowl mix water and eggs with a whisk (if using a home-made prepared mix, add 5 tablespoons of vegetable oil).
2. Add pancake mix and whisk constantly.
3. Do not over mix.
4. Small lumps will still be visible.
5. Heat griddle at medium heat.
6. Grease lightly with butter.
7. Pour 1/3 cup of batter for small pancakes (2/3 for large pancakes).
8. Top with sliced apricots.
9. When bubbles start to burst, turn carefully with a spatula.
10. Finish cooking until golden.
11. Turn over on serving plate with fruit on top.
12. Dust with powdered sugar and sprinkle with cinnamon and sugar.
13. Decorate with a dollop of whipped cream and sliced fruit, if desired.

May also be served with your favorite syrup.

NUTRITION FACTS per serving without whipped cream and extra fruit: 379 calories, 61 calories from fat, 6.9g total fat (11%), 2.8g saturated fat (14%), 113.9mg cholesterol (38%), 984.9mg sodium (41%), 68.6g carbohydrates (23%), 3.9g fiber (16%), 11.2g protein (22%), 2113 IU vitamin A (42%), 7mg vitamin C (12%), 271mg calcium (27%) and 3.1mg iron (17%).

BANANA PANCAKES
Makes 4 servings

Hope Irvin Marston of Black River, New York, picked up this recipe on a trip to *Malaysia*. Canned coconut milk can be substituted for the home-made coconut water.

2 eggs	1/4 teaspoon salt
1 teaspoon sugar	1/2 cup coconut, grated
1/2 cup self-rising flour	1/2 cup water

4 to 5 bananas, mashed

1. Pour water over the coconut; let stand for a few minutes.
2. Squeeze the water out of the coconut and save the water. Save the coconut for another recipe, if desired.
3. Beat the eggs and sugar until light.
4. Combine flour and salt and fold into the eggs along with the coconut water.

5. Add mashed bananas; mix well.
6. Heat a frying pan or griddle over medium heat; oil well.
7. Put 2 tablespoons of batter in the pan.
8. Turn it so the batter forms a thin layer.
9. Cook until lightly browned on both sides.
10. Fold into triangle.

. Serve with slice of lemon or bananas.

NUTRITION FACTS per serving: 217 calories, 55 calories from fat, 6.5g total fat (10%), 4g saturated fat (20%), 106.3mg cholesterol (35%), 267.1mg sodium (11%), 37.5g carbohydrates (12%), 3.9g fiber (16%), 5.4g protein (11%), 251 IU vitamin A (5%), 11mg vitamin C (18%), 47mg calcium (5%) and 1.3mg iron (7%).

BLINTZES
Makes 4 servings

Throughout the Western world people eat crêpe suzettes. Blintzes are the *Jewish* eastern European version of the French treat.

BATTER

1 cup flour	1 cup water, soda water or milk
1/4 teaspoon salt	2 eggs

1. In a bowl, combine flour, water and salt.
2. Add eggs and beat until smooth.
3. Spoon a little batter on a heated, greased 7-inch frying pan (or crepe pan), just enough batter to coat the bottom, tipping to spread thin.
4. Cook on one side only then turn onto a towel.

5. Place about 1 1/12 tablespoons of filling on each pancake, roll up, tucking in ends.
6. Continue until all batter and filling is used.
7. Place on a lightly greased baking sheet.
8. Bake for 10 minutes in a 350°F oven.

NUTRITION FACTS per serving without fruit: 376 calories, 110 calories from fat, 12g total fat (18%), 6.2g saturated fat (31%), 190.3mg cholesterol (63%), 258.6mg sodium (11%), 36.3g carbohydrates (12%), zero fiber, 29.1g protein (58%), 576 IU vitamin A (12%), zero vitamin C, 76mg calcium (8%) and 2.5mg iron (14%).

FILLING

1 pound dry cottage cheese	Cinnamon to taste
3 ounces cream cheese	3 tablespoons sugar
1 egg	Raisins, blueberries or strawberries (optional)

1. Combine cheeses, sugar and egg.

2. Add cinnamon and raisins or berries..

BLUEBERRY BANANA PANCAKES
Makes 18 pancakes

What's better than blueberry pancakes? If you're aboard a *Crystal Cruise Ship*, it's blueberry banana pancakes.

3 cups flour
3 tablespoons sugar
2 teaspoons salt
1 1/2 teaspoons baking powder
1 1/2 teaspoons baking soda

3 eggs, slightly beaten
3 cups buttermilk
4 tablespoons butter, melted
2 bananas, sliced
2 cups blueberries, fresh or frozen, thawed

1. Combine dry ingredients in a large bowl.
2. Add eggs and combine well.
3. Add buttermilk and butter.
4. Let rest 30 minutes.

5. Pour 1/2 cup of the batter on medium heated griddle.
6. Top with banana slices and blueberries.
7. Fry on both sides for 2 to 3 minutes.

NOTE: This recipe can easily be cut into thirds if 18 pancakes are too much for one sitting. Also, try them plain without the fruit.

Serve fruit side up, dust with powdered sugar and serve with syrup.

NUTRITION FACTS per pancake without syrup: 156 calories, 36 calories from fat, 4.1g total fat (6%), 2.1g saturated fat (10%), 43.7mg cholesterol (15%), 452.6mg sodium (19%), 25.4g carbohydrates (8%), .7g fiber (3%), 4.8g protein (10%), 188 IU vitamin A (4%), 4mg vitamin C (6%), 86mg calcium (9%) and 1.2mg iron (7%).

CILANTRO CORN PANCAKES
Makes 12 pqancakes

This Southwestern favorite pancake was created by *Renee Shepherd* (Renee's Garden) and *Fran Raboff*, Felton, California. These pancakes make a colorful and fully satisfying meal.

1/2 cup flour
1 teaspoon baking powder
1/2 teaspoon baking soda
1 teaspoon sugar
1/4 teaspoon salt
1/3 cup cornmeal
1 egg or 2 egg whites

1 cup buttermilk or fresh plain yogurt
2 tablespoons vegetable oil
1 cup corn kernels, cooked & drained
1/4 cup roasted mild chilies, chopped, peeled, seeded
1/4 cup fresh cilantro, chopped
1/3 cup scallions, chopped

Vegetable oil

1. In a large bowl, sift the flour, baking powder, soda, sugar and salt.
2. Stir in cornmeal.
3. In another bowl, lightly beat egg.
4. Add buttermilk, oil, corn, chilies, cilantro and scallions.

5. Add to dry ingredients and stir until combined.
6. Drop by large tablespoons and bake on medium high greased griddle.
7. Cook until tiny holes form.
8. Turn pancakes and brown on other side.

Serve with mild or hot salsa and sour cream.

NUTRITION FACTS per pancake: 85 calories, 27 calories from fat, 3.1g total fat (5%), .5g saturated fat (3%), 18.4mg cholesterol (6%), 156.3mg sodium (7%), 12.1g carbohydrates (4%), .8g fiber (3%), 2.7g protein (5%), vitamin A (2%), vitamin C (21%), calcium (7%) and iron (5%).

CREPE A L'ORANGE
Makes 6 crepes

This *French* favorite comes from *The J.M. Smuicker Company* test kitchen. It's a great combination of fruit flavors.

1/2 cup flour
1/8 cup sugar
1 tablespoon orange zest

1/8 teaspoon salt
1 cup milk
3 eggs, beaten

2 tablespoons vegetable oil

1. In a bowl, combine the flour, sugar, salt and zest.
2. Add the milk gradually and stir until mixture is free of lumps.

3. Add the eggs and oil, blend well.
4. Butter crepe pan lightly and sauté the crepes until yellow on both sides.

RASPBERRY FILLING

2 cups whipping cream
4 tablespoons raspberry jam

4 tablespoons orange marmalade
1 cup raspberries, divided

1. In a bowl, whip the cream.
2. Fold in jam, marmalade and 1/2 cup raspberries.
3. Lay crepes on flat surface.
4. Divide filling onto 6 crepes.

5. Roll crepes firmly and cut in half.
6. Pour orange yogurt sauce onto 4 plates.
7. Place 3 crepe halves on each plate pointing to the center.
8. Decorate with remaining raspberries.

NUTRITION FACTS per serving: 857 calories, 507 calories from fat, 57.9g total fat (89%), 31.2g saturated fat (156%), 334.3mg cholesterol (111%), 259.5mg odium (11%), 75.3g carbohydrates (25%), 2.5g fiber (10%), 14.5g protein (29%), 2231 IU vitamin A (45%), 31mg vitamin C (51%), 306mg calcium (31%) and 1.8mg iron (10%).

ORANGE YOGURT SAUCE

1 cup lowfat yogurt

4 tablespoons orange marmalade

1/2 cup orange juice

1. Combine all ingredients and stir well.

DANISH PANCAKE BALLS
Makes 6 servings

In *Denmark* they are called "*æbleskiver*" and are served as dessert. However, you can enjoy them at breakfast. These pancakes are not flat, but little round balls, and takes a special *æbleskiver* pan (see MAIL ORDER SOURCES, page 248) to cook them. It is believed these pancakes originated with the Vikings. The Vikings often used their dented shields as pans. They would grease the shields, pour on the pancake batter, the batter would sink into the large dents, creating pancake balls. It is unknown if the Vikings served them with powdered sugar and raspberry jam.

5 eggs, separated
3/4 cup milk, cream, or buttermilk
2 cups flour
2 teaspoons baking powder

1/2 teaspoon salt
1/2 teaspoon baking soda
2 tablespoons sugar
1 lemon rind, grated

1/2 teaspoon powdered cardamon

1. In a bowl, beat egg yolks, add milk, sugar, salt, cardamon and lemon rind.
2. In another bowl, sift flour, soda and baking powder together.
3. Add to egg mixture.
4. Beat egg whites until stiff and add last.

5. Place a tablespoon of shortening in each cup of the æbleskiver pan.
6. When pan is hot, pour in about 2 tablespoons of batter into each cup.
7. Turn quickly with knitting needle or poultry fastener as soon as edges are bubbly.
8. Turn ball frequently to prevent burning.

Serve with raspberry jam and powdered sugar, or syrup.

NUTRITION FACTS per serving: 250 calories, 51 calories from fat, 5.6g total fat (9%), 2g saturated fat (10%), 181.2mg cholesterol (60%), 471.9mg sodium (20%), 38.4g carbohydrates (13%), zero fiber, 10.5g protein (21%), 303 IU vitamin A (6%), 1mg vitamin C (1%), 177mg calcium (18%) and 2.7mg iron (15%).

BREAKFAST IN DENMARK

Drive-in hamburger stands do not exist in Denmark, possibly because dining is supposed to be a "*hyggelig*," a friendly, sit down occasion in cheerful surroundings. Although the daily fare in a Danish home is not the elaborate divertissement of cuisine found in the best restaurants and inns, most Danish meals and foods are different from American fare. Home-cooked food, though plain and thrifty, includes the typically Danish dishes, always nicely garnished and served. But if a guest is coming, that is a different story! The whole gamut of Danish specialties is lavishly prepared that would please a king.

The Danes eat six times a day. Breakfast (*morgenmad*) is the most unvaried of the meals. There is an assortment of breads, flavorful cheeses, plenty of butter and marmalade, and, naturally, several kinds of Danish pastry. A boiled egg, served in an egg cup and covered with a cozy, costs extra in a restaurant, but you can be sure it will be fresh. Certainly you must try a dish of pumpernickel crumbs, layered with yogurt and brown sugar – a delicious breakfast dish.

The Danes laugh when told that Americans eat pancakes for breakfast. These treats are definitely a dessert in Denmark, and delightfully tempting they are when embellished with strawberries and gobs of whipped cream. Americans in Denmark stand out immediately by the way they hold their fork in the right hand, instead of the left. Most Europeans don't shift the fork from the left to the right hand after cutting their food. You may hear a native say, "*He's an American. See how awkwardly he eats!*"

DUTCH BABY
Makes 6 servings

Betty O'Dell of Pella, Iowa, says, "*This recipe takes 10 minutes to prepare, 30 minutes to bake and about 10 minutes to assemble.*"

3 eggs, beaten
1/2 cup flour
1/2 teaspoon salt
1/2 cup milk
2 tablespoons butter, melted
1 tablespoon lemon juice

1 1/2 pint strawberries
1 cup sliced peaches, fresh or frozen, drained or other in season fruits
Lemon wedges
Powdered sugar
1/2 cup sour cream or brown sugar & cinnamon

1. Heat oven to 450°F.
2. Put a little butter in a 9-inch iron skillet and place in oven while mixing the batter.
3. In a bowl, sift flour and salt together.
4. Add milk and eggs to the flour; beat until smooth.
5. Stir in melted butter.
6. Pour into pan.
7. Bake on bottom shelf for 20 minutes.

8. Reduce heat to 350°F.
9. Prick shell; bake 10 minutes longer.
10. At the table; have ready the plates of fruit, lemon wedges, sugar and cream.
11. Drizzle the shell with lemon juice; sprinkle with sugar, fill with fruit.
12. Cut in wedges and top with cream.
13. Serve at once!

FLENSJES MET APPELEN
Makes 4 servings

These *Dutch* apple pancakes by *Mina Baker-Roelofs* of Pella, Iowa, have the apples baked right in the batter.

3 eggs	1 tablespoon sugar	2 1/2 cups milk
1/4 teaspoon salt	1 cup flour	1 tablespoon butter, melted
	Cinnamon sugar	

1. In a bowl, beat eggs, salt and sugar together.
2. Blend in flour and stir, adding milk gradually, to a smooth, creamy batter.
3. Stir in melted butter.
4. Heat frying pan, grease with butter, pour 2 to 3 tablespoons batter into pan, tilting pan to make batter spread evenly.
5. Cook 1/2 minute, place apple slices over batter and pour over another 2 to 3 tablespoons of batter.
6. When brown on one side, turn pancake over.
7. Fold or roll pancake and sprinkle with cinnamon sugar.
8. Keep hot.
9. Continue making new pancakes the same way.

APPLE FILLING

| 3 cooking apples | 1 teaspoon cinnamon |
| 1/4 cup lemon juice | 1/2 cup sugar |

1. Peel, core and cut apples in very thin slices.
2. Pour lemon juice over apples and sprinkle with cinnamon and sugar.

NUTRITION FACTS per serving: 464 calories, 109 calories from fat, 12.4g total fat (19%), 6.2g saturated fat (31%), 187.8mg cholesterol (63%), 285.4mg sodium (12%), 77.1g carbohydrates (26%), 3.2g fiber (13%), 13.3g protein (27%), 597 IU vitamin A (12%), 15mg vitamin C (24%), 222mg calcium (22%) and 2.5mg iron (14%).

FRIED MATZOH
Makes 2 servings

"During the Jewish Passover," says *Karen Barnett-Woods*, from Naperville, Illinois, *"Jews must abstain from eating leavened bread, substituting matzoh crackers, since there was no time to bake raised bread during the exodus from Egypt."*

| 2 pieces of matzoh | 1 teaspoon butter | 2 tablespoons milk |
| 2 eggs | 1/4 teaspoon salt | Bowl of warm water |

1. Break the matzoh into small pieces and place them in the bowl of warm water.
2. Let the matzoh soak for about 1 minute, just enough to soften.
3. Do not let it get soggy.
4. Drain all the water from the bowl.
5. In a separate bowl, break the eggs with the milk and salt and mix thoroughly.
6. Add the matzoh; stir well so matzoh is coated with egg.
7. In a skillet melt butter over medium heat until it covers the pan.
8. Pour the matzoh mixture into the pan.
9. As mixture begins to set turn it over so that the uncooked portion can set.
10. Salt to taste.

NUTRITION FACTS per serving: 213 calories, 72 calories from fat, 7.8g total fat (12%), 3.1g saturated fat (16%), 219.7mg cholesterol (73%), 356.8mg sodium (15%), 25.1g carbohydrates (8%), .9g fiber (3%), 0.6g protein (19%), 408 IU vitamin A (8%), zero vitamin C, 47mg calcium (5%) and 1.6mg iron (9%).

GERMAN APPLE PANCAKES

There are many recipes called *German* Apple Pancakes. While many are similar, each is recipe just a little bit different. Try them all and pick out your favorite. Generally, a *German* pancake is one large cake either cooked with apples or topped with cooked apples.

GERMAN APPLE PANCAKE I
Makes 6 servings

Jan Lugenbuhl of Metairie, Louisiana offers her favorite recipe.

3 golden delicious apples, peeled, cored
2 eggs, lightly beaten
2 teaspoons lemon juice
2 teaspoons unsalted margarine
1/2 cup skim milk

1/2 cup flour
1 teaspoon vanilla
1/2 teaspoon lemon rind, grated
1/8 teaspoon cinnamon
1 tablespoon powdered sugar, sifted

1. Cut each apple into 16 pieces.
2. In a small bowl combine apples and lemon juice, tossing well.
3. Coat a large skillet with cooking spray, add apples.
4. Cover, cook over low heat for 5 minutes or until apples are tender.
5. Uncover and cook 2 minutes or until lightly browned; set aside and keep warm.
6. Place margarine in a 10-inch cast-iron skillet coated with cooking spray.
7. Bake skillet at 425°F for about 4 minutes or until margarine melts and skillet is hot.
8. In a medium bowl combine eggs, milk, flour vanilla, lemon rind, and cinnamon.
9. Beat at medium speed until smooth.
10. Pour immediately into hot skillet and bake for about 15 minutes.
11. Remove from oven; top with apples and sprinkle with powder sugar.
12. Cut into 6 equal wedges.
13. Serve immediately.

NUTRITION FACTS per serving: 128 calories, 29 calories from fat, 3.3g total fat (5%), .8g saturated fat (4%), 71.2mg cholesterol (24%), 31.8mg sodium (1%), 21.2g carbohydrates (7%), 1.9g fiber (8%), 4g protein (8%), 252 IU vitamin A (55%), 5mg vitamin C (9%), 41mg calcium (4%) and .9mg iron (5%).

GERMAN APPLE PANCAKE II
Makes 4 servings

Trish Audette of Warwick, Rhode Island prefers to make her pancakes with this recipe.

3 eggs
3/4 cup milk

3/4 cup flour
1 1/2 tablespoons butter

1/2 cup apples, finely diced

1. Preheat oven to 450°F.
2. Put butter into a heavy oven-proof 12-inch skillet.
3. Place the skillet in the oven to melt the butter.
4. Mix remaining ingredients until well combined.
5. Pour into hot skillet.
6. Bake for 10 minutes and drop oven temperature to 350°F for 5 more minutes.

TOPPING

1 pound tart apples, peeled & chopped
1/2 cup raisins

1/4 cup butter, melted
1/4 cup sugar

Cinnamon & nutmeg to taste

1. In medium sauce pan melt butter.
2. Add remaining ingredients and let it simmer while the pancake bakes.

3. When the pancake is ready, serve and pour over the top
.

NUTRITION FACTS per serving: 487 calories, 190 calories from fat, 21.8g total fat (34%), 12.1g saturated fat (60%), 207.7mg cholesterol (69%), 231.7mg sodium (10%), 67.1g carbohydrates (22%), 4.4g fiber (18%), 9.6g protein (19%), 954 IU vitamin A (19%), 8mg vitamin C (14%), 103mg calcium (10%) and 2.4mg iron (14%).

GERMAN APPLE PANCAKES III
Makes 2 servings

Traveling through Oregon, I stopped at *The Original Pancake House* in Eugene and found the secret to making a puff pancakes. Normally this recipe serves two, but it was so good I ate the whole thing.

1 green apple, cored, peeled & sliced thin
2 tablespoons lemon or lime juice
3 tablespoons butter

1/2 teaspoon cinnamon
2 tablespoons sugar

1. In a bowl, toss all ingredients, except butter, together.
2. In an iron skillet sauté apples in butter until tender.
3. Pour Puffy Batter on top of the apples;

sprinkle with brown sugar, if desired.
4. Bake for 25-minutes in 400°F oven until puffy and golden brown.
5. Turn out on plate and sprinkle with powdered sugar

PUFFY BATTER

4 eggs
3 tablespoons vegetable oil

1 cup milk
3/4 cup flour

1. Mix eggs, milk and oil with a whisk until fluffy.

2. Beat in flour until smooth.

NUTRITION FACTS per serving: 820 calories, 466 calories from fat, 52.3g total fat (80%), 18.7g saturated fat (94%), 487.6mg cholesterol (163%), 60.7mg sodium (15%), 67.5g carbohydrates (22%), 2.2g fiber (9%), 21.8gprotein (43%), 1472 IU vitamin A (29%), 12mg vitamin C (20%), 220mg calcium (22%) and 4.1mg iron (23%).

GINGER SPICED PANCAKES
Makes 4 servings

In Pennsylvania's *Amish* community of Intercourse, you will find the *Kling House Restaurant* in the *Kitchen Kettle Village* serving these delicious pancakes every day but Sunday.

2 cups of prepared pancake mix
1 cup molasses

1 tablespoon cinnamon
2 teaspoons ginger

1. In a bowl, stir above ingredients gently.
2. If molasses is too thick, thin with a little water.
3. On a lightly greased griddle, on medium heat, pour a 1/4 cup of batter; cook until bubbles burst.

4. Watch carefully, as these pancakes can burn quite easily.
5. Turn over and cook until done.
6. Serve with lemon pear sauce.

LEMON PEAR SAUCE

1 pear

1 cup lemon pie filling*

1. Peel, core and slice the pear.

2. Heat pears in a saucepan with lemon filling.

*The lemon pie filling can be from a can or from a powder mix (mix according to recipe).

HONEY-BUTTER BLINTZES
Makes 6 servings

From the test kitchens of the *National Honey Board* come these blintzes for the *Jewish Passover* celebration.

1/2 cup butter
1/2 cup honey, divided

3 eggs, beaten
3/4 cup matzo cake meal
Sour cream

1/2 teaspoon salt
1 to 1 1/2 cups water

1. In a bowl, whip butter and 3 tablespoons honey until well blended; set aside.
2. In another bowl, combine matzo cake meal and salt, mixing well.
3. Add matzo meal mixture and water alternately to eggs to make a thin batter.
4. Heat a lightly oiled 6 to 7-inch skillet over medium- high heat.
5. Add about 3 tablespoons batter to skillet and tilt to spread batter.
6. Cook about 30 seconds or until lightly brown on each side.
7. Remove to towel or wax paper.
8. Repeat with remaining batter in lightly oiled pan.
9. Spread each blintz with honey-butter mixture, fold sides and roll up.
10. Pan-fry each in lightly oiled skillet, turning to brown both sides.
11. Serve with sour cream and drizzle with remaining honey.

NUTRITION FACTS per serving: 405 calories, 186 calories from fat, 21.1g total fat (32%), 12.2g saturated fat (61%), 153.5mg cholesterol (51%), 372.8mg sodium (16%), 49g carbohydrates (16%), 1g fiber (4%), 6.8g protein (14%), 843 IU vitamin A (17%), zero vitamin C, 39mg calcium (4%) and 1.5mg iron (8%).

> **Did you know** that honey is the oldest sweetener known to man? The bees suck the nectar from the flowers and deposit the digested liquid in the hives made of wax honeycomb. Honey can be used as a substitute for up to one-half the sugar in most baking recipes. To replace ¼ cup of sugar with ¼ cup of honey, reduce the liquid in the recipe by 1 tablespoons and add 1/8 teaspoon of baking soda to dry ingredients. Double for ½ cup, etc. Also reduce the oven temperature by 25°F to prevent over browning.

HUNGARIAN PANCAKES
Makes 12 pancakes

The most popular breakfast in *Hungary* is pancakes. Their quality is determined by the proper blending of the batter.

2 eggs
1 cup milk
Pinch of salt

4 teaspoons powdered sugar
7 ounces (about 1 ¾ cups) flour
1 cup soda water

Vegetable oil

1. The batter is prepared by breaking the eggs into a glass bowl.
2. Add cold milk, salt and sugar.
3. Beat until smooth.
4. Pour in the flour, stir swiftly, taking care that lumps are not formed.
5. When the batter is thick enough, add soda water until it reaches the consistency of vegetable oil.
6. Pour a little oil into a hot fry pan.
7. Pour in enough batter to cover the bottom with a thin layer.
8. Turn over when golden brown.

Pancakes can be filled with preserves, walnuts, poppy seeds or cottage cheese.

KARTOFFELPUFFER
Makes 4 servings

In the *German* town of Fredericksburg, Texas, tradition is carried on with old world recipes. *Mrs. O.B. Fiedler* provided this potato pancake recipe for the *Fredericksburg Home Kitchen Cook Book.*

4 or 5 potatoes, peeled, grated
1 tablespoon onion, minced
1 egg, beaten
2 tablespoons flour

1/2 teaspoon salt
1/4 teaspoon hot pepper sauce (optional)
1/8 teaspoon nutmeg
3 tablespoons butter

1. Remove excess liquid from the grated potatoes.
2. In a bowl, place potatoes and add the rest of the ingredients, except butter, and mix thoroughly.

3. Drop by a 1/4 cupful into 1 tablespoon of hot butter in a skillet over medium heat.
4. Spread flat with spatula.
5. Fry until golden brown on both sides.
6. Add more butter as needed for frying.

May be mixed in a blender, starting with the egg, then potatoes and the rest of the ingredients.

Delicious with applesauce, peaches or syrup.

NUTRITION FACTS per serving: 197 calories, 88 calories from fat, 10g total fat (15%), 5.8g saturated fat (29%), 76.1mg cholesterol (25%), 385.1mg sodium (16%), 23.4g carbohydrates (8%), 1.8g fiber (7%), 4.4g protein (9%), 401 IU vitamin A (8%), 22mg vitamin C (37%), 19mg calcium (2%) and 1.2mg iron (7%).

You have tried the *German* version, now try the *Jewish* version, less potato, more onion.

LATKES
Makes 4 servings

Originating in eastern Europe, these potato pancakes have been a staple of the *Jewish* diet for many years. Eaten especially during *Hanukah* and *Passover,* these light and scrumptious treats continue to be a favorite on the *Israeli* menu.

3 potatoes, grated
2 tablespoons flour
(Matzo meal during Passover)
1 egg

1 onion, grated
Salt & pepper to taste
Applesauce (optional)
Sour cream (optional)

1. In a bowl, mix potatoes, egg, flour, onion, salt and pepper.
2. Form into patties and fry in vegetable oil until brown on both sides (about 2 minutes per side).

3. Serve with applesauce or sour cream, if desired.

NUTRITION FACTS per serving without applesauce or sour cream: 106 calories, 12 calories from fat, 1.4g total fat (2%), .4g saturated fat (2%), 53.1mg cholesterol (18%), 158.1mg sodium (7%), 19.7g carbohydrates (7%), 1.8g fiber (7%), 4g protein (8%), 79 IU vitamin A (2%), 18mg vitamin C (30%), 29mg calcium (3%) and 1.1mg iron (6%).

Did you know that potatoes originated in Peru? When Spanish conquistador Francisco Pizzaro went searching for gold in the New World, he found Peruvian Quechua natives feasting on strange tuberous roots and took back samples to Europe where they were received with reactions ranging from fear to distrust. The same was said of tomatoes and other New World fruits and vegetables. Now the potato is often called The Eighth Wonder of the World, but it took almost 200 years before it was accepted in Europe. Part of the problem was that few cooks knew what part of the plant was edible.

OATMEAL BLINIS
Makes 12 blinis

"In Ireland," says *Chef Derek Healy*, from the City Club in Los Angeles, California, *"oatmeal blinis can be served as a side dish with breakfast or on their own as the main breakfast course."* In *Scotland*, a similar, simpler recipe is made with out the last seven ingredients and the oatmeal is moisten with buttermilk, not water. Serve hot with sour cream or butter.

3/4 cup quick cooking oatmeal
1 1/2 cups water
3 tablespoons whole wheat flour
1 egg
1/4 cup milk
2 tablespoons maple syrup

Juice of 1/2 lemon
Rind of 1/2 lemon, grated
1/2 teaspoon nutmeg
1 teaspoon salt
Freshly ground pepper to taste
1/2 cup roasted red pepper, julienne

1/2 teaspoon vegetable oil

1. Combine oatmeal and water in a saucepan and cook over medium high heat, bring to a boil.
2. Lower heat and cook for 3 minutes or until thick.
3. Remove from heat and cool.
4. When cool, beat in flour, taking care not to allow lumps to form.

5. Beat in egg, milk and syrup.
6. When well combined, stir in lemon rind and juice, nutmeg and salt; fold in red pepper.
7. Heat oil in a large non-stick pan over low heat.
8. Add batter to form a 2-inch in diameter cake.
9. Cook, turning once, for about 5 minutes or until golden brown and cooked through.

NUTRITION FACTS per blini: 47 calories, 10 calories from fat, 1.2g total fat (2%), .4g saturated fat (2%), 18.4mg cholesterol (6%), 186.1mg sodium (8%), 7.7g carbohydrates (3%), .9g fiber (4%), 1.8g protein (4%), 276 IU vitamin A (6%), 9mg vitamin C (15%), 15mg calcium (1%) and .4mg iron (2%).

ODYSSEY TROPICAL CREPES
Makes 12 crepes

Chef Chris Tasardoulias, executive director for food for *Royal Cruise Line*, says, *"For the gourmet who delights in new taste discoveries, just wait until you try my new tropical treat."*

CREPES

1 cup flour
1 1/2 cups milk

1/4 cup butter, melted
4 eggs

1 tablespoon sugar
Salt to taste

1. In a bowl, combine all ingredients and mix well to form a thin batter.
2. Heat on medium a 7-inch non-stick skillet.
3. Pour in 3 tablespoons of batter, then tilt the pan from side to side so batter spreads evenly.

4. When bottom is golden, about 30 seconds, turn over and cook for another 15 seconds.
5 Repeat until batter is gone.
6. Set crepes aside.

NUTRITION FACTS per crepe without filling: 119 calories, 59 calories from fat, 6.6g total fat (10%), 3.5g saturated fat (18%), 85.2mg cholesterol (28%), 74.7mg sodium (3%), 10.6g carbohydrates (4%), zero fiber, 4.2g protein (9%), 287 IU vitamin A (6%), zero vitamin C, 47mg calcium (5%) and .8mg iron (4%).

FRUIT FILLING

2 1/2 cups low fat cottage cheese
1 cup papaya, diced
1 cup mango, diced
1 cup strawberries, sliced
1/4 cup sugar

1 lemon rind, grated
1 orange rind, grated
1/2 cup walnuts, chopped
1/4 cup brown sugar
1/2 cup honey

1 teaspoon cinnamon

216

1. In a bowl, combine all but the last three ingredients.
2. Spoon a portion of fruit mixture on each crepe.
3. Roll up and place in a greased 9x13-inch baking dish, open edge down.

4. Pour honey over crepes, sprinkle with brown sugar and cinnamon.
5. Bake at 350°F about 10 minutes or until fruit and honey is sizzling.

Garnish with fresh fruit, if desired.

NUTRITION FACTS per filling: 154 calories, 30 calories from fat, 3.6g total fat (5%), .5g saturated fat (3%), 2.1mg cholesterol (1%), 193.9mg sodium (8%), 25.4g carbohydrates (8%), 1.2g fiber (5%), 7.4g protein (15%), 608 IU vitamin A (12%), 20mg vitamin C (33%), 45mg calcium (4%) and .5mg iron (3%).

LOW CALORIE VERSION

The Royal Cruise Line Odyssey Ships all cook to *"Your Heart's Content,"* so if you are watching calories and fat, make the following adjustments.

CREPES

Use skim milk

Use cholesterol-free egg substitute

Use reduced calorie/fat margarine

Use a sugar substitute or just a dash of sugar

A pinch of salt to taste

FILLING

Use non-fat cottage cheese

Omit white sugar or use sugar substitute

OLD FASHIONED BUCKWHEAT CAKES
Makes 30 pancakes

This West Virginia version of the *Russian* and *Polish* "blini" is from *Stephanie Cowell* of Summerville. In *Russia* these buckwheat cakes would be served with sour cream and caviar or smoked salmon. They are also good with your choice of jam. When stuffed they are called *"blinchiki."* In West Virginia these pancakes are sweeten with molasses, whereas in Europe sugar is used.

1 package dry yeast
1/2 cup very warm water (110°F to 115°F)
2 cups water
1 cup flour
2 cups buckwheat flour

1 1/2 teaspoons salt
1 tablespoon molasses
1/4 cup margarine or butter, melted
1 teaspoon baking soda
1/2 cup hot water

1. In a bowl, dissolve yeast in 1/2 cup warm water.
2. Add 2 cups water.
3. Stir in flours and salt, beat well until smooth.
4. Cover and refrigerate overnight.
5. In morning soften soda with 1/2 cup hot water; cool.

6. Stir into flour mixture with remaining ingredients.
7. Let stand at room temperature 30 minutes.
8. Pour from the tip of a large spoon on to the griddle.
9. Turn pancake when puffed, bubbly and brown.
10. Serve immediately.

NUTRITION FACTS per pancake: 71 calories, 17 calories from fat, 2g total fat (3%), .4g saturated fat (2%), zero cholesterol, 167mg sodium (7%), 11.9g carbohydrates (4%), 1.2g fiber (5%), 2.1g protein (4%), 62 IU vitamin A (1%), zero vitamin C, 5mg calcium (1%) and .5mg iron (3%).

PALATSCHINKEN
Makes 2 servings

This *Austrian* Palatschinken pancake is the basis of three recipes. The original is basically a crepe, is followed with a thicker variety and the third, a baked one like a blintze.

3/4 cup flour	Pinch of salt
2 eggs, beaten	1 cup milk

1. In a bowl, mix all ingredients into a smooth batter.

2. If necessary add more flour.
3. Fry thin pancakes.

Fill with jelly, roll them up, sprinkle with sugar and serve.

NUTRITION FACTS per serving without filling: 510 calories, 89 calories from fat, 9.8g total fat (15%), 4.2g saturated fat (21%), 229.1mg cholesterol (76%), 137.9mg sodium (6%), 87.3g carbohydrates (29%), .4g fiber (2%), 17.8g protein (35%), 478 IU vitamin A (10%), 1mg vitamin C (2%), 184mg calcium (18%) and 4.2mg iron (23%).

EMPEROR'S OMELET

1. Ingredients same at palatschiken, but add a little more flour for a thicker batter, along with some raisins.
2. Heat a tablespoon of butter in a fry pan; pour in the batter about finger-deep.

3. Fry until golden brown, turn the omelet over and with 2 forks tear the omelet into little pieces.
4. Serve with stewed fruits.

CURD PANCAKES
Makes 2 servings

3/4 cup ricotta cheese	2 tablespoons sour cream
2 tablespoons sugar	Vanilla, to taste
1 egg	1 cup cream
1/2 cup raisins	2 egg yolks

1. Prepare pancakes as palatschinken.
2. Mix cheese, sugar, egg, raisins, sour cream and vanilla.
3. Spread this filling on the original cooked pancakes, roll them up, put into an oven proof pan.

4. Mix cream and yolks, top on rolled up pancakes and bake in a 350°F oven until golden brown.

NUTRITION FACTS per serving: 190 calories, 91 calories from fat, 10.3g total fat (16%), 5.7g saturated fat (28%), 117mg cholesterol (39%), 48.5mg sodium (2%), 18.5g carbohydrates (6%), .2g fiber (1%), 6.3g protein (13%), 435 IU vitamin A (9%), 1mg vitamin C (1%), 89mg calcium (9%) and 1mg iron (6%).

RUFFED CREPES ISABEL WITH EGG FILLING
Makes 12 crepe cups or 6 servings

When you enjoy these filled crepes from *Sallie and Welling Clark* from the *Holden House* in Colorado Springs, Colorado you might think you are having breakfast in Spain, France or Italy on the Mediterranean coast.

1 1/4 cups flour	Pinch of salt	1 1/2 cups milk
2 tablespoons sugar	3 eggs	2 tablespoons butter, melted
	1 teaspoon lemon extract, optional	

1. In a bowl, blend all crepe ingredients well.
2. Let rest for 5 minutes.

3. Make 5-inch crepes using either a well-greased skillet, crepe pan or crepe maker.

Extra crepes may be stored in refrigerator for later use.

EGG FILLING

7 eggs
1 cup milk
1/2 teaspoon salt
1/4 teaspoon pepper

6 slices turkey bacon, cooked & crumbled
1 cup sharp cheddar cheese
3/4 cup sour cream
Fresh dill, parsley or tarragon

1. In bowl, mix eggs, milk, salt and pepper together.
2. Spray 12 muffin tins with non-stick oil.
3. Press one crepe into each tin.
4. Lightly ruffling edges, but being careful not to tear crepes.
5. Place a small square of cheese on top of each crepe.
6. Pour egg mixture carefully into each muffin tin, filling just to below top of rim.

7. Top with bacon (vegetarian bacon bits maybe substituted).
8. Bake at 375°F for 15 to 20 minutes or until mixture is firm and crepes are just lightly brown.
9. Carefully loosen crepe cups from muffin tins with a fork or a knife, taking care not to break crepe edges.
10. Remove from tins with a spoon, place 2 on each plate and top with a small dab of sour cream and fresh herbs.

NUTRITION FACTS per crepe cup: 274 calories, 144 calories from fat, 15.8g total fat (24%), 7.9g saturated fat (40%), 220.7mg cholesterol (74%), 548.4mg sodium (23%), 16.1g carbohydrates (5%), zero fiber, 16.3g protein (33%), 614 IU vitamin A (12%), 1mg vitamin C (1%), 171mg calcium (17%) and 1.8mg iron (10%)

SAUCIJZE BROODJES
Makes about 80 pigs

Whether you are fixing for a crowd, like *Millie Vande Kieft* of Pella, Iowa sometimes does, or if you just want to have these *Dutch* "pigs-in-the-blanket" ready for a fast breakfast for the kids, this breakfast treat is sure to please.

DOUGH

5 cups flour
1 tablespoon sugar
1 1/2 teaspoon salt

2 teaspoon baking powder
1 1/2 cups margarine
2 eggs, beaten

1 1/2 cups milk

1. In a bowl, mix all ingredients and refrigerate while making the sausage filling.

SAUSAGE FILLING

4 pounds ground beef
2 pounds ground pork
6 Dutch rusks, ground very fine
3 eggs

1 teaspoon salt
1 tablespoon allspice
1 tablespoon sage
1 1/2 teaspoons pepper

1. In a bowl, mix all ingredients.
2. Roll into link-size sausages about 3-inches long.

3. Roll out dough on a floured board, only small amounts at a time.
4. Cut into 3-inch squares, just large enough to completely wrap the pigs.

5. Cut off the extra dough from the edges.
6. Individually place on a cookie sheet and freeze until ready to bake.
7. When frozen, place in air tight plastic bags.

8. When ready to bake, brush the tops of the dough with a beaten egg.
9. Place in 350°F oven for 45 minutes or until golden brown (no need to thaw before baking).

NUTRITION FACTS per pig: 176 calories, 113 calories from fat, 12.4g total fat (19%), 4.2g saturated fat (21%), 43.9mg cholesterol (15%), 156mg sodium (6%), 7.5g carbohydrates (2%), zero fiber, 8.2g protein (16%), 168 IU vitamin A (3%), zero vitamin C, 25mg calcium (3%) and 1.1mg iron (6%).

SOURDOUGH HOT CAKES

Sourdough hot cakes, the main breakfast dish of miners, prospectors, and old-time Alaskans, differ from other hot cakes in that the batter is leavened with a sourdough yeast starter and soda.

Those early day pioneers protected the starter so it wouldn't freeze during the cold winter months. During the day, they kept it under their coat, next to their body, and at night the starter went to bed with them. If they lost the starter there would be no more sourdough hot cakes until spring.

SOURDOUGH STARTER

1 cup all-purpose flour
1 cup warm water

1 package dry yeast (do not use fast acting yeast)
1 tablespoon sugar (optional)

1. Combine all ingredients in pottery bowl with a wooden spoon (never use a metal bowl or spoon).
2. Pour into a non-metallic bowl and place in a warm place covered with cheese cloth.
3. Let it bubble for 1 to 2 days.

4. When ready to use it will have a clean, yeasty, sour odor. The liquid might separate from the batter, just stir in back into the batter.
5. Refrigerate until ready for use. Can also be frozen.

If you replenished after every use, your starter will last a lifetime.

SOURDOUGH HOT CAKES
Makes 4 servings

2 cups flour   2 cups water
Total sourdough starter at room temperature

1. In a non-metallic bowl, mix flour, water and starter.
2. Let stand at room temperature overnight.

3. Put aside 1 cup of starter for the next use.
4. In the morning mix in the following ingredients:

2 eggs, beaten well   1 teaspoon salt
1 tablespoon sugar   1 teaspoon baking soda
2 tablespoons vegetable oil

5. If the batter is too thick, add more water. If too thin, add more flour.
6. Let the batter stand for several minutes.

7. Bake batter on a hot griddle until golden brown on both sides, turn only once.

Serve with hot brown sugar syrup, honey, molasses or jelly and butter.

NUTRITION FACTS per serving without toppings: 317 calories, 70 calories from fat, 7.7g total fat (12%), 4.1g saturated fat (20%), 68.5mg cholesterol (23%), 924mg sodium (38%), 52.1g carbohydrates (17%), .8g fiber (3%), 9.2g protein (18%), 293 IU vitamin A (6%), zero vitamin C, 20mg calcium (2%), and 3.6mg iron (20%).

VLEES PANNEKOEKEN
Makes 4 servings

Mina Baker-Roelofs from Pella, Iowa says, *"These meat filled pancakes are generally served at a Dutch brunch called Koffie Tafel."*

BATTER

1 cup flour
1 1/2 cups milk

2 eggs, beaten
Salt & pepper to taste

1. In a bowl, make a smooth batter of the above ingredients.
2. Heat butter in a 10-inch skillet.
3. Using half the batter, brown the pancake on one side only and cook until done.
4. Place it on a platter, brown side down.

5. Top with hot meat filling on the light side of the pancake.
6. With the remaining batter, cook as with the first pancake.
7. Place light side down on top of the filling.
8. Cut into 4 wedges.

MEAT FILLING

2 cups cooked beef, chopped fine
4 tablespoons butter
1/3 cup flour
Salt and pepper to taste

1/4 teaspoon nutmeg
1/4 cup lemon juice
2 cups beef stock
1/2 cup fresh or canned mushrooms

Parsley for garnish

1. In a skillet, melt butter, add flour, stirring constantly until thick.
2. Add stock, juice and seasonings; it should be quite tart.

3. Keep stirring while adding meat and mushrooms.
4. Remove from heat, but keep hot while making first pancake

NUTRITION FACTS per serving: 574 calories, 300 calories from fat, 33.2g total fat (51%), 16.1g saturated fat (80%), 217.4mg cholesterol (72%), 835.3mg sodium (35%), 38.6g carbohydrates (13%), .2g fiber (1%), 29.4g protein (59%), 707 IU vitamin A (14%), 8mg vitamin C (14%), 142mg calcium (14%) and 4.4mg iron (24%).

Did you know that packaged baking powders have been on the market since the early 1850s? However, it wasn't until 1889 when William M. Wright of Chicago, developed a product with a mixture of baking soda (then called *saleratus*) and cream of tartar that commercial baking powders were reluctantly accepted by the cook. Wright felt a need for a better version. With experimentation, he worked out a formula for a new baking powder, a double-acting one that began its leavening action when mixed into dough, then produced a second leavening in the heat of the oven. Prior to the invention of baking powder, pear lash (or pearl ash) was used as a leavening agents. It was made from leaching wood ashes and was called "potash." Potash was made by adding lye water to wood ashes and letting the water evaporate to a powder. Pear lash was purified potash. It only has some leavening action and did not produce a finished product like today's commercially made baking powder. Baking soda was developed in England and came to America in 1839, packaged in a bright-red wrapper and with a free recipe card. In those early says, soda salesman rode into town in decorated wagons pulled by a team of horses. With the sound of bells and a blast of a trumpet, everyone knew the soda man had arrived. In this day and age, it's hard to imagine that joyous event, since today baking soda comes in a small box easy to overlook on the market shelf.

CHAPTER XV

PUDDINGS

The word "*pudding*" might symbolize in your mind "*dessert.*" However, many of the ingredients found in puddings are the same ingredients commonly found in breakfast recipes: eggs, meats, cereals, breads and dairy products. While puddings are quite popular in other parts of the world, they still haven't caught on in the United States.

Boiled Custard (*West Virginia*) 223

Bread Pudding with Whiskey Sauce (*Louisiana*) 223

Cabbage Pudding (*Sweden*) 224

Capirotada with Piloncillo Syrup (*Mexico*) 224

Cherry Granola Kugel (*Israel*) 225

Chocolate Hazelnut Pudding (*Austria*) 226

Cyprus Pudding (*Cyprus*) 226

Breakfast in Hungry

Jam Pudding (*Hungry*) 227

Lokshen Kugel (*Israel*) 227

Mhallahiyya (*Egypt*) 228

Prune Pudding (*West Virginia*) 228

Queen Pudding (*Cyprus*) 228

Sweet Potato Pudding I (*Antigua & Barbuda*) 229

Sweet Potato Pudding II (*British Virgin Islands*) 229

BOILED CUSTARD
Makes 4 servings

Alice Merryman of Summerville, West Virginia says, "*This is an excellent recipe for those who do not care for bacon and eggs, but would still like protein for breakfast.*" Delicious with fresh fruit or berries.

3 eggs	1/2 cup sugar	1/2 teaspoon vanilla
3 cups whole milk	4 tablespoons flour	Nutmeg

1. Beat eggs until foamy; set aside.
2. In a heavy sauce pan, stir together sugar, flour and milk.
3. Stir constantly and bring milk to scald.
4. Reduce heat and slowly pour in eggs and stir.
5. Add vanilla and a couple of good shakes of nutmeg.
6. Stir often until mixture reaches the consistency of cooked pudding.
7. The pudding thickens as it cools.
8. Serve warm.

NUTRITION FACTS per serving: 294 calories, 89 calories from fat, 10g total fat (15%), 5g saturated fat (25%), 184.3mg cholesterol (61%), 137.3 sodium (6%), 40g carbohydrates (13%), zero fiber, 11.5g protein (23%), 469 IU vitamin A (9%), 2mg vitamin C (3%), 238mg calcium (24%) and 1mg iron (6%).

BREAD PUDDING
Makes 8 servings

This Creole favorite is served to guests at *The Court of Two Sisters* in New Orleans.

5 cups milk	1/4 cup butter, melted
24-inch loaf of day old French bread, cut into 2-inch cubes	4 eggs
1 pound can fancy fruit cocktail, cherries removed, drained	1 cup sugar
29 ounce can peaches, drained, cut into chunks	1/2 teaspoon vanilla
	1 teaspoon cinnamon
	3/4 teaspoon nutmeg
	1/4 teaspoon allspice

2/3 cup raisins

1. Scald the milk in a large heavy saucepan.
2. Remove from heat and allow to cool for 5-minutes.
3. In a bowl, add bread, fruit, butter, raisins and mix thoroughly.
4. In a separate bowl beat eggs with sugar, milk and spices; add to bread mixture.
5. Butter 4-quart baking dish.
6. Pour mixture into the baking dish.
7. Bake uncovered in preheated 350°F oven for 1 hour and 10 minutes or until knife inserted in center comes out clean and top is brown and forms a rough crust.
8. Allow to cool to room temperature.
9. Serve warm or chilled with bread pudding sauce.

NUTRITION FACTS per serving without sauce: 594 calories, 185 calories from fat, 21.1g total fat (32%), 11.6g saturated fat (58%), 158.1mg cholesterol (53%), 573mg sodium (24%), 90g carbohydrates (30%), 5g fiber 920%), 14.7g protein (29%), 1510 IU vitamin A (30%), 10mg vitamin C (17%), 260mg calcium (26%) and 2.5mg iron (14%).

BREAD PUDDING SAUCE

1 1/4 pounds butter	1/2 cup half and half
2 cups sugar	4 teaspoons corn starch mixed
9 egg yolks	in 1/2 cup cold water

1/3 cup whiskey

1. Melt butter and dissolved sugar over water in a double boiler.
2. Add egg yolks and whip vigorously so that egg yolks do not curdle.

3. Add half and half and the corn starch mixture.
4. Cook over double boiler for 5 minutes.
5. Remove from heat and add whiskey.

NUTRITION FACTS per serving: 817 calories, 590 calories from fat, 65.1g total fat (100%), 38.7g saturated fat (193%), 400.1mg cholesterol (133%), 601.2mg sodium (25%), 52.2g carbohydrates (17%), zero fiber, 4.2g protein (8%), 2598 IU vitamin A (52%), zero vitamin C, 59mg calcium (6%) and .8mg iron (5%).

CABBAGE PUDDING
Makes 4 servings

On the weekends in Sweden, breakfast comes alive with all kinds of dishes, that includes this recipe.

2 pounds cabbage, shredded
1/4 cup butter
4 1/2 tablespoons rice
2/3 cup water

2 teaspoons salt, divided
3/4 pound ground beef
1/4 teaspoon white or black pepper
1 cup milk

1. In a skillet, brown the cabbage in butter; set aside.
2. In a saucepan, boil the rice in the water with 1/2 teaspoon salt for about 20 minutes; cool.
3. Mix the ground beef with remaining salt, pepper, cooked rice and milk.

4. Lay the cabbage and the meat in alternate layers in a buttered ovenproof dish.
5. The top and bottom layers should be cabbage.
6. Bake in a 350°F oven for 45 to 60 minutes.

Serve with boiled potatoes and lingonberry jam

NUTRITION FACTS per serving: 504 calories, 324 calories from fat, 36.5g total fat (56%), 17.6g saturated fat (88%), 111.3mg cholesterol (37%), 1310.8mg sodium (55%), 25.5g carbohydrates (9%), .2g fiber (1%), 20g protein (40%), 791 IU vitamin A (16%), 116mg vitamin C (194%), 195mg calcium (19%) and 3.4mg iron (19%).

CAPIROTADA
Makes 8 servings

Every region of *Mexico* has its own version of this bread pudding. This recipe from Chihuahua is unusual in that it includes layers of cheese.

20 to 25 bolillos (hard bread rolls), sliced, 2 days old
2/3 cup butter, soften
10 corn tortillas, toasted (optional)

2 cups queso anejo or Monterey Jack, grated
1 1/4 cups raisins
1 1/2 cups walnuts or peanuts, chopped

Piloncillo Syrup

1. Cover the sides and bottom of a casserole dish with the tortillas. if desired.
2. Dip each piece of bread into the syrup and arrange a layer of bread in the bottom of the casserole.
3. Sprinkle with part of the cheese, raisins and nuts.
4. Continue making layers of bread, cheese, raisins and nuts until all the ingredients have been used.

5. Strain the syrup that is leftover and pour over the top.
6. Cover with foil and bake for 20 minutes at 400°F, uncovering periodically and smoothing the surface with a wooden spoon.
7. Lower oven heat to 300°F and bake for another 30 minutes.
8. Serve lukewarm.

NUTRITION FACTS per serving with tortillas: 853 calories, 383 calories from fat, 43.9g total fat (68%), 17.3g saturated fat (87%), 75.3mg cholesterol (25%), 994.2mg sodium (41%), 96.1g carbohydrates (32%), 6.2g fiber (25%), 25.3g protein (51%), 918 IU vitamin A (18%), 2mg vitamin C (3%), 534mg calcium (53%) and 4.8mg iron (27%).

PILONCILLO SYRUP

1 piloncillo cone (raw sugar), 5 to 6 ounces	1 cinnamon stick
3 cups water	3 whole cloves

1 cup milk

1. Mix sugar, water, cinnamon and cloves in a saucepan and boil, stirring, until the mixture forms a light syrup.

2. Remove from the heat and stir in the milk.

CHERRY GRANOLA KUGEL
Makes 10 servings

Karen Barnett-Woods of Naperville, Illinois says, *"Kugel is very popular during the Jewish holidays and is generally served hot in the evening, either as part of the main course or dessert. My family also likes kugle hot or cold for breakfast."*

12 ounces wide egg noodles	1 to 1 1/2 cups frozen sweet dark cherries, pitted
1/2 cup margarine or butter	4 eggs
8 ounces cream cheese	1 teaspoon cinnamon
12 ounces cherry preserves	1 cup milk

Granola Topping

1. Cook noodles; drain.
2. Put noodles back in the pot over low heat, mix in butter and cheese until melted.
3. Beat eggs and milk together and pour into noodle mixture.
4. Add cinnamon.

5. Stir in cherry preserves and cherries.
6. Pour noodle mixture into greased 9x13-inch pan.
7. Sprinkle granola topping mixture over noodles and bake in at 350°F for 1 hour or until golden brown.

NUTRITION FACTS per serving: 540 calories, 256 calories from fat, 29.2g total fat (45%), 11.4g saturated fat (57%), 157.8mg cholesterol (53%), 279.2mg sodium (12%), 60.9g carbohydrates (20%), 3g fiber (12%), 12g protein (24%), 1105 IU vitamin A (22%), 4mg vitamin C (6%), 93mg calcium (9%) and 3mg iron (16%).

GRANOLA TOPPING

1 cup granola cereal	1/4 cup butter, melted	Cinnamon

1. Mix together butter and granola.
2. Sprinkle over kugel.

3. Sprinkle cinnamon on top of granola.

What do you know about noodles? Noodles for breakfast might sound a bit strange; however, take a look at the ingredients. Flour (used to make bread), eggs and water. A noodle is essentially a narrow dough strip. The word can also apply to all forms of pasta, both Western and Oriental. In the West, noodles are almost always wheat based. In Asia, noodles are more often made with rice flour. You can make your own homemade noodles. It's easy! All you need are egg yolks, flour and salt. Separate two or three egg yolks into a large bowl. Beat until fluffy. Add ¼ teaspoon of salt. Slowly beat 1 ½ cups of flour into the egg yolk until it forms a stiff dough. Use extra flour to prevent sticking. Roll out the dough flat on a floured bread board. Cut into strips about an inch wide (cut any width you desire from 1/4 inch to 2 inches wide). If the dough seems to be thick, roll out each strip to desired thickness. Drop rolled-out strips into salted boiling water until they are cooked through, about 5 to 10 minutes. No need to dry, they are better fresh.

CHOCOLATE HAZELNUT PUDDING
Makes 6 servings

Austria still uses the "*weight system*" for measuring ingredients, hence, spoon and cup measurements in this recipe are approximate. I have tested this recipe and found it makes a tasty breakfast pudding.

1/4 cup butter, unsalted
1/4 cup powdered sugar
3 eggs, separated
2 slices white bread, diced
1/2 cup milk

2 ounces chocolate
3 tablespoons sugar
1/3 cup hazelnuts, grated
1/2 cup bread crumbs
2 tablespoons cake flour

1. In a bowl, whip together butter and powdered sugar.
2. In another bowl, moisten diced bread with milk and beaten egg yolks.
3. In a sauce pan, add diced bread, chocolate and butter, heat gently until chocolate melts.
4. Whip egg whites and sugar to an oily consistency.
5. Carefully fold the whites into the bread mixture.

6. Stir in flour, bread crumbs and hazelnuts.
7. Butter 6 custard dishes, dust sides with bread crumbs.
8. Pour mixture into the molds.
9. Place molds into a large baking pan, filled half way with hot water.
10. Bake in preheated 350°F oven for about 45 minutes.

Serve with chocolate sauce and whipped cream, if desire.

NUTRITION FACTS per serving: 474 calories, 262 calories from fat, 30.2g total fat (46%),12.7g saturated fat (64%), 196.5mg cholesterol (65%), 209.2mg sodium (9%), 44.5g carbohydrates (15%), 3.3g fiber (13%), 10.8g protein (22%), 748 IU vitamin A (15%), zero vitamin C, 106mg calcium (11%) and 2.5mg iron (14%).

CYPRUS PUDDING
Makes 8 servings

In *Cyprus*, the people call this a pudding, however, it is closer to cooked wheat cereal. Semolina is the grain portion left over as the wheat is ground into fine flour.

2 cups milk
1 cup sugar
2/3 cup semolina
1 tablespoon butter

6 eggs
1 cup mixed citrus peel
1/2 cup sultanas or raisins
1/2 cup blanched almonds, chopped

1 1/2 tablespoons baking powder

1. Put the milk, semolina, butter and sugar in a pan.
2. Cook over medium heat, stirring constantly until thick; set aside to cool.

3. When cool, mix in eggs, peel, sultanas, almonds and baking powder.
4. Butter a baking dish, pour the mixture in and bake in a 350°F oven for about 20 to 25 minutes or until set.

Cyprus pudding can be served hot or cold, and if desired, topped with cream.

NUTRITION FACTS per serving without the topping: 334 calories, 31% calories from fat, 12g total fat (19%), 3.8g saturated fat (19%), 172mg cholesterol (57%), 51g carbohydrates (17%), 1.9g fiber (8%), 11g protein (22%), 299mg sodium (12%), 331mg calcium (33%), 2.1mg iron (12%), 17mg vitamin C (29%) and 420 IU vitamin A (8%).

BREAKFAST IN HUNGARY

Hungarian cooking traditions have always included lots of pig fat and paprika. Today paprika still seems to be the main seasoning used in goulashes and other meat dishes, but gone are the days with the fat in favor of vegetable oil.

Hungarian culinary has a tendency to be different with lots of surprises. The inventiveness of housewives tend to take generations of family recipes, improve on them to perfection. Every family has a grandmother who can cook marvelously, and each household have their own different and exquisite variation of flavor, of the shrewdly planned proportion of ingredients and the stratagem of serving. Even the modestly domestic dishes such as apple strudel or cobbler's delight will cause surprise.

JAM PUDDING
Makes 5 servings

While this *Hungarian* recipe is called "*jam pudding*," note there is much more in this bread pudding besides jam.

8 bread rolls, dried, sliced
2 2/3 cups milk, lukewarm
6 eggs, separated
1 1/3 cups sugar, divided
3 1/2 tablespoons butter, melted, divided

Bread crumbs
1 pound apples, peeled, cored, sliced
1 teaspoon cinnamon
1/3 cup rum
5 1/4 ounces apricot preserves, divided

Powdered sugar

1. In a bowl, beat the yolks with 1/2 cup of sugar, milk and 1 tablespoon of butter.
2. In another bowl, pour the mixture over the bread rolls.
3. Coat a baking pan with remaining butter and sprinkle with bread crumbs.
4. Place in the baking pan half of the soaked bread rolls.
5. Top with the sliced apples, 1/2 cup of sugar and cinnamon.
6. Place the rest of the bread on top of the apples, sprinkle with the rum and spread half of the apricot preserves on top.
7. Bake in a 350ºF oven for 25 to 30 minutes.
8. Beat the egg whites and remaining sugar until stiff, mix in the remaining preserves and spread on top of the baked pudding.
9. Put it back into the oven for a few more minutes until golden brown.
10. Sprinkle the top with powdered sugar.

NUTRITION FACTS per serving: 919 calories, 203 calories from fat, 22.5g total fat (35%), 10.4g saturated fat (52%), 294.6mg cholesterol (98%), 524.1mg sodium (22%), 160.8g carbohydrates (54%), 5g fiber (20%), 17g protein (34%), 1041 IU vitamin A (21%), 13mg vitamin C (21%), 267mg calcium (27%) and 3.2mg iron (18%).

LOKSHEN KUGEL
Makes 6 servings

Lokshen Kugel means "noodle pudding" in *Yiddish*. It originated in eastern Europe where the Jewish community spoke that language. This item falls into the category of "grandma's dishes."

8 ounces broad noodles
1 cup pot cheese
1/2 cup raisins
1 egg, slightly beaten

1/2 teaspoon salt
1 teaspoon cinnamon
2 teaspoons sugar
3/4 cup sour cream

1/4 cup margarine or butter, melted

1. Cook noodles as directed on the package; drain well.
2. Stir in remaining ingredients and half of the margarine.
3. Place in a greased casserole.
4. Pour over the remaining margarine.
5. Bake uncovered at 350ºF for 1 hour

MHALLABIYYA
Makes 6 servings

This ancient *Egyptian* recipe is better known as "powdered rice pudding." The finished product will be a bowl of hot cereal. However, the Egyptians prefer to eat it chilled.

1 cup powdered rice
4 cups water
3 cups milk
1 1/2 cups sugar

1 tablespoon rose water or orange bloom water

1. In a pan, combine powdered rice, water and milk.
2. Cook over medium heat, stirring constantly until mixture starts to thicken.

3. Then add the sugar, lower heat and simmer until thick or the consistency of a cream filling, about 30 minutes.
4. Add rose water, bringing it to a fast boil; remove immediately.
5. Pour into a platter or individual bowls.

This breakfast pudding may be eaten warm or cold.

NUTRITION FACTS per serving: 368 calories, 40 calories from fat, 4.5g total fat (7%), 2.6g saturated fat (13%), 16.6mg cholesterol (6%), 60.3mg sodium (3%), 76.7g carbohydrates (26%), .6g fiber (3%), 5.6g protein (11%), 154 IU vitamin A (3%), 1mg vitamin C (2%), 149mg calcium (15%) and .2mg iron (1%).

PRUNE PUDDING
Makes 6 servings

Stephanie Cowell of Summersville, West Virginia says this pudding is a good source for both fiber and iron. Prunes are now called "dried plums."

1 1/2 cups flour
1/2 teaspoon baking soda
1/2 teaspoon salt
1/2 teaspoon cinnamon
1/4 cup butter
3/4 cup sugar
1 egg, beaten well
1/2 cup prune juice
1 cup prunes, cut up
1/2 cup walnuts

1. In a bowl, sift, then measure flour.
2. Sift 3 times with soda, salt and cinnamon.
3. In a bowl, cream butter until light and lemon colored.
4. Add sugar, gradually beating after each addition.

5. Briskly stir in the egg, juice and flour.
6. Fold in prunes and nuts.
7. Pour into an 8x11-inch pan.
8. Bake in 350°F oven for 35 to 40 minutes.

NUTRITION FACTS per serving: 496 calories, 179 calories from fat, 20.7g total fat (32%), 5.8g saturated fat (29%), 56mg cholesterol (19%), 373.2mg sodium (16%), 72.2g carbohydrates (24%), 3.3g fiber (13%0, 10.3g protein (21%), 936 IU vitamin A (19%), 3mg vitamin C (4%), 42mg calcium (4%) and 3.2mg iron (18%).

QUEEN PUDDING
Makes 2 servings

This pudding from *Cyprus* was created and served to queens.

1/2 cup milk
1 tablespoon strawberry jam
2 tablespoons sugar, divided
1 teaspoon vanilla or a little grated lemon rind
2 tablespoons butter
2 eggs, separated

1 cup white bread crumbs

1. In a sauce pan, boil the milk with the butter, and 1 tablespoon of sugar.
2. Pour over the bread crumbs.
3. Allow to stand for 10 minutes.
4. Add the beaten egg yolks and the vanilla.
5. Pour into buttered dish and bake for 30 minutes at 350°F in a pan of hot water.
6. When set, spread jam on the top.

7. In a bowl, beat the egg whites until stiff, add remaining sugar and pile on top of the pudding.
8. Place on bottom shelf of the oven for 20 minutes to set and brown the meringue.

Serve hot or cold.

NUTRITION FACTS per serving: 507 calories, 198 calories from fat, 22g total fat (34%), 10.7g saturated fat (54%), 251.5mg cholesterol (84%), 589.7mg sodium (25%0, 62.3g carbohydrates (21%), 2.9g fiber (11%), 14.9g protein (30%), 824 IU vitamin A (16%), 1mg vitamin C (2%), 144mg calcium (14%), and 3mg iron (17%).

SWEET POTATO PUDDING I
Makes 4 servings

In the Caribbean sweet potato pudding is quite popular. Each country has their own recipe. This one is from *Antigua and Barbuda.*

2 cups sweet potatoes, grated
1 cup coconut, grated
2 cups flour
2 tablespoons margarine, melted
Milk to moisten

1 teaspoon cinnamon
1 teaspoon nutmeg
1/4 teaspoon cloves
1/2 teaspoon salt
1 1/2 cups sugar (more or less to taste)

1. Mix all ingredients into a bowl.
2. Pour into a greased dish.
3. Dot with margarine.

4. Bake in a 350°F oven until firm. Test as for a cake.

. Serve with cream or meringue to which guava jelly has been added.

NUTRITION FACTS per serving: 728 calories, 127 calories from fat, 14.4g total fat (22%), 7.9g saturated fat (39%), 2.1mg cholesterol (1%), 355.7mg sodium (15%), 143.6g carbohydrates (48%), 4.5g fiber (18%), 8.9g protein (18%), 13297 IU vitamin A (266%), 16mg vitamin C (26%), 59mg calcium (6%) and 4.1mg iron (23%).

SWEET POTATO PUDDING II
Makes 10 servings

This *British Virgin Islands* recipe, with just a hint of spices, is for a group of people. Tannia is a tuber and can be found in many supermarkets and Caribbean food stores.

4 cups sweet potatoes, grated
1 tannia, grated (optional)
1 cup pumpkin, grated
1 1/4 cups brown or white sugar
1 cup coconut, grated
1 cup milk
2 tablespoons water
1 teaspoon black pepper (optional)

1/8 teaspoon nutmeg
1 cup flour
1/4 cup butter, melted
1/8 teaspoon cinnamon
1 tablespoon shortening, melted
2 teaspoon vanilla
1 teaspoon salt
2 eggs, beaten

1. Mix potatoes, tannia, pumpkin, sugar, flour and milk in a large mixing bowl.
2. Add remaining ingredients and mix well.

3. Pour into a greased baking dish.
4. Bake at 350°F for 1 hour and 45 minutes.
5. Cool completely before cutting.

NUTRITION FACTS per serving: 283 calories, 94 calories from fat, 10.6g total fat (16%), 6.4g saturated fat (32%), 58.1g cholesterol (19%), 299.9mg sodium (12%), 43.3g carbohydrates (14%), 2.6g fiber (10%), 4.7g protein (9%), 10883 IU vitamin A (18%), 13mg vitamin C (22%), 69mg calcium (7%) and 1.8mg iron (10%).

CHAPTER XVI

VEGETABLES

You might not think vegetables are part of the breakfast menu. What about hash brown potatoes? What about tomato sauce on eggs? Corn flakes are made from corn, right? That's just a sample of some of the vegetables you have probably eaten for breakfast. As you will see from this chapter, vegetables play an important part for breakfast around the world.

Beans for Breakfast

The Bird Flanagan Potato Pancakes (*Ireland*) *231*

Burekas (*Israel*) 231

Cajun Potatoes (*Mississippi*) 232

Chicos (*New Mexico)* 232

Chiles Rellenos Casserole (*Oregon*) 233

Cholay (*Pakistan*) 232

Fadge with Ulster Fry (*Ireland*) 234

Falafil with Variation (*Egypt*) 234

Fried Eggplant with Yogurt (*Egypt*) 235

Leek & Bacon Flan (*Missouri*) 235

Potatoes a la Sutter Creek (*California*) 236

Potato, Cabbage & Irish Bacon Casserole (*Ireland*) *236*

Shakshouka (*Israel*) 236

Stuffed Cabbage Leaves *(Egypt) 237*

Stuffed Tomatoes (*Ireland*) 236 237

Breakfast in the British Virgin Islands

Tanka Soup (*British Virgin Islands*) 238

Vegetable Biryani (Pakistan) 239

Vegetable Salad with Dressing (*Israel*) 239

Yam & Irish Bacon Flan (*Ireland*) 240

BEANS FOR BREAKFAST

Potatoes might be your first vegetable choice for breakfast, and just maybe you wouldn't even consider beans a breakfast food. All you need to do is go south of the border and you will find beans in one form or another on every breakfast plate.

When I traveled throughout Mexico, Central America and South America, restaurants usually included refried beans with almost every egg dish, just like I found grits in America's south and hash browns in the rest of the country.

In northern Mexico, pinto beans seem to be the first choice and were spiced with hot peppers. The further south I went, it was black beans and the beans were less spicy, almost bland in Central American and points south. Sometimes the beans were left whole, other times were mashed. Topping for the beans was either sour cream or a crumbled white cheese.

If you would like to try beans for breakfast, purchase a can from your supermarket. If they are whole beans, drain the liquid and wash, then fry with a tablespoon or two of butter or vegetable oil. If the canned beans are mashed, fry as you would the whole beans.

If you find beans to your liking, than purchase dried beans and start from stretch.

THE BIRD FLANAGAN POTATO PANCAKES
Makes 4 servings

Chef Noel Cullen from Boston University says, *"These up- beat Irish "hash browns' are sure to please everyone at the breakfast table."* Great with sausages!

2 potatoes, peeled, grated
1 egg, beaten slightly
1/4 pound bacon, sliced, finely chopped
1/4 cup cheddar cheese, grated

1 tablespoon onion, chopped
1/4 cup fresh parsley, minced
Freshly ground pepper to taste
2 tablespoons vegetable oil

1. Place grated potatoes in a bowl.
2. Stir in egg and raw bacon.
3. Stir in cheese, onion, parsley and pepper.
4. Mix until thoroughly combined.
5. Heat oil in a crepe pan over medium high heat.
6. When hot, pour in the potato mixture.
7. Pat down to fit firmly into the pan.

8. Lower heat to medium and cook for about 5 minutes or until golden.
9. Turn and cook other side for about 5 minutes or until potatoes are cooked and a crisp crust has formed.
10. Serve immediately.

NUTRITION FACTS per serving: 316 calories, 220 calories from fat. 24.5g total fat (38%), 7.6g saturated fat (38%), 84.7mg cholesterol (28%), 525.6mg sodium (22%), 10.6g carbohydrates (4%), .9g fiber (4%), 13.2g protein (26%), 173 IU vitamin A (3%), 21mg vitamin C (35%), 67mg calcium (7%) and 1.2mg iron (7%).

BUREKAS
Makes 8 servings

This a *Jewish* Sephardic dish which is quite similar to the *Turkish "burak."* Burekas can be prepared with various types of dough; strudel dough (thin leaves), rising dough or with types of prepared dough found in the market. This dish is served on festive occasions, but is widely sold on *Israeli* street corners. To be tasty, burekas must be served hot and fresh.

DOUGH

1/2 pound margarine, melted
1 teaspoon salt

3 cups self-rising flour
Warm water

1. Mix margarine with flour.

2. Add only enough water to roll dough.

3. Roll it and cut out 2 inch circles with a biscuit   cutter.

STUFFING

1/2 cup feta cheese	1 cup cooked spinach	2 egg yolks

4. Mix all ingredients.
5. Put 1 teaspoon of stuffing on each dough circle.

6. Fold in half.

GARNISH

1 egg yolk, beaten	4 tablespoons sesame seeds

7. On top, brush with egg yolk.
8. Sprinkle top with sesame seeds.
9. Place on a well greased cookie sheet.

10. Bake at 350°F for about 15 to 20 minutes or until golden.
11. Serve hot.

NUTRITION FACTS per serving: 444 calories, 263 calories from fat, 29.4g total fat (45%), 6.1g saturated fat (30%), 86.1mg cholesterol (29%), 1306.4mg sodium (54%), 36.7g carbohydrates (12%), 2.2g fiber (9%), 8.8g protein (18%), 2976 IU vitamin A (60%), 4mg vitamin C (7%), 241mg calcium (24%) and 3.3mg iron (18%).

CAJUN POTATOES
Makes 1 serving

Bettye and Cliff Whitney, hosts at *The Corners Mansion* in Vicksburg, Mississippi bring a bit of Louisiana north for their guests. If Cajun seasoning is not available, use a mixture of black and red pepper to suit your taste.

1 potato	1 tablespoon bacon drippings	1/2 teaspoon Cajun seasoning

1. Cook potato in microwave for 15 minutes.
2. Slice in 1/4 inch slices.

3. Cook in drippings in a large pan on top of stove until crisp.
4. Sprinkle with Cajun seasoning and serve.

NUTRITION FACTS per serving: 211 calories, 118 calories from fat, 13.3g total fat (21%), 6g saturated fat (30%), 13.4mg cholesterol (4%), 185.8mg sodium (8%), 21.2g carbohydrates (7%), 2g fiber (8%), 2.5g protein (5%), zero vitamin A, 22mg vitamin C (37%), 8mg calcium (1%) and .9mg iron (5%).

CHICOS
Make 6 servings

The people of New Mexico took a lesson from our Native Americans and came up with their own recipe for chicos. Chicos are sweet corn kernels that have been dried and saved for winter.

2 cups chicos	1 garlic clove, minced
10 cups water	1/2 teaspoon oregano
2 pounds pork, cut into 2 inch cubes	4 chile pods, washed, crushed
1 onion, minced	2 teaspoon salt

1. Wash chicos and soak overnight.
2. Drain and cover with 5 cups of water in a large pot.
3. Bring to a boil and simmer for about 1 hour.
4. In a skillet, fry pork cubes until brown.
5. Drain fat.

6. Stir in 2 cups of water to gather up the flavorful bits at the bottom of the pan.
7. Pour the meat, garlic, oregano, chile, salt and remaining water in with the chicos.
8. Cover and simmer for 2 1/2 hours or until chicos are tender.

CHILE RELLENOS CASSEROLE
Makes 6 servings

A true chile relleno is a long mild green pepper, usually stuffed with cheese, dipped in an egg batter and fried. Sounds easy, but its not as easy as it sounds. *Teresa and Harry Pastorious* from the *Klamath Manor* in Klamath Falls, Oregon have made the recipe easy with almost the same flavor as the real thing.

8 ounce canned whole green chilies,
rinsed, seeded
1 pound Monterey Jack cheese, grated
1/2 pound cheddar cheese, grated

4 eggs, slightly beaten
1/2 teaspoon dry mustard
1 teaspoon salt
1/4 teaspoon black pepper

1. Line bottom of lightly greased 12x7-inch baking dish with half of the chilies.
2. Sprinkle half of the cheeses over chilies.
3. Top with remaining chilies.
4. Sprinkle remaining cheeses.

5. In a bowl, combine eggs, milk and seasonings.
6. Pour over chili/cheese mixture.
7. Bake at 350°F for 30 to 35 minutes or until lightly browned and set.
8. Let cool 5 minutes before cutting into squares.

Top with red chile sauce, if desired.

NUTRITION FACTS per serving: 500 calories, 349 calories from fat, 38.9g total fat (60%), 23.4g saturated fat (117%), 248.7mg cholesterol (83%), 1040.5mg sodium (43%), 5.1g carbohydrates (2%), .6g fiber (2%), 32.9g protein (66%), 1622 IU vitamin A (32%), 92mg vitamin C (153%), 862mg calcium (86%) and 1.8mg iron (10%).

Did you know the chili pepper tropical plant produces pods from mild to hot? The green bell pepper is one of the mildest, while the habañero is the hottest. Jalapeño is one of the most popular, being middle hot to mild. It is said the habañero tastes like apricots, but since they kill all taste buds, it's not known for sure if this is true.

CHOLAY
Makes 6 servings

In *Pakistan*, cholay, a curry made with chickpeas, is usually served free with the purchase of *puri* (see FRIED DOUGHS for PURI, page 104).

1 cup dried chickpeas,
soaked in water overnight
2/3 cup vegetable oil
1 onion, chopped
1 tomato, chopped

1 teaspoon salt
1 teaspoon cayenne pepper
1/4 teaspoon pepper
1/2 teaspoon cumin seeds
3 cups water

1. Drain the water from the chickpeas.
2. Heat the oil in a pan.
3. Add the onion and fry until they start to brown.
4. Add tomato, salt, peppers and cumin.
5. Stir for 3 minutes.
6. Pour the water in the onion mixture.
7. When it comes to a boil, add the chickpeas and lower the heat.

8. Cover the pan.
9. When the water is reduced to less than half a cup and the chickpeas are very tender, about 1 ½ to 2 hours, take off the heat.
10. If the chickpeas are not tender just add more water and cook a little longer.
11. Pour some of the cholay on a plate and eat with the puri.

NUTRITION FACTS per serving: 346 calories, 232 calories from fat, 26.4g total fat (41%), 3g saturated fat (15%), zero cholesterol, 457.1mg sodium (19%), 22.5g carbohydrates (7%), 6.5g fiber (26%), 6.9g protein (14%), 275 IU vitamin A (5%), 7mg vitamin C (11%), 50mg calcium (5%) and 2.4mg iron (13%).

FADGE WITH ULSTER FRY
Makes 4 servings

Chef Joseph Friel from the Plaza Hotel in New York City serves fadge to breakfast diners. Fadge is a knish, a popular potato dish from *Northern Ireland*. See front cover photo.

1 1/2 pounds potatoes
Salt to taste
1/4 cup milk
3 tablespoons unsalted butter
4 tablespoons flour

Freshly ground pepper to taste
2 tablespoons vegetable oil
8 slices bacon
4 sausage links
4 eggs

4 slices black breakfast pudding
4 slices white breakfast pudding
2 tomatoes

1. Peel potatoes, cut into cubes.
2. Place potatoes in a saucepan covered with water.
3. Add salt to taste.
4. Bring to a boil, lower heat and simmer for about 10 minutes or until very tender.
5. Drain well.
6. Pour milk and butter into the same saucepan, bring to a boil, add potatoes immediately.
7. Remove from heat and mash well.
8. Stir in flour and salt and pepper to taste.
9. Turn out onto a lightly floured board and pat or roll out to a circle about 1/2-inch thick.
10. Using a 3-inch biscuit cutter, cut out about 8 cakes.
11. Heat oil in a large sauté pan over medium high heat.
12. When hot, add potato cakes (fadge) and fry turning once for about 5 minutes or until golden brown on both sides.
13. Using the same pan, first fry the bacon, then the sausage and breakfast puddings.
14. Keep meats hot as you fry.
15. Fry tomatoes halves with the breakfast pudding.
16. Cook eggs as desired and serve everything on a large platter along with toasted wheat bread.

NUTRITION FACTS per serving for only the potato cakes: 308 calories, 142 calories from fat, 16.1g total fat (25%), 6.5g saturated fat (32%), 25.1mg cholesterol (8%), 19mg sodium (1%), 37.3g carbohydrates (12%), 2.7g fiber (11%), 4.9g protein (10%), 340 IU vitamin A (7%), 34mg vitamin C (56%), 34mg calcium (3%), and 1.7mg iron (9%).

FALAFIL
(Taamia)
Makes 8 servings

These fava bean patties are quite popular in *Egypt* for breakfast. Falafil patties are delightful as a filling in pita bread. The *Egyptians* also make walnut-sized balls and deep fry them for hors de'oeuvres.

1 pound dried fava beans
1 onion
2 garlic cloves, crushed
1 teaspoon ground coriander seed
1/4 teaspoon cayenne pepper (optional)

1 teaspoon baking soda
1/2 teaspoon cumin
Salt & pepper to taste
1 tablespoon flour
Parsley

Dill

1. Soak fava beans in cold water for 3 to 4 days, changing the water every day.
2. Peel beans and grind with onion, parsley, dill and coriander in a meat grinder.
3. Add remaining ingredients, mixing well.
4. Grind mixture a second time.
5. Form into patties and fry in hot oil.

NUTRITION FACTS per serving: 50 calories, 4 calories from fat, .5g total fat (1%), zero saturated fat and cholesterol, 254.8mg sodium (11%), 8.6g carbohydrates (3%), 2.7g fiber (115), 3.6g protein (7%), 223 IU vitamin A (4%), 20mg vitamin C (33%), 25mg calcium (3%) and 1.3mg iron (7%).

FRIED EGGPLANT WITH YOGURT
Makes 6 servings

Eggplant for breakfast? Yuck! No, it's not, give it a try. However, follow these directions carefully. Eggplant is quite common in *Egypt* and Middle East countries.

3 eggplants	Parsley,	Lemon juice
Salt	2 garlic cloves, crushed	Dried mint, crushed (optional
	Plain yogurt	

1. Cut eggplant into 1/2 inch thick slices.
2. Sprinkle with salt and drain in a colander for 30 minutes.
3. Wipe dry with paper towels.
4. Fry eggplants in hot oil for a few minutes on each side, until lightly browned.
5. Drain and arrange on a platter.
6. Sprinkle slices with parsley, garlic, lemon juice and salt.
7. Top with mint and yogurt.

NUTRITION FACTS per serving: 72 calories, 7 calories from fat, .9g total fat (1%), .3g saturated fat (2%), 1.6mg cholesterol (1%), 371.1mg sodium (15%), 15.8g carbohydrates (5%), 5.8g fiber (23%), 3g protein (6%), 355 IU vitamin A (7%), 9mg vitamin C (14%), 43mg calcium (4%) and 1.3mg iron (7%).

LEEK & BACON FLAN
Makes 4 servings

A specialty from *Teri and Jim Murguia* at *The Branson Hotel* in Branson, Missouri is this recipe.

Quiche crust for 8-inch flan dish (page 139)	1 1/2 teaspoons paprika
3 tablespoons butter	1 teaspoon lemon juice
1 pound leeks, sliced	1/4 cup milk
3 large slices lean bacon, cut into 1/2-inch strips	Salt & freshly ground pepper, to taste
1 1/2 teaspoons flour	2 eggs, beaten

1. Preheat oven to 400°F.
2. Roll out quiche dough on a floured surface to fit and line the flan dish (a pie plate can also be used).
3. Prick base with a fork.
4. Place circle of foil on crust, weight down with dried beans and bake for 10 minutes.
5. Remove beans and foil, return to oven for 10 to 15 minutes until crisp and lightly colored.
6. Melt butter in saucepan, add the leeks, cover and cook until soft.
7. Place bacon in a skillet and cook for about 10 minutes; set aside.
8. When leeks have softened, sprinkle in the flour and paprika and cook for 1 to 2 minutes, stirring.
9. Gradually blend in the juice and milk and bring to a boil, stirring.
10. Add salt and pepper.
11. Remove from heat and stir in the eggs.
12. Lower oven temperature to 350 F.
13. Spread the bacon over the crust and top with the leek mixture.
14. Bake for 20 to 25 minutes.

NUTRITION FACTS per serving: 789 calories, 367 calories from fat, 40.9g total fat (63%), 13.9g saturated fat (69%), 135.4mg cholesterol (45%), 626.1mg sodium (26%), 89.3g carbohydrates (30%), 2.2g fiber (9%), 16.7g protein (33%), 1130 IU vitamin A (23%), 17mg vitamin C (28%), 117mg calcium (12%) and 7.4mg iron (41%).

Did you know the leek, a bulb vegetable, originated in the Mediterranean and is related to onions and garlic? The leek looks like a fat green onion. This mild flavored vegetable is generally used for flavoring soups and salads, however, can be boiled or braised and served as a side dish. Both the root and the leaves are cooked.

POTATOES A LA SUTTER CREEK
Makes 16 servings

In the heart of California's "Mother Lode" country, is the state's oldest bed and breakfast inn, the *Sutter Creek Inn,* in the town Sutter Creek. *Jane Way* fixes a fine breakfast for her guests which includes this recipe.

2 pounds frozen hash brown potatoes, thawed
2 1/2 cups Jack or Swiss cheese, grated
4 cups ham, chopped (optional)
2 cups sour cream

1 can cream of mushroom, celery or
chicken soup
1/2 onion, chopped
2 cups corn flakes, crushed

1/4 cup butter, melted

1. Coat a 7x10-inch casserole dish with oil spray.
2. Mix in a large bowl all ingredients, except corn flakes and butter.
3. Spoon into the casserole dish.

4. Sprinkle the corn flakes on top and drizzle with the melted butter.
5. Bake at 350°F for 45 minutes.

NUTRITION FACTS per serving: 357 calories, 229 calories from fat, 25.7g total fat (40%), 13.6g saturated fat (68%), 63.5mg cholesterol (21%), 945.2mg sodium (39%), 19g carbohydrates (6%), .2g fiber (1%), 13.4g protein (27%), 669 IU vitamin A (13%), 16mg vitamin C (27%), 178mg calcium (18%) and 1.2mg iron (6%).

POTATO, CABBAGE & IRISH BACON CASSEROLE
Makes 4 servings

An *Irish* tradition is "corn beef and cabbage, served with potatoes." Here the corn beef is replaced with bacon. You will find this recipe by *The Limerick Bacon Company* makes a great breakfast and is high in vitamins, minerals and protein.

6 cups green cabbage, shredded
1 onion, chopped
1/4 pound Irish slab bacon,
cut into 1/4 inch cubes
2 tablespoons parsley, chopped

1/4 teaspoon thyme
Salt & pepper to taste
1 pound potatoes, pared, sliced thinly
3/4 cup chicken broth, defatted
1/2 cup low-fat cheddar cheese, shredded

1. Spray a 3 quart casserole dish with cooking spray.
2. Layer with half of the cabbage and onion.
3. Sprinkle with half of the bacon.
4. Sprinkle with half of the seasonings.
5. Arrange half of the potatoes over the top.

6. Repeat layers ending with potatoes.
7. Pour the chicken broth over.
8. Sprinkle with cheese.
9. Cover and bake in a 350 F for 45 minutes.
10. Uncover and bake 15 minutes more or until top is brown.

NUTRITION FACTS per serving: 343 calories, 147 calories from fat, 15.9g total fat (24%), 5.8g saturated fat (29%), 27.6mg cholesterol (9%), 1004.2mg sodium (42%), 29.3g carbohydrates (10%), 2.5g fiber (10%), 18.5g protein (37%), 606 IU vitamin A (12%), 89mg vitamin C (149%), 209mg calcium (21%) and 4.2mg iron (23%).

SHAKSHOUKA
Makes 4 servings

From *Israel* comes this Sephardi favorite. A Middle Eastern dish, but also enjoyed by the Hungarians with lots of paprika. Only fresh tomatoes should be used, not canned.

1 onion, finely chopped
1 tablespoon vegetable oil
3 to 4 slices red pimento (optional)

1 garlic clove, minced (optional)
4 eggs
6 tomatoes, grated

Salt & pepper to taste

1. In a large frying pan, sauté onion, garlic and pimento in vegetable oil until lightly browned.
2. Mix grated tomatoes in the onion mixture, cover and cook over low heat for 25 minutes.

3. Remove cover and break eggs over vegetables.
4. Stir gently to break yolks, cover and cook for about 3 to 4 minutes or until eggs are set.
5. Sprinkle with salt and pepper.

NUTRITION FACTS per serving: 155 calories, 78 calories from fat, 9.1g total fat (14%), 2g saturated fat (10%), 212.5mg cholesterol (71%), 219mg sodium (9%), 11.6g carbohydrates (4%), 2.5g fiber (10%), 8.3g protein (17%), 1843 IU vitamin A (37%), 49mg vitamin C (82%), 53mg calcium (5%) and 1.9mg iron (10%).

STUFFED CABBAGE LEAVES
Makes 6 servings

This recipe from *Egypt* can be made ahead of time, cooked, refrigerated, and reheated in the microwave. Stuffed cabbage leaves are popular in the Middle Eastern countries, as well as parts of southern Europe. In *Greece,* the cabbage leaves would be substituted with grape leaves.

1 medium head of white cabbage
1/2 pound lean ground lamb or beef
1/2 cup rice, washed, drained
1 tomato, skinned, chopped (optional)
1/4 cup parsley
1/4 cup fresh dill, minced or

1 tablespoon dried dill
Salt & pepper to taste
1/2 teaspoon cumin
1/4 teaspoon allspice
2 tablespoons pine nuts or raisins (optional)
Juice of 1 lemon or lime

1. Carefully strip leaves from cabbage and wash them.
2. Dip into boiling, salted water, a few leaves at a time, until they become wilted and pliable.
3. Trim the hard central veins flat.
4. Cut very large leaves in half.
5. Combine meat, rice, tomato, parsley, dill, salt, pepper, cumin and allspice in a bowl.
6. Knead well by hand until thoroughly blended.
7. Add pine nuts.

8. Put a tablespoon of filling at end of each leaf.
9. Fold sides of leaves toward center and roll up.
10. Line a large saucepan with torn or unused leaves to prevent stuffed leaves from sticking.
11. Layer stuffed leaves in pan, packing tightly.
12. Cover with water and lemon juice, mixed with a little salt.
13. Cover pan and cook gently for about 45 minutes to 1 hour, or until rice is done.

NUTRITION FACTS per serving: 222 calories, 87 calories from fat, 10.1g total fat (16%), 3.5g saturated fat (17%), 28.4mg cholesterol (9%), 60.8mg sodium (3%), 23.8g carbohydrates (8%), .7g fiber (3%), 11.1g protein (22%), 323 IU vitamin A (6%), 85mg vitamin C (141%), 120mg calcium (12%) and 3.7mg iron (21%).

STUFFED TOMATOES
Makes 2 servings

Chef Conrad Gallagher from the *Waldorf Astoria Hotel* in New York City has put a new twist on the *Irish* breakfast, tomatoes stuffed with scrambled eggs and bacon.

2 large tomatoes
Salt to taste
4 bacon slices
2 tablespoons unsalted butter, divided
3 eggs, beaten

1/4 cup fresh chives, chopped
1/4 cup heavy cream
Fresh black pepper to taste
2 cups spinach, washed, dried
8 thick slices of black breakfast pudding

1. Preheat oven to 375°F.
2. Wash and dry tomatoes.
3. Trim bottom from tomatoes so that they can sit flat.
4. Slice 1/2-inch off the top to make a lid.

5. Scrape interior pulp and seeds from tomatoes and lids.
6. Season with salt and turn upside down on paper towel to drain.
7. Cut bacon into strips.

8. Melt 1 tablespoon of butter in a saucepan over medium heat.
9. When melted, add bacon, sauté for about 3 minutes or until lightly crisped.
10. Remove and set aside about half the bacon.
11. Add eggs, stir to combine with the remaining bacon.
12. Cook for about 2 minutes or until lightly scrambled.
13. Stir in chives, cream, seasonings; remove from heat.
14. Turn tomatoes up right.
15. Fill each cavity with equal parts of the egg mixture.
16. Place tomato lid on top.
17. Melt remaining butter and brush generously the butter on the filled tomatoes.
18. Place in a baking dish and bake for 5 minutes or until tomatoes are warm, but not cooked and filling has set.
19. Toss spinach with remaining bacon, season to taste.
20. Spread equal amounts of the spinach mixture on two serving plates.
21. Fry black pudding slices over medium-high heat about 1 minute per side or until heated through.
22. Place in a circle in the center of the greens.
23. Place heated tomatoes on top of the breakfast pudding (if breakfast pudding is not available, substitute sausage).
23. Serve immediately.

NUTRITION FACTS per serving without breakfast pudding: 428 calories, 324 calories from fat, 36.8g total fat (57%), 18.6g saturated fat (93%), 401mg cholesterol (134%), 364.9mg sodium (15%), 9.8g carbohydrates (3%), 3g fiber (12%), 16.8g protein (34%), 6130 IU vitamin A (123%), 47mg vitamin C (79%), 128mg calcium (13%) and 3.5mg iron (19%).

BREAKFAST IN THE BRITISH VIRGIN ISLANDS

The British Virgin Islands, known familiarly as the B.V.I., are 50 miles east of Puerto Rico. These islands were first settled by the Arawak and Carib natives. Later the English adventurers, then the Dutch, French and Spanish explorers, followed by marauding pirates, and finally Quakers, plantation owners and other settlers. Much of the food comes the sea, with fish (salt fish), lobster and shellfish topping the list. From the land are tomatoes, garlic, onions, rice, banana, coconut, and tannia (a sweet potato), along with chicken and pork.

TANNIA SOUP
Makes 6 servings

Tannia is a root, similar to sweet potatoes and is native to the Caribbean. This recipe is from the *British Virgin Islands.*

1/2 pound salt beef or pigtail	Sugar (optional)
1 1/2 pounds tannia, quartered	1 chive blade
1 onion, sliced	1 tomato, chopped
1 sprig thyme	2 quarts water
Dumplings (optional)	1 cup milk

Salt & pepper to taste

1. Wash meat with lime and boil in 2 quarts of water.
2. Add onion, thyme, chive and tomato and simmer until meat is tender.
3. Season with salt and pepper to taste.
4. Add tannias and dumplings.
5. Cook until tannias are soft and dumplings float to the top.
6. Add milk and cook for another 3 to 5 minutes.
7. Remove from the heat and sweeten to taste.
8. Serve hot.

There are several dumplings that could be served with this soup. Ducknoor, page 112, is my choice. If you wanted a plain flour dumpling, try Eskimo dumplings, page 113. See "Dumplings, Doughs that are Steamed or Boiled" chapter for more ideas, page 108

VEGETABLE BIRYANI
Makes 10 servings

Shazia Hasan from Karachi, *Pakistan* says, "Biryani is not usually served for breakfast, but to those who like leftovers, like my family, this makes a great breakfast treat."

2 onions, chopped
Water
1 tomato, chopped
1 inch piece of ginger, shredded
3 garlic cloves, minced
2 green chilies, cut length wise,
seeds removed
1 green bell pepper, chopped
2 potatoes, peeled, sliced
3/4 cup green peas

1 carrot, sliced 1/4 inch thick
2 1/4 teaspoons salt, divided
1 teaspoon cayenne pepper
1 teaspoon cumin seeds
1 cinnamon stick
1/2 teaspoon pepper
1/2 teaspoon coriander seeds, ground
1/2 cup yogurt
3/4 cup vegetable oil
2 cups long-grain white rice

1/2 teaspoon orange food color mixed with 1/2 cup water

1. Pour the oil in a large sauce pan.
2. Add the onions and fry gently until they are golden.
3. Add tomato, ginger, garlic, 1 1/4 teaspoon salt, cayenne, cumin, cinnamon, pepper and coriander with 1/2 cup of water.
4. Cover the pan and cook until the liquid is almost gone.
5. Stir into the tomato mixture 2 1/2 cups of water; bring to a boil.
6. Add carrots and peas, cover pan on low heat for 20 minutes.
7. When the carrots are tender, add the potatoes and green pepper.
8. Cover again and cook until all vegetables are tender.
9. If the water dries up, add a little water as needed.
10. When the water is all gone, stir in the yogurt and chilies.
11. Stir for 5 minutes, take off the heat; set aside.
12. In another large sauce pan, fill a little more than half with water, add salt and bring it to a boil.
13. Add the rice and cook until tender.
14. Drain all the water.
15. In a large oven safe baking pan, cover the bottom with some rice.
16. Sprinkle it with some of the orange food coloring.
17. Spread some vegetables over the rice.
18. Repeat the procedure covering the vegetables with more rice, food color and vegetables.
19. Cover, place in a 300°F oven for 20 minutes.
20. Transfer vegetables to a big serving dish, serve with ketchup.

NUTRITION FACTS per serving: 297 calories, 151 calories from fat, 17g total fat (26%), 2.2g saturated fat (11%), zero cholesterol, 604.6mg sodium (25%), 34.8g carbohydrates (12%), 2.2g fiber (9%), 2.3g protein (5%), vitamin A (47%), vitamin C (70%), calcium (5%) and iron (8%).

VEGETABLE SALAD
Makes 6 servings

The idea of salad for breakfast is probably a little strange to North Americans. But this salad is enjoyed by *Israelis* regardless of whether they are from *Russia, Morocco, Yemen* or the United States.

1/2 head lettuce
1/4 head cabbage
4 tomatoes

2 cucumbers
2 carrots
8 radishes

Green onion
2 eggs, hard boiled
2 tablespoons parsley

1. Cut vegetables (except carrots) into small cubes.
2. Grate carrot and egg.
3. Add parsley and salad dressing to salad before serving and mix well.

SALAD DRESSING

2 to 3 tablespoons lemon juice

2 to 3 tablespoons vegetable oil

1. Combine lemon juice and oil, mix well.

NUTRITION FACTS per serving with dressing: 195 calories, 77 calories from fat, 9.5g total fat (15%, 1.5g saturated fat (7%), 70.8mg cholesterol (24%), 77.2mg sodium (3%), 25g carbohydrates (8%), 7.4g fiber (29%), 7.7g protein (15%), 9094 IU vitamin A (182%), 84mg vitamin C (141%), 198mg calcium (20%) and 4.5mg iron (25%).

YAM & IRISH BACON FLAN
Makes 1 servings

Chef Derek Healy from the City Club in Los Angeles came up with this combination of *Irish* heritage and California panache makes this breakfast a special treat.

2 tablespoons unsalted butter
1 yam
1 teaspoon vegetable oil
1/4 cup bacon, julienne
2 tablespoons onion, diced
1 teaspoon jalapeño chile, seeded, minced
1/2 teaspoon fresh thyme, minced

Pinch cayenne red pepper
Freshly ground pepper to taste
Salt to taste
1/4 cup cheddar cheese, grated
2 eggs
1/2 cup milk
Oatmeal Blinis (page 216)

1 tablespoon sour cream

1. Generously butter a 3 1/2-inch round by 2-inch deep soufflé dish or ramekin; set aside.
2. Peel the yam, and slice into very thin slices.
3. Place slices into boiling water, boil until tender, but do not over cook.
4. Immediately drain and wash under cold running water.
5. Pat dry; set aside.
6. Heat oil in saucepan over medium heat.
7. Add bacon, onion and jalapeño.
8. Sauté for about 3 minutes or until vegetables are soft.
9. Stir in seasonings.
10. Scrape from pan into a bowl and allow to cool.
11. When cool, stir in cheese.
12. Beat egg and milk, season to taste; set aside.
13. Preheat oven to 350°F.
14. Place a layer of yam circles, overlapping each circle to make a rosette on the bottom of the prepared dish.
15. Place some cooked bacon mixture on top and press down.
16. Repeat with another layer of yams and bacon mixture on top, pressing down slightly as you go.
17. Pour egg mixture over the yam layers, making sure that it reaches to the bottom and covers the top.
18. Place a circle of buttered aluminum foil over the top.
19. Place dish in another baking dish filled with hot water, water should cover about 1/2 of the dish.
20. Place in oven and bake for about 35 minutes.
21. Cool on a wire rack for 1 to 2 minutes.
22. Run a sharp knife around the edges and invert flan onto serving plate.
23. Tap to loosen.
24. Place 3 blinis around the edge with a dollop of sour cream.

NUTRITION FACTS per serving without blinis: 1134 calories, 749 calories from fat, 83.2g total fat (128%), 38.5g saturated fat (193%), 589.3mg cholesterol (196%), 1404.6mg sodium (59%), 51.5g carbohydrates (17%), 6.5g fiber (26%), 44.9g protein (90%), 2099 IU vitamin A (42%), 55mg vitamin C (92%), 473mg calcium (47%) and 4.1mg iron (23%).

CHAPTER XVII

WAFFLES

Waffles have been made for centuries in Europe. The wealthy had elaborately patterned waffle irons, many with special engravings. The word waffle pertains to an old German word meaning to "weave like a honeycomb." Waffle irons come in various molds: square, round and heart shape being the most common. All nutrition facts refer to 8-inch square waffle irons.

Angel Waffles (*USA*) 242

Basic Waffles with 7 variations (*USA*) 242

Beer Waffles (*USA*) 243

Dutch Buttermilk Waffles (*Netherlands)* 243

Swedish Crisp Waffles (*Sweden*) 244

Whole Wheat Pecan Waffles (*California*) 244

Wizard's Waffles (*USA*) 244

WAFFLE TOPPINGS

Apricot Honey Syrup 245

Sticky Pecan Sauce 245

Simple Sugar Syrup 245

ANGEL WAFFLES
Makes 3 waffles

These waffles have a fresh bread taste, rise nicely, and when first served are crisp. Yes, they are a bit high in fat, just go on a nonfat diet the rest of the day. Enjoy!

1 package yeast
2 tablespoons sugar
1/4 cup warm water (105ºF to 115ºF)
2 cups flour

2 teaspoons baking powder
1/2 teaspoon salt
1 1/2 cups milk
2/3 cup butter, melted

1. In a small bowl soften yeast, sugar in the water for 5 minutes.
2. Mix flour, baking powder and salt in a large bowl.
3. Mix the milk into the yeast mixture.
4. Alternately mix milk mixture and butter to the dry ingredients.

5. Stir until free of lumps.
6. Batter will be thin.
7. Cover, let stand at room temperature for at least 1 hour.
8. Without stirring, spoon the sponge-like batter in the hot iron and bake until crisp.

NUTRITION FACTS per 1/4 square: 192 calories, 101 calories from fat, 11.3g total fat (17%), 6.9g saturated fat (35%), 31.4mg cholesterol (10%), 267.6mg sodium (11%), 19.6g carbohydrates (7%), zero fiber, 3.3g protein (7%), 419 IU vitamin A (8%), zero vitamin C, 99mg calcium (10%), and 1.1mg iron (6%).

BASIC WAFFLES
Makes 3 waffles

Once you master this recipe, you can experiment with variations.

2 cups flour
1 tablespoon baking powder

1/2 teaspoon salt
1 tablespoon sugar
1/2 cup vegetable oil

2 eggs
2 cups milk

1. Combine dry ingredients in a large bowl.
2. Beat together remaining ingredients in a small bowl.
3. Stir into dry ingredients only until flour mixture is moistened, but not lumpy.

4. DO NOT BEAT.
5. Bake per waffle iron instructions. Generally when the waffle iron stops steaming, the waffle is ready to be removed.

NUTRITION FACTS per 1/4 square: 198 calories, 103 calories from fat, 11.5g total fat (18%), 2.2g saturated fat (11%), 41mg cholesterol (14%), 210.5mg sodium (9%), 19.2g carbohydrates (6%), zero fiber, 4.5g protein (9%), 104 IU vitamin A (2%), zero vitamin C, 141mg calcium (14%), and 1.2mg iron (7%).

VARIATIONS

BUTTERMILK WAFFLES: Substitute buttermilk for milk, add 1/2 teaspoon of baking soda and reduce baking powder to 2 teaspoons. Powdered buttermilk culture can also be used. Add 1/2 cup of buttermilk powder to the dry ingredients and replace the liquid measure with 2 cups water.

MEAT FILLED WAFFLES: Fold in 2 tablespoons of cooked meat: ham, bacon or sausage into the batter.

NUTTY WAFFLES: Fold in 1/4 cup of chopped nuts: almonds, pecans or walnuts into the batter.

FRUITED WAFFLES: Fold in 1/2 cup apples (chopped), blueberries, dates or raisins into the batter.

FLUFFY WAFFLES: To make fluffy crisp waffles, separate the eggs, beat the egg whites until stiff with 1 tablespoon of sugar and fold into the batter last, leaving a few fluffs.

CHEESE WAFFLES: Fold in 1/2 cup grated Cheddar or Parmesan cheese into the batter.

SPICY WAFFLES: Add 1 to 2 teaspoons of spice: allspice, cardamon, cinnamon, cloves, ginger or nutmeg into the dry ingredients. Spices can be mixed for a gingerbread taste (1 teaspoon cinnamon, 1 teaspoon ginger, 1/4 teaspoon cloves, and 1 teaspoon nutmeg). Some spices can also be added to fruited waffles, such as cinnamon with apples.

What other combinations can you think of? Waffles are also great at dinner time, topped with creamed tuna or chicken. Kids also like to spread peanut butter and jam on them for an afternoon treat. Left over waffles can also be heated in the toaster.

BEER WAFFLES
Makes 3 waffles

A great waffle for those who do not have time to prepare the batter in the morning. Prepare the batter the night before and refrigerate. The beer acts as the leavening and leaves no trace of the beer taste. These are very light and crisp waffles.

2 ½ cups flour
¼ teaspoon salt

1/3 cup vegetable oil
2 ¼ cups beer
2 eggs
1 teaspoon lemon juice

1 tablespoon orange rind

1. Mix all ingredients in a large bowl.
2. Beat until smooth.
3. Cover and put batter in the refrigerator overnight.

4. Spread batter on iron thin to insure a crisp waffle.
5. These waffles bake quickly and brown fast.

NUTRITION FACTS per ¼ square: 179 calories, 69 calories from fat, 7.2g total fat (11%), 1.8g saturated fat (5%), 35.4mg cholesterol (12%), 57.7mg sodium (2%), 21.8g carbohydrates (7%), .1g fiber (1%), 3.9g protein (8%), 55 IU vitamin A (1%), 1mg vitamin C (2%), 11mg calcium (1%), and 1.3mg iron (7%).

DUTCH BUTTERMILK WAFFLES
Makes 4 servings

Beatrice J. Olsen of Pella, Iowa says, "Dutch settlers introduced waffles to this country. A new bride often received a waffle iron engraved with her initials and the date of her marriage.

1 ¾ cups flour
2 teaspoons baking powder

1 teaspoon baking soda
½ teaspoon salt
2 eggs

1 ½ cups buttermilk
1/3 cup vegetable oil

1. In a large bowl, mix first 4 ingredients
2. Add buttermilk, oil and eggs.
3. Beat until well blended.

4. When the waffle iron is hot, pour batter into center until it spreads to about 1-inch from edges.

Serve at once with jam or syrup.

NUTRITION FACTS per serving: 425 calories, 189 calories from fat, 20.9g total fat (32%), 3.3g saturated fat (17%), 109.5mg cholesterol (36%), 891.6mg sodium (37%), 47g carbohydrates (16%), zero fiber, 11.8g protein (24%), 189 IU vitamin A (4%), 1mg vitamin C (2%), 297mg calcium (30%) and 3.2mg iron (18%).

SWEDISH CRISP WAFFLES
Makes 3 servings

Note the ingredients in this waffle from *Sweden*. Or should I say, *"the lack of ingredients."* No eggs, no sugar, basically just flour and whipped cream. The *Swedes* top the waffle with jam or fruit and whipped cream.

2 tablespoons butter, melted
2/3 cup water

1 cup flour
1 cup whipping cream, whipped

1. Mix water and flour to a smooth batter.
2. Add the melted butter and the whipped cream.

3. Pour the batter, a little at a time into the waffle iron and bake.

NUTRITION FACTS per serving: 547 calories, 336 calories from fat, 37.5g total fat (58%), 23.1g saturated fat (115%), 129.2mg cholesterol (43%), 108.1mg sodium (5%), 45.5g carbohydrates (15%), zero fiber, 7.6g protein (15%), 1452 IU vitamin A (29%), zero vitamin C, 62mg calcium (6%) and 2.7mg iron (15%).

WHOLE WHEAT PECAN WAFFLES
Makes 8 servings

Lisa Smith, the innkeeper at *Country Garden Inn*, Napa, California, has produced the ultimate pecan waffle for her guests. Chopping the pecans, releases the oils for maximum pecan flavor.

5 cups whole wheat flour
2 tablespoons baking powder
1 1/2 teaspoons baking soda
1 teaspoon salt
1/4 cup honey

8 eggs separated
2 cups plain yogurt
2 3/4 cup milk
3/4 cup unsalted butter, melted
2 cups pecans, chopped

1. In a bowl, mix together flour, baking powder, soda, salt, and nuts; set aside.
2. In another bowl mix honey, egg yolks, yogurt, milk and butter.

3. Combine dry and wet ingredients until well mixed.
4. Fold in beaten egg whites well.
5. Spoon into preheated Belgian waffle iron.
6. Cook until golden brown.

Serve with Apricot Honey Syrup or with Sticky Pecan Sauce.

NUTRITION FACTS per serving: 780 calories, 399 calories from fat, 46.4g total fat (71%), 16.8g saturated fat (84%), 277.1mg cholesterol (92%), 911.9mg sodium (38%), 76.1g carbohydrates (25%), 11.2g fiber (45%), 23.6g protein (47%), 1170 IU vitamin A (23%), 2mg vitamin C (3%), 488mg calcium (49%), and 4.7mg iron (26%).

WIZARD'S WAFFLES
Makes 3 waffles

A wonderful waffle, crisp outside, tender inside, that holds up well with toppings. Also makes a great dinner waffle topped with creamed tuna or chicken.

3 eggs
1 1/2 cups flour
1/2 teaspoon salt
1/2 teaspoon baking soda

1 teaspoon baking powder
1 cup buttermilk
1/2 cup sour cream
3/4 cup butter, melted

1. In a small bowl beat eggs until lightly and fluffy.
2. In large bowl combine flour, salt, soda and baking powder.

3. In a small bowl mix buttermilk, sour cream and butter.
4. Alternately add eggs and buttermilk mixtures to flour; mixing thoroughly, but do not beat.
5. Bake until steam stops.

WAFFLE TOPPINGS

Pure maple syrup is probably the number one choice for topping your waffle. However, there are other syrups you will want to try, such as birch syrup. Birch syrup is made similar to maple syrup, only the sap comes from a birch tree. Write to Kahiltna Birchworks, P.O. Box 2267, Palmer, AK 99645 or phone (800) 380-7457 or log on: www.alaskabirchsyrup.com

The following toppings are from the *Country Garden Inn* kitchen of *Lisa Smith*, Napa, California.

APRICOT HONEY SYRUP

This looks like baby food, but it tastes wonderful!

1/2 pound dried apricots	2 cups honey	3 cups simple sugar syrup

1. Soak the apricots in water overnight.
2. Drain off water.
3. Puree apricots.

4. Add honey and syrup.
5. Store in the refrigerator.
Makes 1 1/2 quarts

NUTRITION FACTS per 1/4 cup: 255 calories, zero fats, cholesterol and sodium, and less than 2% vitamins and minerals.

STICKY PECAN SAUCE

This sauce is like a liquid praline. Close your eyes and you will think you are in New Orleans with the first taste.

3 ounces dark corn syrup
3/4 cup pecans, chopped

1 cup unsalted butter, melted
1/2 pound brown sugar

1 cup simple sugar syrup

1. Combine butter, sugar, and syrups; mix well.
2. Mix in pecans.

3. Put in jars and refrigerate.
Makes 1 quart.

NUTRITION FACTS per 1/4 cup serving: 258 calories, 135 calories from fat, 15.6g total fat (24%), 7.8g saturated fat (39%), 32.9mg cholesterol (11%) and 13.8mg sodium (1%).

SIMPLE SUGAR SYRUP

The secret to the above 2 recipes is this simple sugar syrup.

4 cups sugar	2 cups water

1. In a saucepan, bring sugar and water to a boil.
2. Boil gently without stirring for 10 minutes.

3. Cool.

An excellent essence syrup can be made by adding 2 teaspoons of almond, lemon, maple, orange or other extracts to the slightly cooled syrup.

NUTRITION FACTS per 1/4 cup: 193 calories, zero fats, cholesterol and sodium and 50g carbohydrates (17%0, zero fiber, protein, vitamins and minerals.

KID'S BREAKFAST CLUB

"What's for breakfast?" That is a question often asked by kids as they enter the kitchen on their way to school or out to play. The answer might be a bowl of cereal, a plate of bacon and eggs, or maybe a stack of hot cakes.

Today's nutritional marketplace with a barrage of messages is confusing. Decisions must be made to determine what are the best food choices and which are appealing to kids. Nutrition experts agree that fruit, vegetables, cereals, dairy products and grains lead the list of "good for you" foods. Sometimes the problem is making these healthy foods attractive to young appetites. The difference between rejection and satisfaction in children's tastes could be minute. Maybe the rejection is a bitter taste and with an added teaspoon of sugar could correct the problem.

Five hundred kids were asked, *"What do you enjoy for breakfast?"* The answers included cake, soft drinks, popcorn, cold pizza and leftovers. Does not sound like the "good for you" foods, does it? Nevertheless, according to the *American Dietetic Association,* "It is better to eat something, rather than nothing all."

Breakfast provides the energy that kids need to start the day. Dinner was about 12 hours ago and breakfast is a time to break that fast with as nutritious of a breakfast as possible.

The *Iowa Breakfast Studies* have shown that breakfast helps improve mental and physical performance. Kids perform better in school and have more energy to play.

Along with the ideas and recipes in this chapter, you will also want to refer to other chapters as well. Beverages contain a lot of fruits that kids like. Kids like to eat finger foods, so check out the Breakfast Bars, Doughnuts and Muffins chapters. There are many other "kids" ideas throughout this cookbook.

The dual-income family has taken a toll on what kids eat for breakfast. *The National Pork Producers Council* says convenience breakfast foods don't have to be frozen or a fast-food offering. There are many quick and healthful foods that can be made at a moment notice. Some can be made all or part the night before and reheated in the morning. Always start the breakfast with a glass of juice and enjoy any of the following with a glass of milk, a piece of fruit, or maybe a slice of toast:

BREAKFAST PIZZA
Makes 1 serving

Let's start out with the kid's favorite choice, . . .pizza. . . . but with a little different choice of toppings, but just as enjoyable.

1 English muffin, toasted	2 tablespoons raisins
1/2 cup ricotta cheese	2 tablespoons walnuts, chopped
2 teaspoons honey	

1. Spread each half with half of the ricotta cheese.

2. Top with raisins and walnuts
3. Drizzle each with honey.

NUTRITION FACTS per serving: 540 calories, 227 calories from fat, 25.9g total fat (40%), 11g saturated fat (55%), 62.2mg cholesterol (215), 370.8mg sodium (15%), 57.8g carbohydrates (19%), 1.5g fiber (60%), 22.7g protein (45%), 650 IU vitamin A (13%), 1mg vitamin C (2%), 373mg calcium and 2.8mg iron (16%). With a glass of orange juice the child will receive twice the daily requirement of vitamin C. Adding a glass of milk will increase the calcium requirement to 67%.

HAM 'N TORTILLA ROLLUPS
Makes 1 serving

A tortilla replaces bread. Some call this rollup a "wrap" and others might even call it a "breakfast burrito." But whatever you can it, you will like it.

Low-fat cream cheese	Ham, thinly sliced
Flour tortilla	Sprouts or lettuce, chopped

1. Thinly spread low-fat cream cheese on a flour tortilla.
2. Place a piece or two of thin sliced ham on the cream cheese.
3. Top with sprouts or chopped lettuce.
4. Roll up the tortilla.

Can be made the night before, wrap tightly in aluminum foil and refrigerated.

NUTRITION FACTS per serving: 405 calories, 181 calories from fat, 19.8g total fat (30%), 6.7g saturated fat (34%), 87.7mg cholesterol (29%), 2053.8mg sodium (86%), 25.6g carbohydrates (9%), 1.3g fiber (5%), 29.5g protein (59%), 105 IU vitamin A (2%), 41mg vitamin C (68%), 71mg calcium (7%) and 2.9mg iron (16%).

PEANUT BUTTER BREAKFAST SANDWICH
Makes 1 serving

English muffin
Peanut butter

Canadian bacon
Apple, sliced or apple butter

1. Toast English muffin.
2. Spread thinly with peanut butter.

3. Top each half with a slice of Canadian bacon and thinly-sliced apple or a little apple butter.

NUTRITION FACTS per serving: 453 calories, 187 calories from fat, 21.4g total fat (33%), 4.5g saturated fat (23%), 28.4mg cholesterol (9%), 1217.5mg sodium (51%), 44.4g carbohydrates (15%), 3.8g fiber (15%), 24.2g protein (48%), 37 IU vitamin A (1%), 16mg vitamin C (27%), 120mg calcium (12%) and 2.5mg iron (14%).

CINNAMON-SAUSAGE STARTER
Makes 1 serving

2 sausage patties, precooked
Fruit preserves, your choice

Cinnamon-raisin bread

1. Heat sausage patties in the microwave.
2. Place on toasted cinnamon-raisin bread slices.

3. Top each with a tablespoon of fruit preserves.

NUTRITION FACTS per serving: 473 calories, 220 calories from fat, 24.9g total fat (38%), 8.7g saturated fat (43%), 38.1mg cholesterol (13%), 592.3mg sodium (25%), 53.5g carbohydrates (18%), 2.7g fiber (11%), 10.9g protein (22%), zero vitamin A, 5mg vitamin C (8%), 52mg calcium (5%) and 2.2mg iron (12%).

SAVORY BREAKFAST CUSTARD
Makes 1 serving

1 egg
2 tablespoons milk
Dash dry mustard

Salt & pepper to taste
2 tablespoons cheese, grated
1 ounce ham, shredded

1. Beat together the egg and milk with mustard, salt and pepper.
2. Stir in cheese and ham.

3. Spray one-cup custard cups with non-stick oil.
4. Pour egg mixture in custard cup and bake in a 375°F oven for 20 to 25 minutes, until firm.

COTTAGE CHEESE COOLER
Makes 1 serving

This cooler can replace the fruit juice, if desired. The fruit can be prepared the night before and assembled in the morning. Note that the cooler provides 3 times the daily requirement of vitamin C.

1/2 peach or nectarine, chopped
2 strawberries, sliced
1/2 banana, sliced

2 tablespoons orange juice
1/2 cup cottage cheese
1 tablespoon sunflower seeds or wheat germ.

1. Mix fruits and juice.
2. Chill for about 30 minutes or refrigerate overnight.

3. Place fruit mixture in a cereal bowl.
4. Top with cottage cheese and sunflower seeds.

NUTRITION FACTS per serving: 327 calories, 69 calories from fat, 8.1g total fat (12%), 2g saturated fat (10%), 9.5mg cholesterol (3%), 462.9mg sodium (19%), 48.1g carbohydrates (16%), 10.1g fiber (40%), 20.5g protein (41%), 505 IU vitamin A (10%), 193mg vitamin C (321%), 139mg calcium (14%) and 2.2mg iron (12%).

SOUTHWEST STARTER
Makes 1 serving

1 egg, beaten
1/4 cup spicy chorizo sausage

1 flour tortilla
2 tablespoons salsa

1. Scramble egg with chorizo

2. Roll up in a warm flour tortilla.

3. Serve with salsa.

NUTRITION FACTS per serving: 460 calories, 278 calories from fat, 30.4g total fat (47%), 10.3g saturated fat (52%), 262.7mg cholesterol (88%), 954.6mg sodium (40%), 21.8g carbohydrates (7%), 1.3g fiber (5%), 23.1g protein (46), 524 IU vitamin A (10%), 1mg vitamin C (2%), 75mg calcium (7%) and 2.8mg iron (16%).

KANGAROO BREAKFAST SANDWICH
Makes 1 serving

1/4 cup lean meat (ham, roast beef, pork, or turkey, cut into julienne strips
1 tablespoon nonfat salad dressing

1/4 cup lettuce, shredded
1 pita pocket bread

1. Toss meat with salad dressing and lettuce.

2. Cut pita bread in half.

3. Stuff with the meat mixture.

NUTRITION FACTS per serving: 247 calories, 41 calories from fat, 4.5g total fat (7% DV), 1.3g saturated fat (7%), 20mg cholesterol (7%), 933.8mg sodium (39%), 38g carbohydrates (13%), 1.2g fiber (5%), 11.8g protein (24%), 269 IU vitamin A (5%), 12mg vitamin C (20%), 64mg calcium (6%) and 2.1mg iron (12%).

EMBELLISHED EGG SALAD
Makes 1 serving

1 egg, hard boiled
Salt & pepper to taste
1/4 teaspoon mustard
1 teaspoon bacon bits

1 teaspoon nonfat mayonnaise
1 slice whole wheat toast

1. Mash egg with a fork.

2. Add salt, pepper, mustard, bacon bits and mayonnaise.
3. Spread on toast

DUNKIN' BAGELS
Makes 4 servings

4 bagels, toasted and cut into bite size pieces
1 cup plain low-fat yogurt
1 tablespoon mustard

1/4 teaspoon curry powder
Dash red pepper sauce
2 ounces lean ham, diced

1. Except for the cutup bagel, in a small bowl stir all ingredients together.

2. Dunk bagel pieces into the yogurt mixture

Refrigerate leftovers.

NUTRITION FACTS per serving: 260 calories, 34 calories from fat, 3.7g total fat (6% DV), 1.2g saturated fat (6%), 11.5mg cholesterol (4%), 652.7mg sodium (27%), 42.7g carbohydrates (14%), 1.6g fiber (7%), 13.1g protein (26%), 39 IU vitamin A (1%), 4mg vitamin C (7%), 161mg calcium (16%) and 2.8mg iron (16%).

HAM & WAFFLE WALKAWAYS

2 frozen waffle squares

Orange marmalade

Lean ham

1. Toast frozen waffle squares.
2, Spread with orange marmalade

3. Top with lean ham.
4. Place waffles together and eat out of hand.

HAM 'N APPLEWICH
Makes 1 serving

1 English muffin
1 ounce American cheese, slice

1 ounce ham
1 apple slice

1. Toast English muffin.
2. Place slice of cheese on one half.
3. Place a slice of ham and sliced apple on the other half.

4. Place together and microwave for 30 seconds on high power.

NUTRITION FACTS per serving: 312 calories, 118 calories from fat, 13g total fat (20%), 6.7g saturated fat (34%), 42.9mg cholesterol (14%), 822.1mg sodium (34%), 32.8g carbohydrates (11%), .9g fiber (4%), 15.7g protein (31%), 361 IU vitamin A (7%), 10mg vitamin C (16%), 278mg calcium (28%) and 1.9mg iron (10%).

CINNAMON BUNNIES

Susan Bates of Corinth, Mississippi likes to make these little fun-to-eat bunnies.

1 can refrigerator biscuits
4 tablespoons margarine,
　　melted

1/4 cup sugar
1 teaspoon cinnamon
Raisins

Pecans, chopped
Red hot candies

1. Preheat the oven to 350°F.
2. Mix the cinnamon and sugar together in a small bowl; set aside.
3. Cut half of the biscuits into halves.
4. Each half will be a bunny ear.
5. Attach two bunny ears to each remaining whole biscuit by pinching the edges together with fingers.
6. Coat each bunny with melted margarine and

carefully dip the bunny into the cinnamon sugar mixture.
7. Place the bunnies 2-inches apart on a greased cookie sheet.
8. Decorate the bunny faces using the raisins for eyes, a red hot for the nose and bits of chopped pecan for the mouth.
9. Put in the oven and bake for 8 to 10 minutes or until golden brown.

When making the night before, bake the custard, cover and refrigerate. Serve chilled or warm. To serve warm, reheat in the microwave on 70% power for 1 1/2 to 2 minutes. Recipe makes 1 serving. Can be double, tripled, etc.

NUTRITION FACTS per serving: 202 calories, 125 calories from fat, 13.7g total fat (23%), 6.1g saturated fat (31%), 247.7mg cholesterol (83%), 539.3mg sodium (22%), 3.1g carbohydrates (1%), zero fiber, 15.8g protein (32%), 506 IU vitamin A (10%), 8mg vitamin C (14%), 165mg calcium (17%) and 1.1mg iron (6%).

PRETZELS
Makes 16 pretzels

Regie L. Powell of Powell, Ohio says these homemade pretzels are fun to make. They are best when served warm with jam or jelly and also make a great after school snack!

| 1 egg yolk | 1 package dry yeast | 2 teaspoons salt |
| Water | 1 tablespoon sugar | 4 cups flour |

1. Line a cookie sheet with foil.
2. Beat the egg yolk with 1 teaspoon of water; set aside.
3. In a large bowl, dissolve the yeast in 1 1/2 cups of warm water.
4. Add the sugar and salt; mix well.
5. Add flour, a little at a time, to make a firm dough.
6. Turn dough out onto a lightly floured board and knead for about five minutes.
7. Cut dough into 16 pieces and roll each piece with your hands to form a long string.

8. Shape these pieces into pretzel shapes or alphabet letters.
9. Place the pretzels on the foil.
10. When all the dough is on the cookie sheet, brush each piece generously with the yolk mixture.
11. Sprinkle with salt, poppy seeds, caraway seeds, or colored sugar, if desired.
12. Bake at 425°F for 15 to 20 minutes or until golden brown.

NUTRITION FACTS per pretzel: 123 calories, 6 calories from fat, .7g total fat (1% DV), .2g saturated fat (1%), 13.3mg cholesterol (4%), 267.9mg sodium (11%), 24.9g carbohydrates (8%), .2g fiber (1%), 3.7g protein (7%), zero vitamin A and C, 7mg calcium (1%) and 1.6mg iron (9%).

RAINBOW-IN-THE-MORNIN' CAKES

Glenda Smithers of Kingsville, Missouri has a great idea for holidays

| Prepared pancake or waffle mix | Kool-Aid® | Syrups and toppings, you choice |

1. Prepare pancake or waffle batter according to recipe instructions.
2. Divide batter into several bowls.
3. Add a different flavor/color of Kool-Aid powder to each bowl.

4. Cook pancakes or waffles following recipe directions.
5. Serve with a variety of syrups and other toppings (jelly, fresh fruit, etc.).

For the holidays use: orange for Halloween, red for Valentine's Day and the 4th of July, green and red for Christmas morning, and pastels for Easter. Match with holiday napkins and dishes makes it fun!

CHEESY EGGS
Makes 2 servings

Connie Vatthauers of Grand Fork, North Dakota says when grandson, *Travis Turgeon* of Green Bay, Wisconsin, comes to visit, this is his favorite breakfast.

| 2 eggs | 1 teaspoon water |
| 2 slices American cheese, torn into pieces | |

1. Stir briefly with a fork in a microwave-safe bowl the eggs and water.
2. Microwave for 1 minute at medium.

3. Stir; add cheese and microwave for 30 seconds; stir.
4. Microwave a few seconds longer for firmer eggs.

CHICKENS IN THE PEN
Makes 2 servings

Karen Barnett-Woods of Naperville, Illinois makes this fun breakfast for her family.

2 slices white or wheat bread
1 teaspoon butter
2 eggs

Salt & pepper (optional)
1/4 cup mild cheddar cheese, shredded
1 tablespoon water

1. Place rim of a juice glass in the center of the slice of bread.
2. Press down on glass to make a hole in the bread (this is the chicken pen).
3. Remove circle of bread and put aside.
4. Repeat process with second slice of bread.
5. In a frying pan melt butter over medium heat.
6. Place chicken pens in the pan.
7. Turn the pens over so both sides will be buttered.

8. With a spatula press down on the bread to flatten.
9. Carefully crack open each egg and pour into the hole.
10. Sprinkle with salt and pepper, if desired. Let egg partially set, then flip over.
11. Sprinkle shredded cheese on egg.
12. Add water, cover pan and cook over medium heat until the eggs are set.
13. Toast the rounds of bread

NUTRITION FACTS per serving: 215 calories, 114 calories from fat, 12.5g total fat (19% DV), 5.9g saturated fat (30%), 232.7mg cholesterol (78%), 304.8mg sodium (13%), 13.2g carbohydrates (4%), .6g fiber (2%), 11.9g protein

FROZEN GRAPE POPS
Makes 6 pops

All kids like to eat something on a stick, and if it is frozen so much the better. Recipe courtesy of *California Table Grape Commission*

1 pound seedless grapes

1 orange, peeled, cut into chunks

6 Popsicle sticks

1. Puree all ingredients in a food processor.
2. Pour into Popsicle molds and insert sticks.

3. Freeze until firm.

NUTRITION FACTS per pop: 58 calories, 3 calories from fat, .3g total fat (1% DV), .2g saturated fat (1%), zero cholesterol and sodium, 15.6g carbohydrates (5%), 1.4g fiber (6%), .7g protein (1%), 120 IU vitamin A (2%), 15mg vitamin C (24%), 19mg calcium (2%) and .2mg iron (1%).

FRUIT PUNCH POPS
Makes 12 pops

3 cups fruit punch juice

14 ounce can sweetened condensed milk

1/4 cup lemon juice

COOKBOOKS & MAGAZINES

The following cookbooks and magazines all contain breakfast recipes. Call or write for prices and ordering information.

AUNT BEE'S MAYBERRY COOKBOOK
By Ken Beck & Jim Clark
Rutledge Hill Press
211 7th Avenue North
Nashville, TN 37219-1823
244 pages of recipes from viewers of
"The Andy Griffith Show" with many
photographs and comments from the TV show.

THE BERTOLLI OLIVE OIL HANDBOOK
Bertolli Nutrition Center
P.O. Box 2373
Secaucus, NJ 07026-2373
25 Italian recipes with olive oil nutrition.

THE BEST OF NEW MEXICO KITCHENS and
**MORE OF THE BEST OF
NEW MEXICO KITCHENS**
New Mexico Magazine
495 Old Santa Fe Trail
Santa Fe, NM 87503
Recipes from New Mexico's restaurants

THE CENTRAL MARKET COOKBOOK
By Phyllis Pellman Good & Louise Stoltzfus
Good Books
P.O. Box 419
Intercourse, PA 17534
224 pages of recipes from Lancaster's marketplace.

COOKING AT JAMESTOWN SETTLEMENT
Jamestown-Settlement Museum Shop
P.O. Drawer JF
Williamsburg, VA 23187-3631
24 pages of 17th century cooking

COOKING PLEASURES
12301 Whitewater Drive
Minnetonka, MN 55343
Magazine published by the Cooking Club of America

COOK'S ILLUSTRATED
P.O. Box 7446
Red Oak, IA 51591-o446
6 times a year magazine

THE COURT OF TWO SISTERS COOKBOOK
613 Rue Royale
New Orleans, LA 70130
Owner Joseph Fein Caterers presents some of the
restaurant's famous reipes.

THE GOOD EARTH COOK BOOK
By Clyde LeBlanc
Terrebonne Historical & Cultural Society
P.O. Box 2095
Houma, LA 70361
A down home look at Louisiana foods and recipes.

GRATH WOODSIDE MANSION COOKBOOK
Garth Woodside Mansion
11069 New London Gravel Road
Hannibal, MO 63401
56 pages of recipes from this famous B & B inn.

THE KING ARTHUR FLOUR COOKBOOK
P.O. Box 876
Norwich, VT 05055-0876
(800) 827-6836
E-mail: customercare@kingarthurflour.com
www.kingarthurflour.com
608 page cookbook celebrates 200th anniversary

**FREDERICKSBURG HOME
KITCHEN COOK BOOK**
P.O. Box 1152
Fredericksburg, TX 78264
230 pages, with German, American, and TexMex

LINCOLN HERITAGE TRAIL COOKBOOK
Lincoln Boyhood National Memorial
P.O. Box 1816
Lincoln City, IN 47552
32 pages of some of the foods Abe Lincoln liked.

THE MISSISSIPPI COLLEGE COOKBOOK
Mississippi College
P.O. Box 4041
Clinton, MS 39058

THE OLD WASHINGTON RECIPES
Wakefield National Memorial Association
George Washington Birthplace National Monument
1732 Popes Road
Washington's Birthplace, VA 22443
30 pages with 71 traditional recipes

RECIPES FROM A KITCHEN GARDEN and
MORE RECIPES FROM A KITCHEN GARDEN
By Renee Shepherd & Fran Raboff
Renee's Garden
7389 W. Zayante Road
Felton, CA 95018
(888) 880-7228
E-mail: renees@pacbell.net
www.reesgarden.com
Both books content more than 600 recipes

RECIPES FROM GRANDMA SMUCKER'S KITCHEN
Bird-in-Hand Bakery
2715 Old Philadelphia Pike
Bird-in-Hand, PA 17505
(800) 524-3429
www.bird-in-hnd.com/bakery/mailorder.html
68 pages of Pennsylvania Dutch Country recipes.

THE SHARPSTEEN MUSEUM COOKBOOK
1311 Washington Street
Calistoga, CA 94515
Recipes from California's wine growing Napa Valley.

THE STORY OF STEEN'S SYRUP & RECIPES
The C.S. Steen Syrup Mill, Inc.
P.O. Box 339,
Abbeville, LA 70510
(800) 725-1654
E-mail: steens@stensyrup.com
www.steensyrup.com

A TASTE OF THE WORLD
Edited by Mina Baker-Roelofs & Dr. Maxine Huffman
Central College
Pella, IA 50219
330 pages of Dutch & other international recipes.

WINE WAY INN COOKBOOK
By Cecile Stephens
Wine Way Inn
1019 Foothill Blvd.
Calistoga, CA 94515
68 pages of recipes served to guests.

MAIL ORDER SOURCES

Are you looking for an ingredient not found in your local supermarket? Maybe one of the following can help you. Many of these firms sell in case lots only, but sometimes can direct you to a single mail order source.

THE BAKER'S CATALOGUE
P.O. Box 876
Norwich, VT 05055-0876
(800) 827-6836
www.kingarthurflour.com
King Arthur flours & grains, cookbooks.

BALDUCCI'S
42-25 12th Street
Long Island City, NY 11101
(800) 225-3822
Italian bakery & Italian prepared foods.

BIRD-IN-HAND BAKERY
P.O. Box 402
Bird-in-Hand, PA 17505
(800) 524-3429
www.bird-in-hand.com/bakery/mail order.html
Pennsylvania Dutch Country prepared foods

CELTIC FOODS
P>O> Box 119
Tuckahoe, NY 10707-9998
www.celticbrands.com
Irish bacon, sausages & breakfast puddings.

IRISH TEA SALES CORP.
92-16 95th Ave.
Ozone Park, NY 11416
(718) 845-4402
Wholesalers of Irish jams, teas, oatmeal & honey.

KAM MAN FOOD PRODUCTS, INC.
200 Canal Street
New York, NY 10013
(212) 571-0330
www.chinatownweb.com/kamman
A large variety of orient food products

NEWSOM'S OLD MILL STORE
208 E. Main Street
Princeton, KY 42445
(270) 365-2482
e-mail: newsomsham@ziggycom.net
www.store.yahoo.com/newsomscountyham
Smoked ham, bacon, relishes & preserves

OZARK MOUNTAIN FAMILY
P.O. Box 37
Farmington, AR 72730
(800) 643-3437
E-mail: frank@ozarkfamily.com
www.ozrkfamily.com
Smoked hams, bacon, turkey & chicken

RENEE'S GARDEN
7389 West Zayante Road
Felton, CA 95018
(888) 880-7228
E-mail: renees@pacbell.net
www.reneesgarden.com
Herb, vegetable & flower seeds, & cookbooks

THE SUGARMILL FARM
Rt. 16 South, Box 26
Barton, VT 05822
(800) 688-7978
Maple syrup, maple candy & Vermont teas

SHATILA FOOD PRODUCTS
8505 W. Warren
Dearborn, MI 48126
(313) 934-1520
Middle Eastern pastries

SOLVANG RESTAURANT
P.O. Box 436
Solvang, CA 93464-0436
(805) 688-4645
Æbleskiver pans, mixes & Danish jams

THE C.S. STEEN SYRUP MILL, INC.
P.O. Box 339
Abbeville, LA 70511-0339
(800) 725-1654
E-mail: steens@steensyrup.com
www.steensyrup.com
Cane syrup, molasses & cane vinegar

SULTAN'S DELIGHT
P.O. Box 090302
Brooklyn, NY 11209
(800) 852-5046
E-mail: sultansdelight@aol.com
www.sultansdelight.com
Italian, Turkish & Arab specialties including
coffee, spices, olives, nuts, sweets,
dried fruits & cookbooks.

ACKNOWLEDGEMENTS

Hope Abadie, Chelan, WA
Daisy Aguilar, San Salvador, El Salvador
Margarita Aguilar, Leon, Nicaragua
Odilia Aguilar, Leon, Nicaragua
Alabama Bureau of Tourism
Monica Allen,
        British Virgin Islands Tourist Board
Charlotte Altenbernd, Lawrence, KS
American Dairy Association
Laura Amick, Summersville, WV
Camille Appel, McCormick & Company, Inc.
Aron Strait, Inc. Matzo Bakers
A Taste of the World cookbook, Pella, IA
Trish Audette, Warwick, RI
Jeanette Auger, The Sugarmill Farm, Barton, VT
AzarNut Company
Emily Baldwin, Balducci's, New York, NY
Rhona Baptiste, Antigua & Barbuda
Geri Beal, Summersville, WV
Helen E. Becker, Saint Augustine, FL
Robin Belliston, Hyde Park, UT
Aly Bello, Carnival Cruise Lines
Best of New Mexico Kitchens cookbook
Laverne Boos, Fredericksburg, TX
Ann Bouchoux, The Sugar Association
Susan Brown, Bath Street Inn, Santa Barbara, CA
Danna Bransky, Bensenville, IL
Natalie & BJ Burgraf,
        Countryland B & B Resort, Big Fork, MT
Cabin Restaurant, Burnside, LA
California Apricot Advisory Board
California Dried Plum Board
Rosemary Campiformio,
        Saint Orres Restaurant, Gualala, CA
Linda T. Carman, Martha White Foods
Dorothy I. Carpenter, Clinton, MS
Century Souvenir Company, Saint Augustine, FL
Chef Bernard Casavant,
        Fairmont Chateau Whistler, Whistler, BC
Chambered Nautilus Inn, Seattle, WA

Jamie Changler, ConAgra Poultry Company
Shelia D. Chavez, Livermore, CA
Judith Choate
Anne Christian, Figure 3 Ranch, Claude, TX
Sallie & Welling Clark,
        Holden House, Colorado Springs, CO
Coffee Development Group
Goldie Comeaux, Mulate's Cajun Restaurant,
        Breaux Bridge, LA
Andrea Cook, Nestle Beverage Company
Stephanie Cowell, Summersville, WV
Chef Noel Cullen, Boston University, Boston, MA
Paul & Lois Dansereau, Silas Griffith Inn,
        Darby, VT
Tamara Datson, Coffeyville, KS
Susan & William Day,
        Beechmont B & B Inn, Hanover, PA
Diamond Walnut Growers, Inc.
Emily Drabanski, New Mexico Magazine
Sally Dumont, Silver Rose Inn, Calistoga, CA
Mary Ann Eiseman, Israel Government Tourist Office
Kay Engelhardt, American Egg Board
Arie Farr, Hattiesburg, MS
Irv & Diane Feinber,
        Garth Woodside Mansion, Hannibal, MO
Mrs. O.B. Fiedler, Fredericksburg, TX
Teresa Flora, Sawyer, KS
Elsa Foglio, Mexican Government Tourist Office
Chef Michael Foley, Le Perigord & Printer's Row,
        Chicago, IL
Marion Fourestier,
        French Government Tourist office
Boyd Foster, Arrowhead Mills
Rosella Frederick, Cochiti, NM
Fredericksburg Home Kitchen Cook Book
Chef Joseph Friel, Plaza Hotel, New York, NY

Chef Conrad Gallagher,
        Waldorf Astoria Hotel, New York, NY
Paul Germann, McCann's Irish Oatmeal

Kay Gibson, Watson, MO
Tiarra Goble, Idaho Bean Commission
Mrs. Jacob Gold, Sr., Fredricksburg, TX
Grand Marnier Liqueurs
Vivian Greblo, Holland American Line
Cora Habenicht, Fredricksurg, TX
Betty & Lorne Hamilton,
        Hamilton B & B, Port Hardy, BC
Virginia Hammett, Mount Airy, MD
Lucinda Hampton,
        Pennsylvania Dutch Visitors Bureau
Bodil Hartmann,
        Office of Royal Danish Consulate General
Sharia Hasan, Karachi, Pakistan
Chef Derek Healy, City Club, Los Angeles, CA
Chrisine S. Heimann,
        Fredericksburg Visitors Bureau
Boo Heisey, San Diego, CA
Lisa Hess, Summersville Chamber of Commerce
Barbara Hobson, Arkansas City, KS
Emily Holt, National Fisheries Institute, Inc.
Mary R. Humann, National Honey Board
Hungarian National Tourist Office
Irish Trade Board
Jam & Relish Kitchen, Intercourse, PA
Jennifer Jones, Homer, NY
Cheryl Juchniewicw,
        Waldo's Bisto Restaurant, Punda Gordo, FL
Bev & Paul Johnson,
        Sweet Valley Inn, Kelleys Island, OH
Trish Kasper, San Jose, CA
Kitchen Kettle Village, Intercourse, PA
Millie Vande Kieft, Pella, IA
Mrs. Chas. F. Kiehne, Fredricksurg, TX
Carolyn M. Kilgore, Vicksburg, MS
Susan Riogers Killoran, King Arthur Flour
Tom King, Queen Anne B & B Inn, Denver, CO
Kling House Restarant, Intercourse, PA
Margaret Klyn, Pella, IA
Peggy Kuan, Chanticleet Inn, Ashland, OR
Amy Kull, Ketchum Public Relations
Kay & Cliff LaFrance,
        Bosobel Cottage, Monroe, LA
Victoria Lake, Antigua & Barbuda
Clyde LeBlanc,
        The Good Earth Cookbook, Houma, LA
Andrea Levy, Redmond, WA
Cindy Litzie, Crystal Cruises
Karen Lobb, Hazelnut Marketing Board
Robet Logan, Garnett, KS
Jan Lugenbuhl, Metairie, LA
Deborah Lund, National Turkey Federation
Berit Lunde, Norwegian Information Service
Manischewitz
Hope Irvin Marston, Blck River, NY
Hayley Matson, Kansas Department of Agriculture
Sonia & Brian McMillan,
        Sonia's B & B by the Sea, Victoria, BC
Amelia S. Meaux, Crowley, LA
Alice Merryman, Summersville, WV
Clara Lopez de Mier,
        El Patio Restaurant, Saint Augustine, FL

Christie Miller, Dunbar, NE
Chef Paul Mooney, Seabourn Cruises
Ellen & Paul Morissette,
        Five Gables Inn, East Boothbay, ME
Teri & Jim Murguia,
        The Branson Hotel, Branson, MO
Howard Nager, Del Monte Fresh Produce Company
Mrs. W.A. Nettle, Fredericksburg, TX
Diane Douglas, North American Blueberry Council
Tammy Nussbaum & Brenda Huey,
        The Nut Tree, Berne, IN
Liz Oehser, Buttonwood Inn, Franklin, NC
Betty O'Dell, Pella, IA
Beatrice J. Olsen, Pella, IA
Barbara O'Neill, Cypress, CA
Joanne O'Neill, Limerick Bacon Company, Ltd.
Original Pancake House, Eugene, OR
John & Donna Ortiz,
        Riordan House B & B, Penticton, BC
Willie & June Ortiz, La Tertulia, Santa Fe, NM
Monika Pacher,
        Salon of Culinary Art, New York, NY
Palmer House Restaurant, Berne, IN
Ann Parker, SACO Foods, Inc.
Laura Parker, Los Alamos, NM
Tonya M. Parravano,
        National Live Stock & Meat Board
Lynne Pasquale, The Zimmerman Agency
Teresa & Harry Pastorious,
        Klamath Manor, Klamath Falls, OR
P & J Peach Booth, Fredericksburg, TX
Permanent Mission of Cyprus to the United Nations
Karell Phillips, S. Martinelli & Company
Nancy Pierre, Trinidad & Tobago
        Tourism Development Authority
Rae Pittman, Smithfield Packing Company, Inc.
Josie Vander Pol, Pella, IA
Betty & James Provost,
        Wildlife Gardens, Gibson, LA
Publick House Historic Inn, Sturbridge, MA
Barbara Redd,
        La Sal Mountain Guest Ranch, La Sal, UT
Betty Reed, Houma-Terrebonne Tourist Comission
Donna Chowning Reid, National Pasta Association
Anne L. Rehnstrom,
        National Pork Producers Council
Cheryl A. Reitz, Hershey Foods Corporation

June Fallo-Renfro,
        Court of Two Sisters, New Orleans, LA
Tom & Terry Rimel,
        National Pike Inn, New Market, MD
Mina Baker-Roelofs, Pella, IA
Josephine Rosengren,
        Swedish Travel & Tourism Council
Caren Rowland, Eudora, KS
Marie Ruesch, Salt Lake City, UT
Jackie Russell, Chincoteague Island, VA
Nelly Sada, Royal Caribbean Cruises, Ltd.
Anne Salisbury, Perdue Farms Inc.
Mike Salvadore, Walnut Marketing Board
Carol Salazar, Florence, AZ

Carol Salvati, Summersville, WV
Billie Hilburn Sartin, Clarksdale, MS
Hilma Schagen Schakel, Pella, IA
Amy Scherber
Lauren & Joe Scott, Scott Courtyard, Calistoga, CA
Frank Sharp, Ozark Mountain Family
Mr. & Mrs. Harry Sharp,
    The Duff Green Mansion, Vicksburg, MS
Sharpsteen Museum Cookbook
Renee Shepherd & Fran Raboff,
    Recipes From a Kitchen Garden cookbook
Linda Sherwood, West Jordon, UT
Mohamed Shirazi, Egyptian Tourist Authority
Singapore Tourism Board
Joan Sirota, Sun-Diamond Growers of California
Lisa Smith, Country Garden Inn, Napa, CA
Jim Smucker,
    Bird-in-Hand Inn, Bird-in-Hand, PA
Barb Sprunger, Berne Chamber of Commerce
Steamers Seafood Restaurant,
    Chincoteague Island, VA
Debora Steen, The C.S. Steen Syrup Mill, Inc.
Barbara & Marsha Stensvad,
    Chestnut Charm B & B, Atlantic, IA
Cecile & Moya Stephens,
    Wine Way Inn, Calistoga, CA
goodie & Jack Stewart,
    Ashing Cottage, Spring Lake, NJ

Valarie L.V. Stewart, Newark, DE
Dusty Stoughton, Wilmington, CA
Sun-Maid Growers of California
Chef Chris Tasardoulias, Royal Cruise Line
Thierry Tellier,
    Madeleine French Bakery, Dallas, TX
Ken Torbet, Gingerbread Mansion, Ferndale, CA
Carol G. Traub, South Bend, IN
Katey Trushel, Princess Cruises
Fay U. Valley, Barton, VT
Connie Vatthauer, Grand Forks, ND
Mrs. Alex Wamback, Fredericksburg, TX
Jane Way, Sutter Creek Inn, Sutter Creek, CA
George Wheeler, Rhodes International, Inc.
Elizabeh White, J.M. Smuckers
Bettye & Cliff Whitney,
    Corners Mansion, Vicksburg, MS
John Adams Wickham, Saint Augustine, FL
Amanda Beth Wilson, Greenfield, WI
Lois Wirtz, Nome Visitors Bureau
Gabriele Wolf, Austria National Tour Office
Karen Barnett-Woods, Naperville, IL
Alisa G. Zavala, Plano, TX
Luise & Eric Zinsli, Chalet Luise, Whistler, BC

INTERNATIONAL RECIPES INDEX

Most of the recipes listed originated in the country listed. Some international recipes came from United States ethic communities. While other recipes use ingredients from other countries, but the recipes may not necessary be consumed in that country.

Antigua & Barbuda

Baked Fish with Tomato Sauce 181
Boiled Fish 184
Fried Fish Cutlets with Lemon Sauce 185
Salt Fish Pie 188
Steamed Fish with Cucumber Sauce 189
Stuffed Plantains (fruit)) 158
Sweet Potato Fritters 106
Sweet Potato Pudding 229

Austria

Apple Strudel 82
Apricot Dumplings 109
Bohemian Omelets 134
Café Vienna 18
Chocolate Hazelnut Pudding 226
Cottage Cheese Dumplings 112
Cream Strudel 82
Curd Pancakes 218
Emperor's Omelet (pancakes) 218
Germknodel (dumplings) 114
Palatshinken (pancakes) 218

British Virgin Islands

Coconut Bread 39
Conch Fritters 183
Cornmeal Pap 66
Ducknoor (dumplings) 112
Okra Fungi (cereal) 69
Salt Fish & Rice 188
Salt Fish Cundy 187
Sweet Potato Pudding 229
Tannia Soup 238
West Indian Seasoning 194

Canada

Apricot Harvest Pancakes 206
Chalet Luise Scones 29
Double Salmon Pate 184

Good Morning Scones 32
Gooseberry Jam 35
Lemon Thyme Zucchini Bread 42
Mincemeat Muffins 201
Rhubarb & Strawberry Jam 36
Strawberry Mango Tofu Frappe 158
Tourtiere Meat Pie 166

China

Honeyed Fruit 155

Cyprus

Cyprus Pudding 226
Pourgouri *(cereal)* 70
Queen Pudding 228

Denmark

Basic Danish Dough 5
Cockscombs *(pastry)* 7
Fastelaunsboller *(pastry)* 7
Light Rye Bread 47
Pancake Balls 209
Pastry Bread 87
Sourdough Dark Rye Bread 47
Spandauers *(pastry)* 6
Trekanters *(pastry)* 6
White Bread 48
Whole Wheat Bread 49

Egypt

Cornish Hens stuffed with Bulgur 177
Falafil *(vegatable)* 234
Fried Eggplant with Yogurt 235
Ijja *(eggs)* 137
Meatballs 164
Mhallabiyya *(pudding)* 228
Stuffed Cabbage Leaves 237

El Salvador

Empanadas de Pina *(turnover pie)* 88
Quesadilla Salvadorena *(coffee cakes)* 91

England

Breakfast Scones 30
English Muffin Loaves 49
English Muffins 200
Oxford Sausage 170
Scotch Eggs 127

France

A French Breakfast 167
Café Noir *(coffee)* 18
Café-au-Lait *(coffee)* 18
Crepe a L'orange 209
Fish Croquettes 184
French Bread 50
French Country Strata *(eggs)* 130
French Toast 149
Hot Chocolate 19
Marmalade 35
Orange Glazed Ham Steaks 169
Pain Campagnard aux Pommes *(bread)* 54
Poached Eggs with Hollandoise a L'orange 126
Quiche Lorraine 144
Smoked Turkey stuffed French Toast 150

Germany

Apple Pancakes 212 & 213
Homemade Yeast 56
Kartoffelpuffer *(pancakes)* 215
Kolahes *(pastry)* 9
Quiche Alsace 143
Spiced Apple Cider 21
Waffeltoerichen *(pastry)* 13
Weihnachtsstollen *(bread)* 56

Greece

Greek Lamb Skillet Breakfast 191

Guatemala

Banana Bread 41

Hungary

Cheese Dumplings 110
Cobbler's Delight *(coffee cakes)* 84
Grandmas Goulash 164
Jam Pudding 227
Pancakes 214
Plum Ravioli *(dumplings)* 115

Ireland

Absolute Apples *(cereal)* 72
Bird Flanagan Potato Pancakes 231
Corned Beef Hash 162
Fadge with Ulster Fry *(vegetable)* 234

Irish Coffee 19
Low Calorie Mushroom Omelet 138
Oatmeal 68
Oatmeal Blinis *(pancakes)* 216
Oatmeal Souffle 77
Potato, Cabbage & Irish Bacon Casserole 236
Soda Bread 25
Steel Cut Oats 72
Stuffed Tomatoes 237
The Irish "Fry" 168
Yam & Irish Bacon Flan 240

Israel

Bagels 44
Baked Passover Bagels 45
Blintzes 207
Bureka *(vegetable)* 231
Challah *(bread)* 51
Cherry Granola Kugel *(pudding)* 225
Fried Matzoh *(pancakes)* 211
Honey Butter Blintzes 214
Latkes *(potatoes)* 215
Lokshen Kugel *(pudding)* 227
Malawah *(bread)* 101
Matzo Balls 115
Matzo Breil *(eggs)* 125
Mint Tea 20
Rugelach *(pastry)* 12
Shaks Houka 238 ???
Turkish Coffee 21
Vegetable Salad 239

Italy

Almond Cappuccino 17
Apricot Frittata 140
Chicken Scaloppini Palermo 175
Chocolate Almond Biscotti 3
Frittata Omelet 136
Italian Bread 50
Italian Donuts 100
Italiano Eggs Florentine 142
Orange Cappuccino 18
Quihe Italiano 143
Saucy Mediterranean Frittata 132

Korea

Little Korean Omelets 138

Malaysia

Banana Pancakes 209

Mali

Millet 68

Mexico

Arroz con Leche *(cereal)* 65
Banana Breakfast *(beverage)* 15
Capirotada *(pudding)* 224
Carne Asada *(meat)* 162
Chicken Enchiladas 174
Empanadas de Pina *(turnover pie)*88
Fiesta Quiche Ole *(egs)* 141
Huachinango al Perejil *(fish)* 186
Huevos a la Mexicana *(eggs)* 124
Huevos Casas *(eggs)* 124
Huevos Rancheros *(eggs)* 125
Mexican Chicken 179
Mexican Coffee 20
Mexican Steaks 165
Morning Mexican Fiesta *(eggs)* 132
Pollo en Cacahuate *(chicken)* 179
Sweet Tamales 116
Tortillas de Harina *(flour)* 107
Tortillas de Maiz *(corn)* 106

Morocco

Moroccan Honey Chicken 179

Nepal

Jellabies with Cardamon Syrup *(bread)*100

Netherlands

Buttermilk Waffles 243
Crullers 4
Dutch Baby *(pancakes)* 210
Dutch Fritters 99
Dutch Omelet 136
Flensjze met Applen *(pancakes)* 211
Old Fashion Dutch Letters *(pastry)* 12
Olie Bollen *(bread)* 103
Poffertjes *(crullers)*11
Rogge Brood *(bread)* 42
Saucijze Broodjes *(pancakes)* 219
Vlees Pannekoeken *(pancakes)* 221

Nicaragua

Fried Eggs with Creole Sauce 121
Maduro en Gloria *(fruit)*156

Pastel de Maleta *(meat)* 170

Norway

Flatbread 26
Julebrod *(bread)* 51
Rhubarba Strawberry Coffee Cake 92
Risengrynsgrot *(cereal)* 71

Pakistan

Cholay *(vegetable)* 235
Dahi Baray *(bread)* 98
Halwa *(cereal)* 67
Karachi Chicken 178
Paratha *(bread)* 103
Potato Stuffed Paratha *(bread)* 103
Puri *(bread)* 104
Shahi Tukra *(coffee cake)* 93
Vegetable Biryani 239

Russia

Kulich *(bread)* 52
Pashka *(spread)* 53

Scotland

Potato Scones 34

Singapore

Chicken Porridge 176
Chwee Kuey 111
Nasi Goreng *(cereal)* 78
Nasi Lemar *(cereal)* 68
Pork Porridge 171
Roti Prata *(bread)* 105
Teochew Fish Porridge 190

Spain (Island of Minorca)

Bottled Hell 176
Chicken Pilau 175
Crispees 8
Egg Pilau *(cereal)* 66
Fromaardis *(pastry)* 8
Minorcan Pork Cake 169

Sweden

Applecake with Vanilla Sauce 95
Cabbage Pudding 224
Crisp Waffles 244
Curd Cake 86
Gingerbread with Filbunke 88
Rice Porridge 73
Rye Bread 56

Switzerland

Dotted Swiss Chocolate 18
Muesli 63
Oatmeal 73

Taiwan

Yu't'iau *(bread)* 107

Thailand

Son-in-Law Eggs 128

Trinidad & Tobago

Acca 181
Bakes *(bread)* 98
Coo Coo *(cereal)* 76
Floats *(bread)* 99

Zambia

Groundnut Porridge 67

Did you know food information and other facts found in boxes throughout the recipes came from *The ABC's of Food* reference book for both kids and adults. The book is a study of food as history, story, tradition and nutrition. It was compiled, edited and written by Louise Ulmer and Richard S. Calhoun with contributing food experts. It is published by Peach Blossom Publications.

PEACH BLOSSUM PUBLICATIONS

136 Centre Line Ave. • Williamsport, PA 17701

(570) 323-5151

THE ABC's OF FOOD: *A Study of Food as History, Story, Tradition and Nutrition*, by **Louise Ulmer** and **Richard S. Calhoun** with Contributing Food Experts. The ABC's of Food was written for all ages, from elementary school kids through adults. The book is perfect for middle grade and high school cooking classes, and home schooling. This food encyclopedia covers everything from *abalone* to *Zwiebel kuchen*. It's not just a boring reference book, it is filled with food articles, fun tales, recipes, food festivals, food museums, activities and field trips. It's a one-volume course in American cookery and belongs in every school and home.. . . . .560 pages **$24.95**

CHEECHAKO: An Alaskan Adventure, a true story by Richard S. Calhoun
Clark's father is offered a summer job in Alaska. When the family arrives, they are taken into the wilderness. Dad's job is a watchman at an aging gold mine. Clark's new friends teach him Alaskan ways. While learning to fish, Clark's boat appears to incur the wrath of a Tlingit god, who causes an earthquake that sends the boat riding a tidal wave over an island and out to sea. Clark steps on a sacred bug and, according to Tlingit myth, someone will die. Clark witnesses a death, causing him to wrestle with superstitions and personal guilt. By summer's end, Clark has come to love Alaska, along with new respect for his parents and for a new culture... . . . . .157 pages **$16.00**

THE GLOBSTER OF GLASSY BEACH, by Louise Ulmer
(Ages 8-12) Based on marine history, the story presents a fascinating mystery from the sea. Jimmy becomes a local legend when a giant "blob" or "globster" washes up on the shimmering black sands of Glassy Beach, Maine. The globster looks like a beached whale, but doesn't have a head. However, has gills. Soon people come to look at it. Some think it's a giant oyster without a shell, while others think it is part of a dead whale. Jimmy camps out on the beach to protect his discovery. But there are some thing he can't protect the globster from... . . . . 56 pages **$6.95**

SHAKER WINTER by Louise Ulmer
Life was hard enough for Daisy since Mama died and Papa went to fight in Mr. Lincoln's army. But then Aunt Paratine sold her lovely Victorian home and moved in with the strange "shaking Quakers." Set in the historic Pleasant Hills Shaker Village, it's a story about "hands to work and hearts to God," about freedom, especially freedom to worship in a free land. . . . . 101 pages **$7.50**

JOHNSTOWN SUMMER, 1889 by Louise Ulmer
A story about the Johnstown (Pennsylvania) flood that leveled the town. It's a story about when bad things happen to good people. . . . . 120 pages $7.50

Payable with check or money order. Add 10% for postage and handling in USA, 15% in Canada, 20% in other countries. Pennsylvania residents add 6% sales tax.